USING CONSENSUS BUILDING TO IMPROVE UTILITY REGULATION

ACEEE Books on Energy Policy and Energy Efficiency

Series Editor: Carl Blumstein

Transportation and Global Climate Change
Regulatory Incentives for Demand-Side Management
Energy Efficiency and the Environment: Forging the Link
Efficient Electricity Use: A Development Strategy for Brazil
State of the Art of Energy Efficiency:
Future Directions
Energy-Efficient Motor Systems:
A Handbook on Technology, Programs,
and Policy Opportunities
Residential Indoor Air Quality and Energy Efficiency
Electric Utility Planning and Regulation
Energy Efficiency:
Perspectives on Individual Behavior
Energy Efficiency in Buildings:
Progress and Promise

ACEEE also publishes numerous reports on a variety of topics
addressing energy policy and energy efficiency:
for a catalog of publications write
ACEEE, 2140 Shattuck Avenue, Suite 202,
Berkeley, California 94704.

USING CONSENSUS BUILDING TO IMPROVE UTILITY REGULATION

JONATHAN RAAB

American Council for an Energy-Efficient Economy
Washington, D.C. and Berkeley, California
1994

Using Consensus Building to Improve Utility Regulation

Copyright © 1994 by the American Council for an Energy-Efficient Economy.

All rights reserved. Reproduction in whole or in part is strictly prohibited without prior written approval of the American Council for an Energy-Efficient Economy (ACEEE), except that reasonable portions may be reproduced or quoted as part of a review or other story about this publication, and except where specific approval is given in the text.

Published by the American Council for an Energy-Efficient Economy,
1001 Connecticut Avenue, N.W., Suite 801, Washington, D.C. 20036
and 2140 Shattuck Avenue, Suite 202, Berkeley, California 94704.

Cover art copyright © 1994 M.C. Escher Heirs/Cordon Art—Baarn—Holland

Cover design by Chuck Myers
Printed in the United States of America by Edwards Brothers, Inc.

Library of Congress Cataloging-in-Publication Data

Raab, Jonathan, 1957–
   Using consensus building to improve utility regulation/by Jonathan Raab.
     p.317   23 cm.
   Includes bibliographical references and index.
   ISBN 0-918249-19-8: $28.00
   1. Electric utilities—Government policy—United States—Citizen participation.
   2. Electric utilities—Law and legislation—United States.
   3. Consensus (Social sciences) I. Title
HD9685.U5R27   1994
363.6'0973—dc20   94-15737
                                                                                       CIP

NOTICE

This publication was prepared by the American Council for an Energy-Efficient Economy. Neither ACEEE, nor any person acting on behalf of ACEEE: a) makes any warranty, expressed or implied, with respect to the use of any information, apparatus, method, or process disclosed in the publication or guarantees that such use may not infringe privately owned rights; b) assumes any liabilities with respect to the use of, or for damages resulting from the use of, any information, apparatus, method, or process disclosed in this publication.

♻   Printed on recycled paper.

to Ingrid, for Joshua

Acknowledgments

Many people deserve credit for contributing to this book in different ways. I am grateful to all my friends and colleagues from the Massachusetts Department of Public Utilities who taught me how to be a regulator and inspired some of my best work. In particular I thank former commissioners Susan Tierney, Bob Werlin, and Bernice McIntyre; co-workers Susan Coakley, Tim Woolf, and Henry Yoshimura; and the rest of the staff at the DPU.

I thank Richard Cowart and Michael Dworkin along with Paul Peterson, Rick Weston, and other members of the Vermont Public Service Board, who were delightful to work with. Their frequent phone calls served as a necessary counterpoint to my initial book-writing process. Later, my mediation work in Vermont along with my rewarding work for the indefatigable Mary Kilmarx of the Rhode Island PUC on two DSM collaboratives provided me with additional insights during the final stages of this project.

Support for the original research leading to the demand-side management collaborative case study in this book came from the U.S. Department of Energy via Oak Ridge National Laboratory. My work with Martin Schweitzer and Eric Hirst of ORNL finally put me in gear and allowed me to test many of the theories on measuring success I had been pondering for some time. Additional funding for this book came from fellowships provided by the Switzer Foundation, the Center for International Studies at MIT, and the Edison Electric Institute. I am grateful to them all.

I also thank the seventy-five-plus people I interviewed for this effort. Without their good work, I would have had little to write about. Ron Elwood of the New York PSC, David Pritzker of the ACUS, and Robert Burns of NRRI provided invaluable literature and data and served as occasional sounding boards.

Lawrence Susskind opened up new and exciting vistas when he introduced me to alternative dispute resolution at MIT. He chaired my Ph.D. committee and provided me with insightful feedback on my various tomes and musings over the years. Richard Tabors also served on my committee, providing good humor and even daring to participate in some of my consensus-building experiments. Lyna Wiggins both taught and advised me well at Stanford, and was invaluable on my Ph.D. committee at MIT.

Many others have provided inspiration over the years, including Denis Hayes, Amory Lovins, Ralph Cavanagh, and Connie Smyser. At Stanford, Gil Masters introduced me to decentralized energy planning and the joy of teaching. Ken Tolennaar lured me to the University of Oregon to work and teach, and then encouraged me to return to school for my doctorate just as I was getting comfortable.

Special thanks go to Carl Blumstein and Glee Murray of ACEEE for orchestrating this publication, and to Ed Kahn of LBL for steering me their way. I also thank my editors Susan Benjamin and Seth Zuckerman, and copyeditor Mary Anne Stewart.

I am indebted to Susan Tierney for taking the time from her endless responsibilities at DOE to write the book's foreword.

Most importantly, I am grateful to my family and friends, who have supported me during my life's assorted challenges and accomplishments—including this book. In particular, I thank my grandparents, Gert Raab and Sydney Leff; my parents, Gail and Martin Raab; Nina and Evan Fox; and my wonderful wife and son, Ingrid and Joshua Raab.

Preface

The electric utility industry and its regulatory environment are at a number of complex, controversial, and critically important crossroads. Utilities, intervenors, and even public utility commissions are no longer able to initiate and sustain changes unilaterally. Meanwhile, traditional approaches to regulation—adjudication and rulemaking—are often contentious, costly, and produce results that stakeholders do not perceive as either legitimate or practical.

Consensus building and alternative dispute resolution have the potential to help utilities and their regulators resolve the host of issues confronting them in the 1990s and beyond. Technical sessions, settlements, collaborative processes, and negotiated rulemaking are several consensus-based options currently being tried.

As described in Chapter 2, consensus prevailed by default on electricity issues facing society in the early to mid-1900s. In the last two decades, the consensus fell apart; only in recent years have utility regulators, advocacy groups, and the utilities themselves tried to rebuild a modicum of consensus, using a variety of directed methods and techniques. This book presents the theory behind alternative dispute resolution (ADR) and its relationship to electric utility regulation, and offers a framework for evaluating the successes and failures of attempts to employ these processes.

To show how this theory has been put into practice and to test the analytic framework presented, I have described in detail four cases of alternative dispute resolution in the electric utility industry: the Pilgrim nuclear power plant outage settlement, the demand-side management collaborative processes, and the formation of integrated resource management rules in Massachusetts, and in New Jersey, the resource bidding policy settlement. These examples also provide evidence to support eight principles that would improve and expand consensus building in electric utility regulation, described at the end of the book. The framework, the analysis that follows, and the final recommendations are rooted not only in the evidence that I present, but also in my seven years of working for public utility commissions and wrestling with these issues every day, as well as in my experience leading dispute resolution trainings and serving as a neutral third party in resolving contentious disputes.

Contrary to conventional wisdom, consensus-building processes do not tend to save process-related resources in the short run, even though long-term benefits can be positive and substantial. Supplemental consensus building can enhance the legitimacy of electric utility regulation and produce more practical remedies and plans. To cultivate consensus more actively, regulators and stakeholders will need to make a paradigm shift, but the evidence suggests that the effort would be well spent.

Foreword
Susan F. Tierney

It is fairly common in utility regulation for all of the parties in a case to be disgruntled with the final decision rendered by the regulators. In fact, it is just that kind of uniformly unhappy postdecision reaction that has led many a regulator to exclaim with some degree of relief, "Well, then, the decision must have been just about right after all."

As a former state public utility commissioner, I have to admit to having said, or at least thought, those very words on more than one occasion. And yet, when I look back on my years as a regulator, I think that some of the best decisions I ever made were not ones in which a carefully reasoned and balanced regulatory decision was met with universal disdain among the parties. In fact, the particular decisions I have in mind were cheered by the parties—which was no surprise, since the parties had actually written them in the first place.

I am not embarrassed to say that some of my best decisions were ones reasoned and written by others. In so saying, I should note that I took my public interest responsibility very seriously and was not in the practice of having parties write my decisions. However, on a few occasions—such as those described by Jonathan Raab in two of the case studies in this book (the DSM collaboratives in Massachusetts and the Pilgrim settlement)—I concluded that it was indeed in the public interest to graciously and judiciously embrace as my own the creative thoughts and consensual words of others.

These were not cases in which I and my colleagues at the Department of Public Utilities sat back and let things happen. We were actively involved in the formal proceedings although we participated not at all in the behind-the-scene settlement processes. The formal proceedings touched on important, contentious, and complicated matters, as did the informal ones. Ultimately, the truly innovative work that led to the crafting of a decision acceptable to all parties, includ-

---

Dr. Susan F. Tierney is the Assistant Secretary for Policy, Planning, and Program Evaluation at the U.S. Department of Energy. Previously, she held positions in Massachusetts, both as a commissioner of the Department of Public Utilities and as the Secretary of Environmental Affairs.

ing the commission, took place off-line in the informal collaborative setting, not in the hearing room. Our essential role in making the consensus-building effort happen was to signal clearly to the parties that we would value their work if they sat down to devise a solution together.

There is nothing particularly new about parties getting together during the pendency of a case to negotiate a settlement. But one thing that is new, exciting, and hopeful about the type of settlements analyzed by Jonathan Raab is that they explicitly built into their agreements a participatory role for the parties in shaping consensus on key issues in the future. These settlements set up new processes designed to enable stakeholders to collaborate in creating and buying into workable strategies to solve important problems down the road.

The lessons learned from the 1980s collaborations on electric utility regulatory issues have important applications for the 1990s. The electric industry is now on the edge of a storm, with the pressures and promises of increased competition looming large all around the country. There is clear consensus among stakeholders that tension is high. Yet there is no consensus on a shared vision of what the electric industry should look like in the future, nor on the best path to take it there.

Given these tensions and uncertainties, the collaborative processes used effectively in making some of the dicey utility regulatory policies in the 1980s offer a promising means for helping interested groups build workable consensus on the critical issues facing the electric industry in the 1990s.

To motivate parties to spend the time and resources necessary to engage effectively in—and trust—consensus-building processes, regulators need to send clear messages that they welcome and will do every reasonable thing they can to support the products of collaboration. Dr. Raab, whom I worked closely with at the Massachusetts DPU when I was a commissioner and he was the assistant director of its Electric Power Division, suggests useful ways in which regulators can send such signals.

Creative consensus-building processes hold promise not just for resolving issues in electric utility regulation. They are appropriate for other public policy arenas as well. In my own experience in Massachusetts, such processes were extremely useful in shaping thorny environmental regulatory policy. Regulators and interest groups worked collaboratively and aggressively over a two-year period to design a new regulatory and managerial approach for the state's hazardous waste clean-up process. The fact that this new "21E" process in now up and running, having been enacted by the legislature with the support of various interest groups, and that the process is making it possible for lands to actually be cleaned up, is a testament to the benefits of collaboration.

At the federal level as well, the Environmental Protection Agency has had some success in developing clean air and other regulations through negotiated rulemaking, known colloquially as "reg negs." The Department of Energy has also experimented with reg negs in the area of setting appliance efficiency standards and has indicated its intention to use more reg negs in the future.

The Clinton administration is now encouraging agencies to search proactively for issues on which negotiated rulemaking and consensus-building processes will be productive. A recent example in which the administration hopes to use such consensus building is with regard to the car. As promised in the administration's 1993 Climate Change Action Plan, the White House during 1994 will bring parties to the table to try to build consensus around workable ways to improve the fuel economy, emissions performance, and safety of personal automobiles.

Our understanding of the promises and challenges of using consensus to build better regulatory approaches will be enriched by the thoughtful analysis presented in this book. We owe a debt to Jonathan Raab and to the American Council for an Energy-Efficient Economy for advancing our understanding and, hopefully, our reliance on such productive methods of public policy making.

Contents

CHAPTER ONE

Introduction: Can Consensus-Building Processes Improve Utility Regulation? 1
    Issues in Consensus-Building Processes 2
    Applying Consensus Building to Other Regulatory Areas 3
    Overview of the Book 3

CHAPTER TWO

The Decline of Consensus in Electric Utility Regulation 7
    The Birth of Electric Utility Regulation 7
    The Era of Implied Consent 9
    The End of Consensus 11
    Interventionism 13
    Problems with Interventionism 18
    Current Controversies in Electric Utility Regulation 19

CHAPTER THREE

Introduction to the Theory, Practice, and Evaluation of Consensus Building in Electric Utility Regulation 27
    Toward a New Negotiation Paradigm: Getting to Yes 28
    How Principled Negotiation Has Been Applied to
        Consensus Building in Electric Utility Regulation 34
    The Practice of Consensus Building in Electric
        Utility Regulation 36
    Evaluating the Success of Consensus-Building Processes 41
    Toward a Workable Evaluative Model 49

CHAPTER FOUR

Adjudication 53
    Adjudication Defined 53

Rise of PUC Adjudication 55
Shortcomings 57
The Role of Settlement 61
Expanding and Formalizing Consensus Building 61
Introduction to the Case Studies 64
The Pilgrim Settlement 65
Background 66
Pilgrim Cases Before the DPU 69
The Settlement 73
DPU Approval 77
The Postsettlement Era 79
Evaluating the Success of the Pilgrim Settlement 85
DSM Collaboratives in Massachusetts 93
Background 95
Formation and Approval of the DSM Collaboratives 97
Phase I 102
Phase II 108
Phase III 117
Ongoing Collaboratives 123
Evaluating the Success of DSM Collaboratives
   in Massachusetts 125
Summary 138

CHAPTER FIVE

Rulemaking 141
Differentiating Agency Rulemaking from Adjudication 141
The Evolution of Agency Rulemaking at the Federal Level 142
Alternative Rulemaking Procedures 146
State PUC Rulemaking 149
Introduction to the Case Studies 150
IRM Rulemaking in Massachusetts 151
Background 152
The Traditional Process (Formation of Preapproval Rules) 155
The IRM Rulemaking Process 159

The IRM Proposal 160
The Decision to Use Technical Sessions 162
The Technical Sessions 165
Substantive Results of the Technical Sessions 170
Formal Rulemaking Process and Final Rules 176
Evaluating the Success of the IRM Rulemaking Process 177
The New Jersey Bidding Settlement 187
Background 189
Settlement Process 192
The Settlement 195
Postsettlement Process 201
Implementation Experience 203
Future Revisions 207
Evaluating the Success of the New Jersey
    Bidding Settlement 208
Summary 215

CHAPTER SIX

Improving Electric Utility Regulation: Cultivating Consensus 217
Challenges Facing Society on Electricity Issues 217
Shortcomings of Current Regulatory Approaches:
    Interventionism Revisited 218
Benefits of Supplemental Consensus-Building Processes 220
Cultivating Consensus 222
Principles for Designing Consensus-Building Processes
    to Improve Electric Utility Regulation 223
Parting Comment: One State's Evolution 235

APPENDIXES 237
ENDNOTES 243
REFERENCES AND BIBLIOGRAPHY 273
INDEX 295
ABOUT THE AUTHOR 317

Chapter 1

Introduction: Can Consensus-Building Processes Improve Utility Regulation?

Electricity is vital to our society. It runs the lights, motors, computers, and VCRs that we rely on for productivity and pleasure. It is also one of our largest single expenditures. In 1990 alone, U.S. ratepayers paid utilities $179 billion for electricity (U.S. Department of Energy 1991).

Not surprisingly, electricity issues engender some of our most impassioned debates. Beginning with discontent over rapidly increasing electricity rates in the early 1970s (after over half a century of declining costs), electricity-related disputes have expanded tremendously. Examples of these controversies include utility investments in nuclear power plants, the environmental impacts of electricity resources, the role of demand-side management as an alternative to supply-side resources, and the introduction of competition.

Attempts to resolve electricity-related disputes usually occur in adjudicatory and rulemaking proceedings before state public utility commissions (PUCs).[1] Adjudicatory (contested case) proceedings generally involve the application of PUC rules and policies to individual utilities, whereas rulemaking proceedings commonly develop policies and procedures that apply across all utilities. However, traditional adjudicatory and rulemaking proceedings often prove unsatisfactory. Specifically, both utilities and intervenors (such as consumer groups, environmental organizations, independent power producers, and public advocates) contend that the processes are expensive and produce results that are unfair, inefficient, and difficult to implement. Appeals of PUC decisions to the courts are not uncommon.

Recently, utilities, intervenor groups, and PUCs have initiated supplemental consensus-building processes. Although negotiated settlements among litigants in rate cases are not new, such settlements are now occurring with increasing regularity. Moreover, new and expanded forms of consensus building are being tried. These efforts include facilitated technical sessions, collaborative processes, and negotiated rulemaking and address a broad array of substantive issues.

Issues in Consensus-Building Processes

Neither participants nor scholars have directed much effort at evaluating supplemental consensus-building processes in electric utility regulation, despite their increasing application. The primary purpose of this book is to investigate whether such processes can improve upon traditional methods of adjudication and rulemaking in resolving disputes.

To address this central question, the book identifies current controversies in electric utility regulation and assesses the shortcomings of the approaches traditionally used to resolve them. It then focuses on a difficult methodological question: how should the success of supplemental consensus-building efforts be measured vis-à-vis traditional processes? For instance, is it adequate to look solely at whether a consensual agreement has been achieved among traditional adversaries and whether participants have saved time and money? Or is it necessary to look more deeply at both the process and the results? This book explores the methodological issues in some detail and then recommends and applies an analytic framework in evaluating four case studies of alternative dispute resolution.

The last set of issues this book addresses is prescriptive. If consensus building has potential benefit, how can its application be expanded and improved? The ensuing chapters examine the range of consensus-based processes that are available and evaluate when each is appropriate. Finally, the book explores how such processes can best be structured. It poses, analyzes, and provides recommendations on questions regarding the timing and content of negotiations, inclusion of interested parties (including the PUC itself), use of facilitators and mediators, and the dovetailing of consensus-building processes with traditional regulatory and adjudicatory procedures.

These and other issues inherent to consensus-building processes are explored through four detailed case studies representing a spectrum of approaches to consensus building in electric utility regulation. The methodology combines formal case records (such as testimony, exhibits, and PUC orders), over seventy-five in-depth interviews, personal observations, secondary literature, and other data. These four cases represent the cutting edge in consensus-building efforts rather than typical rate case settlements. The cases are diverse and innovative, and the significance of both their processes and outcomes is nationally recognized.

As senior economist and later assistant director of the Electric Power Division at the Massachusetts Department of Public Utilities, I had the opportunity to participate in all three of the Massachusetts cases reported in this book and was instrumental in the design of the consensus-building process in one of them. This participant-observer status has provided unique insights that have greatly assisted my analysis. As a participant, I feel uniquely qualified to write about the issues involved in regulatory disputes. In addition to the perspectives I gained as a participant-observer in these cases, my varied experience in the field of alternative dispute resolution has also helped me to evaluate the cases and to craft this book.[2] Ultimately, the recommendations I make are backed by evidence from secondary and primary sources but are also rooted in the perceptions and judgments I have formed over years of first-hand involvement in these issues.

Applying Consensus Building to Other Regulatory Areas

This book stands at the intersection of two fields of inquiry—electric utility regulation and public dispute resolution—and I have structured the material to make contributions to both. The findings should be relevant to several additional areas as well. One is the regulation of other activities under the jurisdiction of PUCs (such as natural gas, telecommunications, and water), in which regulatory procedures are identical to those used in resolving electricity-related disputes. The material should also be of interest to those involved in regulatory matters before the Federal Energy Regulatory Commission, which uses similar adjudicatory and rulemaking procedures to regulate interstate electricity and natural gas transactions. Finally, federal and state administrative agencies that are involved in regulating other areas (such as environment, health, and safety) should find the book useful, given both the pervasiveness and similarity of adjudicatory and rulemaking procedures.

Overview of the Book

Chapter 2, "The Decline of Consensus in Electric Utility Regulation," provides a brief history of electric utility regulation and traces the decline of widespread support for the electric utilities (and the laissez-faire policies of state regulators) that began in the early 1970s in the face of rising costs, environmental concerns, and other factors. It introduces the concept of interventionism by state regulators and identifies its strengths and potential shortcomings. In closing, the chapter presents five current controversies in electric utility regulation that highlight the difficult choices now facing society with respect to electricity issues.

Chapter 3, "Introduction to the Theory, Practice, and Evaluation of Consensus Building in Electric Utility Regulation," begins with a description of alternative dispute resolution theory as presented by Roger Fisher and William Ury in their popular book *Getting to YES* and a discussion of the theory's relevance to electric utility regulation. It then explains the direct link between this theory and consensus-building experiments in electric utility regulation. The chapter describes in detail the range of consensus-building mechanisms currently in use and presents criteria for evaluating the successes and failures of consensus-based supplements to traditional regulatory processes.

Chapters 4 and 5, "Adjudication" and "Rulemaking," examine respectively the use of consensus building in adjudicatory and rulemaking proceedings before state PUCs. Chapter 4 begins by documenting the rise in major contested-case proceedings before state PUCs over the past decade and then examines some of the shortcomings of traditional adjudicatory approaches to resolving disputes. A description of the concurrent growth in consensus-based settlements is followed by two detailed case studies illustrating such processes.

The first case study analyzes a settlement of litigation over the prudence of Boston Edison Company's extensive expenditures during a thirty-two-month outage at the Pilgrim nuclear power plant. This settlement, reached among long-standing adversaries after extremely protracted and contentious litigation, illustrates numerous potential benefits of using supplemental consensus building in the context of traditional adjudicatory proceedings.

The second adjudicatory case in Chapter 4 involves a series of collaborative processes used to design state-of-the-art DSM programs for electric utilities in Massachusetts. In contrast to the Pilgrim nuclear power plant case, the DSM collaboratives represent a new and growing type of settlement process that occurs prior to a contested-case proceeding and that focuses on future utility plans rather than on past decisions. The DSM collaboratives are also unique in that they represent ongoing consensus-building efforts (several have lasted over five years so far) and in that the utilities have spent over $5 million for the nonutility parties to procure their own outside technical experts.

Chapter 4 concludes by briefly summarizing the major findings regarding the use of consensus building in adjudicatory proceedings.

Chapter 5, "Rulemaking," opens with the history of agency rulemaking, from its inception in 1946 with the passage of the federal Administrative Procedures Act to the present, noting the increasing judicialization of the administrative rulemaking process and presenting some key criticisms of its effectiveness. The chapter then presents an alternative, negotiated rulemaking model popularized by Philip Harter and practiced with increasing regularity in some federal agencies. It then examines two cases in which consensus building was used to formulate regulatory rules and policies.

The first of these cases involves the development of complex integrated resource management (IRM) rules by the Massachusetts Department of Public Utilities. The DPU used a series of structured technical sessions attended by over one hundred interested parties and incorporating outside facilitation, both before and after formulating proposed rules.

The second case study in Chapter 5 is of the negotiated settlement process used to develop comprehensive resource bidding policies for the New Jersey Public Utility Board. Thirteen parties, representing a broad range of stakeholders, spent over half a year negotiating the detailed mechanisms and actual wording for new state policies.

Chapter 5 concludes with a brief summary of the major findings regarding the use of consensus building in rulemaking proceedings.

Chapter 6, "Improving Electric Utility Regulation: Cultivating Consensus," highlights the benefits to intervenors, utilities, and PUCS of using supplemental consensus building to resolve current and future disputes in electric utility regulation. The chapter and the book conclude by proposing eight principles for improving consensus building in electric utility regulation. It is my hope that these recommendations—resting as they do on the evidence I present and the experience I have accumulated in the field—will help better the regulatory process both within the electric utility industry and beyond.

Chapter 2

The Decline of Consensus in Electric Utility Regulation

Over the last few decades, society's widespread support for electric utilities (and the laissez-faire policies of regulators) has declined because of rising costs, environmental concerns, and other factors. A broad spectrum of interested parties have increasingly intervened before regulatory agencies to press their concerns. Regulators are also pushing their own agendas more forcefully than ever before. But this rise of interventionism has met with only limited success, and the future promises to be even more challenging than the past. Current controversies faced by society regarding electric utility regulation include minimizing societal costs, utility investment in demand-side management, competition in electricity generation, interjurisdictional conflicts, and incentive ratemaking.

The Birth of Electric Utility Regulation

The regulation of industry in the United States began at the state rather than the federal level, and the initial focus was on regulating railroads. Although state regulation of railroads began in 1839 with a short-lived commission in Rhode Island, it was most prominently pioneered after 1869 in Massachusetts under the influence of Charles Francis Adams (McCraw 1984). At the time, the railroads were accused of exploiting their monopoly position by charging high and discriminatory prices and providing poor service (Barkovitch 1989). However, in contrast to today's relatively independent and powerful state public utility commissions (PUCs), the railroad commissions of the nineteenth century were built around the notion that the appropriate role of government was to persuade business through negotiation rather than to coerce it (id.). Apparently this approach was not a rationalization in the wake of weak enabling legislation, but a philosophic belief of Adams and others that regulation should focus on policy formation through independent investigation, advice, and direct negotiation (id.)

It is not uncommon today for electric utilities and other regulated industries to bemoan the excesses of regulation. However, the initial impetus of state regulation came largely from the electric utilities themselves. Beginning in 1898, Samuel Insul, head of Commonwealth Edison in Chicago and president of the National Electric Light Association (NELA), led a crusade to establish state regulatory oversight of electric companies in exchange for exclusive production and distribution franchises (D. Anderson 1981, Hirsh 1989). In 1907, apparently convinced more by the threat of continued local regulation or even municipalization (that is, having local governments own and operate electricity systems) than by Insul's original pleadings to eliminate interutility competition, the NELA unanimously approved a strong statement by its Policy Committee supporting the concept of state regulation of businesses (D. Anderson 1981, Hirsh 1989).

However, the upswell of support for state regulation of electric utilities did not begin and end with the utilities. Also instrumental was the reputable National Civic Federation, which appointed a diverse and prominent group to study the issue for two years (D. Anderson 1981).[1] In 1907 the federation adopted a majority report, signed by nineteen of its twenty-one members, that recommended replacing the status quo of unsupervised competition with either state regulation or public ownership:

> Public utilities are so constituted that it is impossible for them to be regulated by competition. Therefore, they must be controlled and regulated by the government; or they must be left to do as they please; or they must be operated by the public. There is no other course. None of us are in favor of leaving them to their own will, and the question is whether it is better to regulate or to operate. (id., p. 45)

In addition to its overall recommendation, the report included many specific suggestions for crafting new state commissions that were used as the basis for the commission structures ultimately adopted (id.).

The growing consensus for state regulation of electric utilities was capped by the support of progressive governors in New York, Wisconsin, California, and New Jersey. Apparently each governor used his support of government control of private enterprise to establish his political reputation—each eventually ran for president of the United States (id.).[2]

In 1907, Wisconsin and New York became the first states to pass laws creating comprehensive commissions to regulate electric power and other utilities (D. Anderson 1981). The Wisconsin statutes simply expanded and strengthened the authority of the state's railroad commission to cover electricity, whereas New York created a new commission to regulate gas and electricity. Over the next six years, and with support from all sectors of society (excepting some municipalities that viewed the movement as a preemptive strike on local ownership), two-thirds of the states passed similar enabling legislation, and the rest of the states were not far behind (McCraw 1984).[3]

The Era of Implied Consent

Electric utility regulation was relatively noneventful from 1907, when state PUCs began regulating electric utilities, through the early 1970s, when a series of trends and events converged to shatter the calm. During this period, electricity use expanded tremendously, reaching beyond its initial roots in lighting services until it was tightly related to every facet of American life. A recent book by David Nye, *Electrifying America*, vividly describes how the integration of electricity into society transformed the city, the farm, the industrial base, and our domestic lives (Nye 1990).

The increased demand for electricity resulted in the construction of ever larger and more efficient plants (Hirsh 1989, A. Kahn 1988). Through numerous technological breakthroughs, economies of scale, and falling fuel costs, utilities were continuously able to bring down the cost of producing electricity until the early 1970s. The price of electricity to consumers correspondingly fell in nominal terms from approximately $.25/kWh in 1910 to less than $.05/kWh in the early 1970s (E. Kahn 1988). The real decrease in rates to consumers, however, was much more dramatic, as can be seen in Figure 2-1. The figure also shows the large corresponding growth in electricity generation.

Although state PUCs had the authority to regulate utilities' services and rates (primarily to make sure that utilities did not make excessive profits and that rates were "fair and reasonable"), there existed a laissez-faire approach to regulation. This may have been due in part to inadequate resources at the PUCs and some judicial debate about the scope of their authority.[4] But there was also little public pressure to "rein in" the utilities. Between electricity's perceived usefulness and its declining price, the public held both the product and its producers in high esteem throughout this period, and there was little or no intervention before the PUCs (Hirsh 1989, E. Kahn 1988).[5]

Rate cases were rare during this period. When they did occur, they were noncontroversial compared with today's often hotly contested cases. As late as the mid-1960s, only three or four rate cases per year were initiated in the entire nation (D. Anderson 1981). The PUCs

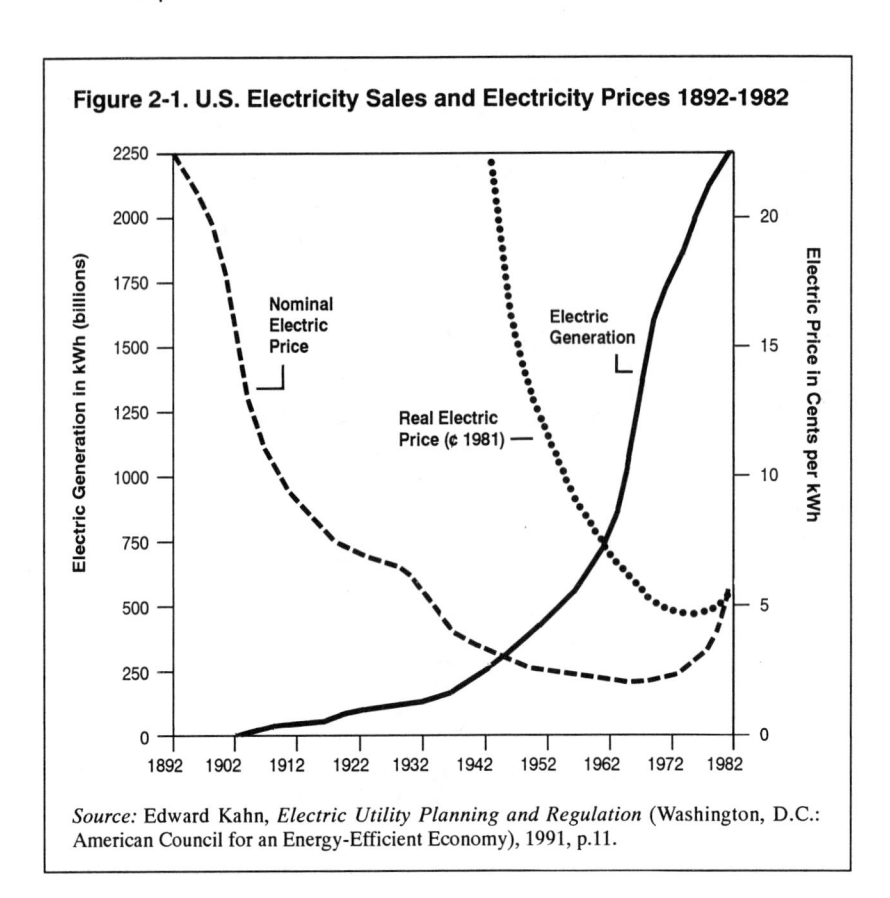

Figure 2-1. U.S. Electricity Sales and Electricity Prices 1892-1982

Source: Edward Kahn, *Electric Utility Planning and Regulation* (Washington, D.C.: American Council for an Energy-Efficient Economy), 1991, p.11.

probably could have justified requiring utilities to lower rates more frequently during this period,[6] but they rarely instigated investigatory proceedings, waiting instead for the utility to file a case (id.). When cases did occur, the regulators concentrated solely on a utility's rate of return and level of service. Pricing, operations, and planning issues were left to the utility managers' discretion. "Unintrusiveness" was the norm of PUC regulation (Barkovitch 1989).

If rate case adjudications were rare prior to the early 1970s, the use of rulemaking and other techniques by the PUCs to articulate and advance electricity-related policies and standards was virtually nonexistent (Trebing 1967). There was an implicit consensus that utilities were performing satisfactorily or that it wasn't the place of regulators to judge their strategies. All parties saw little need for active PUC intervention, either to restructure the industry or to second-guess utility decision making. Richard Hirsh, in his book *Technology and Transformation in the American Electric Utility Industry*, writes:

> . . . The stakeholders in the electric power matrix had formed an implicit consensus about the technological system and its management. Benefits accrued to all: consumers enjoyed electricity whose unit price declined gradually. Investors profited from steadily increasing dividends and share prices of utility stocks. Managers congratulated themselves for their aptitude in running a complex technologic enterprise . . . and regulators sat quietly on the sidelines, providing little interference in what appeared to be one of the best examples of natural monopoly. It was an elegant system . . . . (Hirsh 1989, pp. 176–177)

The End of Consensus

Hirsh's book describes how the initial seeds of the ensuing discontent were technological in nature and were sown in the 1960s, despite the common belief that a series of financial, economic, and regulatory problems during the early 1970s led to the end of the implicit consensus on matters concerning the electric utility industry and its regulation (Hirsh 1989). Specifically, the technological innovation that was the driving engine of the electric utilities' success during the preceding half century reached a plateau. Both plant size and the thermal efficiency of new units peaked during the 1960s and maintained a status quo throughout the 1970s.[7] Utility rate cases rose dramatically from three to four per year during the mid-1960s to forty-five to ninety-four per year between 1970 and 1972, largely as a result of this leveling off and prior to the sharp rise in oil prices in the wake of the OPEC oil embargo during 1973–1974 (D. Anderson 1981, p. 70).

The quadrupling of oil prices in the 1973–1974 period immediately increased fuel costs to utilities—particularly in the Northeast, where utilities had recently converted many of their coal-burning plants to oil for environmental reasons. Other fuels essentially tracked the rise in oil prices: rising energy prices in turn sparked inflation. Inflation increased the cost of capital to utilities, at a time when many of them were building new plants to meet anticipated load growth, and increased their nonfuel operating costs as well. As a result, utilities turned to regulators for permission to raise rates and pass their increasing costs directly along to consumers. Alfred Kahn in the new introduction to his classic text *The Economics of Regulation: Principles and Institutions* explains the predicament:

After two decades of relative quiescence, during which regulators were comparatively complacent about costs falling faster than rates and earned rates of return tending systematically to exceed levels determined previously to be "just and reasonable," requests for rate increases began suddenly to press hard one upon the other, as each award proved to be inadequate even before it went into effect, and achieved returns fell systematically short of the cost of capital. (A. Kahn 1988, p. xxiii)

By the mid-1970s, consumer advocate groups were springing up throughout the country to protest utility rate increases. They were joined by a burgeoning environmental movement that had succeeded in getting Congress to pass the Clean Air Act in 1970 and that had recently turned some of its attention to electric utility regulation. Environmentalists sought to force utilities to better account for environmental externalities through more skillful pricing, planning, and investment (Lovins 1976, Roe 1984). Consumer and environmental forces joined to oppose capital-intensive nuclear power plants, which many utilities were banking on, but which proved to be lightning rods for citizens concerned about increasing prices and potential environmental disasters. Increased citizen protest led to more difficult and time-consuming siting procedures for new plants (both nuclear and other technologies), as well as to prolonged construction periods.

In 1974, the year after the OPEC oil embargo sent energy prices skyward, residential electricity usage actually decreased for the first time in the century. Though the decrease was not large, 0.1 percent, the change was shocking to an industry that had grown accustomed to a 7 percent annual growth over the preceding two decades, a growth that had amounted to a doubling of electricity use each decade (Hirsh 1989). The electric utility industry was suddenly faced with the disconcerting specter that customers would respond to rising electricity prices by conserving electricity (through lifestyle changes and investments in energy efficiency), by self-generating electricity, or by substituting fuels. Consumer cutbacks on electricity usage forced utilities to reconsider their ambitious plans for new plant construction, as well as to discontinue some plants already under construction.

The increasing confrontation between citizens and utilities was exacerbated in the late 1970s and early 1980s by the second oil price shock during the Iranian crises, the Three Mile Island nuclear plant accident in 1979, and double-digit inflation. Some of the frustrations culminated in demonstrations at nuclear power plants, such as Seabrook in New Hampshire and Diablo Canyon in California, where arrests often followed acts of civil disobedience. However, much of the confrontation occurred in the hearing rooms of the state PUCs. Richard Hirsh describes the transformation as follows:

> Once a benign and polite activity that ratified decisions already made by power companies, utility regulation became a hornet's nest as commissioners relearned the nature of their business . . . hesitated to pass along rate relief . . . [and] companies' earnings suffered. (Hirsh 1989, pp. 112–13)

Hirsh assigns much of the blame for the ensuing conflict to the management of the utilities. He argues that they failed to acknowledge the technological stasis upon them[8] and then failed to appreciate "that their industry was a publicly regulated industry in which an active consensus was necessary, especially during unusual times like the crises-laden 1970s" (id., p. 148).[9] Some of the blame, however, must rest with the regulators, who also failed to recognize the technological stasis and, when they did, responded poorly. In the end, assignment of blame is less significant than the recognition that the broad support for the electric utility industry, together with a laissez-faire approach to regulation assumed by state PUCs, ended rather abruptly in the 1970s.

Interventionism

In the 1970s, state PUCs were inundated with a tidal wave of requests for rate increases. Besides the unwelcome attention these rate cases brought to the utilities, the requests drew attention and public scrutiny to the commissions themselves, whose job it was to resolve these contentious cases, usually by granting an unpopular rate hike. Whereas in the past, efficiency improvements at generating facilities had allowed real electricity rates to decrease for all customers, society was now forced to decide how to distribute increasing costs between utilities and ratepayers, among existing customers, and finally between present and future generations. Moreover, there was a growing debate about whether the electric utility industry should continue to rely on large, centralized generating facilities that utilized nonrenewable resources (such as oil, coal, and nuclear energy), or whether the industry should switch to a system built on renewable energy (such as solar, wind, or hydro power) and energy efficiency (Lovins 1976).[10] Intervenors—such as residential and industrial ratepayers, environmentalists, and other government agencies—turned to the regulators for support because they did not trust utilities to plan well for the long term or to distribute costs and benefits fairly among different classes of ratepayers, stockholders, and other stakeholders.

Regulators, in turn, were required to make decisions in areas that they had previously left to utility managers. These areas broadly included rate design and cost allocation issues, and utility planning, procurement, and operating decisions. To resolve these issues, regulators had to take a much more active role, both as judges and as policymakers, than they had in the past. In 1974, economist Paul Joskow observed that regulators were somewhat reluctantly forced into abandoning their previous passive style of minimizing conflict in favor of a more activist approach to regulation (Joskow 1974). However, as Barbara Barkovitch points out in her book *Regulatory Interventionism in the Utility Industry: Fairness, Efficiency and the Pursuit of Energy Conservation*, although regulators may have been reluctant at first, beginning in the mid-1970s, many rose to the occasion:

> Writing in the early 1970s, he [Joskow] did not anticipate the shift in ideology that would lead to regulators who craved the limelight and actively pursued major regulatory policy changes—rejecting the traditional paradigm. For such regulators, intervention was not an aberration but an integral part of the job. (Barkovitch 1989, p. 49)

Barkovitch's book focuses on the "interventionism" (as she calls it) of the California PUC in energy conservation matters (more commonly labeled today as demand-side management or DSM) during the mid-1970s and early 1980s. However, the history of electric utility regulation since the mid-1970s is replete with parallel examples in other states. The following three sections briefly describe three of the most significant early interventions, including that of the California PUC, to illustrate the phenomenon and to make several points about this period.

Marginal Cost Pricing in New York

The New York Public Service Commission pushed to change the way electricity was priced. Prior to the arrival of Alfred Kahn, the preeminent regulatory economist from Cornell, as chairman of the New York PUC, electric utilities throughout the country priced electricity at flat or declining block rates. The rates were also not differentiated by time of day or season. Although this made sense in a constantly declining-cost industry, promotional rates made little sense during times of increasing cost, when higher use meant higher costs.

According to Thomas McCraw in *Prophets of Regulation*, when Kahn arrived at the New York PUC in June 1974, he immediately set about converting the PUC commissioners and staff, the utilities, and the intervenors to the notion of marginal cost pricing (McCraw 1984).[11] He initiated a series of generic hearings at which he personally presided to take testimony on the issue and to engage in a dialogue with interested parties (id.). At the beginning of the hearings, Kahn made a statement that was to set the tone throughout: "I hope we can proceed as cooperative seekers of truth rather than as adversaries seeking an advantage over one another" (id., p. 251).

By the end of the generic hearings, the concept of marginal cost pricing had the strong support of a strange coalition, including the Long Island Lighting Company (LILCo) and the Environmental Defense Fund; tacit support from most of the other utilities; and continued strong opposition, primarily from large commercial and industrial users who feared paying higher rates (McCraw 1984). Rather than moving to a rulemaking procedure to promulgate standards that would apply industrywide, Kahn preferred to institutionalize the concept on a case-by-case basis. In LILCo's next rate case, time-of-use pricing was established, allowing the utility to charge higher rates during the summer months and peak hours when the cost of generation was highest and lower rates in other times. Kahn agreed that the target revenue extracted from any one customer class would remain unchanged after the new rates went into effect (that is, the extra amount paid by on-peak users in a single customer class would be balanced by the amount saved by the off-peak users in that class), apparently in an attempt to gain the support of the large commercial and industrial consumers, but somewhat in violation of pure marginal cost theory (id.).

The adoption of marginal cost pricing in New York in the mid-1970s was an important substantive change in PUC regulation and would be accepted in various forms in most other states over the next decade. Kahn had worked successfully to shape a political consensus on his ideas (id.). Still, a separate PUC order requiring Consolidated Edison to abandon its declining block rate structure for residential rates issued during the original generic hearings was indicative of Kahn's intentions to intervene on this issue and institutionalize marginal cost pricing—whether or not he could persuade everyone else of its virtues.

Demand-Side Management in California

In California, under the leadership of Robert Batinovich and Leonard Ross, who were appointed shortly after Governor Jerry Brown took office in 1975 (and after intervention from environmental and consumer groups), the California PUC pushed the utilities (both gas and electric) to begin aggressive DSM programs (Barkovitch 1989, Roe 1984). In 1978, for example, the California PUC ordered all utilities to weatherize 90 percent of the homes in their service territories in five years by offering 8 percent loans to customers for installing ceiling insulation and by supplying low-flow showerheads and water heater blankets free of charge (Barkovitch 1989). Although the PUC's order was appealed in 1979 to the state supreme court, which ruled that the PUC had exceeded its authority by ordering utilities to undertake aggressive DSM programs, the California legislature shortly afterwards explicitly granted the CPUC that authority. The CPUC immediately continued its quest to have utilities install DSM as an alternative to new supply and as a way of mitigating customer rate increases (id.).

In 1980, under the leadership of another Brown appointee, CPUC chair John Bryson, the PUC pushed PG&E, the largest investor-owned utility in the country, to enhance its residential weatherization programs by offering zero-interest loans to its customers (id.). Many other DSM programs were also ordered by the CPUC as it continued to become involved in both the oversight and the program formulation of the utilities—refusing to play either a passive or disinterested role (id.).[12] By 1984, California utilities' expenditures on electricity DSM alone had reached $127 million per year, which was probably an order of magnitude higher than expenditures in any other state (Calwell and Cavanagh 1989, Raab et al. 1994). Other state PUCs eventually followed California's lead and began pressuring utilities to invest in DSM.

Although many utilities could see advantages to DSM as a means of mitigating rising customer bills, and some perhaps could understand the advantages of load management (that is, shifting customer use from peak to off-peak periods), it took more than a decade until any of them concurred with the CPUC's new philosophy that DSM was as good as, if not better than, existing supply-side resources. The CPUC, particularly under Bryson, still made some attempts to build consensus by addressing the fears and concerns of the utilities.[13] However, the CPUC's intended interventionism on this issue was inevitable and virtually unstoppable as Jerry Brown saw his election as a mandate to pursue DSM and renewable resources.[14]

Nuclear Power Plant Cost Disallowances Across the Country

The treatment of the utilities' nuclear power plant investments perhaps captures the intensity of this period and the regulators' growing interventionism as does no other issue. Originally touted as the next great technological breakthrough and promising to produce electricity that would be "too cheap to meter," nuclear power was criticized first for being unsafe and later for being both unsafe and too costly. Although substantial debate goes on regarding the causes of the escalating costs associated with nuclear power (as well as the safety and health risks), between the early 1970s and the mid-1980s the real cost of nuclear power increased sixfold (Flavin 1987). Plants that were completed after the mid-1970s were consistently and substantially over budget and late. Furthermore, since 1974, no new nuclear plant has been ordered by U.S. utilities that has not subsequently been canceled: over one hundred reactors have been canceled—including many that were under construction (id.).

Whenever utilities came before PUCs to request rate increases to recover their nuclear investments, parties intervened to argue for major disallowances on the grounds that the utilities had acted, and continued to act, imprudently by embracing nuclear power. By 1986, PUC disallowances were projected to total as much as $35 billion for both canceled and completed nuclear plants—amounting to almost 54 percent of the utilities' total equity in those plants (A. Kahn 1988, p. xxvii).[15] These massive disallowances marked a significant departure from what was virtually a guaranteed pass-through of new plant costs to ratepayers prior to the 1970s.

Previously, PUCs had rarely disallowed imprudent expenditures despite having had the authority and the responsibility to do so. Because imprudence is difficult to prove, the PUCs' willingness to apply a prudence standard to disallow tens of billions of dollars of nuclear investment was a sign of the contentiousness of the times and of regulatory interventionism.[16] Moreover, several states, including Massachusetts, Pennsylvania, and Kansas, added new and more rigorous standards (known as "used and useful" standards) to justify disallowing even larger portions of nuclear investments than the prudence standard alone would have permitted (Kalt et al. 1987). In addition to disallowing costs associated with imprudent management decisions made throughout the course of construction and operation, PUCs could disallow costs if the plants were not currently needed to meet demand or cheaper sources were available under new "prudent, used, and useful" standards.

Utilities and others argued that these new standards unfairly transferred risks once shouldered by the ratepayers to the utilities and constituted a breach of the regulatory bargain (that is, the utilities' agreement to accept financial returns that were below monopoly rates in exchange for guaranteed recovery of prudently incurred expenses) (id.). The disallowances threatened to have a chilling effect on investment in new facilities (id.). Moreover, the disallowances (which were also applied occasionally to coal plants) continued to further fracture relationships between consumers, utilities, and regulators, which had started to deteriorate as prices began rising in the late 1960s and early 1970s.

Problems with Interventionism

The increased involvement of intervenors in the regulatory process, combined with the interventionism of PUCs beginning in the mid-1970s, led to many significant changes in the electric utility industry. Such changes included the movement toward marginal cost pricing, the offering of DSM programs by some utilities, and major disallowances for past expenditures in new supply-side facilities. However, no consensus had been reached about how the electric industry should be structured or regulated. Basic values and principles were in dispute. Despite decisions on many contentious cases by the state PUCs, underlying electric utility issues often remained controversial and unresolved. Even where the PUCs' new-found interventionism appeared to have resolved disputes, this seeming consensus eventually proved illusory.

In California, for example, the utilities' investment in DSM programs declined considerably after 1984 despite continued public interest (Calwell and Cavanagh 1989). In fact, it was not until 1990 that California's DSM programs were revitalized after the four largest California utilities and thirteen representatives of public and private interests reached an agreement through an innovative and extensive DSM collaborative process (Raab 1991, Raab and Schweitzer 1992, Raab et al. 1994). Included in the collaborative agreement were provisions to provide utilities with financial incentives based on shared savings. This represented a major inducement that had not been present when the CPUC pushed utilities to run DSM programs in the late 1970s and early 1980s (Raab et al. 1994). The California PUC endorsed the collaborative process and suggested that it would be willing to provide financial incentives to the utilities for successful DSM performance. The California DSM case illustrates the potential difficulty of sustaining changes ordered through regulatory interventionism without broad support.

A second example of the shortcomings of regulatory interventionism occurred in Massachusetts in connection with its "prudent, used, and useful" standard and illustrates the potential of regulatory interventionism for producing unintended and undesirable results. Beginning in the early 1980s, Massachussetts law required utility investments to be subjected to a test of whether the expenditures had been prudent, used, and useful before they could be incorporated into the rate base on which the utility earned its return. In the mid-1980s, Massachusetts regulators disallowed substantial nuclear-related costs through this test. Subsequently, the fear of seeing their investments disallowed scared the state's utilities away from building new capacity. As a result, in the late 1980s, while Massachusetts was still experiencing the "economic miracle" that Governor Dukakis boasted about during his bid for the presidency, the capacity situation was tight: brownouts had already occurred in the summer of 1987.

To create a climate in which utilities would be willing to invest in new resources, the Massachusetts Department of Public Utilities (DPU) opened a rulemaking process. As discussed in detail in Chapter 5, this four-year rulemaking process completely revised the rules for the ratemaking treatment of new facilities and also produced integrated resource management (IRM) rules, developed through an elaborate technical negotiating process that actively solicited the views of interested parties and sought to build consensus.

The point of these illustrations is not to make a case for the failure of regulatory interventionism or to call for a return to the days of laissez-faire regulation. Such a return would be neither possible nor desirable given the complexity and controversy of the current issues in the electric utility industry and the regulatory environment. It is, after all, the PUCs' job to regulate by acting quasi-judicially in rate cases (and other adjudications) and quasi-legislatively in rulemaking (and other policy deliberations). More importantly, regulators often bring unique and insightful ideas to the regulatory arena.

Instead, this book examines the usefulness of consensus in resolving contentious regulatory disputes. Clearly, some of Alfred Kahn's success was due to the consensus building he was able to pursue along with his interventionism. Kahn's experience, and the case studies laid out in this book, show that it is likely that DSM in California and IRM in Massachusetts will be more successful now that regulators and others have begun to supplement their traditional regulatory efforts with consensus building.

Current Controversies in Electric Utility Regulation

There is probably consensus in society that the electric utility industry is in transition, with many issues begging for resolution. Substantive controversies now facing the industry and its regulatory environment cover the planning, operation, and ratemaking treatment of electricity-related investments. Current controversial issues can be grouped into five areas: (1) minimizing societal costs, (2) utility investment in demand-side management resources, (3) competition in electricity generation, (4) interjurisdictional conflict, and (5) incentive ratemaking. This list is not meant to be exhaustive—other important and controversial issues certainly exist—but it provides a flavor of the current challenges facing society regarding electric utility issues. Moreover, it offers a preview of many of the substantive issues at the core of the case studies that follow.

Minimizing Societal Costs

Traditionally, the goal of electric utility power planning, acquisition, and operation decisions has been to minimize the direct cost (that is, out-of-pocket costs) of electricity for consumers. Additional social costs or benefits associated with electricity production, distribution, and consumption were not explicitly accounted for in the decision-making calculus. However, since the mid-1980s, many utilities have been required by regulators to expand their evaluation criteria to explicitly incorporate other costs and benefits—most notably environmental externalities (S. Cohen et al. 1990, Raab 1993). This required expansion of evaluation criteria has taken several forms, including (1) looking to environmental factors as a tie breaker when choosing between resources with comparable direct costs (New Hampshire); (2) explicitly favoring less-polluting resources with a simple cost credit for cleaner resources or a penalty for dirtier resources (Northwest Power Planning Council, Wisconsin PSC, Vermont PSB);[17] and (3) using cost adders based on emissions ($/ton of pollutant) that must be combined with direct costs when comparing resources (New York PSC, Massachusetts DPU, Nevada and California PUCs).

Many states now require that utilities minimize social costs; others are considering such action. However, both the underlying rationale for including externalities and the methods for doing so remain controversial among regulators and within society (NARUC 1990). Some argue that states that have included such considerations have already gone too far (Browne 1991, Joskow 1991, A. Kahn 1991, Maine PUC 1991). These critics generally argue that state PUCs lack the authority and expertise to regulate pollution beyond already stringent federal and state standards. They also question the efficacy and fairness of requiring utilities to further internalize externalities without also imposing such restrictions simultaneously on all sectors of the economy across the country. Finally, these critics argue that the use of cost adders is technically flawed because there is little basis for setting the cost per unit of pollutant.

Meanwhile, supporters of including environmental externalities in utility decision making often argue that even the most stringent approaches taken by some states do not go far enough (Bernow et al. 1991, Chernick and Caverhill 1992, Krause et al. 1991, Pace University 1990). Specifically, these critics argue that the most aggressive approaches currently required apply only to new resources and do little to address decisions about existing resources (that is, retrofit, fuel substitution, retirement of existing plants, and system dispatch). Some also argue that the methods need to be expanded to (1) incorporate pollution over the entire fuel cycle instead of focusing solely on smokestack emissions, and (2) apply to all environmental impacts (for example, nuclear waste and habitat destruction from hydro development) instead of focusing solely on air pollutants. Finally, these critics argue that some of the environmental externality adders being used by states may be too low, and that other externalities besides environmental ones should be included (for example, economic and security).

It is unlikely that the controversy surrounding environmental factors in electric utility regulation will dissipate anytime soon, given the growing public concern over environmental issues and the fact that electricity generation still accounts for a significant portion of pollution in the United States (two-thirds of sulfur dioxide, one-third of nitrogen oxide, and one-third of carbon dioxide) (Moskovitz et al. 1991). PUCs will probably continue to push utilities to include environmental externalities in their resource decision making, if for no other reason than to internalize the cost of complying with more stringent regulations anticipated in the future.[18]

Utility Investment in Demand-Side Management Resources

Amory Lovins's article "Energy Strategy: The Road Not Taken?" published in *Foreign Affairs* in 1976 sparked extensive debate over the technical feasibility and the appropriateness of substituting DSM resources for supply-side options. A virtual consensus has emerged that *society* should pursue energy conservation opportunities that cost up to the price of new supply. However, there is no consensus regarding the appropriate role of *electric utilities* in delivering and financing DSM programs.

The proponents of active utility involvement argue that utilities are well situated to broker DSM programs by helping overcome substantial market barriers that keep ratepayers from investing in DSM (for example, inadequate information, split incentives between landlords and tenants, or limited access to capital) (Cavanagh 1988, Lovins and Gilliam 1986, Lovins and Hirst 1989, Northwest Power Planning Council 1988). They further contend that utilities should be willing to pay up to their avoided cost (that is, the cost of additional new supply-side resources) to procure DSM. Such a strategy, proponents assert, should result in the minimization of the overall cost of delivering electricity services to society and lower the average customer's bill, even though electricity rates may rise in the process.

Opponents generally argue that utilities are in the business of selling kilowatts and are not particularly well suited for delivering DSM, or "negawatts," as Lovins calls them (D. Anderson 1991, Costello 1987, Joskow 1988, A. Kahn 1991, Ruff 1988). Moreover, they contend, a utility's obligation to finance DSM programs should be limited to the difference between its avoided cost of new supply and the current rates.[19] Such a limitation, they assert, will avoid raising rates for everyone and increasing the bills of customers who do not participate in the DSM programs; moreover, it will send the proper price signal to customers who do participate.

As the debate continues, electric utility investment in DSM in the United States has grown to more than $2 billion per year (Moskovitz et al. 1991).[20] At least ten utilities are spending over 3 percent of their revenue on DSM investments (id.). PUCs are generally requiring utilities to spend up to their full avoided cost on DSM if necessary to gain customer participation. However, as both rates and nonparticipant bills continue to rise, customer backlash against utility DSM programs—particularly in these difficult economic times—is likely. In addition, the recent push by some intervenors and PUCs for utilities to include fuel substitution measures in their DSM programs (that is, requiring utilities to pay to switch customers using electricity for certain end uses, such as water heating or space heating, to alternative fuels) is intensifying the debate on DSM (Raab and Cowart 1992).

Competition in Electricity Generation

In 1978 Congress passed the Public Utilities Regulatory Policy Act (PURPA), requiring utilities to purchase power at avoided cost from cogenerators, and from small power producers using renewable resources (Qualifying Facilities, or QFs). At that time, utilities essentially produced all the electricity delivered to their customers through the power grid.[21] Since the passage of PURPA, however, an increasing percentage of new generating resources is being provided by QFs and other independent power producers (IPPs) that do not meet PURPA's definition for QFs. There are currently 43,000 MW of IPP generation on-line, representing 8 percent of total generation (RCG/Hagler, Bailly, Inc. 1992). With nearly half the state PUCs requiring or permitting utilities to solicit the majority of new resources through bidding systems open to QFs, and often to other IPPs and even to DSM providers, the new generating resources supplied by nonutility entities should continue to increase.[22] Estimates of the market share of nonutility generators for new generation over the next decade range from 25 to 50 percent (Joskow 1989; RCG/Hagler, Bailly, Inc. 1992; USGAO 1990).

In addition to these changes, there have been hearings on the prospect of requiring electric utilities to open their transmission lines for "wheeling"—the delivery of power directly from a utility or private generator to a utility or another customer, much as pipeline owners and other common carriers are required to transport anyone's goods. These and other changes in the vertical integration of generation, transmission, and distribution challenge the electric utilities' monopoly-like position.

This major restructuring of the electricity generation sector in the United States is not occurring without substantial controversy. The controversy falls into two general areas: (1) the appropriateness and design of the processes—most notably bidding—to accomplish this restructuring and (2) concerns with the restructuring itself. Some of the controversial questions at the heart of the debates on bidding are listed in Table 2-1. Different PUCs and utilities (in the absence of state rules) have addressed these questions in diverse ways (Duane 1989).

The concept of infusing competition into electricity generation is generally accepted. However, there is a debate on how far and how fast it should be done (Gerber 1988, Hamrin 1989, Joskow 1989, E. Kahn 1990, Naill and Belanger 1989, Stalon and Lock 1990, Tierney 1989). Some fear that increased dependence on IPPs could jeopardize system reliability and raise electricity prices (Gerber 1988, Joskow 1989). Others argue just the opposite (Hamrin 1989, Naill and Belanger 1989). Some question whether competition should apply only

---

Table 2-1. Controversial Questions on Bidding

1. Is it appropriate to integrate DSM into supply-side bidding?
2. Should utilities participate in their own bidding processes?
3. If utilities do not participate, how will it be determined what portion of need will be bid and what portion will be delivered by utilities?
4. Should bidding processes use self-scoring systems, or should utilities be given greater flexibility in resource selection?
5. What nonprice factors should be evaluated, and how should they be structured? Also, how should price factors be weighed against nonprice factors when comparing resources?
6. Should utilities be allowed to negotiate contracts for power outside of, or even instead of, a bidding framework?

to new resources, or whether existing resources should also be subject to competition. Finally, many argue that unfettered competition would be unwise before transmission access and pricing issues, and other issues that touch on the question of interjurisdictional authority, are resolved (Hempling 1990, Steinmeier 1990).

Interjurisdictional Conflict

The primary focus of this book is on intrastate PUC regulation. However, an analysis of the major controversies facing society on electricity regulatory matters would be incomplete without mentioning some of the interjurisdictional conflicts that currently exist between the state PUCs and the Federal Energy Regulatory Commission (FERC), and also among the states.

Federal-state conflicts stem from a separation of authority between federal and state regulators on electric utility issues, an authority that is fuzzy in many areas and that has required increasing intervention from the courts in recent years to sort out (Stalon and Lock 1990, Vince et al. 1990). A central issue is the right of state PUCs to review the prudence of investments by multistate holding companies under FERC's jurisdiction as they relate to retail subsidiaries under state jurisdiction. A recent court case ruled that states cannot second-guess FERC in its allocations of project costs among various subsidiaries of a single utility holding company.[23] However, states continue to argue that this infringes on their prerogative to regulate utility supply planning.

Transmission issues are another source of friction. States have jurisdiction over transmission certification and siting. FERC has authority over interstate electricity transmission access and pricing. The two jurisdictions have butted heads over state-sponsored efforts to push utilities to provide IPPs with open access to transmission at market-based prices (Stalon and Lock 1990, Tierney 1990). The National Association of Regulatory Utility Commissioners (NARUC) and others have opposed reforms to the Public Utility Company Holding Act of 1935 (PUCHA)[24] until states' concerns over transmission access and pricing, and the future of state oversight of utility energy planning, are adequately addressed (Hempling 1990, Stalon and Lock 1990, Steinmeier 1990, Vince et al. 1990).

A third set of issues entails the implementation of PURPA. FERC has challenged some states on the consistency of their implementation procedures with federal law (for example, New York PSC's requirement that utilities pay QFs prices above avoided cost). Finally, mergers between utilities in different states require approval both by the

PUCs in the affected states and by FERC—giving each entity an effective veto. Recent merger cases have proven extremely contentious both between federal and state entities and between states (for example, the PacifiCorp and Utah Power & Light merger, and the Northeast Utilities and Public Service of New Hampshire merger).

Jurisdictional tensions between states also exist, although usually they are driven more by concerns over the interstate distribution of costs and benefits than by underlying principles of legal authority. The merger cases are a good example of this phenomenon. Another good example is disputes over the selection of supply-side resources or the design of DSM programs by PUCs in neighboring states in which retail companies are serviced by a common multistate company—particularly when states have different preferences and planning rules. Differing regulations on environmental matters are also a source of concern among states. States with relatively tough environmental standards can increase the cost of electricity for others and can even cause the export of pollution to states with lower standards.

Given the current trends to merge and consolidate utilities into holding companies and power pools on the one hand, and to infuse competition in generation on the other, jurisdictional disputes between federal and state entities and between state PUCs will undoubtedly remain in the limelight throughout the 1990s.

Incentive Ratemaking

Traditional cost-of-service ratemaking essentially reimburses electric utilities for their expenditures and provides a reasonable return on long-term investments. Regulators typically can disallow recovery for imprudence and other factors. The ratemaking system is based almost exclusively on the threat of regulatory reprisal and does not inherently encourage utilities to control costs or pursue least-cost resources (Joskow and Schmalensee 1986, Moskovitz 1989). Over the past decade, however, state regulators have begun to experiment with modifications to the ratemaking process by providing utilities with more direct incentives to minimize the cost of service.

By 1986, over twenty states had imposed modest operation and maintenance incentives for some generating facilities under their jurisdiction (Joskow and Schmalensee 1986). Regulators in some states have expanded incentive ratemaking to cover investments in new resources. For instance, Massachusetts adopted rules in 1988 that require utilities to seek preapproval for new resources and major capital additions through a process that would fix before the fact the price that utilities would be paid for delivering electricity (Massachusetts DPU

1989). Twenty-three utilities in fifteen states are allowed to earn incentives on their DSM investments, which share the savings (that is, the difference between the next supply plant and the cost of DSM) with their ratepayers (Destribats and Rosenblum 1992, Nadel et al. 1992). In 1991, PUCs in Washington and Maine adopted the most sweeping ratemaking incentive mechanisms to date when they approved proposals to decouple profits from sales by fixing utility revenue at a set amount per customer (Moskovitz and Swofford 1991).[25]

Traditional adversaries on the electric utility regulatory battlefield now support initiatives to design and implement incentive-oriented ratemaking schemes. However, others continue to maintain that incentive schemes are unnecessary. They argue that utilities' obligation to serve requires them to provide least-cost and reliable service. But even those who agree that experimentation with incentive ratemaking schemes is appropriate and necessary continue to disagree over when and where incentives should be applied, and also over how incentives should be structured and sized. These five controversial issues—minimizing societal costs, utility investment in demand-side management, competition in electricity generation, interjurisdictional conflict, and incentive ratemaking—represent some of the opportunities for better consensus building in electric utility regulation. The next chapter explores ways that these issues can be resolved, using techniques that bring the parties together to forge a solution instead of trapping them solely as adversaries in the PUC hearing room.

Chapter 3

Introduction to the Theory, Practice, and Evaluation of Consensus Building in Electric Utility Regulation

As the old consensus on utility regulation disappeared, the need arose for some way of resolving disputes over electricity issues such as the controversies described in the preceding chapter. At first an adversarial process was tried, but it suffered from the drawbacks of ill feeling, delay, and expense. Subsequently, parties have often attempted to settle the outstanding controversies while ameliorating the drawbacks of adversarial proceedings before the regulators. These strategies aimed to infuse supplemental consensus-building processes into traditional regulatory procedures. In this way, the parties sought a consensus that was not the result of happy historical accident, as the old utility consensus had been, but rather the carefully and deliberately constructed product of focused effort by the stakeholders involved.

The rise in settlement and other consensus-based processes within the context of electric utility regulation reflects the new paradigm for consensus-based negotiation that has emerged in the literature during the last decade under numerous banners, including "principled negotiation," "integrative bargaining," "win-win or mutual-gain negotiation," and "alternative dispute resolution" (ADR). In fact, utilities, regulators, and intervenor groups have been experimenting with a broad array of consensus-building options, described in the literature. However, evaluating the success of these efforts relative to standard practice poses significant practical and theoretical challenges. Ultimately, evaluations should try to assess the overall legitimacy of the process and its results; the practicality of the remedies, plans, and policies; and the process-related savings.

Toward a New Negotiation Paradigm: Getting to Yes

Negotiation has always been used in our society to resolve both private and public disputes,[1] and, as described in Chapter 4, negotiated settlements have been a fixture in the landscape of electric utility regulation for a long time. There have been many critiques of traditional negotiation practices and suggestions for improvements. However, the publication in 1981 of *Getting to YES: Negotiating Agreement Without Giving In*, by Harvard professors Roger Fisher and William Ury, succeeded in crystallizing and popularizing an approach to negotiation that has enjoyed increasing influence over the past decade.[2] The central tenet of Fisher and Ury's "principled negotiation" approach is that disputes can be more successfully resolved when parties shift their focus from "distributive" to "integrative" bargaining. Distributive bargaining (which has also been called "win-lose" or "zero-sum" negotiation) is based on the premise that there is a fixed pie or pot of money such that an increase in one person's share can only be achieved by decreasing the shares of others. Integrative bargaining assumes that the pie is not fixed, but rather can be expanded in ways that can make everyone's portion larger.

In the absence of a negotiated settlement, Fisher and Ury contend, a certain resolution will prevail (perhaps enforced by regulators, or perhaps dictated by external circumstance) that will not benefit either party very much. They call this point the "best alternative to a negotiated agreement" (BATNA), denoted by point C in Figure 3-1. This point serves as a benchmark against which to compare the results of a negotiation.

Fisher and Ury demarcate the outer limit of possible solutions to the dispute by the line ADEB, which constitutes a frontier of sorts determined by external factors, such as costs and laws. Any solution to the dispute that lies to the left of the line CD would be worse for party B than the BATNA; any solution that lies below line CE would disadvantage party A. Any resolution in the wedge CDE is an improvement for both parties.

In economic terms, the resolutions in the wedge CDE are called Pareto improvements: changes that improve the lot of one party without harming the other. These improvements can be made until the Pareto curve, DE, is reached, which represents a set of outcomes that are all equally efficient.

Improvements can be made because most disputes are multi-issued, and to the extent that parties value issues differentially, efficient trades can be made.[3] Howard Raiffa, in *The Art and Science of Negoti-*

Figure 3-1. Integrative Bargaining

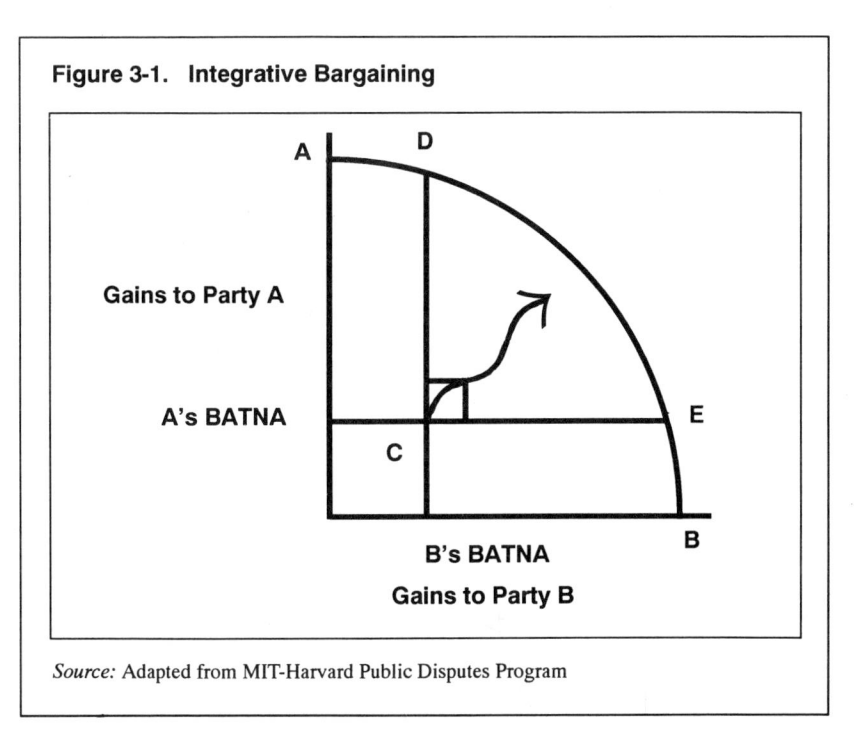

Gains to Party A

A's BATNA

B's BATNA

Gains to Party B

Source: Adapted from MIT-Harvard Public Disputes Program

ation (1982), provides the following examples of where such trades are possible:

> . . . The potential of finding joint win-win situations depends on the exploitation of differences between beliefs, between probabilistic projections, between tradeoffs, between discount rates (a special case of intertemporal tradeoffs), between risk preferences. (Id., p. 286)[4]

To succeed in shifting to a more integrative bargaining paradigm, Fisher and Ury suggest that disputants must abandon traditional positional bargaining and adopt a more collaborative, joint problem-solving orientation. This somewhat radical concept is based on the assumption that we can better satisfy our own interests only through seeking to better satisfy the interests of our opponents. *Getting to YES* articulates a strategy for approaching this task that is paraphrased in Table 3-1.

Fisher and Ury's original treatise on principled negotiation stands as the major pillar of the alternative dispute resolution (ADR) literature. However, numerous other important works have focused on refining Fisher and Ury's concepts and on creating ways to incorporate them into traditional procedures. Most notable from the perspective of this book are works by Philip Harter on the use of ADR in administra-

Table 3-1. Fisher and Ury's Strategy for Integrative Bargaining
1. Focus on underlying interests rather than on positions.
2. Invent options for mutual gain.
3. Decide on objective criteria or underlying principles for resolving any remaining distributive components to a negotiation.
4. Separate the people from the problem (i.e., be hard on the issues and soft on the people).
5. Seek to strengthen your own negotiating power by improving your best alternative to a negotiated agreement (BATNA) while better understanding the BATNAs of those you are negotiating with.
Source: Adapted from Fisher and Ury, Getting to YES (1981).

tive agency decision making, particularly those on negotiated rule-making,[5] and works by Lawrence Susskind on resolving public disputes, the advantages of using assisted negotiation (for example, mediation), and the use of ADR specifically in the context of electric utility regulation.[6] (Since aspects of these important works will be discussed in various places throughout this book, detailed descriptions are omitted here.)

Three Criticisms of Alternative Dispute Resolution

Fisher and Ury's overall approach to negotiation has generally received wide support. However, it has also been criticized in several ways. Three major issues are (1) the problem of power imbalances in negotiations, (2) the handling of distributive questions within the context of integrative bargaining, and (3) fundamental limits to the use of ADR. These criticisms, along with their rejoinders, are relevant to consensus building efforts in an electric utility regulatory context. Other potential criticisms have been raised, but these are more narrowly focused and are discussed at appropriate places in subsequent chapters.

Power Imbalances

Fisher and Ury have been accused of paying insufficient attention to preexisting power imbalances between parties (Amy 1987, Bazerman 1987, Fiss 1984, McCarthy 1985, White 1984).[7] These power imbalances, it is argued, can undermine any real progress toward equitable, integrative settlements. In an article entitled "Negotiating Power," Fisher acknowledges the potential problems of differential power relations but claims that negotiating power is not a function of actual control over the situation, but rather of how other parties perceive one's power (Fisher 1983). Thus negotiating power is not static and can be enhanced in several ways: through skill and knowledge, good relationships, development of strong alternatives to a negotiated agreement, creation of elegant solutions, emphasis on the legitimacy of a proposed approach, and construction of affirmative commitments (that is, reasonable offers) (id.). In a separate article, Susskind adds to this list the ability to form coalitions and the use of mediation as two additional methods to temper power imbalances (Susskind 1985).

The initial distribution of power is often unclear in public policy disputes generally, and in electric utility regulation specifically. For instance, although electric utilities certainly have more resources at their disposal than most intervenors, it would be wrong to assume that utilities are always the most powerful players in the regulatory arena. It is more appropriate to assess the relative distribution of power in the regulatory context against the benchmark of the party's ability to persuade the PUC, or the courts on appeal, to decide in its favor. To the degree that significant uncertainty exists in this regard, as I would argue is usually the case, the starting distribution of power is less clear. If parties can muster sufficient resources to intervene in a case in the first place,[8] and if all the parties agree to try and settle (that is, reach a consensus), the ability to veto that consensus immediately gives all parties significant power. In addition, the more patient a party can afford to be, the stronger its negotiating position will be. Its power can be further enhanced by resorting to some of the negotiating techniques that Fisher and Susskind have identified. In the cases in the following chapters, we will see exactly this phenomenon.

Inadequate Attention to Resolving Distributive Issues

A second criticism of the theory of "principled negotiation," as originally defined in *Getting to YES*, is that it pays insufficient attention to the facts that some negotiations are largely distributive and that all negotiations have distributive elements (Bazerman 1987, Lax and Sebenius 1986, Raiffa 1982, White 1984). As can be seen in Figure 3-1, even if joint problem solving could succeed in expanding the pie all the way to the Pareto curve of efficient solutions (arc DE), parties would still need to decide where along this curve they should end up—any movement along the arc results in a gain to one party with a corresponding loss to the other. Such tension, it is argued, is never totally absent from even the most integrative negotiating process, since it is unlikely that parties will stop worrying about how the pie they are jointly focused on expanding will ultimately be divided, even when they are still far from the Pareto curve (Bazerman 1987, Lax and Sebenius 1986, Raiffa 1982). In a chapter entitled "The Negotiator's Dilemma: Creating and Claiming Value," in their book *The Manager as Negotiator* (1986), Lax and Sebenius describe the problem:

> There is a central, inescapable tension between cooperative moves to create value jointly and competitive moves to gain individual advantage. This tension affects virtually all tactical and strategic choice. . . . Neither denial or discomfort will make it disappear. (Id., p. 30)

Fisher acknowledges that distributive elements are present in virtually all negotiations but maintains that such tensions can be tempered without resorting to traditional "hard" bargaining (Fisher 1984, Fisher et al. 1991). First and foremost, Fisher emphasizes that disputes are usually multi-issued and that expanding everyone's options by focusing on integrative solutions will relieve some pressure from distributional tensions. What distributional tensions remain can be eased by refocusing the debate away from deciding who gets the last dollar to a question of how to jointly decide on objective criteria for resolving the distributional questions (id.). By starting with the parties' underlying interests, rather than their proposals or negotiating positions, further discussion can revolve around how to satisfy those interests rather than on who will get more advantage than the other. Fisher acknowledges that attaining this goal is not always easy. However, he argues that by refocusing the debate, distributional questions can be approached in a more principled and productive way (id.). Other authors, most notably Raiffa and Lax and Sebenius, have attempted to provide both elaborations and variations on Fisher's recommendations for dealing with this inescapable tension between creating and claiming value.[9]

This issue is directly relevant to electric utility regulation, particularly to rate cases, in which the overall focus on determining a rate of return, a level of disallowance, or a cost allocation appears extremely distributive. But as will be seen in the cases in the following chapters, particularly the Pilgrim nuclear power plant outage settlement case in Chapter 4, rate cases need not be solely distributive. The initial focus of the Pilgrim outage litigation involved a seemingly distributive question on how the money associated with a nuclear outage should be divided among utility stockholders and ratepayers. Parties to the case negotiated an extremely integrative settlement that involved tying shareholder earnings to future performance of Pilgrim and commencing an aggressive DSM effort. In so doing, the parties were able to better satisfy their own long-run interests while settling the narrower distributive question de facto. Even the most mundane rate cases generally involve several parties and a multitude of issues that parties value differentially, thus raising the possibility of integrative settlements to seemingly distributive problems. Still, difficult distributive issues must constantly and ultimately be resolved in electric utility regulation.

Fundamental Limits to Alternative Dispute Resolution
A third criticism of Fisher and Ury's integrative bargaining approach is that certain types of cases are not appropriate for ADR and should be considered off-limits. In an article entitled "Against Settlement" in the *Yale Law Journal*, Owen Fiss makes such an argument:

> My universe [where I do not think ADR is appropriate] includes those cases in which there are significant distributional inequalities; those in which it is difficult to generate authoritative consent because organizations or social groups are parties or because the power to settle is vested in autonomous agents; those in which the court must continue to supervise the parties after judgment; and those in which justice needs to be done, or to put it more modestly, where there is a genuine social need for an authoritative interpretation of law. I imagine that the number of cases that satisfy one of these four criteria is considerable. (Fiss 1984, p. 1087)

There is general agreement even among ADR advocates that certain disputes involving questions of fundamental constitutional rights (for example, civil rights and abortion) are not good candidates for ADR, although many would quibble with Fiss about where to draw the line (Fisher and Ury 1981, Menkel-Meadow 1985, Susskind and Cruikshank 1987). In addition, as Susskind and Cruikshank point out, once courts have defined what is legal and illegal with respect to these rights, consensus building might assist in protecting them or in reconciling them with other valid interests. The authors also observe that people often try to obfuscate what are essentially distributional questions by coating them in the vernacular of constitutional rights (Susskind and Cruikshank 1987, p. 17).

Although electric utility regulation may involve questions of rights, it is not immediately clear where those rights are so fundamental that they preclude attempts at ADR. Rate cases, for instance, which involve the distribution of costs and benefits between ratepayers and utility shareholders, and among ratepayers, can hardly be considered as addressing a fundamental right. A 1989 Supreme Court decision, Duquesne Light Co. v. Barash, indicated the Court's willingness to allow PUCs substantial latitude in disallowing utility investment prior to considering it a "taking" of property (Kolbe and Tye 1991). Utilities often argue that measures such as the inclusion of environmental externalities in resource planning or requirements that utilities pay for their customers to substitute fuels as an energy efficiency measure violate the rights of the utilities to sell their product without unnecessary or overburdensome regulation. However, it is not clear that embracing environmental externalities or substituting fuels actually threatens fundamental rights, and as the cases in the following chapters demonstrate, settlements have already been forged between traditional adversaries in some states even on these contentious issues.

There may, however, be particular instances in which a fully litigated electric utility case is preferable to a negotiated settlement. Former New Mexico PSC commissioner Marilyn O'Leary, an enthusiastic supporter of using ADR, has argued that in certain instances in which cases are extremely controversial or in which there is a need to publicly illuminate the details of utility actions or proposals, ADR may be inadvisable (O'Leary 1986). However, there do not appear to be any types of electric utility adjudications or rulemaking in which a categorical exclusion of ADR is necessary a priori. In 1992, for example, the New York Public Service Commission in its revised settlement guidelines and rules reversed its earlier decision to exclude rate design issues from settlements (NYPSC 1992).[10] In 1993, a consensus study completed by a forty-six-member committee of regulators, utilities, consumers, and legal practitioners on the use of settlement in PUC proceedings identified twenty-two different types of PUC proceedings and concluded that settlement negotiations "can be beneficial in virtually every case" (Center for Public Resources 1993).

How Principled Negotiation Has Been Applied to Consensus Building in Electric Utility Regulation

Since the mid-1980s, the theoretical literature on ADR has begun to influence the resolution of disputes in electric utility regulation. These disputes had been contentious and at times bloody for two decades; besides the numerous controversies before PUCs, the siting of electric generating plants had also stirred major controversy (Bacow and Wheeler 1984). It is therefore not surprising that many of those involved in the electric utility industry and its regulatory environment, particularly the utilities, began to look to ADR for assistance.

Initial exposure to ADR theories for many has been through

Fisher and Ury's original *Getting to YES*, which has sold over 2 million copies. More importantly, numerous direct attempts have been made to train participants in these techniques and to develop actual procedures at various state PUCs based on ADR theories. For example, in 1985–1986 the Edison Electric Institute contracted with the Public Disputes Program at Harvard Law School's Program on Negotiation to conduct well-publicized experiments using assisted negotiation on a variety of issues in three states. The issues included (1) the negotiation of a rate shock moderation plan in New Mexico associated with the "coming on line" of the Palo Verde nuclear power plant;[11] (2) the negotiation of a demand forecasting methodology and resource selection criteria for Boston Edison Company in Massachusetts; and (3) a resource planning rule for the PUC in Colorado (Susskind and Morgan 1986a, 1986b). The experiments met with mixed, short-term success because of several complicating factors. However, they were successful in familiarizing participants with ADR techniques and turned out to have numerous long-term benefits (O'Leary 1986; Richardson 1991; Susskind and Morgan 1986a, 1986b; Technical Development Corporation 1987), as in the Palo Verde case in New Mexico, which was actually settled five months after the formal assisted negotiations ended (Richardson 1991).

Since the late 1980s, many of the participants in the electric utility regulatory arena have been trained in ADR techniques. Lawrence Susskind, a professor at MIT and director of the MIT-Harvard Public Disputes Program, conducted ADR training workshops for the PUC staffs and commissioners in Maine in 1988 and New York in 1990. In 1989 and 1990, the Public Disputes Program conducted two 2-day trainings on using ADR in utility ratesetting, rulemaking, and least-cost planning. Over 115 state regulators, utility representatives, public advocates, and others attended these two sessions from thirty states; Washington, D.C.; and Canada.[12] Half-day trainings in ADR and electric utility regulation have been conducted at two of NARUC's national conferences and at two seminars for senior PUC staff at Lawrence Berkeley Laboratory, reaching over 100 additional people.[13] Other ADR-related trainings have also included participants from the electric utility regulatory arena.[14]

The concepts embodied in ADR have clearly filtered into the language and practice of many utilities and PUCs. In 1990, when PUC commissioners from thirteen states were asked about ADR, they showed both a considerable familiarity with the theory and a surprising amount of experimentation with ADR approaches at the PUCs (Public Utilities Fortnightly 1990).[15] There has also been a steadily increasing stream of articles in the literature and papers delivered at national conferences, primarily by participants in these processes (Bergmann 1992, Boucher and Weedall 1991, Chouteau 1991, A. Cohen and Chaisson 1990, A. Cohen and Townsley 1990, Cowell 1990, Ellis 1989, Endispute 1991, Hicks 1990, Lehr 1990, McIntyre and Reznicek 1992, Nogee 1990, O'Leary 1986, Raab 1989a, Raab and Schweitzer 1992, Raab et al. 1994, Richardson 1991, Schweitzer and Raab 1992).

The Practice of Consensus Building in Electric Utility Regulation

Settlements, which by definition represent a consensus among disputants, were used to resolve electric utility rate cases prior to the early 1980s, when Fisher and Ury popularized the concept of ADR. However, it would not be accurate to assume that all settlements prior to 1981 were distributive and that today's settlements are expansive and integrative. Undoubtedly there are more similarities than differences between past rate case settlements and current settlements, both in terms of the issues addressed and the degree to which integrative bargaining (even though past disputants may not have called it that) was utilized.

What has changed, however, is that there is now a more conscious recognition of both the theory of and the need for consensus building in the regulation of electric utilities. This recognition has led to numerous efforts by regulators, utilities, and intervenors over the past decade to develop both formal and informal consensus-based processes.

Consensual Options

Table 3-2 provides an overview of the range of consensus-building mechanisms currently in use. All of the activities listed in Table 3-2 (with the exception of case settlements) are appropriate supplements to rulemaking proceedings, whose objective is to set guidelines that will apply to all utilities in a state. Similarly, all of these activities (except policy dialogues and negotiated rulemaking) are appropriate supplements to adjudicatory proceedings, whose focus is applying the existing rules to a rate request from a specific utility. The list provides a spectrum of consensus-building activities, beginning at the top with seminars and conferences, which represent the least intensive activity in terms of seeking consensus, and ending with negotiated rulemaking, which represents the most intensive.

Seminars and conferences are occasionally used to provide participants with information about a particular subject or issue. Dialogue is not the primary focus, although contrasting perspectives are often pro-

Table 3-2. Consensus-Building Mechanisms in Electric Utility Regulation

Seminars and conferences
Technical sessions and workshops
Policy dialogues
Advisory committees
Case settlements
Prospective collaboratives
Negotiated rulemaking

vided. Technical sessions and workshops in the context of adjudicatory or rulemaking proceedings are often provided to give parties the opportunity to explore technical issues outside the hearing room (usually off the record, and occasionally at great length). In addition to attempting to illuminate factual matters, technical sessions and workshops generally expose participants to each other's perspectives while providing an opportunity to engage in dialogue. Policy dialogues allow for similar exploration but focus on policy issues.

Convergence of opinion will often surface in technical sessions, workshops, and policy dialogues even though consensus is not necessarily actively pursued. Often areas in which there is some convergence serve as the basis for subsequent settlement in adjudications, or as the basis for policy proposals in rulemaking. However, even when no consensus emerges, such processes can still help to focus the subsequent formal proceedings more sharply by providing a greater common understanding of the facts, parties' interests, and the areas of agreement and disagreement. This sharper focus can in turn make it easier for PUCs to decide unresolved issues intelligently.

Advisory committees are used often by utilities and occasionally by PUCs to review past activity and to provide suggestions for future action. Although advisory committees often strive to attain consensus recommendations from their members, that is not always the case. Many advisory committees never aspire to provide anything more than feedback, albeit in an organized fashion. Moreover, even when advisory committees do strive for consensus, the entity seeking advice (the utility or the PUC) is rarely a formal party to the consensus. Still, such processes can be extremely helpful in building consensus on an informal basis.

Settlements in rate cases and other adjudicatory proceedings are based on reaching a formal consensus among the utility and the various intervenors on as many issues as possible. Settlements happen before, during, or after hearings in contested cases. When PUCs have advocacy staffs (people who are empowered to litigate cases as full parties but who are precluded from discussing the cases with their commissioners)[16] involved in a case, they are usually party to any settlement that may be forged. Uncontested settlements (that is, those in which all parties to a proceeding are in accord) are subsequently submitted to the commissioners for their review and approval, often after review by a hearing officer. Contested settlements follow a similar path but generally involve an opportunity for dissenters to file written objections or cross-examine the signatories of a settlement in subsequent hearings.

For reasons that will be described in Chapter 4, the use of settlement to resolve contested cases on electric utility matters is rapidly becoming the rule rather than the exception. Over the past decade, a majority of major electric utility cases before the New York Public Service Commission have had settlement discussions, and many were settled by most parties on most issues (Elwood interview). At the Federal Energy Regulatory Commission, parties have consistently settled 70 to 80 percent of the contested electric cases since the mid-1980s (Orecchio interview). It is worth noting at this juncture, however, that despite the extensive use of settlements, only a few state PUCs and FERC currently have formal settlement guidelines (Elwood and Marland interviews).[17]

Prospective collaborative processes are a relatively new form of consensus building in electric utility regulation and represent an extension of the settlement concept. Settlements in traditional contested rate cases generally involve resolving issues associated with past decisions and expenditures. In contrast, prospective collaboratives involve designing future plans or programs for utilities, or policies for PUCs. A second distinguishing feature of prospective collaboratives is that they often occur outside of an immediate contested case or rulemaking proceeding. However, like other settlements, collaborative results are generally subject to PUC review and approval.

The best examples of prospective collaboratives to date are the demand-side management (DSM) collaborative processes that have sprung up across the country since 1988 (Raab and Schweitzer 1992). A DSM collaborative brings together a utility (or group of utilities) with its traditional adversaries to jointly design comprehensive DSM programs for its customers. The utility almost always provides funds for the nonutility parties to secure their own independent technical experts. Chapter 4 explores the prospective collaborative processes through a case study of DSM collaboratives in Massachusetts. Such approaches are likely to become increasingly popular in resolving DSM issues as well as other issues related to a utility's upcoming actions.

The final consensus-building mechanism on the list is negotiated rulemaking, in which parties come together to reach consensus on a new rule. If consensus is reached, the rule is issued as the PUC's own proposed rule for public comment. Negotiated rulemaking is not yet common practice at state PUCs. However, the continued increase in rulemaking activities at the PUCs, combined with a growing acceptance of negotiated rulemaking at federal agencies (in the wake of numerous recent applications and the passage of a federal law in 1990 requiring federal agencies to consider negotiated rulemaking),[18] is likely to result in future experimentation with this consensus-building mechanism. Chapter 5 discusses negotiated rulemaking at length and includes a case on the formation of bidding policies for Qualifying Facilities (QFs) and other energy sources in New Jersey that in most respects was similar to federal agency use of negotiated rulemaking.

Assisted Consensus Building

All of the mechanisms for consensus building described in the previous section can be conducted exclusively by the parties themselves, or parties to a dispute may seek the assistance of facilitators or mediators. Reasons for considering the use of assisted negotiation to resolve public policy disputes, such as electric utility regulatory issues, are many and various:

> Most public disputes are highly complex, for example, and the affected groups are hard to identify and difficult to represent. Disputing parties often have great difficulty initiating and pursuing discussions. Emotional, psychological, or financial stakes may be so high that the disputants are unable to sustain the collaborative aspects of unassisted negotiation. Finally, power imbalances may preclude direct and unassisted dealings among disputants. (Susskind and Cruikshank 1987, p. 136)

Professional neutral parties can help provide facilitation, mediation, nonbinding arbitration, or some combination of these services (id.).

To date, most consensus-building endeavors in electric utility regulation have relied on unassisted negotiation. Where assisted negotiation has been used, the assistance has usually come from within the regulatory agency itself. For instance, New York occasionally uses a settlement judge other than the administrative law judge presiding over a rate case to oversee settlement activity. Currently, less than 10 percent of settlements in New York use settlement judges (Crary and Elwood interviews). At FERC, which has a similar internal settlement judge option, approximately 10 to 20 percent of the electricity cases that are settled use settlement judges (Orecchio interview).

Outside neutrals have rarely been used by PUCs in the past. However, this policy appears to be changing gradually. The Edison Electric Institute experiment mentioned above made use of the MIT-Harvard Public Disputes Program to provide mediation services in three cases. One of the DSM collaboratives also used an outside mediator with some success (Raab and Schweitzer 1992). The Massachusetts DPU employed outside neutrals when developing its integrated resource management rules (this case is featured in Chapter 5), and in 1992 the Arizona commission hired former Colorado commissioner Ron Lehr to facilitate meetings of a task force on environmental externalities.

In 1991, the Ohio PUC hired Endispute, Inc., to mediate rate settlements among intervenors and three utilities regarding a potential $590 million annual rate increase associated with the construction of the multi-billion-dollar Zimmer power plant, which began as a nuclear plant and was converted to coal midstream (Endispute 1991). Intervenors settled the case with one utility in a pact that was subsequently approved by the PUC; the cases involving the other two utilities were not settled and ultimately were litigated (Bergmann 1992, Endispute 1991).[19]

From September 1992 through June 1993, I was hired as a mediator by the Vermont Public Service Board to assist a diverse group of utilities, intervenors, and state agencies craft a board rule on the incorporation of environmental externalities in utility resource decisions. Despite not reaching a final settlement, the parties sent the board a letter indicating their belief that the process had been a success because they had come close to agreement on extremely complicated and contentious issues, and because as a result of the process, they had come to a better understanding of each other's positions as well as of the major issues and their consequences (Vermont parties 1993). The parties praised the mediating effort and encouraged the board "to be alert for situations which lend themselves to such processes in the future" (id.).[20]

Notably, in 1992, the New York PSC issued an order concerning its new settlement guidelines and rules that included an option for participants to use settlement judges from outside the PSC (NYPSC 1992). The role of assisted negotiation will be revisited in more detail both in Chapter 5 and in the concluding chapter.

Evaluating the Success of Consensus-Building Processes

Little effort has gone into rigorously evaluating whether the addition of settlement and other supplemental consensus-building processes in electric utility regulation (such as those described in the previous section) have been successful. Yardsticks for measuring success are rarely articulated beforehand or explored afterwards. The literature on the subject is primarily descriptive and has been written almost exclusively by participants in the processes (Bergmann 1992, A. Cohen and Chaisson 1990, Cowell 1990, McIntrye and Reznicek 1992, Wall and Griffin 1990). Finally, efforts to comment on the successes and failures of consensus-building processes have often focused on a narrow subset of criteria—that is, whether consensus was reached, whether the regulators approved the programs, and whether time and money were saved in the process.

A broader set of criteria can provide a fuller picture of the success of consensus-building supplements. Chief among these expanded criteria is whether the search for consensus produced substantive improvement in the ultimate solution. If the result is an improved solution, the consensus-building process can be said to be a success even if it required more resources. Evaluators can apply a variety of both objective and subjective criteria, including participants' stated satisfaction, to assess the success of consensus-building efforts. Each has its own unique analytic challenges. But ultimately, what is needed is a combination of criteria that together look at the overall legitimacy of the process and its results; the practicality of the remedies, plans, and policies; and the process-related savings.

Process-Related Resource Savings

Consensus-building activities, such as settlement, are most commonly advocated as a way to streamline the adjudicatory and rulemaking procedures of administrative agencies such as PUCs (Harter 1982, Susskind and McMahon 1985). Specifically, it is argued that time and resources related to the process itself can be saved. Any attempt to analyze this hypothesis must first accurately assess the time and resources that the consensus-building process typically requires. As the cases in the following chapters illustrate, these resources are often substantial and include those associated with the parties' participation as well as any outside technical or process-oriented (for example, mediation) expertise used.

The analysis must then compare the time and resources for consensus building against what would have been expended had the cases been resolved conventionally. Assessing the likely time and costs that would have been incurred without the consensus-building activity (that is, in the traditional adjudicatory or rulemaking process) is complex because it is by nature hypothetical. The first step is to determine the costs that would have been necessary to complete the proceeding before the PUC. In an adjudicatory proceeding such as a rate case settlement, savings over the traditional process might include a less substantial PUC final order, the absence of legal briefs, fewer hearings, or possibly less discovery, depending on when during the process the settlement occurs. Similar savings must be assessed in a rulemaking proceeding, although as we will see in Chapter 5, since rulemaking is rarer than adjudication and since PUCs have more flexibility in shaping rulemaking procedurally, establishing a baseline is more difficult.

Obviously, the further along in the process a settlement occurs, the smaller the potential for savings. Since, as explored in Chapter 4, most settlements in major electric utility cases happen after hearings are completed, savings may not be as large as is often assumed.[21] If consensus building does not result in settlement, the savings associated with the PUC process may be even smaller and may possibly even amount to net cost increases, since participants will still need to litigate (or in rulemaking, comment on) unresolved issues (Raab and Schweitzer 1992).

However, the framework for analyzing whether a particular consensus-building process saved time and resources must extend beyond the PUC's immediate proceeding. Such a framework should also incorporate savings associated with any reduced subsequent litigation, including appeals to the courts, as well as any savings associated with implementation of the settlement or a PUC order or rule. To the extent that consensus building in general, and settlement in particular, reduces appeals, subsequent litigation, and implementation problems, the long-run process-related savings from consensus building may be more significant than any short-term savings.

Potential long-term, process-related savings seem likely. However, they are even more difficult to ascertain than the initial savings in the PUC process. With respect to appeals, one must estimate both the probability of an appeal and its likely cost. Estimating the savings from avoiding or streamlining future litigation and from maximizing implementation compliance is highly speculative and difficult. Furthermore, these two types of savings must be analyzed over a sufficiently long time frame (at least several years) to adequately trace the effects of the consensus-building process involved. It would be worthwhile to describe these benefits at the very least, even if it is not possible to estimate them. The distribution of savings among the actors will have obvious ramifications for the support that the settlement process garners.

Finally, even when a thorough evaluation of the process-related costs and savings along these lines can be completed, they still tell only part of the story. Such savings do not represent a net benefit analysis from a societal perspective. A more thorough net benefit analysis must also include the benefits (or costs) to society from any changes in the substantive outcome as a result of the consensus-building process. In other words, even if consensus building costs more than a traditional process (using the approach described above), if the outcome can be shown to be substantively superior, the net benefits to society are also likely to be positive. The question of net societal benefits is far more important than the much narrower, but more commonly asked, question of whether process-related savings have been achieved. The remainder of this chapter focuses primarily on ways to approach this critical assessment.

Attainment of Consensus

Since the object of consensus-building supplements to traditional regulatory procedures is by definition a search for consensus, any evaluation must look at whether consensus was attained. The more comprehensive a consensus is, both in terms of the issues it resolves and the parties it includes, the greater the potential for success. However, failure to reach consensus should not automatically be seen as indicating a fatal flaw in a consensus-building process. Often agreement is not the formal goal in such processes as technical sessions, policy dialogues, and advisory committees. Even when agreement is the goal, as in settlement, prospective collaboratives, or negotiated rulemaking, consensus often is not reached on all issues or by all parties. One must look closely at both the resolved and the unresolved issues before judging how successful such processes were.

A collaborative process cannot be judged by consensus alone, since a partial settlement in which some issues must be litigated or further disputed may be preferable to a complete consensus in which critical issues, however thorny, were never on the table (Honeyman 1990). It must be determined whether important issues were omitted from what otherwise appears to be a complete consensus or, alternatively, whether the unsettled issues in a partial settlement were inappropriate for settlement or unrealistic. One must also look at whether all relevant interests were adequately represented. Complete consensus only on select issues, by select parties, or both, could result in an unstable agreement over time.

Consensus-building processes in which consensus is not achieved can also succeed in educating the participants about the substantive issues as well as the interests of all parties. This effort can help better focus everyone's input into the formal process before the regulators. It can also contribute to settlement at a later date (Richardson 1991). In the end, consensus, like savings in process-related resources, is an important but incomplete factor in evaluating the success of consensus-building processes.

PUC Approval and Judicial Review

Consensus-building processes do not exist in a vacuum; rather, most are embedded in traditional regulatory procedures and must ultimately stand the test of both regulatory and judicial scrutiny. If consensus is reached, for instance in a rate case settlement, it must be approved by the PUC. If a PUC decision approving a settlement is appealed, it in turn must be sustained by the courts.[22] It would be difficult to consider a consensus-building process successful if it were in large part rejected by the regulators or overturned in the courts. Such a rejection would be indicative of a failure of the process to adequately reflect political and judicial reality (Raab 1991). However, if the parties were able to reconvene to address the issues raised in the rejection of the initial consensus, success could be salvaged.

For these reasons it is critical that any analysis of a consensus-based process trace the results all the way through the traditional regulatory and judicial channels. That said, as Chapters 4 and 5 explain in more detail, uncontested rate case settlements or rules are rarely rejected by PUCs. This appears to be particularly true at PUCs where there are advocacy staffs that directly represent the PUC's perspective in negotiations. In other states, such as Massachusetts, where the Department of Public Utilities has historically had an advisory staff, but not an advocacy staff, the commission may show a greater willingness to reject otherwise uncontested settlements. Appeal to the courts would not be an issue since parties would generally not have this right unless a PUC rejects an uncontested settlement or other type of consensus.

PUC rejection of settlements or other consensual agreements that are contested by one or more parties, or that do not resolve all issues, are still relatively rare. The likelihood of appeals to the courts when there is a contested settlement increases but also is not that common; such appeals are certainly much less frequent than in contested cases absent any settlement or consensus-building procedures.[23]

In judging the relative success of a consensus-based process, one must carefully scrutinize the reasoning behind any rejection or call for modification by a PUC. To the extent that the concerns raised by a PUC could have been better accommodated in the consensus-based process, it could be concluded that the process had some shortcomings. The question of how to better integrate PUC perspectives into consensus-based processes is examined in more detail in the final chapter of this book.

Interpreting the meaning of judicial review vis-à-vis the consensus-based process, if and when it occurs, is more challenging. Inference is complicated, since the courts will be ruling on the PUC's decision about the settlement, rather than on the settlement itself. There is also underlying tension in the courts regarding their role in reviewing agency decision making—over the issue of deferral to agency expertise, on the one hand, versus interpreting legislative intent while guaranteeing due process on the other (Breyer 1987).[24] Against this backdrop, whether courts need to take a "hard look" at agency decisions involving negotiated settlements has been debated in the literature and is discussed in more detail in Chapter 5 (Harter 1986, Sturm 1991, Susskind and McMahon 1985, P. Wald 1985). Again, the important point here is that if a court overturns an agency decision related to a settlement, it must be carefully analyzed to see how it reflects on the consensus-based process itself.

Substantive Improvement

Although the three criteria for success described in the previous sections—saving process-related resources, reaching consensus, and surviving regulatory and judicial scrutiny—are all important and must be examined, they are insufficient by themselves for gauging success. The criteria do not directly address whether the outcomes of a consensus-building process were actually "good," or at least "better" than what would have occurred without the processes. This is not to say that saving time and money, and getting traditional adversaries to come to a consensus, are not important ends in themselves; however, any judgment of success of a consensus-building process should also examine how it resolved the substance of the controversies.

Selecting an Appropriate Baseline

To analyze how successfully a consensus-based process resolved substantive disputes, a comparative baseline is needed. It is not enough to determine whether the outcome of a consensus-based process is "better" than the preexisting conditions and arrangements. At a minimum, the substantive outcome of a consensus-building process must be compared to the outcome that might have resulted if the traditional regulatory process had run its course without the consensus-building supplement. Such an approach would need to speculate about what a utility, the PUC, and possibly even the courts would have done absent the consensus-building activity.[25] Decisions in comparable past cases or the resolution of similar controversies in other states can be examined to try to determine such a baseline. Empirical studies could be used, for example, to evaluate the DSM programs of utilities that participated in collaborative processes and those that did not.

An absolutist comparison that assesses whether the resolution was as "good" as possible is an alternative to the relativist comparison that focuses on what would have happened without the consensus-based process. This approach, which has been described most eloquently by Howard Raiffa in the theoretical literature, examines whether all the joint gains have been captured by the parties (that is, have the parties negotiated their way to the Pareto optimality curve shown earlier in Figure 3-1?) (Raiffa 1982). Specifically, one would attempt to identify changes in the final resolution of the substantive issues that represent improvements for some parties without making other parties worse off.[26]

Together these two analytic approaches can provide important insights by comparing the consensus-based decision with the status quo and some notion of optimality. However, the relativist comparison by itself is adequate to determine whether adding such supplements can improve regulatory processes. It is the primary baseline used in this book. The absolutist approach can help point to ways to improve the consensus-building process itself, and it too is pursued here, although less rigorously.

Searching for Objective Criteria

It is challenging to determine whether the resolution of the substantive controversies handled through a consensus-based process were successful, regardless of which baseline is used. An evaluator should define evaluative criteria without relying solely on the views of the participants themselves, a topic that is the subject of the concluding section of this chapter. Criteria related to notions of efficiency, fairness, wisdom, and stability seem appropriate for analyzing public policy disputes generally, and electric utility regulation in particular (Susskind and Cruikshank 1987).[27]

Before these criteria can be effectively applied, however, they must be more rigorously defined, a task that is far from straightforward. In Deborah Stone's insightful book *Policy Paradox and Politi-*

cal Reason (1988), the author describes the difficulty in defining fairness by explaining how chocolate cake could be distributed to her class according to at least eight entirely defensible definitions of fairness (for example, equal slices, unequal slices but equal value, unequal slices but equal statistical chances). Stone points out that similar, ultimately subjective, determinations must be made even with respect to efficiency:

> Efficiency is . . . always a contestable concept. Everyone supports the general idea of getting the most out of something. But to go beyond the vague slogans and apply the concept to concrete policy choice requires making assumptions about who and what counts as important. There are no correct answers to these questions. The answers built into analyses of efficiency are nothing more than political claims. By offering different assumptions, sides in a conflict can portray their preferred outcomes as being more efficient. (Stone 1988, p. 53)

This dilemma is not new to electric utility regulation, which makes value-laden determinations and tradeoffs with respect to distributional and other issues constantly (Trebing 1981, Zajac 1978). After all, what is a "just and reasonable rate" in the end, if not a judgment? A more concrete example regarding cost allocation may be useful here. To decide whether a utility's DSM expenditures are equitably distributed among ratepayers, one needs to decide if a fair cost allocation of the DSM expenditures is (a) to all customers by a fixed cents/kWh, (b) directly back to the participating customers, (c) on a fixed cents/kWh, but only back to the customer class eligible for a particular DSM program, or (d) a portion of the expenses to all customers and a percentage back to the customer or customer class. One's perspective on this issue would undoubtedly be influenced by one's view about whether DSM is a resource that all ratepayers should pay for, a service that only participating customers should pay for, or some combination of the two.

How is an outside analyst supposed to choose independently among seemingly internally consistent, but mutually exclusive criteria? For simplicity, analysts could adopt the yardsticks (that is, the cost-effectiveness test and cost allocation policies) of the jurisdiction in which the case they are analyzing occurred. However, where consensual processes cross jurisdictions in which regulators use different yardsticks, analysts would need to apply different tests in the same analysis. If the yardsticks themselves are the subject of controversy in the case, as is common, the selection of criteria by an outside evaluator would be even more confounded. Yet, without such criteria, evaluation cannot readily proceed.

The main point is that some fairly subjective decisions must be made to develop presumably objective criteria. Analysts can and should develop criteria to evaluate the success of consensus-based processes and public decision making generally. However, I am not convinced that criteria definitions that are essentially selected by an evaluator can be considered objective, even if they can be objectively applied subsequent to selection. For these reasons, evaluators must at a minimum be explicit about the criteria they choose to apply. Such criteria, as illustrated in the cases in Chapters 4 and 5, must not only be explicit but must usually be finely tailored to the relevant issues in each case. An alternative, discussed in the following section, is to turn to the participants themselves to help define the evaluative criteria.[28]

Tapping the Insight of Participants

Notions of fairness, wisdom, stability, and possibly even efficiency are inherently subjective and in the end are political determinations (Schuck 1979, Stone 1988). It therefore is essential for evaluators to focus their attention directly on the participants when analyzing the success of a consensus-based process (Raiffa 1982, Sturm 1991, Susskind and Cruikshank 1987). Susskind and Cruikshank, for instance, conclude:

> In our view, it is more important that an agreement be perceived as fair by the parties involved than by an independent analyst who applies an abstract decision rule. (Susskind and Cruikshank 1987, p. 25)

Ultimately, the success of a consensus-based process must be tied to how well the substantive outcome satisfies the various interests in society.[29] An analyst therefore must attempt to see the process and its results through the eyes of the participants in addition to using the other evaluative criteria discussed above. Interviews are essential to accomplish this end. Affected parties who were not participants to the process, including the regulators themselves, must also be interviewed. Focusing only on the participants when assessing the success of a consensus-based process may reveal little more than the "collective irrationality of the negotiators" (Forester and Stitzel 1989), particularly when important stakeholders have been excluded.

Legitimate stakeholders (that is, participants plus other affected parties) can provide invaluable insights about the substantive results. An evaluator should ask interested parties whether resolution of the issues in dispute produced results that satisfied their interests better than they would have expected through the traditional process. In addition, stakeholders can help identify potential improvements to the final resolution of the substantive disputes and serve as a sounding board for possible improvements suggested by the analyst or others. In this way, a much richer picture of the process and its results emerges.

Often, however, there is not consensus among participants about the outcome. Different participants usually feel differentially satisfied and see various shades of success even when a consensus is reached. It is then the evaluator's task to better understand the nature and scope of any dissent to qualify the characterization of a consensus-based process as "successful."

Another potential problem is related to the old adage that "hindsight is 20-20." It would be preferable to establish a baseline by interviewing parties at the outset of a consensus-building process as to their interests, aspirations, and expectations, as well as their own definitions of other evaluative criteria, such as equity, efficiency, and wisdom. However, such a baseline is rarely created because most evaluations are initiated after the fact. Even if a baseline could be determined at the outset, parties are often not clear about their objectives or are unwilling to discuss them for fear of compromising their positions. This generally leaves evaluators in the difficult position of having to rely on hindsight to ascertain both the baseline interests and the satisfaction of those interests. Finally, since things always look different on the ground than on paper, participants and affected parties should also be interviewed several years after a final consensus or PUC decision to garner the benefits of hindsight in the face of implementation experience.

This approach to measuring substantive success should not be used in isolation, even if interviews of participants are expanded to include parties that were not directly involved in the negotiations and even if such interviews can be repeated several years after the process has concluded. Other factors already discussed must also be used, including attempts by evaluators to objectively apply other predetermined criteria, even if these criteria are not objectively conceived.

Toward a Workable Evaluative Model

As should be clear by now, measuring the success of adding consensus-based processes to traditional electric utility regulatory procedures is not a simple task. This chapter has suggested a series of evaluative criteria that can each provide important insights. These criteria include the degree to which consensus was reached, the reaction of the PUCs and the courts, and whether the substantive resolution of contested issues represents an improvement from what would have happened in the absence of consensus building.

These important evaluative factors are weighed for each of the four case studies in Chapters 4 and 5, and the conclusions of each case study combine factors to address three overarching questions: (1) Were process-related resources saved? (2) Did the supplemental consensus-building process enhance the legitimacy of the traditional process and of the final results? (3) Were the final remedies, plans, and policies more practical because they used a consensus-building process? The question of saving process-related resources has already been discussed in detail in this chapter. As additional background to the case studies, however, some further definition of the questions of legitimacy and practicality will prove useful.

The legitimacy of traditional regulation is enhanced by supplemental consensus building when the overall process and the final results are considered fairer than they might otherwise have been. The starting point for assessing this question must be with the participants themselves. Whether consensus was reached, and whether the participants believe that their interests were better served by the results of a modified process are essential questions for making this initial judgment. Ultimately, however, evaluating the legitimacy of a consensus-building process requires casting a broader net to include other parties who are affected by a decision but who may not have directly participated, including future generations.

To a certain extent, the reactions of the PUCs and the courts serve as a proxy for this broader net because these bodies act as, among other things, checks against egregious damage to nonparticipants. Lack of support from the PUCs and the courts would not bode well for a finding of enhanced legitimacy. PUC and court actions are therefore integral to an analysis of legitimacy. However, the case studies in the following chapters also incorporate direct feedback from nonparticipants in the analyses whenever such feedback is relevant and available.

Final remedies, plans, and policies become more practical when they are more implementable from both a technical and a political vantage point. However, practicality means something more than just being practicable (that is, capable of being put into effect or implemented). To be considered practical, an approach must prove not only that it can be put into practice but that doing so will more effectively resolve the substantive issues at hand. As such, a truly practical improvement implies both implementability and a certain dose of wisdom and efficiency.

The assessment of practicality in this book's case studies rests primarily on the question of whether the decisions represent a substantive improvement over what would have been likely to occur without the consensus-based process. In making this difficult appraisal, the analyses in the case studies draw on the opinions of participants and other affected parties, along with other appropriate benchmarks when available. The analyses also evaluate whether the process itself used the best available information when framing options and agreements. Finally, additional insights come from examining any experience with implementing the remedies, plans, and policies to assess how they perform in the field.

In addition to an evaluation of outcome using these three central criteria of process-related resource savings, legitimacy, and practicality, each case study concludes with a brief process evaluation, the purpose of which is to highlight important features of the consensus-based processes and to explain critical connections with the overall successes and failures of the cases.

In the end, no pat formula or recipe can be used to evaluate the success of consensus-building processes in electric utility regulation. Instead, the approach used to analyze the cases in the next two chapters more closely resembles that of creating a montage or patchwork quilt. When all the factors are carefully analyzed, findings surface regarding the process-related resource savings, legitimacy, practicality, and ultimately the overall success of both the cases themselves and the use of consensus building in electric utility adjudicatory and rulemaking procedures.

Chapter 4

Adjudication

Chapter 3 discussed the opportunities for consensus building in traditional PUC regulation in broad-brush terms and analyzed criteria for evaluating the success of consensus-based processes. This chapter focuses on PUC adjudication—first by defining it and then by recounting its history, including the increase in the frequency and controversy of contested cases in recent years and the turn to settlement. A discussion of the opportunities to enhance consensus building specifically in adjudicatory matters precedes an in-depth analysis of two cases. The first of these is the settlement resolving issues related to an extended outage at the Pilgrim nuclear power plant in Massachusetts. The second is the development of comprehensive demand-side management (DSM) programs for utilities in Massachusetts by means of a unique collaborative process.

Adjudication Defined

Unlike rulemaking procedures, in which industrywide policies are promulgated (the focus of the next chapter), adjudicatory proceedings, in theory, involve applying those policies to specific cases. When agencies such as state PUCs adjudicate cases, they act quasi-judicially and must adhere to due process requirements that are similar to those followed by the courts:

> [A]gencies when they adjudicate individual cases must use procedures that involve the traditional legal attributes of judicial due process: public notice; an unbiased decision maker; a public record upon which the decision is based; opportunity to present evidence, witnesses, and argument, and to challenge those presented by the opposing side; right to counsel; right to a reasoned decision; and increased judicial review of the decision. (Breyer 1982)

Despite many similarities between agencies like PUCS and the courts on due process requirements, there are some important differences. Agencies generally grant intervention more freely than judicial courts and have more flexibility in deciding what to allow into evidence in a proceeding (Strauss 1989). Also, in more than half the states, PUCs are bound by "open-meeting" or "sunshine" laws, and commissioners confer with each other only in public meetings, unlike the situation in multijudge judicial courts, where judges are permitted to confer with each other privately prior to rendering a decision.[1] Still, all PUC commissioners, like judges in the judicial branch of government, are forbidden from ex parte contacts with utilities and intervenors (that is, written or oral communication that is not on the public record) during the course of adjudicatory proceedings and are required to base their decisions on the evidence in the record.

A state PUC's primary interface with the industries it regulates and with the public has historically been through adjudicatory proceedings, rather than rulemaking cases. Over the past decade, for example, the Massachusetts Department of Public Utilities (DPU) has conducted almost a thousand adjudicatory cases, but only two rulemaking ones. Although the rulemaking cases were extremely complex and time consuming, as is discussed in the integrated resource management (IRM) rulemaking case study in Chapter 5, the fact remains that the majority of the DPU's time (and correspondingly the utilities' and intervenors' time) is still dedicated to adjudicatory proceedings.

The most common adjudications have traditionally been rate cases.[2] A rate case is used to determine what costs an individual utility should be able to recover from its ratepayers; what return on its investment it deserves; how its costs, along with its return, should be allocated to different customer classes; and how rates should be structured within each customer class. The procedural structure of a typical rate case is provided in Table 4-1.[3] Other adjudications before the PUCs generally follow the same procedural process.

Rate cases generally focus on examining historic facts, such as past expenditures and whether utilities complied with preexisting policies. Rate cases traditionally do not focus on future plans and objectives.[4] Other traditional adjudications that fit into the mold of focusing on past actions include prudence and performance investigations.

More recently (that is, over the past half decade), utility-specific adjudications involving future plans in addition to past performance have come before state PUCs with increasing frequency.[5] Such adjudications are generally associated with the implementation of new PUC rules. Often they involve approval of a utility's resource plan or its resource bidding proposal, or approval of specific utility resources prior to investment (both supply-side and demand-side). These new cases reflect greater involvement in utility decision making ex ante rather than ex post, as was traditional. Although these cases follow the same

Table 4-1. Traditional Rate Case Process

1. Case filed, including testimony of utility, and given docket number; stakeholding parties given notice
2. Parties intervene
3. Discovery conducted: parties ask each other questions and receive responses, usually in writing
4. Testimony submitted by intervenors
5. Contested hearings held: parties cross-examine each other's witnesses; PUC asks questions
6. Briefs, and often reply briefs, describing final positions submitted by utility and intervenors
7. PUC decides case and issues order
8. Period provided for parties to request PUC to reconsider its decision, and for appeal to courts

procedural steps as rate cases and other adjudications involving historic performance, I believe they constitute a distinctly different substantive focus.

Rise of PUC Adjudication

As mentioned in Chapter 2, beginning in the late 1960s, when the era of declining electricity production costs ended, the number of rate cases before the state PUCs increased dramatically. Although the number of rate cases fluctuates annually, the national trend has been upward since 1970. For 1990, forty-three states reporting to the National Association of Regulatory Commissioners (NARUC) listed more than 100 major electric rate cases, compared with less than 50 per year reported by all states prior to 1970 (D. Anderson 1981; Bauer 1991, pp. 344–351).[6]

The total number of electricity-related cases before the PUCs, including the new breed connected to utility planning and future procurements, is much larger than the number of general rate cases. For example, states reported over 2,000 electricity-related cases to NARUC for 1990 (1,390 were concluded in 1990, and 774 were pending at the end of the year) (Bauer 1991, pp. 22–66).[7] Although many cases may be fairly routine (for example, fuel charge proceedings) in terms of requiring only limited PUC, utility, and intervenor resources, many are not.

Table 4-2 shows the number of adjudications before the Massachusetts DPU over the last decade, broken down into major adjudica-

Table 4-2. Electric Utility Adjudications Before the Massachusetts DPU, 1982–1991

Case Type	1982	1983	1984	1985	1986	1987	1988	1989	1990	1991	Total
Major adjudications											
General rate cases	7	4	4	1	2	2	5	4	3	2	35
Prospective resource cases[a]	0	0	1	0	3	5	2	8	8	9	36
Subtotal major adjudications	7	4	5	1	5	7	7	12	11	11	71
Other adjudicatory cases[b]	89	80	87	83	99	97	91	95	87	84	892
Total Adjudicatory Cases	**96**	**84**	**92**	**84**	**104**	**104**	**98**	**107**	**98**	**95**	**963**

Source: Massachusetts DPU card catalog, compiled by Henry Yoshimura and author.

[a] Prospective resource cases include DSM and supply-side preapprovals, QF RFPs, and IRM approvals.

[b] Other cases include fuel charges, power purchases, financings, ownership transfers, power contract approvals, zoning exemptions, power plant goal setting and performance, and other miscellaneous cases.

tions (general rate cases and prospective resource cases) and other, minor adjudications. Although the number of total cases is surprisingly consistent, the number of major cases has increased substantially during the past decade (from 4.4 per year during the first five years to 9.6 per year in the second five years).[8] Of particular interest is the increase in major cases related to forward-looking resource issues, such as preapprovals, Qualifying Facility (QF) requests for proposals (RFPs), and most recently, integrated resource management plans.

It is also important to point out that electricity is only one of many industries that PUCs regulate. Rate cases and other adjudications associated with natural gas and telephone regulation have also increased concurrently with rising electricity-related case loads. For 1990, forty-three states reporting to NARUC listed altogether more than 40 major telephone rate cases, 80 major gas rate cases, and hundreds of water cases (Bauer 1991, pp. 352–381). Some PUCs also regulate cable TV, motor carriers, sewer, and even solid waste (id., pp. 22–166). If cases related to all industries and of all case types (rate cases, other adjudications, and a sprinkling of rulemaking cases) are considered, cases reported to NARUC by states in 1990 totaled over 30,000 (id.).[9]

Shortcomings

Since PUC staffing has generally not kept pace with the increasing number and complexity of cases, PUC resources have been unduly strained in recent years. Table 4-3 shows the number of adjudications and the number of full-time staff at the Vermont Public Service Board between 1988 and 1991. The numbers show dockets increasing by 16 percent, hearing days increasing by 74 percent, and decisions and non-docket reviews more than doubling in less than four years (rising by 111 percent and 119 percent respectively). Meanwhile staff increased only 10 percent, from nineteen full-time equivalents to twenty-one. Although the Vermont PSB is smaller than most PUCs, the trends shown in Table 4-3 are probably typical.

Meanwhile, the number of commissioners on state PUCs has remained constant over the last two decades, with a median of 3 and a mean of 3.2 (Bauer 1991). It is therefore not surprising that rapidly increasing case loads threaten to compromise PUCs' ability to do their jobs effectively. Former commissioner Ron Lehr of Colorado explains:

> [PUC commissioners] are faced with issues of unbelievable scope, spanning several major industries, a mass of technical detail, and calendars which are so loaded with meetings and hearings as to

Table 4-3. Vermont Public Service Board Caseload and Staffing, 1988–1991

	1988	**1989**	**1990**	**1991**	**Change**
Hearings Held	191	247	291	333	+ 74%
Decisions Issued [a]	210	275	293	444	+111%
Dockets Processed	176	185	190	205	+ 16%
Non-Docket Reviews	120	132	173	263	+119%
Staff [b]	19	19	20	21	+ 10%

Source: Vermont Public Service Board, Board Clerk Susan Hudson and General Counsel Michael Dworkin.

[a] Decisions issued include proposals for decisions issued by hearing officers, as well as electric, gas, telecommunication, water, and cable TV cases.

[b] The PSB has one full-time and two half-time commissioners.

leave insufficient time for reading, preparing and thoughtful consideration. (Lehr 1990)

Not only have the number of PUC adjudications increased dramatically over the past two decades; the cases themselves are usually more controversial and more complex. This trend began when rate cases no longer meant rate decreases but signaled inevitable increases. Utilities, and ultimately the PUCs, are now forced to decide how to allocate cost increases among customer classes as well as among customers within each customer class. In addition, as Chapter 2 discusses, rate cases and other PUC adjudications have become the place where the prudence of past utility decisions is contested. When PUCs weigh the prudence of past utility decisions, they must allocate the costs between ratepayers and utility shareholders—inevitably a controversial process. Finally, PUC adjudications are made even more contentious when the commission ponders a utility's decisions about the future, resolving disputes over demand forecasts and the way the utility chooses among possible resources.

Most electric utility cases today are met with intervention by opposing parties and close scrutiny by regulators. These contested cases are conducted through an adversarial process in which each side (or sides) makes every effort to present its own perspective favorably while discrediting the opinions of others. This approach is taken regardless of whether historic facts, remedies for past decisions, or future plans are the subject of dispute. After each side issues often-exhaustive discovery requests, testimony is prepared by witnesses (often by outside experts), who are then subject to detailed cross-examination. When the hearings are complete, the parties argue their cases in written briefs. The PUC staff and commissioners must then wade through what is inevitably a voluminous and conflicting record and render a decision that strives to be efficient, fair, and consistent with the record.

The adjudicatory process itself is often extremely resource-intensive for utilities, intervenors, and regulators alike. The first case in this chapter describes adjudications associated with an extended outage at the Pilgrim nuclear power plant in Massachusetts, a process that required over ninety days of hearings, over 1,300 exhibits, and more than twenty-five witnesses. The Pilgrim adjudications are probably situated at the more intensive end of the spectrum (although they are by no means alone). However, the average rate case lasts between eight and nine months[10] and requires weeks of hearings and hundreds of exhibits. Written decisions by PUCs at the end of rate cases are usually hundreds of pages long, even for small utilities (Raab 1989b).[11]

Intensive litigation does not always adequately illuminate the issues in ways that facilitate the PUCs' decision making. Instead, cases usually end with considerable disagreement over the historic facts, and PUCs are left to pick and choose among alternative views. Lawrence Susskind and Allan Morgan described the problems caused by this lack of clarity in an article that appeared in Edison Electric Institute's *Electric Perspectives* in the spring of 1986:

> The adversarial process also encourages the parties to discredit each other's scientific or technical studies. Indeed, the tendency in such situations is to spend a great deal of time and money undermining the claims of others rather than improving the quality of the information available to everyone. Unfortunately, challenges to the technical work submitted by others merely confirm the general public's view that all studies are nothing more than polemics prepared on behalf of one client or another. This jockeying is very dangerous: it can lead to politically expedient but technically or economically unsound decisions. . . . (Susskind and Morgan 1986b, p. 23)

Where cases focus on future utility plans that rely on unknowable facts and uncertain forecasts, the problem of discovering what is correct via litigation borders on pointlessness. Although adjudication can help weed out gross forecasting deficiencies, inevitably a wide range of forecasts and subsequent options will exist. Adjudication can do little more than clarify parties' differing expectations and preferences.

Even where there is some convergence on the facts, the parties rarely agree on the appropriate remedies. Such disagreement is not surprising given the subjectivity inherent in many of the decisions in rate cases and other adjudications. Despite the ultimate need for regulatory discretion, adjudications still tend to obsess over these subjective decisions in unproductive ways, attempting to resolve issues through computation instead of acknowledging that they are fundamentally value judgments. In *Regulation and Its Reform*, Judge Stephen Breyer demonstrates this point with his discussion of how a rate of return is "derived":

> . . . Setting a rate of return cannot—even in principle—be reduced to an exact science. To spend hours of hearing time considering elaborate rate-of-return models is of doubtful value, and suggestions of a proper rate, carried out to several decimal places, give an air of precision that must be false. (Breyer 1982, p. 47)

Such subjectivity is inherent not only because PUCs must make distributional decisions involving various parties, but because they must make difficult tradeoffs between oftentimes competing objectives, such as efficiency and equity. Decision makers can look to rules and precedents for guidance, but their ultimate decisions must reflect the record developed in the case. However, as former New Mexico commissioner Marilyn O'Leary explains, the adjudicatory process itself does not generally help commissioners make these difficult tradeoffs:

> The result of parties' taking extreme positions is that the decision maker feels as if he or she is living out the story of the blind man and the elephant. It is difficult, if not impossible, to get the whole picture. The commissioners' role of balancing the interests of the parties who do not reveal their true interests is difficult. (O'Leary 1986, p. 11)

Lastly, PUCs often—de facto—use contested cases to promulgate new policy initiatives that affect the entire industry. When PUCs try to wrestle with policy issues through adjudication, at least two problems arise besides the legal question of whether a rulemaking process is required to make industrywide policy (discussed in the next chapter). First, not all parties who will be affected by the regulations are likely to be parties to an adjudication, since adjudications normally focus on an individual utility. Second, as just discussed, adjudication tends to obscure parties' true interests and polarize positions. This polarization can stifle creative approaches to policy formation.

Together these shortcomings often overwhelm PUCs, making it difficult for them to craft decisions that will be perceived as legitimate or praised as practical.[12] An indication of this frustration is that parties frequently request PUCs to reconsider adjudicatory decisions or appeal them to the courts. In 1990, for example, more than half of the twenty-two PUCs that reported to NARUC on this issue had at least one appeal filed against their adjudicatory decisions in the courts.[13] Since virtually all courts decide appeals based on the record established by the PUC (usually with supplemental briefs and possible oral argument before the court) rather than de novo, the cost of appeals generally pales compared with the initial litigation. However, appeals are often contentious and increase regulatory uncertainty by further delaying final resolution of important issues. Between 1985 and 1990, the average time required to process an appeal of a state PUC decision was 14.3 months—significantly longer than the 8.6 months it takes PUCs, on average, to render their decisions (Bauer 1991).[14]

PUCs usually walk a thin line in their adjudicatory decisions—attempting to balance the interests of parties within the context of existing rules and policies. This balancing is extremely difficult when parties obscure their true interests by taking exaggerated positions. PUC decisions rarely leave all or even most parties satisfied. Even when cases are not appealed, dissatisfaction often leads to implementation problems and general intransigence. Issues that have supposedly been reconciled by a PUC decision in a case or cases often reemerge in subsequent proceedings.

The Role of Settlement

One way that parties attempt to reduce the time, cost, uncertainty, and general dissatisfaction of litigation in rate cases and other adjudications is to voluntarily settle the cases. When settling, they reach a consensus among themselves with respect to the disposition of some or all contested issues and submit the settlement to the regulators for approval. Although settlements in civil matters before the courts usually occur prior to trial, this is not generally the case in traditional rate case settlements before state PUCs. In rate cases, settlements usually occur after a utility and the intervenors have presented their cases and a record has been established (that is, after discovery and hearings). However, settlement can occur at any time prior to a PUC's final order in a case. Recently, with the advent of more forward-looking, resource-planning cases, such as the DSM preapproval case described later in this chapter, prefiling settlements of a new variety are beginning to occur.

Settlement on regulatory issues began at the federal level. The Federal Power Commission (FPC), the precursor to the Federal Energy Regulatory Commission (FERC), originally promulgated settlement procedures in 1949. However, it was not until the early 1960s that the FPC actively promoted settlements as a way of resolving cases. At that time, it had been swamped by requests for rate increases by pipeline companies following the rise in gas prices at the wellhead during the 1950s. Due to the FPC's huge backlog, over $1 billion had been collected by gas pipeline companies subject to future refund (Freeman 1965).[15] Largely as a result of this backlog, the FPC was singled out in a report by James Landis (then special advisor to President-elect Kennedy) as "the outstanding example in the federal government of the break-down of the administrative process" (Landis 1960).

According to S. David Freeman, the assistant to the chairman of the FPC at the time, by the mid-1960s, through a combination of increased staffing and active use of settlement procedures, the case backlog was erased, and the agency's credibility had largely been restored (Freeman 1965). The use of settlement continued to grow at the FPC and later at the FERC, and by the mid-1980s approximately 80 percent of FERC's caseload was resolved through settlement (Burns 1988, Harter 1984). In 1980, FERC's settlement guidelines were amended to provide parties the option to use settlement judges to facilitate negotiations (Joseph and Gilbert 1990). Today, FERC is still settling 70 to 80 percent of its major electric cases, with only 10 to 20 percent of settlements using settlement judges (Orrechio interview). FERC rarely rejects a settlement reached by all, or even most, parties (id.).

Although I have not found any reports detailing the early use of settlement in state PUC adjudications, I suspect that settlements in electric utility cases increased substantially after rates began to rise during the 1970s. Representatives of PUCs interviewed in seven states all indicated a rise in settlements over the past five to ten years.[16] Table 4-4 shows the number of settlements submitted to the New York Public Service Commission (PSC) for approval between 1981 and 1990.

Of the thirty-nine electric utility settlements in New York shown in Table 4-4, 21 percent were resolved before hearings, 26 percent during hearings, and 54 percent after hearings. In addition, 62 percent of the electric utility settlements were complete settlements resolving all outstanding issues, whereas 38 percent were partial, leaving some issues unresolved. Less than 10 percent of all the cases shown in Table 4-4 used settlement judges, and only two settlements have been re-

Table 4-4. Settlements in Cases Before the New York Public Service Commission, 1981–1990

Year	Electric Cases[a]	Other Cases	Total Cases
1981	1	2	3
1982	1	8	9
1983	2	8	10
1984	3	8	11
1985	6	6	12
1986	4	5	9
1987	5	11	16
1988	10	11	21
1989	6	10	16
1990[b]	1	4	5
TOTAL	**39**	**73**	**112**

Source: Compiled by author from data supplied by the New York PSC, courtesy of Ron Elwood.

[a] Included in the electric cases are seven combined gas/electric rate cases.

[b] Part year.

jected by the PSC (Elwood and Crary interviews).

The electric-related settlements in New York represent approximately 70 percent of the utilities' major electric cases during this period.[17] This rate is probably higher than that in many other states, given New York's active encouragement of settlement. In Massachusetts, for example, there was settlement in only 14 percent of major electric cases between 1982 and 1991.[18] However, as in Massachusetts, I suspect the frequency of settlement is increasing across the country.

In addition, the diversity of issues being settled is expanding (Burns 1988). For instance, the thirty-nine electricity-related settlements in New York covered the following broad range of issues: avoided costs, cost allocation, cost-of-service, customer complaint procedures, decommissioning of a nuclear reactor, electric line routing and construction procedures, phase-in of a nuclear power plant into rates, rate of return, rate design, rate moratorium, replacement power costs, and sales forecasts. Settlements in Massachusetts have also included initial resource plans and the preapproval of utility DSM programs.

Expanding and Formalizing Consensus Building

Settlement is obviously already part of the landscape of resolving adjudicatory proceedings on many issues before state PUCs. However, it is relatively new and evolving. Most cases are still probably not settled, and many are often only partial settlements. Some PUCs even consider certain topics off-limits. For instance, until recently, rate design settlements were considered taboo in New York and Massachusetts, according to sources at those commissions (Elwood and Werlin interviews).[19]

The increased use of settlement would seem to require state PUCs to have clearly articulated procedures and techniques for conducting settlements and integrating them into traditional adjudicatory proceedings. Yet, as of this writing, despite statutory authority to allow them in most states, only California and New York have been identified as having formal settlement guidelines and rules that apply to electric utilities (Elwood and Marland interviews).[20] The remaining states apparently oversee settlements on an ad hoc basis (id.).

Without such guidelines or rules, many important issues, including the following, remain rather nebulous and must be revisited on a case-by-case basis: (1) What subjects, if any, does the PUC consider off-limits for settlement? (2) When during proceedings can settlements occur, and how will they mesh with ongoing adjudication? (For example, does the clock stop during settlement discussions?) (3) What is the appropriate role of staff and commissioners in settlement proceedings? (4) Who should be included and noticed regarding settlements? (5) How should the confidentiality of information revealed during settlement negotiations be protected?

Even New York's detailed settlement guidelines, which were first established in 1983, have room for improvement, as a New York Telephone case in 1989 and 1990 revealed. In that case, the New York PSC rejected a settlement when a significant dispute arose regarding whether intervenors to the case who were not parties to the settlement (which had been settled by the company and the commission's own advocacy staff) had received proper notice of the settlement process and had been included in it (NYPSC Opinion No. 90-14, April 26, 1990; Elwood interview). As a direct result of that case, the New York PSC opened an investigation into its own guidelines and approved new rules and guidelines in February 1992 (NYPSC Opinion No. 92-2, March 24, 1992; Elwood interview). The new rules and guidelines, among other things, require that all parties receive notice and be given an opportunity to participate in settlements.

New York is not alone. In April 1991, the FERC opened a notice of proposed rulemaking to revisit its settlement guidelines. That same month, NARUC's Staff Subcommittee on Administrative Law Judges issued model settlement guidelines for states to consider.[21] Settlement rules and guidelines are not yet common, however. Debates over what such rules and guidelines should entail go to the heart of the value of settlement in PUC regulation and address the question of how best to tap its potential advantages while avoiding potential problems.

Introduction to the Case Studies

The case studies described in this chapter illuminate the fundamental question, What benefits, if any, can settlement and other consensus-based processes add to traditional PUC adjudication?[22] These case studies, along with those in Chapter 5, also serve as the basis for the recommendations made in the conclusion of this book on how best to structure settlement and other consensus-building processes.

The first case study involves a settlement resolving extremely lengthy and controversial proceedings on expenditures made by Boston Edison Company during a thirty-two-month extended outage at its Pilgrim nuclear power plant in Massachusetts. This settlement was reached after the parties' cases were fully developed on the record and represents a more traditional, albeit creative, settlement. In the second case I examine demand-side management collaboratives among Massachusetts utilities and various intervenors. These collaboratives represent a new type of settlement process that has arisen to deal with forward-looking planning and implementation issues. The case is important for many reasons, including the fact that the settlements occurred prior to the utilities' filing their plans with the Massachusetts Department of Public Utilities.

THE PILGRIM SETTLEMENT

In 1989, the Boston Edison Company (BECo), the Massachusetts Public Interest Research Group (MASSPIRG), the Attorney General's Office, and the Division of Energy Resources (DOER)[23] crafted a settlement resolving several complicated and controversial issues being adjudicated before the Massachusetts Department of Public Utilities (DPU) involving the Pilgrim Nuclear Power Plant (Pilgrim). The settlement discussions began after approximately ninety days of contentious hearings in a general rate case and a simultaneous proceeding addressing replacement power costs incurred during a thirty-two-month outage at Pilgrim. Intervenors asserted that Pilgrim was no longer cost-effective compared with alternative resources and challenged BECo's decision to invest hundreds of millions of dollars more in it. Intervenors also challenged BECo's right to recover over $100 million in replacement power costs, charging that the thirty-two-month outage was a consequence of management imprudence.

After months of negotiations, the parties settled all the issues in both cases, and the DPU approved the settlement. Although the process used by the parties resembles traditional adjudicatory settlements in many respects, the scope of issues and the solutions that the parties invented make this case unique.

Did the settlement process enhance the adjudicatory process and result in a better resolution of the issues (consistent with the criteria laid out in Chapter 3) than if the DPU had decided the cases? I conclude that the settlement did not necessarily save process-related resources in the short run. However, the settlement appears to have produced a more creative and practical solution that was also more palatable to all parties, including the DPU itself.

The following analysis rests on a wide range of primary documentation, such as DPU orders, excerpts from the enormous record in the case (for example, transcripts, exhibits, testimony), and internal DPU memos. It also relies on several secondary sources, including testimony written by the participants to the settlement and newspaper articles.

In addition, I conducted personal interviews with representatives of the four major parties to the settlement, as well as a lead staffperson

Table 4-5. Interviews for Pilgrim Settlement

Brian Abbanat	Chief Engineer, Electric Power Division, Massachusetts Department of Public Utilities
George Dean	Director of Regulated Industries Division, Massachusetts Attorney General's Office
Thomas May	Executive Vice-President, Boston Edison Company
Alan Nogee	Energy Program Director, MASSPIRG
Rachel Shimshak	Director of Policy and Planning, Division of Energy Resources
Robert Werlin	Attorney, private law firm; former Commissioner and Chair, Department of Public Utilities

Note: Positions and affiliations are as of the time of the interviews.

and a former commissioner at the DPU. The names of those interviewed, including their affiliations and titles, are given in Table 4-5. All interviewees reviewed an earlier draft of this case, and their comments have been incorporated as appropriate.

Finally, as a staff member at the Massachusetts DPU at the time these cases and the internal review of the Pilgrim settlement took place, I was involved in several hearings in the rate case (related to demand-side management) and participated in numerous internal discussions and meetings about the cases and the settlement. Although confidentiality obligations preclude the direct use or quotation of those discussions, meetings, and internal memos,[24] they helped shape the analysis presented here—particularly with respect to what may have happened absent the settlement.

Background

On April 11, 1986, BECo began a gradual shutdown of the Pilgrim nuclear reactor to investigate a leak in one of its cooling systems. The following day, the reactor unexpectedly scrammed (that is, an automatic emergency shutdown occurred) after valves in the main steam line running between the reactor and the turbine suddenly and unexpectedly closed. After unsuccessfully trying to reopen the valves, reactor operators were forced to use a backup emergency cooling system to control the pressure in the reactor.

This event was not unique at Pilgrim. Apparently a similar chain of events had occurred only two weeks before at the reactor (Nogee and Brach 1988). In fact, during the early-to-mid-1980s, Pilgrim was regarded by the Nuclear Regulatory Commission (NRC) as one of the most troubled nuclear reactors in the country, and its workers had the highest collective radiation exposure of any nuclear plant (Nogee 1990).[25] In 1982, the NRC fined Pilgrim's operators $550,000 (the largest fine ever issued by the NRC at the time) for numerous problems, including design errors, inadequate procedures, plant failures, and lack of sound management.[26] It also ordered BECo to develop a "performance improvement plan" in 1982 and a "radiological improvement program" in 1984. In 1984, BECo shut down Pilgrim for an entire year, during which over $200 million of repairs and capital improvements were made to the plant (Nogee and Brach 1988).

The NRC was not the only regulatory body critical of BECo's management. At the time of the April 1986 reactor scram, BECo had just completed a contentious general rate case before the Massachusetts DPU. During the case, intervenors criticized BECo not only on Pilgrim issues, but also on its energy planning process and failure to pursue other resources—most notably demand-side management (DSM). In a scathing order, the DPU concluded, "It is clear that the Company does not believe it's accountable either to its customers or the Department" (Mass. D.P.U. 85-271-A/86-266-A [1986b], p. 14]). In addition to reducing BECo's return on equity to the bottom of its allowable range, the DPU insinuated that a change of management at the company was in order. The DPU even took the unprecedented step of distributing its order directly to each of the members of BECo's outside board of directors.

The day after the reactor scram, on April 12, the NRC sent BECo a confirmatory action letter ordering a special investigation into the causes of the incident and requiring the company to seek formal NRC approval before restarting the reactor (NRC 1986). Two weeks later, on April 26, 1986, the Chernobyl nuclear reactor accident occurred in the Soviet Union, igniting a heightened sense of concern regarding reactor safety in the United States—especially at plants like Pilgrim.[27]

In keeping with recommendations made by an independent review panel initiated by its board of directors in the aftermath of the DPU's scathing order, BECo restructured its upper management in 1987 (while Pilgrim was still off-line). The company brought in Admiral Ralph Bird, a twenty-eight-year veteran of nuclear operations at the navy, to oversee Pilgrim as senior vice-president for nuclear operations. BECo also hired executives from outside the company, including Bernard Reznicek as chief operating officer, and accepted the resignation of several other executives.[28]

However, at the same time that BECo was attempting to revitalize its management, it continued to have problems with state regulators.

In April 1987, the Energy Facilities Siting Council (EFSC), the agency responsible for overseeing utility energy planning, rejected BECo's 1985 and 1986 supply plans and its planning process generally (Mass. EFSC 1987). In addition, public resentment of Pilgrim grew. In November 1987, MASSPIRG, a statewide consumer and environmental group, published a report entitled "Nuclear Lemon: Ratepayer Savings from Retiring the Pilgrim Nuclear Power Plant" (Nogee 1987). MASSPIRG's report added an economic twist to the public controversy surrounding Pilgrim, which until that time had focused primarily on safety concerns. The report claimed that ratepayers could save as much as $1.5 billion over Pilgrim's anticipated lifetime if the plant was retired immediately and cheaper alternatives were procured (id.). MASSPIRG also filed a petition at the NRC that, if it had been accepted, would have required BECo to "show cause" as to why Pilgrim should not be shut down.[29]

BECo originally anticipated that the outage at Pilgrim would last only a few weeks. However, repairs and other changes spiraled in time and cost, and the restart date was pushed back more than twenty-five times. Pilgrim was not officially restarted until December 21, 1988—thirty-two months after the outage began. Data provided in Table 4-6 indicate that BECo made over $200 million in capital improvements to Pilgrim between 1986 and 1988 (the period that was the subject of the adjudications before the DPU). In addition, almost $300 million was spent on operation and maintenance at Pilgrim during the outage.[30] Finally, $115 million was spent on replacement power (the cost BECo had to pay to secure power from the spot market to replace

Table 4-6. BECo's Spending on Pilgrim During Outage, 1986–1988

Year	Capital Expenditures	Operation and Maintenance	Replacement Power
1986	$46	$78	na[a]
1987	$150	$172	na[a]
1988[b]	$15	$38	na[a]
TOTAL	$221	$288	$115

Source: Capital expenditure and operation and maintenance data from Nogee and Brach 1988, based on a Boston Edison Company response to an information request from the Massachusetts Public Interest Research Group.

[a] Annual distribution of replacement power costs were not readily available.

[b] 1988 expenditures do not represent the entire year.

Pilgrim power)—for a total of over $600 million in outage-related expenditures.

Between ongoing safety concerns, BECo's substantial investment during the outage, the regulators' dim view of BECo's management, and allegations that Pilgrim was not projected to be cost-effective into the future, the stage was set for a major battle over BECo's past actions and the future of both the plant and the company.

Pilgrim Cases Before the DPU

The DPU took up the issues surrounding Pilgrim primarily in two cases. The first, which is often referred to as the "outage" or "replacement power" case, was an investigation into the causes of the Pilgrim outage and the conduct of BECo while Pilgrim was off-line (Mass. D.P.U. 88-28 [1989a]). Hearings for this case began in January 1989. The immediate objective was to determine the refunds, if any, of the $115 million the company spent to replace Pilgrim power during the outage and passed along to ratepayers through the fuel clause.[31] Both MASSPIRG and the Attorney General intervened in this case to oppose BECo's request to retain all but $7.6 million of the replacement power costs it collected during the outage.[32]

The second case was a general rate case, filed in April 1989 (Mass. D.P.U. 89-100 [1989a]). BECo requested an $86 million (8.4 percent) rate increase, which it justified almost entirely on expenditures associated with Pilgrim since the last rate case.[33] The immediate objective of this case was to determine the portion of the capital expenditures and operating and maintenance costs that should be included in Pilgrim's base rates.

A third and earlier investigation, which had been initiated by the DPU before the end of the outage and after it had received a petition by state senator William Golden on behalf of twenty BECo ratepayers (February 25, 1988), was merged into the rate case (Mass. D.P.U. 88-48 [1989a]). The Golden petition specifically requested that all expenditures and investments in Pilgrim be removed from rate base and that the company provide rebates for damages allegedly sustained by ratepayers as a result of the operation of Pilgrim.

The Division of Energy Resources (DOER) joined MASSPIRG, the Attorney General, and Senator Golden in opposing BECo's request for the largely Pilgrim-related rate increase.[34] Although the two cases focused on the appropriateness of BECo's historic expenditures with respect to Pilgrim—particularly during the outage—the interests of the intervenors were clearly broader in scope. Golden's original petition, for instance, wanted to take Pilgrim completely out of rate base and provide rebates to customers for costs charged to ratepayers even prior to the outage. DOER was concerned primarily with whether Pilgrim would be economic for ratepayers in the future. Alan Nogee, director of energy policy at MASSPIRG, bluntly described his organization's interest in Pilgrim and their decision to intervene in the cases:

> Our primary interest was to shut Pilgrim down and generally see a decreased reliance on nukes and fossil fuel generation and an increased reliance on renewables and DSM. Our strategy was to cut off ratepayer subsidies, which allowed the company to charge ratepayers whether or not Pilgrim operated. We hoped to do this by challenging BECo's ongoing investments, changing its incentives in the future, and penalizing it for past mistakes. Saving money for ratepayers in the short run was a secondary interest. (Nogee interview)

The two cases followed typical adjudicatory procedures used by PUCs in rate cases (summarized in Table 4-1). Largely because of the contentiousness of the Pilgrim issues, both cases required extensive commitments of resources by all the parties and the DPU. Although rate cases often require many days of hearings, these cases were much more intensive than usual. For instance, the outage case required thirty-four days of hearings, filling twenty-seven volumes of transcripts and including 651 exhibits and 209 record request responses (that is, requests for more information made during the hearings) (Mass. D.P.U. 88-28/88-48/89-100 [1989a], p. 2). The rate case required fifty-eight days of evidentiary hearings, with twenty days specifically focused on Pilgrim, and had 653 exhibits and 299 record request responses (id.). In the rate case alone, BECo sponsored eleven witnesses and nine panels with multiple witnesses, and the intervenors sponsored five individual witnesses and one panel.

Despite the extensive time spent in hearings, during which both sides had the opportunity to air their views and question the other parties, as is typical in adjudicatory proceedings, the positions of BECo and the intervenors remained separated by a wide chasm. BECo maintained that it had acted prudently throughout the outage. It promised that its newly refurbished nuclear power plant would perform better in the future than it had in the past, bringing its ratepayers $400 million in benefits over the remainder of its economic life, as compared with alternatives. The company argued that it should be granted nearly all of its replacement power costs and allowed to place all Pilgrim-related capital expenditures and incremental operation and maintenance costs into base rates.

From the intervenors' perspective, BECo acted imprudently by sinking so much money into Pilgrim before, during, and after the outage without adequately exploring potentially less costly alternatives. Even before the outage, Pilgrim was only marginally cost-effective compared with alternatives, the intervenors asserted, citing an internal BECo staff report completed in October 1985 to back up their claim. In the rate case, DOER sponsored testimony by consultants Paul Chernick and Jonathan Wallach, who presented evidence that Pilgrim could cost ratepayers $2.3 billion more than the cost of alternatives if it did not substantially improve its historic performance. In the outage case, the Attorney General sponsored testimony by MHB Technical Associates, who claimed that virtually the entire outage was caused by BECo's imprudence, both in causing and prolonging the outage and in the company's decision not to evaluate or pursue alternative resources. Because of the availability of cheaper alternatives, the intervenors argued that BECo should be denied virtually all the monies it had requested.

From the DPU's perspective, these were extremely important cases because of the large amount of money at stake, the public concern over Pilgrim and nuclear power generally, and the commission's ongoing concerns over BECo's management and planning capabilities. These concerns are evident in the commission's decision to have Commissioner Susan Tierney spearhead the investigation into whether BECo's Pilgrim investments met the "prudent, used, and useful" test.[35] Such a decision was unusual because at the time, in rate cases and other adjudications before the DPU in Massachusetts, technical staff usually heard the cases and then made recommendations to the commission.[36]

Toward the end of the rate case, and after hearing conflicting testimony on the myriad of variables on which the economic viability of Pilgrim hinged (Pilgrim's future capacity factor, future operation and maintenance expenditures and capital additions, the future price of fossil fuels, and the amount of cost-effective DSM, to name a few), Commissioner Tierney asked BECo to rerun its model on the economics of Pilgrim, this time using a set of prespecified parameters. The new model runs were based on assumptions less favorable to Pilgrim than BECo had originally proposed, but not as damaging as those used by the intervenors. These new runs indicated that the plant could put ratepayers at risk for over $1 billion if Pilgrim's lackluster historic performance did not significantly improve.[37]

Although Commissioner Tierney's request, and BECo's response, appeared to foreshadow at least the possibility of substantial DPU disallowances for BECo, the outcome of the cases remained uncertain for several reasons. First, even if the commission decided that BECo's imprudence had caused and prolonged the outage, or that BECo had acted imprudently in its decision not to analyze and pursue alternatives to Pilgrim, the commission would still need to determine the portion of the costs that should be disallowed. Second, of the costs that were considered prudent, the commission would need to decide what portion should be considered "used and useful" (that is, needed and economic compared with alternatives) and therefore eligible for BECo to earn a return on. Even with the extensive record, these decisions would not have been straightforward (Abbanat interview).

Since the DPU is traditionally limited to ruling only on past expenditures, at most the DPU could have disallowed less than $0.5 billion (roughly $100 million in replacement power plus $100 million in incremental operation and maintenance costs plus $300 million in capital expenditures). However, a disallowance of this magnitude was highly unlikely since the DPU would have probably found only some portion of the expenditures to be imprudent and uneconomic. Even if a substantial disallowance had occurred, the penalty would have paled next to the $1 to $2 billion in potential costs to ratepayers that the intervenors alleged (that is, compared with pursuing more cost-effective alternatives over Pilgrim's expected life). Moreover, a major financial penalty might have done little to guarantee better performance of Pilgrim in the future. In fact, it might have aggravated the situation by forcing the utility to skimp on operation and maintenance costs and by raising its cost of capital for future investments.

The DPU would undoubtedly have considered the following alternative in its deliberations if the case had not been settled: removing all or a portion of Pilgrim from traditional cost-of-service regulation and requiring that BECo be compensated only for the value of electricity that it actually delivered. This was in many ways consistent with a new set of ratemaking preapproval rules that the DPU had adopted in October 1988, which required new utility generating facilities and major additions to existing facilities to be paid on the basis of a fixed price for delivered electricity and capacity (Mass. D.P.U. 86-36-E [1988c]). However, the new rules were not designed to be applied retroactively, although the expenditures on Pilgrim would have probably qualified as a major addition in terms of the size of the investment.[38] It was therefore not clear whether the DPU had either the legal authority or a sufficient record in the case to order BECo to change the status of Pilgrim with respect to future cost recovery (Werlin interview).

The Settlement

In late June 1989, after the close of hearings in the replacement power case and while the rate case hearings were winding down, BECo's new chief operating officer, Bernard Reznicek, telephoned Attorney General James Shannon to explore the possibilities of entering into settlement discussions on both Pilgrim cases. Soon after Reznicek's phone call, the Attorney General, DOER, and MASSPIRG began meeting with BECo.[39] This "core" group of nonutility parties (NUPs) represented those who were most active in the cases.

According to Tom May, executive vice-president at BECo, although the company felt it had put on a strong case before the DPU, it had several reasons for initiating settlement discussions with the parties:

> As part of a new management team brought on largely in response to an extremely critical DPU order in 1986, we were trying to turn the company around. We felt that the company was too focused on defending its past action, without enough vision for the future. We saw settlement as a way to turn this around. Secondarily, we hoped to remove a large uncertainty that we faced if the DPU decided the case. . . . Though we thought we had put on a strong case, you cannot have a plant down for three years and not have some serious regulatory risk. We felt there would be some disallowances but were not sure how much. (May interview)

The NUPs also felt that they had put on a strong case and that BECo faced substantial disallowances. However, they too were uncertain about the ultimate size of the disallowance, or the DPU's ability to go beyond a simple disallowance to address some of their more fundamental concerns. Rachel Shimshak, director of policy and planning at DOER, explains:

> We were worried the DPU's orders would not be strong enough. We thought there was sufficient evidence to close Pilgrim down on economic grounds, but we doubted the DPU would do that since there was little precedent for such an extreme remedy. We also continued to have serious concerns about the safety of Pilgrim—an area where the department does not have much jurisdiction, if any. (Shimshak interview)

George Dean, chief of the Regulated Industries Division of the Attorney General's Office, pointed out that even if the DPU had ordered major disallowances as the NUPs requested (and as he fully expected), the victory would have been a Pyrrhic one. He explains: "If we had won big at the department, we would have earned ratepayers a few hundred million dollars and turned BECo into a financial basket case" (Dean interview). Nogee agreed with both Shimshak and Dean about both the possibilities and problems of a major disallowance by itself, and explained that a more creative resolution of the issues was needed than was likely to emerge from the DPU:

> I believed that the department was likely to deal with the decision conventionally—allocating the costs of past mistakes between the company and ratepayers. Although I expected large disallowances, there would be no tangible incentive for improving future performance. Given that it was unlikely that Pilgrim would be shut down immediately, I felt we needed a creative approach to establishing incentives for future performance. (Nogee interview)

The utility, represented by three of its top executives—Bernard Reznicek (chief operating officer), Tom May (then senior vice-president), and Douglas Horan (deputy general counsel)—engaged in settlement discussions directly with Alan Nogee of MASSPIRG, Rachel Shimshak of DOER, and George Dean of the Attorney General's Office.[40] Senator Golden, Massachusetts Citizens for Safe Energy (MCSE), the Energy Consortium, and the U.S. General Services Administration—all of whom were intervenors in one or both of the Pilgrim cases (but who did not play an active role in the cases, except for the Energy Consortium, which was active primarily on rate design issues)—were not included in the negotiations until the basic settlement had been structured by the four core parties. Since some of these parties were represented in the core negotiating group (for example, MCSE and MASSPIRG were closely allied), and all the parties ultimately signed the settlement, this selective approach does not appear to have caused any significant problems.

During the summer, the parties met as often as several times a week at the Attorney General's offices—sometimes until eight at night. Between negotiating sessions, the NUPs often caucused, and BECo's executives met with their staff. Both the NUPs and the utilities were required to do extensive financial computer modeling to assess the tradeoffs from different settlement packages. Participants interviewed for this study reported that the negotiations were intensive and occupied over half of their time between July, when the negotiations began in earnest, and October 3, when a settlement was filed with the DPU.

Given the historic animosity between BECo and the NUPs (which intensified during the Pilgrim hearings), the fact that the discussions took place at all, let alone functioned fairly smoothly and ended in settlement, is impressive. In the end, the NUPs commented that they felt that BECo had put its best people forward and had negotiated in good faith. BECo also praised the NUPs for negotiating in an "honest and reasonable manner" (May interview).

Still, the negotiations were extremely difficult and complex. As Shimshak points out, "There was no easy issue. It was a package deal, and everything was fluid until the end" (Shimshak interview). Yet, despite what appeared in the hearings to be an unresolvable $2.7 billion difference in the value of Pilgrim to the ratepayers (that is, the difference between BECo's positive $400 million value and the NUPs' negative $2.3 billion value), the parties were able to find fertile ground for compromise. At least three major areas of basic agreement emerged during the negotiations, which together allowed a settlement to crystallize. First, the parties agreed that if BECo was confident in its ability to improve Pilgrim's performance, it should be willing to base at least part of its future earnings directly on that performance. Second, parties agreed that the NUPs' desire for greater health and safety at Pilgrim and a more serious pursuit of DSM was not inconsistent with BECo's own desires. Lastly, the parties agreed that the NUPs should be willing to relinquish part of the current disallowances they had been insisting on in return for satisfaction on the first two points.

With these underlying principles in mind, the parties were able to forge a comprehensive settlement that effectively resolved all of the outstanding issues in both the replacement power and general rate cases. The major components of the settlement are outlined in Table 4-7.

The four core parties' signatures on the settlement demonstrate their belief that it represented a better resolution of the issues in the cases than they would have expected from a DPU decision. If they believed otherwise, it is not likely that they would have signed. When asked to rank how well the settlement satisfied their underlying interests, all four parties gave it high marks (7 to 8 on a scale of 1 to 10) and expressed a high degree of satisfaction.[41] Even after three years, the parties still felt extremely positive about the overall settlement and each suggested only a couple of relatively minor issues they might have changed if they could have better predicted certain future events, such as the economic downturn and the rapid growth of utility DSM programs in Massachusetts.

The settlement promised to remove a huge uncertainty regarding the content of the DPU's final order in both cases. More importantly, the settlement allowed the parties to act proactively in designing tolerable penalties and incentives. From BECo's perspective, it averted yet another potentially hostile DPU order. Also, settling such important cases with the company's traditional adversaries was an invaluable

Table 4-7. Major Components of the Pilgrim Settlement

1. BECo would withdraw its previously filed rate increase ($86 million) and be precluded from filing a new rate case for three years, until April 1992. (BECo would also be permanently precluded from retail recovery of $101 million in Pilgrim operating and maintenance expenses incurred during the outage and would write off the unamortized accrued balance.)

2. A performance-based cents/kWh charge would be applied to all retail sales between 1990 and 1992 based on the following performance adjustment factors:

    a. A base component would recover $20 million, $42.5 million, and $67.5 million in 1990, 1991, and 1992 respectively.

    b. If Pilgrim's capacity factor fell below 60 percent, BECo's revenues would decrease $1 million for each percent of performance shortfall, down to a $30 million decrease. If the capacity factor was better than 76 percent, revenue would increase $1 million for each percent, up to a $15 million maximum annual increase.

    c. BECo could reap up to $4.5 million in bonuses or suffer as much as $9 million in penalties based on six measures of management performance at Pilgrim related to health and safety indicators.

3. BECo would retain the $115 million collected through the fuel charge for replacement power during the outage and through the power ascension program.

4. BECo would spend $75 million on DSM programs over three years with no recovery from ratepayers. At least $25 million would be targeted to elderly customers, low-income customers, public schools, state government facilities, and multifamily residences (at $5 million for each customer class). A settlement board comprised of the Attorney General, MASSPIRG, DOER, Senator Golden, and BECo would be set up to oversee these investments.

5. BECo would be permitted to adjust its amortization of certain property taxes and its reserve for deferred income taxes if necessary to boost its return on equity to 11 percent in 1990, 11.5 percent in 1991, and 12 percent in 1992.

6. After November 1992 and before November 2000, BECo's cost recovery for one-third of the company's capital investment in Pilgrim during the outage, and one-third of its share of any postoutage capital additions and operating and maintenance costs, would be put on a performance basis. The performance factors are similar to those used for the 1989–1992 period (that is, capacity factor and management performance indicators) and are specified in the settlement. All other Pilgrim costs (that is, the remaining two-thirds of the costs incurred since the outage and all costs prior to the outage) would continue to be collected.

7. None of the pre-1989 capital additions to Pilgrim would be subject to disallowance on the grounds of prudence.

harbinger for the new executive team, with ramifications, both inside and outside of BECo, beyond the immediate issues at hand (May interview). From the NUPs' perspective, major financial concessions had been gained from BECo, in a way that did not threaten the company's economic viability. In addition, the NUPs received many unexpected benefits, such as direct control over the company's DSM effort and the tying of cost recovery to general performance requirements, including health and safety indicators. All parties also avoided the need for contentious rate case litigation with each other during the next three years.

The settlement is important because it managed to resolve some extremely difficult issues in the context of a controversial case with a great deal of creativity and innovation. For instance, instead of rebating customers for the replacement power costs that BECo had collected from ratepayers during the outage, the parties agreed to allow the company to keep that money and provide $75 million dollars in DSM to its ratepayers (without recovery in rates) through programs approved by the parties to the settlement.

Another important example of the parties' innovation was the decision to tie rates during the following three years to Pilgrim's actual performance. The settlement's inclusion of additional health and safety performance factors was unique in the nation. In theory, the inclusion of these factors could provide additional incentive to maximize long-run performance while reducing the incentive for a utility to manage a plant solely to maximize its capacity factor in the short run (Nogee interview).

Finally, another important innovation was the parties' decision to tie cost recovery on one-third of any incremental investments made in Pilgrim since the outage began, and into the future, to Pilgrim's performance between 1992 and 2000. Although two other nuclear facilities, Diablo Canyon in California and Fort St. Vrain in Colorado, had been similarly "cut loose" from traditional cost-plus ratemaking (except that those two plants had 100 percent of their costs tied to performance), Pilgrim was the only plant in which performance was tied, at least in part, to health and safety indicators.[42]

DPU Approval

The Pilgrim settlement was submitted to the DPU for review and approval on October 3, 1989, and was signed by the core negotiating group and all of the other parties to the cases, except for the Massachusetts Bay Transportation Authority, which did not raise any objections. In the accompanying cover letter, the parties said that this Settlement Agreement is far-reaching in effect, and achieves the Department's goals of performance-based ratemaking and investment in cost-effective DSM programs. The value to all interested parties of this global settlement is very substantial. It permits the parties and the Department to put these disputes behind us and focus our collective efforts on better serving the public in the future. (BECo et al. 1989, cover letter, p. 3)

Since a commission cannot delegate its authority to make the final decision on adjudicatory affairs, it is obligated to carefully review settlements prior to approval and make a finding that the settlement is essentially just and reasonable and in the public interest:

Thus, a settlement agreement among the parties, however well wrought, does not oust the Department's jurisdiction nor absolve the Department of its statutory obligation to conclude its investigations with a finding that a fair outcome will result. (Mass. D.P.U. 88-28/88-48/89-100 [1989a], pp. 8–9)

Obviously, to come to such a conclusion in cases as complicated and controversial as these, the DPU must determine a reasonable range of acceptable outcomes. Since the settlement discussions started after the hearings and the DPU was obligated to issue an order in the rate case by January 23, 1990—or BECo would legally be entitled to its entire rate increase request—the DPU had already had substantial internal discussions on the cases and was preparing a draft order (Werlin interview).

However, in Massachusetts, rate case orders are rarely issued before the last day of the suspension period, and significant issues are often not resolved until the waning hours. Therefore, although the commissioners may have had a general notion of the direction and rough magnitude of how they wanted to resolve these cases, specific numbers had not been finalized when the settlement was received. Lastly, given the uncertainty about the DPU's legal authority to order BECo to (1) tie Pilgrim cost recovery to its performance, or (2) link performance to health and safety indicators, or (3) invest in DSM expenditures without charging ratepayers, it cannot be presumed that the DPU was contemplating taking such actions on its own initiative.

After careful scrutiny, the DPU approved the settlement on October 31, 1989, concluding that

the benefits to BECo customers envisioned by the settlement agreement are consonant with reasonable findings, taken as a whole, had the cases taken the customary course. (Mass. D.P.U. 88-28/88-48/89-100 [1989a], p. 10)

In addition to finding that the settlement "fairly repairs the harm to ratepayers that Boston Edison's decisions during the outage may reasonably be said to have caused," the DPU praised the settlement for its innovative performance features (id.).

Still, the DPU spent nearly half of the eighteen-page order chastising BECo for its actions during the outage (id., pp. 11–17).

> The information before us shows a pattern of inadequate planning and chaotic execution of major projects that persisted well into 1987. . . . The Company's resource planning continued to suffer from failure to assess all reasonable alternatives, failure to conduct cost-effectiveness and feasibility analyses before embarking on major investments, ... (id., p. 12)

In doing so, the DPU was clearly informing the parties and the public of its predisposition to require major disallowances in absence of the settlement. Still, the order ends on a positive note, praising BECo for the settlement and hoping that it may be a symbol of a brighter future for the company and its ratepayers:

> Indeed, the settlement agreement itself may be the bellwether of a change in practice and attitude from one of confrontation to one of conciliation, a recognition by the Company that the consequences of its own actions must be squarely reckoned with, resolved, and put behind it. (id., p. 16)

The Postsettlement Era

Since the adoption of the Pilgrim settlement, several developments have transpired that together provide additional insight into the legitimacy and practicality of the settlement. These include the emergence of opposition to the settlement, Pilgrim's actual performance, the fate of the plans laid out in the settlement under New England's economic downturn, and the trials and tribulations of the DSM settlement board.

Outside Opposition

Although the signatories, the DPU, and the press were positive about the settlement, representatives of some local citizen groups and the NRC voiced opposition. On October 31, 1989, the day the settlement was approved by the DPU, Janice Nickerson and other representatives of local citizens' groups faxed the department a letter claiming that there could be "serious consequences to the health and safety of the public" if the settlement were approved and asking the department to stay its decision and allow for additional public input. The NRC's criticism came later in public speeches and direct contact with the DPU (Werlin and Shimshak interviews).

Ironically, although one of the settlement's self-proclaimed strengths was the linkage it established between health and safety at Pilgrim on the one hand and BECo's economic return on the other, health and safety issues were central to the opposition by these seemingly disparate groups. The local citizens, who were primarily interested in shutting Pilgrim down, worried that the performance incentives—particularly the capacity factor incentives—would encourage BECo to run the plant unsafely to maximize its bonuses (Allen 1991). The criticisms, particularly from the local citizen groups, deeply stung MASSPIRG and other intervenors, given their obvious concern over health and safety issues at Pilgrim (Nogee interview).

The NRC was not receptive to the idea of linking health and safety indicators directly to economic returns. It had successfully opposed a proposal in New York to link nuclear plant performance to financial management incentives (NRC 1987, p. 40), arguing that utilities should strive for safe plants for their own sake. Like the citizen groups, the NRC was concerned that the performance formulas would provide incentives for BECo and other utilities to run plants just to improve their indicators and might also provide incentives that could undermine accurate logging of the health and safety indicators that the NRC required them to track.

Pilgrim Performance

One of the NUPs' primary objectives in crafting the settlement was to create a system of incentives that would force BECo either to turn Pilgrim into one of the best-run plants in the country or to retire it. However, as Nogee describes, the NUPs remained skeptical that BECo could turn Pilgrim around:

> Our bet was they couldn't do it, and were likely to have to shut the plant down. No plant in the country had made the kind of turnaround Boston Edison projected. (Quoted in Allen 1991)

During the first two years after the settlement, as Nogee points out in the same article, Pilgrim's performance showed overall improvement compared with its historic record. In both years, BECo earned bonuses, albeit small ones, in accordance with the performance formulas. During the first year, the company earned $470,000 in bonus money over the $20 million base component. During the second, it earned $142,000 in bonus money over the $42.5 million base.

Pilgrim's historic capacity factor of approximately 57 percent increased to 68 percent during the first year and fell slightly to 64 percent during the second year;[43] both of these figures are in the neutral zone (60–76 percent) that provides neither bonus nor penalty. Table 4-8 shows Pilgrim's performance with respect to all of the indicators tracked in the settlement. During the first year, the plant was in the neutral zone in four categories and the bonus zone in three others. In the second year, performance slipped slightly: it was in the neutral zone in three categories, in the bonus zone in two categories, and in the penalty zone in two categories (safety system failures and collective radiation exposure). There also appeared to be little consistency in the indicators between the first two years, since only the capacity factor remained in the same category (neutral) in both years.

Still, Rachel Shimshak of DOER claims: "Pilgrim has made a miraculous turnaround" (Shimshak interview). Moreover, the NRC,

Table 4-8. Pilgrim Performance Indicators

Indicator	Neutral Zone	First Year[a]	Second Year[a]
Capacity factor	60%–76%	68% (N)[b]	64% (N)
SALP[c]	1.6–1.8	1.70 (N)	1.57 (B)[d]
Automatic scrams while critical	1–3	2 (N)	0 (B)
Safety system failures	2–4	3 (N)	7 (P)[e]
Safety system actuations	1–2	0 (B)	1 (N)
Collective radiation exposure (person-rems)	345–575	221 (B)	578 (P)
Maintenance backlog (more than 3 months)	49.4%–59.4%	41.2% (B)	52.4% (N)

Source: BECo et al. 1989; personal correspondence from Tom May, BECo, February 6, 1992.

[a] First year = 11/89–10/90. Second year = 11/89–10/90. Slightly different time periods were used for some indicators.

[b] (N) = in neutral zone. The neutral zones for some factors float over time to track industrywide performance.

[c] SALP = NRC's Systematic Assessment of Licensee Performance scores.

[d] (B) = bonus zone.

[e] (P) = penalty zone.

which in the mid-1980s considered Pilgrim one of the five worst plants in the country, now considers it "above average." However, it is probably premature to determine whether Pilgrim is cured of the problems that have plagued it. Although the plant is operating better than previously, its capacity factor hovers in the lower-to-mid-range of the neutral zone (that is, 64–68 percent). Since, as BECo maintains, Pilgrim is only economic above a 60 percent capacity factor, given its base case assumptions (BECo 1990), it may remain only marginally cost-effective in the long run. Table 4-8 also indicates that Pilgrim continues to experience some health and safety problems (for example, during the second year, there were seven safety system failures, and collective radiation exposure was above the neutral range defined in the settlement).

It remains unclear what role, if any, the settlement has played in Pilgrim's improvement. Obviously, at either extreme, BECo stands to gain or lose tens of millions of dollars per year from the performance incentives. However, around the neutral zone, the incentives probably provide little financial motivation.

At least three other factors besides the settlement have probably contributed to Pilgrim's improvement. First, as discussed previously, significant changes occurred in BECo's upper management and in the management and operation practices of the plant prior to the settlement. Second, throughout the outage, the NRC vigilantly oversaw Pilgrim's improvements, and the NRC continues to monitor operations since the plant has come back on-line (as it does for every other nuclear facility in the country). Lastly, it is hard to imagine hundreds of millions of dollars of improvements having been made in Pilgrim without an improvement in its performance!

Perhaps the greatest benefit of the performance factors in the near term is that they are being more closely scrutinized by the public and the regulators, a factor that may be more effective than any direct financial impact. Probably because of the NRC's and some local citizen groups' outspoken concerns about performance incentives, BECo appears reluctant to acknowledge publicly that it pays much attention to them. Recently, George Davis, chief executive at Pilgrim, claimed that plant managers do not base decisions on the state bonus system, saying "we do not allow ourselves to even consider it" (Allen 1991).

The Economy Sours

When the parties signed the settlement in 1988, none of them suspected that the Massachusetts economy was about to sour. However, soon after the settlement, BECo's sales growth plummeted along with the Massachusetts economy. In 1990 the company experienced its first decline in sales in over twenty years (May interview). However, the settlement precluded BECo from requesting a rate increase (that is, to spread its fixed costs over the smaller sales volume) for three years. The company's unanticipated loss, which conversely was ratepayers' unexpected gain, may be on the order of tens of millions of dollars.

Tom May claimed that, had BECo realized the economy would worsen, the company probably would not have agreed to a three-year rate freeze in the settlement or would have insisted on the inclusion of an accounting mechanism that would fully compensate BECo regardless of sales volume.[44] But ironically, as May agrees, the rate freeze may prove to be one of the healthiest things that have happened to the company. Not only did it allow BECo, in May's words, "three years of peace with respect to rate case litigation," but it forced the company to substantially cut its costs. Since all the other utilities in Massachusetts have had rate increases during this period, BECo, which had some of the highest retail rates in Massachusetts, now has rates that are among the lowest. For example, although the company's residential rates are still approximately 10 cents/kWh, as they were in 1988 when BECo had the highest residential rates in the state, only one company now has lower rates. A similar pattern can be found in BECo's commercial and industrial rates.

Largely as a result of BECo's cost-cutting initiatives and low rates in the wake of the settlement and the economic downturn, BECo's stock prices rose sharply several years after the settlement. In addition, BECo's top twenty-two executives received substantial bonuses worth $2 to $3 million during 1991 (Allen 1991).

DSM Settlement Board

The original purpose of the DSM settlement board was to make sure that the $75 million BECo agreed to spend on DSM without recovery from ratepayers was spent wisely, and that one-third of the DSM was distributed to the "hard-to-reach" sectors (for example, low-income). The board has been responsible for initiating numerous program design innovations, especially in BECo's residential programs. Also, BECo has spent more than double the $75 million stipulated in the settlement on DSM between 1990 and 1993.

Despite these apparent successes, the participants I interviewed agreed that the DSM settlement board has proven to be the most frustrating part of the settlement implementation process. It has turned out to be time consuming and contentious. BECo claims that the NUPs are trying to micromanage the company's DSM efforts, and the NUPs claim that the company is being recalcitrant and withholding important information. Some issues, such as designing an appropriate cost-effectiveness tool to screen DSM measures, engendered a two-year debate between the company and the other board members.[45]

Notably, the same parties who were able to forge a creative and comprehensive settlement during the Pilgrim cases appear to be stumbling over relatively small DSM issues on the settlement board. There appear to be three possible reasons why this consensual process in the postsettlement implementation phase has faltered. First, whereas the Pilgrim settlement was time constrained since a settlement had to be reached in a matter of months or the DPU would decide the cases, the three-year duration of the settlement board has allowed many issues to remain unresolved. Many of them were policy-related disputes, which in hindsight most of the parties claimed should have been brought to the DPU for resolution early on.

Second, concurrent with the settlement board's oversight, a DSM collaborative process has also been designing DSM programs for BECo (see the DSM collaborative case later in this chapter). The parties to both processes were almost identical, and the NUPs on the settlement board intended to allow most program design issues to be resolved in that collaborative. However, they occasionally added additional program elements—often to the consternation of BECo, and sometimes even the Conservation Law Foundation (CLF) (which was instrumental in the collaborative, but not part of the settlement board). Also, the NUPs often could not participate effectively because they were spread too thin by their settlement board commitments on top of their other substantial workloads. Finally, to the degree that the settlement precluded BECo from collecting additional financial incentives associated with its DSM programs besides the $75 million in direct costs, the company's enthusiasm for DSM programs may have been less than that of other Massachusetts utilities that participated in DSM collaboratives but were not constrained from earning such incentives.[46]

Third, shortly after the settlement board began, in May 1990, BECo filed plans with the regulators to build a 306 MW, gas-fired, combined-cycle generating unit known as Edgar Station (Edgar). The Attorney General, MASSPIRG, and CLF intervened in the cases before the Energy Facilities Siting Council (EFSC) and DPU to oppose Edgar. Since the primary justification for the plant was a projected need for power that hinged in part on the amount of available DSM, the parties were suddenly litigating many of the same issues they were trying to more peacefully resolve at the settlement board. But instead of a few million dollars' worth of DSM riding on the settlement board's decisions, the parties now also felt they had the fate of a major new supply-side plant in tow.

Evaluating the Success of the Pilgrim Settlement

The overall success of the Pilgrim settlement may be assessed by considering whether process-related resources were saved and whether the settlement resolved the issues raised during the case in a way that was more legitimate and more practical than if the DPU had decided the cases.

Process-Related Resource Savings

As discussed in Chapter 3, using settlement and other consensus-building methods within the adjudicatory process is often touted as being able to save substantial time and resources. At first blush, it is difficult to imagine drawing such a conclusion in cases such as Pilgrim's, which required over ninety days of evidentiary hearings. However, the proper framework for analysis is to compare the resources used in the settlement process with the likely resources that would have been expended had the DPU resolved the cases. The enormous amount of time and money spent on the cases prior to the inception of settlement discussions should be considered a sunk cost with respect to this question.

In both cases, when the settlement discussions began, the hearings had concluded, and all that remained was for the parties to write legal briefs. In such cases, the preparation of briefs, in which the parties explain why their positions should be upheld and their opponents' positions rejected, would undoubtedly have cost the parties substantial time and effort. Still, such an effort probably would not have required as many resources as the intensive three months of settlement negotiations. All those I interviewed claimed it took more than half of their own time and substantial resources from their respective organizations.

In theory, the Pilgrim settlement should also be credited with savings from the litigation that would have occurred had the DPU's decision been appealed. Placing a value on this factor requires estimating both the probability of such a challenge and its likely cost. Certainly in cases as controversial as these, appeals are fairly common—particularly if a PUC's order leans heavily toward one party or the other. At the same time, according to Tom May, given BECo's overwhelming desire to put Pilgrim behind it and make peace with both the intervenors and the regulators, the company's tolerance in these cases would have been much higher than it had been historically (Tom May interview). Since appeals can be costly (though usually much less so than the original adjudication), despite perhaps a low probability of appeal, the Pilgrim settlement certainly should be afforded some positive benefit in this area. However, it is probably not enough when combined with the additional resources consumed during the settlement process itself to conclude that the settlement saved process-related resources.

If there are to be any process-related savings from the settlement, they will probably occur during the implementation phase. Since BECo itself helped craft the settlement, there is a greater likelihood of enthusiastic implementation than if the DPU had ordered comparable changes. Therefore, the result should be less regulatory oversight and litigation. Clearly, if the settlement had not frozen BECo's rates for three years, given the economic downturn, the parties would have engaged in additional and costly rate case proceedings sooner.[47] The DSM settlement board is the one place where the implementation of the settlement may actually be sapping more resources than if there had been no settlement. The board has been more time consuming and more frustrating than any of the parties had anticipated. However, these costs must be compared with accomplishing similar results through costly litigation. (See the DSM collaborative case later in this chapter for further discussion of this last point.)

On balance, it appears that the Pilgrim settlement did not save resources related to the adjudicatory process itself in the short run but may save resources in the long run by avoiding or deferring future litigation. Moreover, because the settlement improved participant relations, as everyone interviewed claimed, potential savings might occur in other, subsequent proceedings between BECo and the intervenors. However, the preceding analysis, which focuses only on the process-related savings vis-à-vis traditional litigation, is incomplete since it does not represent a net benefit analysis. A more complete and important analysis must focus on how successful the settlement was in enhancing the legitimacy of the traditional process and improving the practicality of the final results.

Legitimacy

PUCs can occasionally craft orders in the wake of contentious adjudications that are able to satisfy the wide range of interests in a case. More often, cases like Pilgrim push parties to take extreme positions, and the PUC's final decision has a "split-the-baby" quality.

In the Pilgrim settlement process, parties were forced to get beyond the extreme positions taken during the cases to probe each other's underlying interests. For example, during the cases, the primary focus was on an appropriate level of compensation or disallowance for BECo's past decisions. However, during the settlement discussions, the parties were forced to deal directly with their true underlying interests—the future of Pilgrim and the utility's DSM plans, as well as the company's overall viability and reputation. Without recognizing where these underlying interests converged and diverged, the parties could not have crafted a settlement.

The fact that consensus was reached between BECo and the intervenors is testimony to the participants' enhanced perception of the legitimacy of the settlement process, compared with the range of likely outcomes had the DPU decided the cases. As mentioned, all of the parties I interviewed felt that the settlement was extremely successful in satisfying their underlying interests. Although the implementation phase, most notably with the DSM settlement board, has sometimes been frustrating, all the parties I interviewed retain great enthusiasm for the original settlement that they created.

The DPU's approval and praise of the settlement further enhances its legitimacy, as does the absence of any appeals. There were, however, two blemishes related to this enhanced legitimacy. First was the discontent voiced by some of the local citizen groups, who felt that their health and safety concerns over Pilgrim's continued operation were ignored. Second was the NRC's concern over the legitimacy of tying cost recovery to performance-based approaches generally, and to the NRC's own health and safety indicators specifically.

With respect to the local groups, it is difficult to sustain an argument that their concerns were ignored, since those groups were members in the Massachusetts Citizens for Safe Energy, one of the signatories of the settlement. In addition, the citizens' interests to see Pilgrim preferably shut down, but otherwise made safer, were obviously shared by the NUPs. Since the DPU did not have the authority to shut the plant down on health and safety grounds, these parties would probably not have been satisfied by the likely range of DPU decisions in the absence of settlement. Furthermore, the addition of health and safety indicators to the performance formulas was an obvious improvement to using capacity factors alone. Lastly, the local groups' total opposition to the use of performance indicators in the settlement is surprising, since Senator Golden's original petition on behalf of the local citizens was to move all of Pilgrim out of rate base and on to a performance basis (rather than the relatively small portion moved out in the settlement).

The NRC's concerns, though couched in language that appears to question the legitimacy of the Pilgrim settlement and the DPU order approving the settlement, are really about the practicality of linking performance to cost recovery. According to the NRC, performance incentives could cause nuclear plant operators to jeopardize safe operation for short-term economic gains. Adding health and safety indicators did little to allay the NRC's fears. Although they raise important empirical issues, the NRC's worries seem somewhat unfounded given their own continuing obligation to oversee health and safety at Pilgrim and other nuclear facilities. In the end, the NRC's concern has more to do with the conflicting jurisdiction between the state and federal government on regulatory issues related to nuclear power plants than with the legitimacy of the settlement itself.

Practicality

The Pilgrim settlement seems to have developed superior remedies that were both easier to implement and more effective than whatever redress might have been expected from a DPU order. If the decision had been left exclusively to the DPU, while probably well reasoned and judicious, the order would most likely have focused largely on an appropriate level of disallowance for BECo. It might have laid out certain expectations with respect to BECo's future performance, but it probably would still have focused primarily on BECo's past actions. It is unlikely that the DPU would have formally linked Pilgrim's cost recovery directly to its performance, particularly to health and safety indicators, nor would it have included anything on DSM expenditures. These linkages were unlikely in large part because they were not articulated in the case record and thus would not necessarily have been prominent in the minds of the DPU staff and commission. However, even if the commission had considered comparable options, problems regarding its legal authority could have constrained it. This may have precluded the commission from such experimentation, despite its obvious sympathies for what those changes represented.

The members of the core settlement group were much freer to explore alternatives to resolving the contentious issues in the case. They ultimately also agreed on a de facto disallowance range, but they were able to package it in a way that better satisfied their interests. All the parties agreed that the settlement they signed resolved the outstanding issues more creatively and practically than could have been expected from a DPU order. Even the NUPs were clear that major DPU disallowances alone, without any formal incentive structure for future performance, would not have served their interests well, even though that is exactly the remedy they were formally seeking in the cases!

Rather than force the DPU to make a prudence determination, in large part on future projections of unknowable variables that would determine the cost-effectiveness of Pilgrim, the settlement ties BECo's cost recovery directly to the plant's future performance. The settlement added six health and safety performance indicators to counterbalance concerns that this tying could provide BECo perverse incentives to operate the plant unsafely. This addition was the first in the country.

Perhaps even more impressive than the overall structure of this performance approach is its detailing. Not only did the parties agree on the appropriate indicators for the performance approach; they agreed on explicit formulas for each of them. These formulas specify the zones in which BECo would earn neither bonus nor penalty and the value for each bonus and penalty step outside that neutral zone. Formulas of this detail would have been extremely difficult for the DPU to derive on its own, even if it had been so inclined, and would have never emerged consensually in the contested-hearings process.

Another example of the creative practicality embodied in the settlement is found in the combined treatment of the replacement power and the DSM issues. The parties agreed to provide BECo's customers with $75 million of essentially free DSM services rather than refund a portion of the replacement power monies collected during the outage to BECo's ratepayers, as the Attorney General had originally requested. This quid pro quo allowed BECo to save face by avoiding the perception that it imprudently overcollected money from its ratepayers during the Pilgrim outage and, in fact, gave BECo the opportunity to bolster its image by actively promoting DSM. The NUPs felt that it still allowed them to show their constituencies that they secured something tangible. In addition, by establishing a DSM settlement board, the NUPs gained more control over the shape of BECo's DSM programs than they otherwise would have.

However, the DSM settlement board has been the source of some friction among the parties during implementation. Much of that friction is being driven by issues other than those anticipated in the settlement itself, such as the possibility of a large new supply-side facility whose future partly depends on the amount of DSM available. Nonetheless, even here the settlement board has fulfilled its obligation to oversee the spending of $75 million on DSM; and the board, despite much bickering, has even managed to produce several important program design innovations.

Together, all these practical innovations distinguish the Pilgrim settlement from ordinary rate case orders that emerge from PUCs after adjudication, and also from typical rate case settlements. However, whereas the concepts and directions established during the settlement appear to have practically resolved many of the thorny Pilgrim-related issues, it is still early to tell how they will actually work. Although Pilgrim's overall performance has improved, it has been uneven (that is, the capacity factor is up, but Pilgrim was penalized in 1991 for continuing to expose some of its workers to radiation, as well as for other safety problems). In addition, several other factors besides the settlement—including new management, vigilant regulatory oversight, and large capital investments—have simultaneously played a part in Pilgrim's improved performance.

In theory, the settlement should provide financial incentives for BECo to either improve the operation of Pilgrim or retire it and replace it with less expensive alternatives. However, the magnitude of the incentives, the portion of Pilgrim's embedded and future costs exposed to the performance requirements, or both may be too small to ultimately motivate the company.

Process Evaluation

In many respects, the Pilgrim settlement was an extension of a traditional process used to resolve rate cases and other adjudicatory matters before state PUCs. Although the frequency differs from state to state, rate case settlements are not uncommon. However, traditional rate case settlements are usually narrowly focused on selecting essentially a few numbers, such as the magnitude of the change in the cost of service or the rate of return. Occasionally the settlements venture into more complicated areas, such as cost allocation and rate design.

The uniqueness of the Pilgrim settlement rests in large part on its success in resolving a broad array of contentious and complicated issues in one fell swoop. More importantly, its distinctiveness stems from the parties' use of consensus-building techniques to identify those issues they really cared about—even though some of those issues were not represented directly in the proceedings before the DPU. As a result, the solution enhanced the final resolution of those issues, rather than merely serving as a convenient substitute for the DPU's judgment on more narrowly defined questions (for example, selecting an appropriate level of disallowance).

It is important to emphasize why the parties chose to settle the case. Despite over ninety days of hearings, the parties remained uncertain regarding what the DPU would ultimately order. More importantly, the reasonable range of likely outcomes from the DPU, given precedent and other legal constraints, was not really attractive to any of the parties because it was unlikely to satisfy their underlying interests. For both these reasons, the parties chose to act proactively by seeking a mutually agreeable settlement on their own.

Several features of the settlement process itself helped the parties achieve what in the end must be considered a fairly successful settlement. First, all the participants put forward competent and senior personnel; BECo's new chief operating officer, for example, attended all the settlement discussions. Second, the participants were able to make room in their busy schedules to participate fully in the settlement process—spending, on average, half their time over a three-month period. Third, the negotiations were clearly timely and time constrained since the DPU was required to decide the case itself and issue an order by the end of the six-month suspension period.

Fourth, the nonutility parties acted as a coalition, with a core subgroup of the original intervenors working out any minor discrepancies among themselves separately from the direct negotiations with BECo. The coalition approach helped to further streamline the meetings between BECo and the intervenors. The only shortcoming of the representative coalition approach was that even though all the parties ended up signing the settlement, some of the neighborhood groups behind Senator Golden's original petition felt that they had not been adequately represented and were not happy with the final settlement (even though Senator Golden himself supported the settlement). Better communication within the strict confines of protecting the confidentiality of the settlement negotiations themselves should have been possible.

Several features of the negotiation strategy are worth highlighting. First, the parties gained by their decision to initially focus on key principles from which a subsequent settlement could be molded, rather than continuing to haggle over the appropriate level of disallowance. Once they had agreed on several major principles and objectives, though the negotiations were never easy, the focus shifted to how to best reach the agreed-on objectives. In this way the difficult distributive questions, which were the exclusive focus of the contested hearings, were temporarily suspended so that parties could identify areas where integrative bargaining could occur. Second, once integrative bargaining began, the parties did not try to solve each issue sequentially. Rather, they recognized from the beginning the value of packaging proposals in ways that allowed them to take advantage of their different relative valuations of particular issues right up until the end. Finally, and perhaps most importantly, the parties took advantage of their freedom to reach beyond the confines of the narrow questions addressed in the contested cases (that is, how much money should BECo be given or denied?). By grasping innovative remedies that made sense vis-à-vis the parties' true interests, such as Pilgrim's future performance and BECo's DSM plans, the parties were able to find fertile ground for trading.

In closing, it is worth pondering for a moment whether the settlement could have occurred earlier in the contested-case process—sparing everyone considerable expense and aggravation. Although some of the hearings could have probably been circumvented, it is unlikely that in these cases a settlement would have been possible or productive early on. Parties needed the opportunity to present their own cases and to probe each other's cases. This ventilating was probably necessary to get numerous facts and opinions on the table and to allow the parties to more realistically assess their relative strengths in the cases. In this regard, the DPU's own information requests and cross-examination, although not definitive with respect to the commission's ultimate intentions, also helped parties to reassess their strengths and weaknesses.

All of those I interviewed were skeptical about the usefulness of initiating settlement discussions much earlier in the process. Alan Nogee articulately captured this commonly held view:

> A settlement would not have made sense either prior to or early in the hearings. We needed to get all the information out on the table. Otherwise, the settlement would have become a back-room deal, and not a creative solution based on the evidence and the parties' different expectations of the future. Until we had developed the case on paper, we would not have known how to set all the parameters in the settlement, and it would have been rather arbitrary. (Nogee interview)

I agree with the parties' assessment that it was critical for them to have thoroughly ventilated the issues prior to settling. However, I question whether that ventilation really necessitated such exhaustive discovery and so many days of evidentiary hearings. Perhaps the use of technical sessions during the cases could have helped establish the facts more quickly and completely. More importantly, such sessions might have allowed parties to understand each other's underlying interests faster than the highly contentious and positional hearings allowed. There might have even been other, more direct ways for the commission to convey its concerns to the parties, such as the use of an expanded prefiling conference.

These suggestions along with other possible improvements to adjudicatory consensus building, including mediation, are explored in more detail throughout this book. The next case, on a DSM collaborative process, specifically examines the use of a settlement process prior to the initiation of a contested case.

DSM COLLABORATIVES IN MASSACHUSETTS

Since 1988, eight Massachusetts utilities have been involved in unique collaborative processes with their traditional adversaries to design comprehensive demand-side management (DSM) programs outside the traditional adjudicatory process. The utilities concerned are the Boston Edison Company (BECo); Cambridge Electric Company and Commonwealth Electric Company (together COM/Electric); Fitchburg Gas & Electric (FG&E); Eastern Edison Company (Eastern—the Massachusetts retail company of Eastern Utilities Associates Service Corporation [EUA]); Nantucket Electric Company (Nantucket); Western Massachusetts Electric Company (WMECo—the Massachusetts retail company of Northeast Utilities [NU]); and Massachusetts Electric Company (MECo—the Massachusetts retail company of New England Electric System [NEES]). The nonutility parties (NUPs) include the Conservation Law Foundation (CLF); the Office of the Attorney General (Attorney General); the Division of Energy Resources (DOER—known as the Executive Office of Energy Resources [EOER] until late 1989); and the Massachusetts Public Interest Research Group (MASSPIRG).

The collaborative processes used to develop these DSM programs differed significantly from historic litigation strategies, in which the NUPs intervened in virtually every case before the Massachusetts Department of Public Utilities (DPU) to force utilities to improve their DSM efforts. The DSM collaboratives, which occurred in the wake of a history of litigation, had at least three unique features. One was their attempt to settle contentious issues prior to litigation rather than at the end of a litigated case, as is the general rule with traditional settlements. A second was that the utilities agreed to provide over $5 million in funds for the NUPs to secure outside technical experts. Finally, in contrast to traditional settlement processes, which generally end when the case is resolved, some of the collaboratives with individual utilities have already lasted more than five years.

The usefulness of collaboratives rests on whether they represent an improvement to the traditional adjudicatory procedures previously used to resolve these issues, and whether they produce superior results. Despite significant variability and room for improvement among the individual DSM collaboratives, it appears that they have helped the utilities' DSM programs become more practical while at the same time enhancing the legitimacy of the adjudicatory process.

Analysis of the collaboratives relies on relevant documentation, including DPU orders, written testimony, transcripts of hearings, utility filings, speeches by participants, and journal and newspaper articles. In addition, I conducted thirty-one (primarily face-to-face) interviews with twenty-eight representatives of the utilities, the NUPs, former DPU commissioners, and other intervenors during the summer and fall of 1991. The interviewees are listed in Table 4-9, along with their affiliations and titles.[48] I originally conducted these interviews as part of a larger study on DSM collaboratives, entitled *Public Involvement in Integrated Resource Planning: A Study of Demand-Side Management Collaboratives*, that was funded by the U.S. Department of Energy and published by Oak Ridge National Laboratory (Raab and Schweitzer 1992).[49] Some key findings from that cross-collaborative analysis, which included nine cases involving twenty-four utilities and approximately fifty NUPs in ten states, are woven into this analysis.

Table 4-9. Interviews for Massachusetts DSM Collaboratives

Utilities

John Cagnetta	Senior Vice-President for Corporate Planning and Regulatory Relations, Northeast Utilities
Al Destribats	Vice-President for Planning, NEES
Peter Flynn	Director of Conservation and Load Management, NEES
L. Carl Gustin	Senior Vice-President for Customer Savings, Marketing, and Corporate Relations, BECo
Elizabeth Hicks	Director of Demand Planning, NEES
Kathleen Kelly	Manager of Evaluation and Monitoring, BECo
Lydia Pastuszek	President of Granite State Electric Company (former Director of Demand Planning), NEES
John Rowe	President and CEO, NEES
Richard Sergel	Treasurer (former Director of Rates), NEES
Earle Taylor	Director of Conservation and Load Management, Northeast Utilities
Ben Tucker	Technical Assistant to L. Carl Gustin, BECo
Wendy Watts	Director of Conservation, Nantucket Electric Company
Carol White	Supervisor of Demand-Side Planning and Evaluation, EUA Services Corporation
Mort Zajac	Manager of Demand Program Administration, COM/Electric

Nonutility Parties

Steve Burrington	Attorney, CLF
Joseph Chaisson	Consultant, lead coordinator of NUP consultants

Finally, as the lead staffperson responsible for questioning witnesses and drafting orders for the DPU on the Massachusetts utilities' DSM programs during most of the period covered by these cases, I was a "participant-observer" to the collaboratives.[50] As such, my observations regarding the external collaborative process, the hearings, and the internal DPU decision-making process helped shape my perspectives on this case.

Background

During the mid-1980s, none of the Massachusetts utilities viewed DSM as a significant resource. Programs tended to focus on (1) load management, (2) research, or (3) audits related to implementing fed-

Table 4-9. (continued)	
Susan Coakley	Consultant, coordinator of NUP consultants for BECo, COM/Electric, and EUA collaboratives (former staff DPU)
Armond Cohen	Senior Attorney, CLF
Stephen Cowell	President (former lead residential consultant), Conservation Services Group, Inc.
Douglas Foy	Executive Director, CLF
Alan Nogee	Energy Program Director, MASSPIRG
Jerrold Oppenheim	Assistant Attorney General, Massachusetts Attorney General
Rachel Shimshak	Director of Policy and Planning, Massachusetts Division of Energy Resources
Regulators	
Janet Besser	Manager of Energy Planning, New Hampshire Public Utilities Commission
Mary Kilmarx	Director of Energy Policy and Planning, Rhode Island Public Utilities Commission
Susan Tierney	Secretary for Environmental Affairs (former Commissioner, Department of Public Utilities)
Robert Werlin	Attorney, private law firm (former Commissioner and Chair, Department of Public Utilities)
Other Intervenors	
Andrew Newman	Attorney for lighting retailers and large industrial consumers

Note: Positions and affiliations are as of the time of the interviews.

eral and state statutes (for example, Residential Conservation Services) (Cohen and Chaisson 1990). Unlike the California utilities, which collectively spent hundreds of millions of dollars on DSM in the early-to-mid-1980s, ramping down their expenditures during the late 1980s (Raab and Schweitzer 1992, Raab et al. 1994), electric utilities in Massachusetts spent relatively little. Not until 1987 did several of the utilities begin to offer systemwide programs with limited financial incentives, largely in the form of rebates. That year, as indicated in Table 4-10, the Massachusetts utilities still spent less than $18 million on DSM—representing less than 1 percent of their total revenue.

Beginning back in 1984, virtually every time that a utility filed a rate case at the DPU, parties such as the Attorney General and DOER would protest the company's inadequate DSM efforts. The cases became acrimonious and resulted in a series of orders with increasingly stronger language in which the DPU chastised the utilities for not aggressively pursuing DSM resources.

In 1986, in a case that received much local and national public attention, the DPU penalized BECo's rate of return, primarily for not adequately pursuing DSM (Mass. D.P.U. 85-271-A/86-266-A [1986b], pp. 10–15). Other utilities also received harsh criticisms and penalties for not aggressively pursuing DSM.[51] According to John Cagnetta, senior vice-president for Northeast Utilities, WMECo's parent company:

> During this period, the DPU carefully probed our DSM programs and continuously questioned the underlying economic, policy, and technical assumptions. The cases were highly contentious, with a

Table 4-10. DSM Expenditures of Massachusetts Utilities in 1987

Utility[a]	DSM Expenditures ($ million)	Total Revenue ($ million)	DSM/Revenue (percent)
BECo	$ 5.2	$1,181	0.4%
COM/Electric	0.8	361	0.2%
MECo	9.4	1,086	0.6%
WMECo	2.4	295	0.8%
TOTAL	$17.8	$2,923	0.6%

Source: All data provided by utilities.

[a] Eastern, FG&E, and Nantucket had essentially no DSM programs in 1987 except for the federally mandated Residential Conservation Services residential audit program.

lot of intervenors, and were extremely burdensome for all. (Cagnetta interview)

Progress was slow, however, despite increasing litigation and pressure from the DPU, including financial penalties and requirements for the utilities to run specific DSM pilot programs. Robert Werlin, former DPU commissioner, describes the DPU's frustration:

> While we required various pilot programs, the DPU didn't really know what would work. The companies remained unenthusiastic, and up through the 1986–1987 period, while we continued to operate in an action-reaction-action mode, there was really no significant movement toward pursuing DSM. (Werlin interview)

Meanwhile, the New England region was in a capacity-tight situation, and the prognosis for the future was not hopeful (New England Governors' Conference 1986). In 1986, the DPU opened a generic docket (Mass. D.P.U. 86-36 [1986c]) to explore options for utilities to recover supply-side resource costs in ways that might encourage resource development while better protecting ratepayers. Before new rules could be promulgated,[52] a series of brownouts occurred in Massachusetts in the summer of 1987.

With constrained supplies, highlighted by the brownouts, the pressure for utilities to pursue DSM more aggressively continued to mount. After an investigation of the brownouts, prompted by petitions from the Attorney General and DOER, the DPU reiterated that each utility was obligated to pursue all cost-effective DSM (Mass. D.P.U. 87-169 [1988e], p. 72).

Formation and Approval of the DSM Collaboratives

In July 1987, the New England Energy Policy Council (NEEPC), consisting of twenty-six environmental and consumer groups, released a study on potential energy conservation savings in New England entitled *Power to Spare: A Plan for Increasing New England's Competitiveness Through Energy Efficiency*.[53] The study claimed that total projected electricity demand in 2005 (that is, existing demand plus utility projections of approximately 2 percent per year) could be cut by 37 to 57 percent by adopting technically feasible DSM measures. Although the utilities and others disputed the magnitude of some of the numbers, no one disputed the overall thrust of the study—that there existed a large reservoir of untapped DSM.

Half a year later, in February 1988, the Connecticut PUC ordered Connecticut Light and Power (CL&P, the Connecticut retail company for NU, and WMECo's sister retail company) to increase its DSM expenditures and undertake a collaborative process with several intervenors. This collaboration, which came at the end of a contentious rate case in which parties pressed for more DSM, was the first full-scale "DSM collaborative" (Raab and Schweitzer 1992). Its presence in a neighboring state ultimately influenced Massachusetts' utilities, intervenors, and regulators to undertake similar collaboratives.

In the spring of 1988, hearings were held in Massachusetts on DSM and least-cost planning issues in an expanded and bifurcated rulemaking process (Mass. D.P.U. 86-36 [1986c]).[54] Douglas Foy, executive director of CLF, who followed a panel of national experts,[55] asked the DPU to order the eight private electric utilities[56] in the state to do the following: (1) enter into a joint planning process with NEEPC, (2) implement the results of such a process, and (3) provide NEEPC with funds to hire outside experts.

The NUPs viewed collaboration as an alternative to litigation for accomplishing their common objective of having the utilities procure comprehensive, cost-effective DSM as expeditiously as possible. Douglas Foy explains why an alternative was necessary:

> Our guerrilla warfare was not working well on DSM. We could stop new supply-side projects, and we could show the inadequacy of existing DSM programs in litigation, but we had neither the in-house expertise nor the funding to tell regulators about better DSM programs. (Foy interview)

Uncertain about its authority to order a funded collaborative effort, the DPU requested written comments from interested parties on the legal findings necessary to require the utilities to comply with CLF's request. The NUPs filed comments claiming that no new findings were necessary. The utilities, however, argued against CLF's request for various reasons, including (1) the DPU's lack of authority to order a collaborative in a rulemaking proceeding (as opposed to an adjudicatory proceeding) and (2) the DPU's lack of authority to order intervenor funding. In addition, several utilities were already of their own accord considering a collaboration with the NUPs.

During another hearing in the generic rulemaking proceeding, with the DPU still deliberating on the fate of CLF's request, John Cagnetta of WMECo volunteered to participate in a collaborative process and coordinate the utility parties.[57] While encouraging Cagnetta, the DPU staff posed numerous issues for the parties to address in designing a voluntary collaborative process regarding representation, scope, deadlines, and the role of the DPU. On July 19, 1988, a proposed collaborative agreement was jointly submitted by CLF,

DOER, the Attorney General, MASSPIRG, and seven of the eight private electric utilities in the Commonwealth.

MECo, the second-largest utility in Massachusetts (on the basis of revenue), decided not to join the joint-utility collaborative but to engage in a separate but parallel DSM collaborative through NEES (its parent holding company) with CLF alone. NEES decided not to join the joint-utility collaborative for two reasons. First, NEES maintained that its programs would be slowed down because they were further along than those of the other utilities. Second, although 75 percent of NEES's retail sales are in Massachusetts, its programs still have to pass muster in New Hampshire and Rhode Island (Destribats, Pastuszek, and Rowe interviews).[58]

CLF favored keeping the collaborative with NEES distinct from those of the other utilities because NEES was likely to go the farthest, the fastest, and do the best job—thus being the flagship for the other utilities to emulate (Foy interview). CLF also feared that the other NUPs would slow down the collaborative process (Chaisson interview). Not surprisingly, the two organizations' decisions did not sit well with the other utilities or NUPs, or necessarily with the regulators.

Participants and Their Interests

Although the joint-utility collaborative may have been more inclusive than the NEES collaborative, other parties with interests in the outcome of the process still were not invited to join—most notably the energy service companies (ESCOs) (that is, the deliverers of DSM services) and industrial customers. At one point, an ESCO actually petitioned the DPU to be admitted into the joint-utility collaborative, and numerous other ESCOs expressed interest in participating at some level.[59] The NUPs, however, as a whole saw themselves as essentially a residential consumer and environmental coalition with a common perspective on the role of DSM in the utility industry. In the NUPs' opinion, the differently focused interests of the ESCOs and industrial intervenors could not easily be accommodated within a collaborative that was largely structured as a two-party negotiation (that is, the utilities and the NUPs). In the interviews, some of the NUPs agreed that they could have done a better job soliciting input from others—although none wanted to admit them as full parties to the joint-utility collaborative. The utilities, in contrast, with the possible exception of NEES, generally regretted omitting others and were more interested in getting direct involvement from representatives of their other customers (that is, nonresidential customers) and ESCOs in the future.

The parties' different perspectives on representation largely reflected their underlying reasons for participating in a collaborative process in the first place. As mentioned, the NUPs' primary motivation was to expeditiously procure all cost-effective DSM. The NUPs differed only slightly in the relative importance of certain common interests underlying their strategic objectives, such as environmental preservation, reducing ratepayer bills, and avoiding outages while delaying the need for new supply-side resources. Strategically, the NUPs hoped to procure the best technical expertise on DSM in the country and help the utilities forge state-of-the-art programs.

In contrast, the utilities' primary reasons for participating in a collaborative were more political. Though interested in honing their technical competence and designing better programs, they wanted to engage in a process that could improve their relationships with the NUPs and the regulators, thereby dampening future litigation. Most of the utility representatives I interviewed felt the NUPs and the regulators in prior proceedings had unfairly judged and misunderstood their DSM efforts and hoped that better communication would help in the future (Cagnetta, Gustin, Rowe, and Zajac interviews).

It is noteworthy that although the utilities were interested in securing better financial treatment for their DSM resources, they were more motivated to avoid future disallowances of DSM expenditures and penalties on their rates of return. The notion of providing positive financial incentives for superior DSM performance, such as shared savings, was not explicitly on the table as it has been in subsequent DSM collaboratives across the country (Raab and Schweitzer 1992) or in later phases of the collaboratives involving individual utilities.

Phases and Funding

The joint-utility collaborative agreement initially proposed structuring the collaborative process in two phases. During Phase I, which was expected to commence on July 18, 1988, and end on December 15, 1988, all parties would work together to design a generic portfolio of comprehensive DSM programs. In an optional Phase II, the NUPs would work with individual utilities to tailor the generic program designs to their circumstances. (In the NEES collaborative, the parties proposed refining NEES's existing programs and supplementing its current portfolio with new programs from the start.) Phase III, unanticipated at the outset, consisted of the refinement of each utility's DSM designs in response to the DPU's rulings and orders after the utilities sought the DPU's preapproval of their proposed programs.

As part of the agreement, the utilities consented to provide the NUPs with money to secure outside technical expertise. In the joint-utility collaborative, for example, the utilities agreed to provide the NUPs with $385,000 for a technical assistance fund for Phase I to be managed by CLF. Contributions were divided among the utilities in proportion to their size. NEES also agreed to provide substantial monies for CLF to secure similar expertise. None of the monies provided by any of the utilities, however, were for the NUPs' internal staffing needs, and the utilities retained veto power over the NUPs' proposed consultants.

Funds for outside technical expertise had been made available in the Connecticut collaborative and in most other DSM collaboratives (Raab and Schweitzer 1992), and they have proved critically important to the NUPs' ability to participate effectively in collaborative processes. Such funds allow organizations that have the political interest in pursuing a DSM agenda, but not the in-house technical expertise, an opportunity to participate in the regulatory process more productively.

Approval of the Joint-Utility Collaborative Agreement

The commission was relieved that it was not forced to decide CLF's original motion (particularly with respect to ordering utilities to provide funding for the NUP consultants, which it considered comparable to intervenor funding)[60] and hopeful that the proposed collaborative process could be successful in accelerating the DSM efforts of Massachusetts utilities in ways in which the DPU itself had not succeeded. The DPU approved the joint-utility collaborative agreement on August 4, 1988 (Mass. D.P.U. 86-36-D [1988b]).[61] According to former DPU commissioner Susan Tierney:

> All of us [commissioners] were frustrated because we were doing a lot of hammering on the utilities to do more DSM, and we were still not getting sufficient cost-effective DSM. We were willing to give the collaborative process a try, recognizing that even if it failed, the commission would still have greater leverage to try other regulatory approaches. (Tierney interview)

However, unlike the regulatory staff in many other DSM collaboratives, who were present as full parties or as observers (Raab and Schweitzer 1992), the Massachusetts DPU staff did not participate in either the joint-utility or the NEES collaborative. As discussed in the Pilgrim case, the absence of an advocacy staff at the DPU limited its ability to have staff participate in rate case settlements. Since the DSM collaboratives were viewed as front-end supplements to potential future adjudicatory proceedings on the utilities' DSM programs, the commission determined that staff could not participate in the collaboratives and then advise the commission in subsequent related proceedings.

The DPU obviously had strong feelings and some in-house expertise regarding DSM issues. Its inability to participate directly in the collaboratives meant that the participants were forced to second-guess its interests. The DPU meanwhile tried to make its expectations clear wherever possible. For instance, in the order approving the joint-utility collaborative, the DPU expressed numerous concerns and directives.[62] Evidence presented later in this case study will show that participants' consistent lack of access to DPU perspectives resulted in some settled issues that were unacceptable to the DPU and could have been avoided through better linkages.

Phase I

During Phase I of the joint-utility collaborative, the seven utilities met regularly with the NUPs to try to design a portfolio of DSM programs and to attempt to resolve numerous underlying policy issues. The collaborative between NEES and CLF proceeded concurrently and focused on similar technical and policy issues.

Structure

Phase I of the joint-utility collaborative had an oversight committee, as well as a working group with five subgroups focused on (1) residential programs, (2) commercial and industrial programs (later split into two groups), (3) load management and rate issues, (4) data base and monitoring issues, and (5) policy issues. The utilities and the NUPs were represented on the oversight committee and were part of the working group and its subgroups. The oversight committee met only once at the beginning of the process, whereas the working groups met regularly throughout Phase I.

In many ways, the structure of the Phase I joint-utility collaborative resembled that of a two-party rather than a multiparty negotiation. By design, the utilities and NUPs each acted as separate coalitions—reaching internal consensus on issues prior to negotiating between the coalitions. At both the working-group level and in each subgroup, a pair of utility and nonutility representatives coordinated all activities and co-facilitated the meetings. Outside neutrals were not used at all during Phase I.

Among the NUPs, CLF clearly played the lead role, not only in initiating the joint-utility collaborative, but in managing the day-to-day operations as well. CLF was responsible for identifying the consultants and overseeing their work, whereas the other NUPs signed off on the consultants prior to hiring and reviewed their major work products. Some tensions, however, arose during Phase I between CLF and the other NUPs regarding CLF's dominant role. The NUPs occasionally felt that CLF was overly controlling and asserting disproportionate influence over the process. Specifically problematic were CLF's efforts to simultaneously represent its own interests while being the shuttle diplomat between the NUPs and the utilities, on the one hand, and between the NUPs and the consultants on the other.

In subsequent phases of the joint-utility collaborative, during which each utility worked independently with the NUPs, although the NUPs continued to support CLF's management of the process, given CLF's greater resources and skills in that area, several changes were made. In addition to the hiring of separate NUP coordinators for each of the individual utility subcollaboratives, the internal NUP process was revised to provide the non-CLF NUPs with greater access to the consultants, as well as more direct access to the utilities. This reduced CLF's role as shuttle diplomat and alleviated some of the friction that had developed between the organizations.

In the NEES collaborative, where CLF was the only NUP, a hierarchical oversight structure was also used, consisting of three successively senior pairings of representatives from NEES and CLF and ending in John Rowe, the CEO of NEES, and Douglas Foy, the executive director of CLF. Most problems were resolved at the lowest level of oversight, involving the CLF coordinator and the NEES DSM manager, but occasionally, on issues of great importance (for example, the appropriate incentive level for the company, environmental externalities, and fuel substitution), the issues were bumped all the way up to the top. As shown later in the case, the NEES/CLF structure worked well for the parties, and they achieved a high degree of consensus throughout their joint effort.

Early in both collaboratives, participants spent a majority of their time in detailed technical discussions between the NUPs' consultants (most of whom were from the Pacific Northwest, where aggressive DSM programs had been run by utilities in the mid-1980s) and the utilities' technical staff. This joint fact-finding phase was used to familiarize the NUPs with the utilities' programs and to update everyone on the strengths and weaknesses of DSM programs being implemented elsewhere in the country. According to all interviewees, this period was technically enlightening and strategically critical, as it allowed the utilities and NUPS to begin to build constructive relationships.

Developing Programs and Grappling with Controversial Issues

The main goal of the joint-utility collaborative during this first phase was to design a set of comprehensive programs that could subsequently be fine-tuned to fit the particularities of the individual utilities during Phase II. Ultimately the parties were able to reach consensus on a portfolio of twenty-five separate DSM programs that covered most end uses in new and existing buildings and facilities. This consensus was a major accomplishment in its own right, given the long history of litigation and animosity between the NUPs and the utilities. Moreover, the scope of the consensus included a portfolio of programs that was far more comprehensive than any of the efforts offered by the individual utilities at that time. Finally, it was obvious that the program designs utilized the best available information from around the country and offered numerous innovative design features.

Phase I of the joint-utility collaborative had relatively little trouble ironing out broad-brushed program designs. However, it was less successful at reaching consensus on many details that relied on underlying policies. Table 4-11 lists a spectrum of issues that were at least touched on in Phase I of the joint-utility collaborative. The relative ranking of the issues from the least difficult to the most difficult to reach consensus on (as determined by interviews with participants in the collaboratives) was also found to hold across the broader range of collaboratives studied in the Oak Ridge National Laboratory project (Raab and Schweitzer 1992).

The utilities and the NUPs exchanged position papers on various policy-related issues early in the Phase I joint-utility collaborative but made little headway in finding common ground. The two most controversial and time-consuming policy debates involved selecting an appropriate cost-effectiveness test for screening DSM measures and programs, and designing an appropriate cost-recovery method for utility investments in DSM.[63] There was as much controversy among the NUPs as there was between the NUPs and the utilities on cost-recovery issues (Cohen, Nogee, and Oppenheim interviews). The intra-NUP disagreement turned on whether utilities needed and deserved additional financial incentives for pursuing DSM resources.

On November 30, 1988, a month before the parties completed Phase I, the DPU issued an interim order (Mass. D.P.U. 86-36-F [1988d]) as part of its ongoing rulemaking proceedings. In the order, the DPU defined an appropriate cost-effectiveness test for comparing resources, including DSM, and provided some guidelines for DSM-related cost recovery. Although the DPU's order did not resolve all the policy issues bogging down the Phase I joint-utility collaborative, it provided sufficient definition with respect to a cost-effectiveness test to allow the program design process to continue.[64] It also provided adequate assurance concerning the DPU's willingness to guarantee cost recovery, thus allaying some of the utilities' biggest fears about being required to pursue aggressive DSM agendas without compensation.[65]

According to Kathleen Kelly, manager of evaluation and monitoring at BECo:

> Although we [the utilities] did not completely agree with all the policies in D.P.U. 86-36-F, we were somewhat relieved when it came out because it appeared that the collaborative was not going to come to agreement on most of these policy issues. The order at least set a direction that we all had to live with. (Kelly interview)

Table 4-11. Spectrum of Issues Addressed by DSM Collaboratives

Least Difficult to Resolve
1. Identifying potential DSM technologies and inefficient end uses
2. Designing research and development efforts
3. Packaging measures into programs and designing marketing and delivery strategies
4. Screening measures and programs for cost-effectiveness (using previously adopted cost-effectiveness test)
5. Designing evaluation and monitoring plans
6. Choosing customer incentives for programs
7. Detailing cost-effectiveness tests for measure and program screening (including method for determining long-run avoided cost)
8. Selecting annual budgets for individual DSM programs and overall DSM effort
9. Ratemaking and cost-recovery issues (also in ascending order):
   A. Allocating DSM expenditures to rate classes
   B. Expensing versus amortizing DSM expenditures
   C. Recouping lost revenue caused by DSM savings
   D. Other utility incentives (shared savings, bounty)
10. Valuing environmental externalities
11. Valuing fuel substitution as a DSM measure

Most Difficult to Resolve

Source: Adapted from Raab and Schweitzer 1992.

However, the joint-utility collaborative continued to attempt to iron out a cost-recovery proposal that was consistent with the DPU order but which more specifically met the needs of the parties. Parties were unable to reach consensus on such a proposal prior to the Phase I filing, apparently in large part because of the reluctance of the Attorney General and MASSPIRG to commit to providing utilities with lost-revenue and positive financial incentives (Cohen and Oppenheim interviews).

Fuel substitution (that is, changing electric end uses—such as electric water and space heating—to alternate, potentially less costly fuels, such as gas, as a DSM measure), which has been the bane of many other collaborative DSM processes, was not on the table for long in either the joint-utility or the NEES collaborative. The utilities made clear from the outset that they were not interested in discussing fuel substitution and that little else would get resolved if it were made part of the collaborative agenda (Kelly, Taylor, and Chaisson interviews). According to Douglas Foy, the NUPs decided not to push the issue in these collaboratives since there was a large enough reservoir of DSM opportunities to pursue without factoring in fuel substitution. "You can't eat the elephant all at once," he said (Foy interview).[66]

Environmental externalities were similarly relegated to a second-tier issue in both collaboratives until the DPU order (Mass. D.P.U. 86-36-F [1988d]) that required that externalities be included in cost-effectiveness calculations. But instead of promulgating a method or set of values, the DPU chose instead to take advantage of the collaborative spirit and directed all interested parties to work together to propose both a method and specific values, if possible. In April 1989 (after the Phase I filing), the members of the joint-utility collaborative and other parties, along with NEES, came together in a minicollaborative to explore environmental externalities. In June 1989, the minicollaborative disbanded after an impasse over several issues. The most central was whether externalities needed to be priced before they could be included in resource comparisons.[67]

By the end of December 1988, the joint-utility collaborative had accomplished its primary objective for Phase I: agreement on a portfolio of technically sophisticated program designs. Many of the touchier policy-related issues spilled over into the Phase II subcollaboratives and into the ongoing NEES collaborative. Some of the issues were resolved by the parties during subsequent rounds of collaboration. Other issues that were not resolved by the DPU in its interim order (Mass. D.P.U. 86-36-F [1988d]) or by the collaboratives themselves were addressed in orders issued at the end of the DPU's "DSM preapproval" reviews following the adjudicatory proceedings in subsequent phases of the collaboratives. At least one policy issue, fuel substitution, remains unresolved, whereas others have been reexamined by both the DPU and the parties (for example, environmental externalities, customer incentives, program budgets).

Filing at the DPU

The generic portfolio of DSM programs designed during Phase I of the joint-utility collaborative was completed on schedule and filed at the DPU on December 23, 1988. All eleven parties (seven utilities and four NUPs) agreed to these preliminary program designs, as well as to a set of minimum guidelines on program monitoring and evaluation. The future of a collaborative with all the utilities except NEES, which was involved in an ongoing collaborative with CLF, was somewhat unresolved at the time of the Phase I filing. Participants agreed that work plans for Phase II would be submitted by companies that wished to continue with Phase II collaboratives on or before June 19, 1989, instead of with the Phase I filing.

In January 1989, the DPU held a public hearing on the Phase I filing and agreed to provide comments but not to issue an order, as the filing was deemed purely informational. On March 22, 1989, the DPU staff provided a letter to all interested parties stating that the DPU was "impressed by the success of the collaborative process to date" and emphasizing several areas of DPU concern that needed more attention during Phase II.[68]

Still outside of the collaborative process, the DPU could only send signals regarding its interests and concerns through occasional orders and letters. These messages were often considered cryptic or ambiguous by the participants and, in any case, were incapable of addressing all the subtleties that come up when policies are transformed into implementation details. On April 4, 1989, the DPU commissioners hosted a rare technical session on the DPU's ratemaking policies with respect to DSM program costs in an attempt to clarify its policies (which had been causing some confusion despite the DPU's interim order) and to solicit feedback.

This half-day session, which was facilitated by someone outside the DPU,[69] successfully created a useful dialogue distinctly different from the traditional hearing and order-writing process. The use of facilitation freed the commissioners and staff from running the sessions and allowed them to focus more attentively on the substantive issues. In hindsight, the DPU could have effectively used more technical sessions throughout the DSM collaboratives to stay informed about the process and to informally provide feedback on contentious issues.

However, as discussed in Chapter 6, such sessions need to be designed carefully to avoid case-related discussions between the decision makers and litigants outside the hearing room (ex parte contacts) and other potential improprieties.

Phase II

The primary objective of Phase II was to take the generic portfolio of programs agreed to during Phase I and adapt them to the particularities of individual utilities. Although the participants considered Phase II voluntary, the utilities all entered into separate collaborative processes with the NUPs (see Table 4-12), except for FG&E, which decided not to engage in further collaboration, and NEES, which simply continued its collaborative with only CLF.

All of the Phase II collaboratives shared a similar structure. Each had an oversight group consisting of the utility and a representative from each of the four NUPs. Each also had four or five working groups including both NUP consultants and utility staff and focusing on such areas as commercial and industrial programs, residential programs, and evaluation and monitoring. The utilities continued to provide funds for the NUPs to secure outside technical expertise. Some of the utilities also hired their own consultants, particularly the smaller ones that did not have adequate in-house expertise.

Table 4-12. Phase II Timeline: Agreements, Filings, and DPU Orders

Utility	Agreement	Filing	DPU Order
BECo[a]	June 1989	March 1990	—
COM/Electric	March 1989	November 1989	July 1990
Eastern[a]	June 1989	March 1990	—
FG&E[b]	—	—	—
NEES[c]	—	September 1989	March 1990
Nantucket[d]	September 1989	May 1991	December 1991
WMECo	March 1989	September 1989	June 1990

[a] BECo and Eastern filings were informational only, and no DPU action was ever taken on either of them.

[b] FG&E did not enter into a Phase II agreement.

[c] NEES did not have a distinct Phase II agreement separate from the original agreement signed August 1988.

[d] The Nantucket collaborative ended before the Phase II filing.

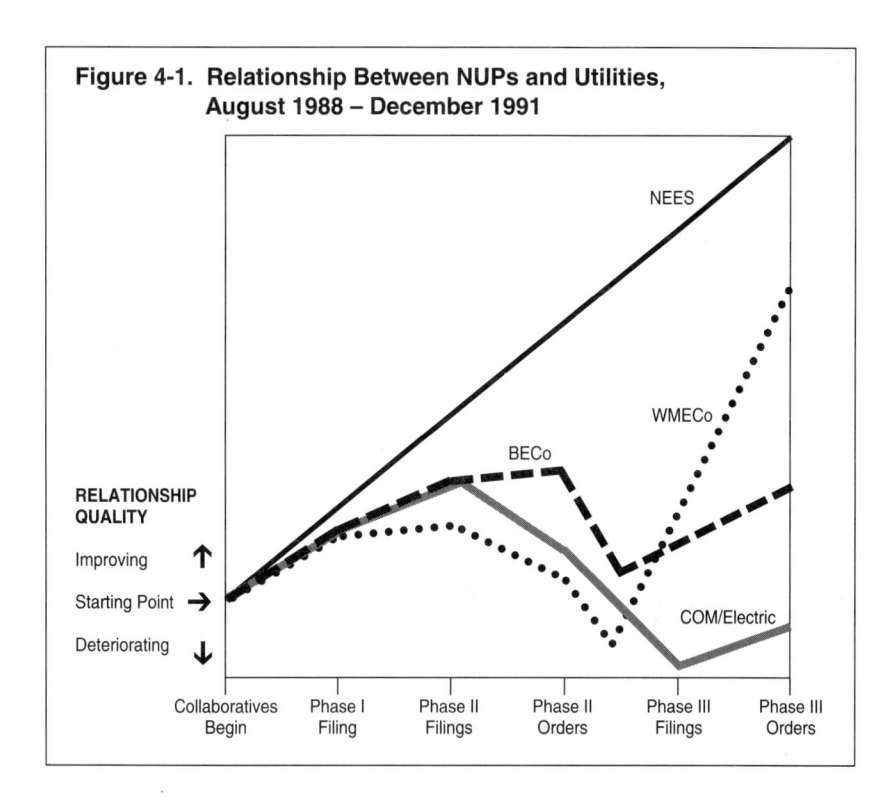

Figure 4-1. Relationship Between NUPs and Utilities, August 1988 – December 1991

A NUP coordinator was hired for each subcollaborative to oversee consultants' work and act as a liaison between the process and the NUPs. The coordinator was also a liaison between the NUPs and the utilities—often working through technical issues directly with the utility coordinator, who was generally a senior staffperson. Only BECo hired outside consultants to coordinate its internal staff, but this arrangement did not work well and was terminated after several months (Coakley interview). Again, no outside mediators were used in any of the collaborative processes.

Despite similar structures and common agendas, the Phase II collaboratives rapidly evolved their own individual paths. Some succeeded where others failed. Figure 4-1 provides a basic road map of the historic relationships between the NUPs and each of the four largest utilities from the time the collaboratives began in mid-1988 through the end of 1991.[70] As can be seen in the figure—and as will be explored in greater detail below—each collaborative took on a distinctly different character indicative of its unique set of problems and accomplishments. During periods of strong or improving relationships, consensus building was at its best, whereas during periods of low or deteriorating relationships, the collaboratives were marked by conflict or even hostility.

The NEES collaborative is the only one with steadily improving internal relationships overall. The WMECo collaborative, in contrast, was virtually shut down after a contentious case before the DPU following Phase II but was revitalized and strengthened after a brief hiatus. COM/Electric's collaborative was somewhat countercyclical to WMECo's: it filed a consensus plan at the end of Phase II but fell apart shortly thereafter. The BECo collaborative followed a rocky road throughout: it did not have the radical swings experienced in the COM/Electric and WMECo collaboratives, but neither did it experience the steady improvement that occurred in the NEES collaborative.

NEES

The collaborative between NEES and CLF, which began prior to any of the other individual utility collaboratives, was less contentious than the others, in part because the intra-NUP squabbles evident in Phase I of the joint-utility collaborative were absent (since there was only one NUP: CLF), and in part because of a good relationship that developed early on between NEES and CLF (including CLF's consultants) (Chaisson, Cohen, Destribats, and Pastuszek interviews). Still, each conservation program took months of joint fact finding and program design negotiations. Apparently it was also much easier for NEES and CLF to reach agreement on new programs for commercial and industrial customers than it was in areas in which NEES had preexisting programs, which it was often reluctant to change (Chaisson interview).

NEES and CLF ultimately agreed on a portfolio of ten programs that would cover all customer sectors, for both new and existing structures. The consensus between the two parties included many significant innovations. For instance, most of the programs were designed around the concept of "direct investment," in which NEES would purchase DSM resources from its customers by paying, in most cases, the full incremental cost of the measures. This approach differed conceptually from that of most of the utility programs across the country during the previous decade, which had used partial rebates and low-interest loans.

Another major innovation from the NEES collaborative was an actual financial incentive for NEES to aggressively pursue DSM based on the concept of shared savings. Shortly after John Rowe became CEO at NEES in February 1989, he made clear to his staff that he could not continue to support DSM unless they found a way to make it profitable (Pastuszek and Rowe interviews). Since Douglas Foy of

CLF concurred with Rowe's assessment that "the rat must be able to smell the cheese" (explaining why utilities needed incentives), the two organizations were able to forge a creative incentive approach.[71] Prior to their effort, such an approach, while touted in the literature (Moskovitz 1989), had not been adopted and, as mentioned earlier, was controversial among the NUPs.

Through NEES, in September 1989 MECo became the first utility in Massachusetts to file for preapproval of its programs. NEES proposed spending $37 million in Massachusetts in 1990. CLF filed jointly with NEES in complete support of its programs and its cost-recovery proposals. However, the Attorney General, which had not been invited to participate in the collaborative, intervened to protest NEES's incentive proposal and what it considered poorly designed and inadequately funded residential DSM programs. The Energy Consortium, a group of large industrial users, also intervened, primarily to get NEES to reduce its proposed incentive. Finally, a group of lighting vendors argued that having the company distribute lights for free in many of its programs would violate antitrust law.

WMECo

In March 1989, WMECo became the first utility to sign an agreement to begin a Phase II collaborative with the NUPs. In the first six months of their collaborative, they were able to hammer out most of the program details. However, several issues remained unresolved and highly controversial. The most contentious revolved around the pace at which WMECo pursued DSM. The NUPs argued that WMECo should pay the full incremental cost for DSM measures and run its DSM programs at full throttle (that is, not cap the annual DSM budgets, but allow "maximum exploitation of conservation opportunity . . . subject only to constraints of C&LM [conservation and load management] infrastructure availability" (CLF 1990, p. 2). The company, meanwhile, facing an overcapacity situation (due primarily to the start-up of its nuclear power plant, Millstone III) wanted to proceed slowly in acquiring DSM resources and to find ways for customers receiving the services to pay as much of their cost as possible.

Evaluation and monitoring plans and DSM cost recovery were also much in dispute. The NUPs proposed using end-use metering and traditional statistical sampling techniques for measuring savings. WMECo found this unreasonably expensive and proposed an alternative, but untried, approach.[72] With respect to cost recovery, the NUPs disagreed among themselves and with the company about whether

WMECo deserved to recover lost revenue associated with its DSM programs and earn an additional positive financial incentive.

Despite a lack of consensus, WMECo filed for preapproval in September because it feared disallowances on its preexisting DSM programs (Cagnetta interview). The NUPs did not jointly file with the utility in support of its programs, as CLF had done with NEES. Instead, CLF and the Attorney General intervened to express their concern that WMECo's investment posture did not reflect the maximum commitment to pursuing all cost-effective DSM over the next few years and that the future of the collaborative seemed uncertain.[73] The only other intervenor was the Energy Consortium, which argued that portions of the DSM programs were anticompetitive.[74]

In an effort largely to appease the NUPs prior to the start of hearings, WMECo unilaterally increased its proposed 1990 DSM budget from $4.7 million to $6.1 million and agreed to do more DSM if possible (Cagnetta interview). Although generally appreciated by the NUPs, the midcourse changes came too late to be adequately reviewed before the hearings. According to Joe Chaisson, the NUP coordinator, the NUPs' inability to review the changes on time was due partly to the lateness of the changes and partly to the fact that the NUPs were stretched too thin to respond in a timely fashion (Chaisson interview). The result was a relatively confusing and fractious hearings process that lasted eight days. During this time, the DPU staff attempted to ferret out the details of the company's revised proposals as well as the evolving positions of CLF and the other NUPs.

In the end, the NUPs still maintained that WMECo's filing did not commit to fund conservation to the maximum extent feasible (CLF 1990, pp. 7–8). DOER, the Attorney General, and MASSPIRG recommended against providing WMECo with any positive financial incentive because their "preliminary" review of the filing "does not permit the conclusion that the company proposes exemplary or above-average performance" (id.). CLF, however, split from the other NUPs and decided that, despite the shortcomings in WMECo's filing, it would support the company's request for recovering its direct DSM expenditures, any lost revenue associated with those expenditures, and a financial incentive (id., p. 3).

COM/Electric

In contrast to the WMECo collaborative, the Phase II COM/Electric collaborative went relatively smoothly, ending in a virtual consensus filing in November 1989. CLF intervened in support of WMECo's proposal, as it had done in the NEES case.[75] Although the Attorney General also intervened, it did not get very involved because it considered COM/Electric's DSM plans and projections a "shining star" among the utilities (Oppenheim interview). The company requested preapproval for sixteen programs at an estimated cost of $11 million for 1990.

However, the filing was made in the midst of a snowballing ratepayer revolt sparked by recent rate increases made by Commonwealth Electric (as approved by the DPU). These were unrelated to DSM but doubled the bills of some electric heat customers.[76] On January 11, 1990, after the DSM preapproval request was filed but prior to the hearings, the Massachusetts legislature (with Governor Dukakis's blessing) overturned the DPU's rate case order for Commonwealth Electric in an unprecedented move. The legislators reallocated costs and reinstated the previous rate design, including "discounts" for electric space heating.

Whereas customers generally had praised most other utilities for proposing aggressive DSM programs, two residential ratepayer groups, IRATE and RATEBUSTERS, intervened in COM/Electric's DSM preapproval case to protest against the company's attempt to raise rates for DSM. In addition, they accused the company of falsely advertising that it would deliver DSM to its customers for "free" while, in fact, they argued, it had every intention of recovering those costs through rates.

COM/Electric requested direct cost recovery for its DSM expenditures in the year that the monies were spent, as was permitted other utilities. However, unlike WMECo, COM/Electric did not request any compensation for lost revenue, nor did it request a positive financial incentive, as both NEES and WMECo had done.[77]

BECo

The BECo Phase II collaborative started later than the COM/Electric and WMECo collaboratives for two reasons. First, both BECo and the NUPs were preoccupied with other proceedings (for example, the Pilgrim nuclear outage cases discussed earlier in this chapter). In addition, BECo was somewhat ambivalent about continuing with the collaborative process (Kelly interview). When it finally began, the BECo collaborative was slower and more contentious than the others. The problems were due, in large part, to bad blood between the utilities and the NUPs as a result of nearly a decade of vitriolic litigation over BECo's Pilgrim nuclear power plant, its commitment to DSM, and the management of the company generally.

Also, the NUPs were less willing to defer to CLF on many of the decisions than they were in the other subcollaboratives. Here the NUPs were involved in every detail, partly because of their historic interest in BECo—the largest utility in Massachusetts regulated by the

DPU[78]—and partly because the NUPs had already cut their teeth in the other, earlier Phase II subcollaboratives (Nogee and Shimshak interviews). In some ways, the NUPs appear to have held BECo to a higher standard than the other utilities during Phase II.

In October 1989, the non-CLF NUPs gained additional incentive to focus on the BECo collaborative when the DPU approved the Pilgrim settlement (described in detail in the previous case study). The settlement required BECo to spend $75 million on DSM without recovering the costs from its ratepayers and to set up a DSM settlement board including the Attorney General, DOER, and MASSPIRG (but not CLF, which was not a party to the Pilgrim cases) to oversee the spending.

Whereas WMECo and COM/Electric concluded their Phase II collaboratives and filed for preapproval in the fall of 1989, BECo did not conclude the second phase of its collaborative until March 1990. Although the parties had completed the bulk of their effort the previous fall, they continued to seek agreement in several elusive areas—most notably the role of performance contracting in BECo's commercial and industrial programs and the company's cost-effectiveness screening tool (Gustin and Coakley interviews). The participants had not agreed to all the final details when BECo finally filed its programs in March 1990. However, since the company was obligated to provide $75 million worth of DSM without reimbursement from the ratepayers, the March filing did not seek the DPU's preapproval, and no formal review was ever conducted.

Phase II Preapproval Cases

Most of the Phase II collaboratives ended in requests for DPU preapproval.[79] As mentioned, several parties intervened in the NEES, WMECo, and COM/Electric cases, and, despite a considerable degree of consensus within the respective collaboratives, the cases were all marred by controversy. Parties outside the collaboratives raised many of these issues; however, some were also raised by the NUPs themselves.

The cases followed traditional adjudicatory procedures used in rate cases, including discovery, testimony, hearings, and the filing of legal briefs. Over half a dozen days of evidentiary hearings transpired in each case, during which parties cross-examined each other and the DPU staff questioned everyone.

The DPU's tasks during the hearings were twofold. First, it needed to resolve contested issues raised by intervenors. Second, the DPU was obliged to guarantee that the resultant rates would be just and reasonable and that the settlement was consistent with the DPU's DSM policies. Therefore it had to scrutinize all the other settled issues. This task was tantamount to making sure that the DPU's own "interests" and the "interests" of ratepayers were accommodated by the settlement.

In most traditional rate case settlements, PUCs are required to accept or reject the entire settlement, but no such restriction was placed on the DPU by the parties to the collaboratives. The DPU ultimately approved the majority of the details submitted in the DSM preapproval filings and generally praised both the process and the results. However, it also required significant changes in all three cases. In fact, the Massachusetts DPU probably required more substantial changes than any other state PUC that has reviewed a DSM collaborative as of this writing (Raab and Schweitzer 1992). (In contrast, the Rhode Island and New Hampshire portions of the NEES collaborative filing were resolved in traditional postfiling settlements including the advocacy staffs of the PUCs. These settlements were in turn approved by the commissions without any substantive changes.)

The changes required by the DPU fall into two broad categories of issues: program design and ratemaking. With respect to program design, the DPU actually rejected two of WMECo's and three of COM/Electric's programs for not meeting the DPU's cost-effectiveness criteria.[80] The DPU also refused to approve at least one of the collaboratively designed programs for each of the utilities because it concluded that they were not complete in all their details.

The DPU often required modifications on the programs it did approve. For instance, it ordered WMECo to enrich the customer incentives in its commercial and industrial programs. Generally, the DPU required the utilities to accelerate the implementation of many of their programs and include additional, potentially cost-effective measures. In one instance, it ordered WMECo to include motors and building shell measures in addition to lighting measures in its Small Commercial Retrofit program. The DPU also ordered the companies to examine DSM opportunities in entirely new areas that were not covered by the collaboratives, such as street lighting and voltage reduction on the distribution systems. Finally, the DPU ordered all three companies to improve their monitoring and evaluation plans, which it considered an integral part of program design.

Whenever the DPU ordered modifications, it essentially returned the issues to the collaborative participants for further resolution and improvements. The DPU either ordered the utilities to resubmit new programs or program revisions in interim compliance filings, or to wait until the utility's next preapproval filing the following year.[81]

The DPU also ordered substantive changes on ratemaking issues.

It significantly modified NEES's cost allocation proposal and NEES and WMECo's financial incentive proposals. Although NEES's original cost allocation proposal was to spread DSM costs equally over all energy sales (that is, on a per kWh basis), the DPU decided that the costs should first be divided among the customer classes eligible to participate in each program and then spread equally within them on a per kWh basis.[82]

NEES's request for a financial incentive was one of the most hotly disputed issues in the proceeding, and it was also controversial within the DPU. According to former commissioner Robert Werlin:

> The incentive that NEES proposed represented a fundamental break in the way rates were set. We had three commissioners with three different views on the strengths and weaknesses of the original proposal. Eventually we were able to come to a consensus that if the company does a good job, it would be o.k. for it to make a little more money. (Werlin interview)

However, the commission required several major changes, including (1) halving the requested incentive amount plus requiring a threshold that would allow bonus recovery only on savings exceeding 50 percent of projected savings; (2) scrapping NEES's proposed shared-savings incentive formula and replacing it with a fixed ¢/kWh and $/kW bonus; and (3) requiring that savings be based on after-the-fact measurement rather than prespecified estimates.[83]

The DPU also approved a bonus incentive for WMECo but required it to pass a higher threshold of accomplishment to get that bonus than it had required of NEES. NEES was required to meet 50 percent of its targeted savings prior to earning a bonus on all additional savings in Massachusetts, whereas WMECo was required to achieve 75 percent of its targeted savings before it could earn a comparable bonus. The more stringent bonus hurdle was justified primarily because of the commission's finding that although WMECo's proposed DSM efforts showed substantial improvement over prior efforts, they appeared less aggressive than NEES's (Mass. D.P.U. 89-260 [1990d], p. 123). The DPU's decision turned largely on the testimony of the NUPs since it had little other than the NEES case to use as a benchmark.

Through its preapproval orders, the DPU finally had direct input into the collaborative program designs and ratemaking proposals of the utilities and the NUPs. The DPU's directives occasionally reinstated objectives relinquished by the NUPs during the negotiations. In other instances, all the collaborative parties felt somewhat disdainful of the DPU's strong intervention.[84] If the DPU had directly participated in the collaborative processes, it is likely that some of the collaborative programs and ratemaking proposals would have been designed to better reflect the regulators' interests or that the DPU would have been more receptive to the collaborative designs as submitted, or both.

Phase III

In Phase III, the utilities and NUPs had the opportunity to take the DPU's rulings and use them to reshape and implement the companies' DSM plans. For NEES and BECo, Phase III began immediately after Phase II ended. The WMECo process restarted after a brief hiatus, whereas the COM/Electric collaborative never restarted.

NEES: Growing Stronger

The collaborative process between NEES and CLF intensified and improved after what both parties perceived as major victories. These victories occurred not only in Massachusetts but also before the Rhode Island and New Hampshire PUCs, where even fewer changes were made to their collaborative filings and where almost all issues were settled with the PUC advocacy staffs and other intervenors after the filing, but prior to a commission ruling. NEES and CLF worked together during Phase III to (1) formulate the compliance filing in Massachusetts, particularly in the design of an evaluation and monitoring plan, which had not been filed prior to the 1990 preapprovals; (2) work through the myriad of details necessary to implement the approved programs; and (3) begin to refine the programs and budgets in preparation for the 1991 preapproval filing.

In October 1990, NEES and CLF jointly filed in Massachusetts, Rhode Island, and New Hampshire a 1991 proposal for review that represented a consensus on all issues. NEES proposed increasing its expenditures in all three states to $85 million, which represented a 30 percent increase over its $65 million 1990 budget (a 20 percent increase over the $71 million that was actually spent in 1990). The $85 million represented almost 5 percent of NEES's gross revenue and was among the highest expenditures by any utility in the country (Moskovitz et al. 1991).[85] It is also important to point out that NEES agreed to increase the budget despite its calculation that the souring New England economy would result in its load leveling off for the foreseeable future.

NEES and CLF jointly filed their consensus proposals at the DPU. Again the Energy Consortium (that is, the large industrial users) intervened. This time they pushed for an energy service charge that would effectively reallocate DSM expenditures directly back to the actual recipient of the DSM service. The Attorney General did not intervene, but Boston Gas Company did to press NEES to include fuel substitution in its DSM programs in Massachusetts. The DPU decided to bifurcate the preapproval proceeding and put the controversial fuel substitution issue on a separate track. As of this writing, the fuel substitution proceeding has not been resolved, and more than twenty parties have intervened (including CLF in support of fuel substitution and in opposition to NEES's position).

WMECo: Hiatus and Rejuvenation

After the DPU's Phase II order, the collaborative between WMECo and the NUPs screeched to a halt. The parties stopped talking to each other for several months (Chaisson interview). According to Earle Taylor of Northeast Utilities, WMECo's parent company, WMECo was disappointed with the lack of support it received from the NUPs in the hearings:

> We were extremely upset over the NUPs' stance during the hearings. The NUPs had been pushing us to pay 100 percent of the cost of DSM and to run our programs at more aggressive levels. We finally gave in at the eleventh hour and agreed to run our programs full throttle, although we didn't give in on the customer incentive payment issue. Still, the hearing process was more contentious than we wanted, and we felt somewhat betrayed by not getting more support from the NUPs. We started to feel like we got little out of the collaborative. (Taylor interview)

At the same time, the NUPs were frustrated with the company for making many changes without consulting them or giving them sufficient time to review the changes prior to the hearings. More importantly, they continued to be frustrated over WMECo's lack of movement on customer incentives and several other issues.

Apparently the collaborative of WMECo's sister retail company, Connecticut Light and Power (CL&P), which had also stopped during this period, was revived after the PUC chair, Peter Boucher, called all the parties together and pressured them to reconvene. The CL&P collaborative brought in an outside mediator to help with this task. The reasons and mechanisms behind the resurrection of the WMECo collaborative, which happened subsequent to the Connecticut revival, are less clear-cut (for example, the DPU did not pressure the parties, nor was an outside mediator brought in). However, William Ellis, CEO of parent company Northeast Utilities, apparently pushed to reconvene the group prior to the next preapproval filing (Taylor and Chaisson interviews). A new NUP coordinator and CLF attorney were brought on board, both of whom had substantially more time to invest in the process than their predecessors, and a new WMECo coordinator was selected.

Once resuscitated, the WMECo collaborative progressed smoothly, and the second preapproval filing was the first fully consensual filing that included all the NUPs in Massachusetts (Chaisson interview).[86] In sharp contrast to the 1990 preapproval case, CLF, DOER, and the Attorney General all intervened before the DPU in support of WMECo's entire preapproval package. The Attorney General and MASSPIRG, which had previously refused to support positive financial incentives or even lost-revenue adjustments for any utility, signed off on both for WMECo. In contrast to his comment after the first preapproval case, Taylor was far more sanguine about the collaborative after the second time through:

> We were very happy to have their endorsement in the second preapproval. It would've been extremely hard on us if their support or testimony was either absent or negative. As a result, we have decided that it's worth the price over the next few years to get the NUPs' "good housekeeping" seal of approval. (Taylor interview)

COM/Electric: The Unraveling

Whereas the WMECo collaborative went from contentiousness in Phase II to creative consensus building in Phase III, the COM/Electric collaborative moved in the opposite direction. Despite a relatively harmonious and productive Phase II collaborative between COM/Electric and the NUPs, the parties were unable even to reach an agreement to engage in subsequent collaboration. According to Mort Zajac of COM/Electric, both the NUPs' proposed level of oversight and the price seemed unreasonably high:

> The NUPs' proposal for ongoing collaboration included what we considered to be an unreasonable level of oversight and micromanagement. We felt that they were proposing a continuous level of review—equivalent to the IRS sitting here every day waiting for you to do your taxes. We felt that it would paralyze the staff. In addition we found their proposal too expensive and didn't feel that some of the experts they proposed to use were as proficient as our own staff. (Zajac interview)

COM/Electric's reluctance to engage in subsequent collaboration with the NUPs was rooted in frustration and dissatisfaction with certain aspects of the Phase II collaborative. Specifically, the company maintained that it had been difficult to get the NUPs' focused attention or to reach a consensus on certain issues (id.).[87]

The NUPs acknowledged that they had some internal problems during Phase II of the COM/Electric collaborative, including the fact that some of their consultants were tardy and a few of their number, most notably the Attorney General and MASSPIRG, were more focused on the BECo collaborative. However, all the NUPs were still interested in pursuing an ongoing collaborative with COM/Electric and were frustrated by COM/Electric's unwillingness to go forward at a level of engagement comparable to the Phase II effort (Chaisson and Coakley interviews).

The parties never did reach agreement, and no collaboration occurred after Phase II. Instead COM/Electric hired its own consultants and filed for preapproval unilaterally in March 1991. It proposed to limit its DSM expenditures to $23 million for both its companies and to run only four programs.[88] The company's proposal did not include several programs previously ordered by the DPU, nor did it include three programs that were preapproved in 1990, at the parties' request, for immediate implementation.

CLF intervened to make the unprecedented request that the DPU find COM/Electric's implementation of its prior preapproval contract and its 1991 DSM preapproval proposal imprudent, and that the company's entire DSM effort be placed under the direction of an outside receivership.[89] COM/Electric defended its decision as part of its need to restrict its DSM effort in the face of mounting public opposition to rate increases of any sort and severe limitations on its ability to retain the additional staff necessary to run new programs. However, it pointed out that despite this decision, the programs it did run were successfully implemented.[90] Finally, COM/Electric maintained that, given its current financial condition, it needed to continue to streamline and prioritize its programs and maintain a budget cap in the future.

Other intervenors, in what turned out to be an acrimonious proceeding, included the Attorney General; DOER; the Massachusetts Executive Office of Economic Affairs; the Energy Engineers Task Force; the City of Cambridge Public Schools; IRATE; Cape United Elderly, Inc.; and an industrial ratepayer group called Save Our Regional Economy (SORE). More discovery requests (over three hundred) were served on the parties, and more hearings were held (three days of public hearings and fourteen days of evidentiary hearings) than in any other DSM-related case that had ever come before the DPU.

After the hearings but prior to the DPU issuing its order in the case, a cross-section of parties representing a diverse group of interests forged a settlement resolving many of the most contentious issues. The most significant features of the settlement included (1) setting up a formal task force, comprised largely of the parties to the settlement, to work with COM/Electric on improving its DSM programs and its relations with ratepayers; (2) setting aside $250,000 to hire an independent DSM expert to provide ongoing scrutiny of COM/Electric's DSM efforts, to furnish advice, to act as a liaison to the task force and the DPU, and even to mediate disputes when necessary; and (3) minimizing future rate impacts through cost caps and the amortization of expenses while expanding the scope of its programs. The settlement left certain issues for the DPU to decide, such as the prudence of COM/Electric's past DSM activities.

BECo: Same As It Ever Was?

Much of the debate from Phase II carried over into Phase III, particularly with respect to the policy ramifications of the screening tools used to choose which demand- and supply-side resources to draw on. In fact, the issues intensified substantially after BECo informed the DPU and the Massachusetts Energy Facilities Siting Council of its intent to construct a 306 MW gas-fired combined-cycle generating facility at the site of its retired plant, Edgar Station (Edgar). The amount of cost-effective DSM available to the company was a central issue in the Edgar case.[91] The intervention of CLF, the Attorney General, and MASSPIRG to oppose Edgar at the DPU and the siting council was not well received by BECo and further strained an already-stressed collaborative.

Although Edgar seemed to reopen old wounds among the participants, they continued to try to settle remaining DSM issues, such as the screening tool and the evaluation and monitoring protocols, and to help BECo ready its new DSM programs for implementation (Coakley interview). Concurrently, the company was working through the details of its programs with the DSM settlement board established in the Pilgrim case, creating additional coordination problems despite the fact that both the collaborative and the board contained many of the same members.

In an attempt to gain greater control over the process, BECo insisted that when the NUPs' consultants visited the company, they brief BECo's senior management on their findings prior to reporting back to the NUPs (Gustin interview). This request caused an uproar with the NUPs, which did not want the company to control their consultants. The final resolution was to hold "exit interviews," in which the consultants briefed the company in the presence of the NUPs. This change apparently helped the process. It allowed the parties to work from the same information base, thereby accelerating the transfer of information from the consultants to all parties, and provided the company and the NUPs with greater face-to-face interaction (apparently, prior interaction was often through CLF or the NUP coordinator).

In March 1991, BECo filed its revised programs with the DPU for preapproval. This time, since the company's projected 1991 expenditures exceeded the DSM it promised to deliver at no cost to its ratepayers under the Pilgrim settlement, BECo sought preapproval on the incremental investment, including recovery of lost revenue and a financial bonus. The parties had reached consensus on virtually all issues, with the NUPs filing a joint brief supporting BECo's filing. However, the NUPs raised concerns regarding the company's load management programs and other matters that were not directly part of the collaborative effort (Gustin interview).

Phase III Preapproval Decisions

Table 4-13 shows the filing and order dates for the Phase III collaboratives.

With its Phase III preapproval orders, the DPU continued to inject its own concerns and interests into the DSM activities of the utilities, despite substantial consensus in the NEES and WMECo collaboratives and the settlement of the COM/Electric case. Nowhere was this more apparent than in the NEES order, in which—even without the intervention of the Attorney General—the DPU continued to push the company to (1) make its Massachusetts programs as comprehensive as possible (that is, pursue all cost-effective measures rather than merely the most cost-effective measures); (2) offer them to all its customers as quickly as possible; and (3) cover enough of the measure costs through direct investment to guarantee high participation and measure acceptance (Mass. D.P.U. 89-260 [1990d]).[92] In contrast to the DPU's

Table 4-13. Dates for Phase III Filings and DPU Orders

Utility	Filing Date	Order Date
BECo	April 1991	April 1992
COM/Electric[a]	March 1991	January 1992
NEES	October 1990	January 1991
WMECo	March 1991	July 1991

[a] The COM/Electric filing was not a collaborative effort.

continued push for pursuing all cost-effective DSM, the Rhode Island PUC had just approved a settlement crafted by its staff that pushed NEES to go after the most cost-effective programs and measures within programs rather than comprehensive treatment spread over all customer classes (Kilmarx interview, Kilmarx and Wallis 1991). This different direction is important to note because it highlights the nonhomogeneity of the regulators themselves and underscores the need for including them in the process. In the NEES case, the Massachusetts DPU rejected the appliance labeling and multifamily programs submitted by the collaborative for not being cost-effective. The DPU also ordered NEES to refine its cost-effectiveness analysis in several important respects,[93] lowered its financial bonus from $6.1 million to $5.4 million, approved its evaluation and monitoring plans with some modifications, and granted the company a preapproval for one year instead of the five it had requested (id.). Overall, despite the changes, the DPU continued to find that if NEES met its targets as modified by the DPU's order, it would be doing an "exemplary" job.

Even in the COM/Electric case, while ultimately approving the fairly comprehensive settlement, the DPU issued a 146-page order in which it thoroughly analyzed and made findings on every aspect of the case. The DPU went through each program and provided guidance to COM/Electric and other parties to the settlement as to the DPU's expectations.

In stark contrast to its order at the end of Phase II, the DPU's Phase III WMECo order was extremely supportive of the unanimous settlement reached by the company and the NUPs. Although the DPU rejected the energy service charge notion raised by the Energy Consortium in its intervention, it made only several minor modifications to the collaborative proposals. This positive order, with its lack of DPU-required modifications, was due primarily to the settlement of the issues between WMECo and the NUPs in a way that was responsive to past DPU directives.[94]

Ongoing Collaboratives

More than five years after the DSM collaboratives began in the summer of 1988, the BECo, NEES, and WMECo collaboratives continue. The COM/Electric, Eastern, and Nantucket collaboratives have been terminated. (FG&E never entered a separate Phase II collaborative.) However, the ongoing collaboratives' focus has changed from program design to implementation oversight and program refinement. Since the utilities are offering programs that are on the cutting edge of those offered nationwide, the NUP consultants' earlier role of bringing in the experiences of other utilities is less relevant today.

All three remaining utilities funded collaboratives in 1992 and 1993. However, the future of these collaboratives remains uncertain. Both BECo and WMECo continue to question the benefits they receive compared with the costs they incur (Taylor and Gustin interviews). Neither company is interested in having the NUPs continuously looking over its employees' shoulders; both expressed the desire for greater control (id.). BECo also expressed a desire during the interviews to expand the process to include more of its consumers as well as DSM service providers, but to concurrently restructure the process to resemble an advisory board more than a consensus-based collaborative.

The NUPs also believe that the remaining collaboratives can and should wind down over the next several years. However, they are not particularly interested in an advisory board structure, in which they would have much less influence (Chaisson and Nogee interviews). In California, where the utilities set up advisory boards directly after the conclusion of the collaborative, most of the NUPs expressed extreme dissatisfaction and frustration over the change (Raab and Schweitzer 1992, Raab et al. 1994). Although advisory boards can undoubtedly play an important role in utility DSM programs, they do not appear to be a substitute for a consensus-based collaborative.

The only collaborative that does not show major fatigue despite various stresses is the NEES collaborative, which continues to involve only CLF. After submitting its third consensus DSM preapproval filing (this time for 1992), NEES and CLF were able to settle the case with all the intervenors in Massachusetts, including a newly formed DPU advocacy staff (Mass. D.P.U. 91-205 [1991b]).[95] Armond Cohen of CLF expressed confidence that the two organizations, which now agree on everything except environmental externalities, fuel substitution, and perhaps program scale, would continue their collaboration for the foreseeable future. Unlike the other utilities' collaboratives, the NEES collaborative seems truly ingrained. John Rowe, NEES's CEO, speculated about its future:

> If our collaborative is now 70 percent for political legitimacy reasons and 30 percent for substantive reasons, that's a good combination. Since the need for legitimacy and good ideas will never change, I expect that the collaborative will continue. In fact, I hope that we can expand it to other areas, like environmental externalities. (Rowe interview)

Evaluating the Success of DSM Collaboratives in Massachusetts

As discussed in Chapter 3, the success of the DSM collaboratives in Massachusetts can be evaluated by examining whether, in comparison to a fully adjudicated alternative, the collaborative processes saved process-related resources; enhanced the legitimacy of the traditional process and the final results; and improved the practicality of the final policies.

Process-Related Resource Savings

The collaboratives required extensive commitments of time and resources from all parties. Although Phase I of the joint-utility collaborative process took only half a year, the NUPs have been actively engaged in negotiations with WMECo, BECo, and NEES for over five years as of this writing. The NUPs were also involved for almost two years with COM/Electric, Eastern, and Nantucket before those collaboratives ended. As can be seen in Table 4-14, almost $5.4 million was spent by the utilities to hire DSM experts to advise the NUPs through September 1993. During this period, the utilities spent an additional

Table 4-14. Massachusetts Utilities' Expenditures for NUP Consultants, August 1988–September 1993

Utility	Phase I ($1,000)	Phase II and Beyond ($1,000)	Total All Phases ($1,000)
BECo	$215	$1,647	$1,862
COM/Electric	66	368	434
Eastern	42	323	365
FG&E[a]	7	na	7
MECo[b]	na	1,484	1,484
Nantucket	1	36	37
WMECo	54	1,154	1,208
TOTAL	$385	$5,012	$5,397

Source: Expenditures from Mass. D.P.U. 91-80 (IR-2-11) (1992a), updated by NEES staff and NUP coordinators.

[a] FG&E did not engage in a collaborative after Phase I.

[b] MECo through August 1993. All expenditures for MECo shown in Phase II. MECo estimated at 75 percent of NEES expenditures.

$3 to $4 million to cover their own staffing and consultant needs (utility interviews). Each of the NUPs also estimated dedicating approximately one-third to one-half of a full-time-equivalent staffperson's time to the collaboratives, with CLF devoting significantly more (NUPs interviews).

Virtually all those interviewed concluded that although the collaboratives were extremely resource-intensive, having to litigate all the issues would probably have required even more resources in total. This possibility appears substantiated by both the historic DSM-related litigation prior to the collaboratives, as well as the contentious postcollaborative DSM-related litigation, such as the recent COM/Electric case[96] and the ongoing adjudications over fuel substitution in Massachusetts. Also, whereas traditional settlements usually occur at the end of a contested case, these collaboratives are unique in that they represent prefiling settlements. As such, they have a greater potential to save resources associated with litigation than a traditional settlement.

Some short-term process-related resources may have been saved. However, several important factors mitigate this conclusion. First, not all the collaboratives consistently resulted in full consensus filings. When filings occur without consensus, such as in WMECo's first filing, the litigation process can be intensive. Second, even when the collaboratives did reach consensus, since they did not include all interested parties, a litigated case was always put on by outside intervenors. The intervention by the Attorney General after the first consensus filing by only NEES and CLF is a prime example of this phenomenon. Last, even when there was a consensus and little or no third-party intervention, as was the case in WMECo's and NEES's second preapproval filings, both cases required more than a week of hearings because of the DPU's lack of direct representation in the collaboratives and its intense interest in DSM. Also, final DPU orders in virtually all the DSM preapproval cases were not issued until the end of the DPU's self-imposed deadline, regardless of how controversial the cases were. Thus little, if any, time was saved in the approval process itself. In other states, where collaboratives achieved consensus among a broader range of parties, including the regulatory staff, and where no self-imposed decision deadlines were in effect, more litigation before the PUCs was usually avoided than in Massachusetts (Raab and Schweitzer 1992).

As discussed in Chapter 3, a careful analysis of the process-related savings must look beyond the immediate PUC process to embrace the appeals and implementation processes as well. Monsanto Company unsuccessfully appealed the PUC's decision to allow a provision in one of

WMECo's DSM programs that restricted industrial self-generation (as a condition for participation) as a violation of state antitrust law and as discriminatory.[97] This was the only appeal regarding the DPU's decisions on the collaboratives, and it was a rather narrow appeal of a design feature of a single program that could have been waged against many noncollaboratively designed DSM programs with similar elements. Therefore, it should not be inferred that the collaboratives increased process-related costs associated with appeals. On the other hand, since appeals of DSM-related issues in Massachusetts happened rarely, if ever, prior to the DSM collaboratives,[98] these collaboratives may not have saved significant resources in terms of avoiding future appeals.

To the extent that programs have been implemented more rapidly, at a greater scale, and more comprehensively than they might have otherwise, the collaboratives probably avoided some long-term litigation. At the same time, the litigation that has occurred when the collaboratives have gone astray (for example, WMECo after Phase II and COM/Electric after Phase III) has been conducted at a level of exhaustive detail that would be unlikely, if not inconceivable, had the collaboratives never transpired in the first place. On balance, the collaborative processes will probably save some long-term, process-related resources as compared with an approach that used only litigation.

However, it is worth noting that if the NUPs were forced to litigate every DSM issue, they probably could not afford as comparable a level of involvement as they were able to muster for the collaboratives. Their limited resources would have required them to be more selective in picking their battles. In addition, if everything were litigated, the NUPs most certainly could not have afforded all the outside technical expertise the utilities funded during the collaboratives. So if the cases had been litigated, the NUPs would probably have spent less than they actually did, whereas the DPU and the utilities would likely have spent more. On balance, the collaborative route appears to have lowered total spending by all parties combined as compared with what it would have been had the cases only been litigated.

More importantly, even if the NUPs had pursued litigation and had been able to afford the requisite outside technical expertise, regardless of whether it cost more or less than collaboration, litigation might never have been able to produce results qualitatively comparable to those the collaboratives produced. To the extent that the process was perceived as fairer, and that better DSM programs resulted from the collaboratives, total net benefits were probably positive (and potentially substantial), regardless of whether the process-related costs were slightly more or less than traditional litigation.

Legitimacy

As discussed, DSM issues in Massachusetts have historically been vehemently contested in rate cases and other proceedings before the DPU and other agencies (for example, the Energy Facilities Siting Council), rarely leaving any of the participants I interviewed with positive feelings about the regulatory process or its results. Despite some ongoing battles within the DSM collaboratives, the parties frequently reached a surprisingly high degree of consensus on program design and program scale issues. For example, Phase I of the joint-utility collaborative, Phase II for COM/Electric, Phase III for both WMECo and BECo, and all phases of the NEES collaborative were essentially consensual filings. These agreements are no small feat, and they potentially enhance the legitimacy of the traditional adjudicatory proceedings used to resolve these issues by better satisfying the participants' interests.

The few cases in which consensus fell apart prior to a utility filing (for example, the WMECo Phase II filing and COM/Electric's Phase III filing) raise some concerns about whether this legitimization process can be sustained. Nonetheless, the fact that WMECo was able to recover from its hiatus after its contested case in Phase II and come to the first fully consensual filing in Phase III (which included all the NUPs) is testimony to the potential long-term prospects for collaboration in this area. Even in the COM/Electric Phase III case, which was strongly opposed by the NUPs and other intervenors in the most contentious DSM case ever to come before the DPU, a settlement was reached after hearings but prior to a DPU order.

Still, the collaboratives did not make an effort to include all potentially interested parties. In the NEES collaborative, only CLF was included, and the Attorney General, an active member in the other collaboratives, intervened against NEES in its first collaborative filing. All the collaboratives experienced intervention by other parties, such as energy service companies, industrial consumers, and residential ratepayer groups. Because the interests of these groups were not adequately represented within the collaboratives themselves, some of the legitimization that the collaboratives could have provided was definitely compromised. Attempts to garner that support through other means, such as advisory groups, could not take the place of more active involvement through the actual collaboratives.

In contrast to many other states, the Massachusetts DPU staff did not participate in the collaboratives, primarily because the DPU lacked an advocacy staff (Raab and Schweitzer 1992). The DPU's lack of direct involvement may ironically have compromised the legitimization of the process to some degree both by inadequately inoculating the collaborative participants with the DPU's interests and by not giving the DPU the direct benefit of the substantive knowledge learned during the collaboratives or the difficult tradeoffs made while building consensus. Instead of direct DPU involvement in the collaboratives, the DPU's interests were conveyed with each successive order. Ultimately the DPU required many modifications to the collaborative filings—sometimes even when the parties themselves had reached consensus.

In the end, however, the DPU's overall enthusiastic support for most of the collaborative agreements contributes to the conclusion that the collaboratives helped enhance rather than hinder the legitimacy of the DPU's adjudicatory processes. In a recent article in *Public Utilities Fortnightly* entitled "Collaborative Approaches to Conservation" (March 1, 1992), a heretofore unlikely duo—former DPU chair Bernice McIntyre and BECo's CEO Bernard Reznicek—wrote:

> Today, just five years later [after the collaboratives began], few would argue that the Massachusetts commission lost control when it created the opportunity for dialogue. In fact, many might argue that the commission, the utilities, and the advocates became more informed and were better able to define and offer solutions to problems.[99] (p. 18)

The lack of appeals, except for one in the WMECo case in which the Massachusetts Supreme Judicial Court upheld the DPU's decision, can be construed as further testimony to the success of the collaboratives in satisfying the interests of various segments of society and working within regulatory and judicial constraints. Also, where collaboratives were ongoing, the implementation problems were resolved much more expeditiously and productively (for example, NEES) than where the collaboratives had disbanded (for example, COM/Electric). The greatest animosity was found between parties who tried to reach consensus and failed—possibly as a result of their unmet expectations of agreement. Finally, the improvement of interpersonal relationships among most of the collaborative participants, as many interviewees reported, is likely to have positive spillover into subsequent regulatory procedures related to DSM and other matters. These spillover effects may in the long term be the most important testimony regarding whether the DSM collaboratives enhanced the legitimacy of the DPU's adjudicatory procedures and may be the collaboratives' most lasting legacy.

Practicality

The DSM collaboratives seem to have produced many practical improvements to utility DSM programs that might not have surfaced had the cases simply been litigated. The practicality of the collaborative results can be seen most clearly in the increased scale, comprehensive design, and resulting success of most of the DSM programs. And although the collaboratives did not resolve certain basic underlying policy issues, they did succeed in educating all parties and in strongly focusing the litigation before the DPU.

Program Scale

The DSM programs of Massachusetts electric utilities have increased substantially since the inception of the DSM collaboratives in the summer of 1988. As can be seen in Table 4-15, the utilities' annual DSM expenditures increased approximately tenfold between 1987 and 1991, from $18 million to $174 million (in nominal dollars). Measured as a percentage of revenue, the increase represents approximately an eightfold increase in expenditures, from 0.6 percent in 1987 to 4.7 percent in 1991. As the last three columns in the table indicate, those expenditures resulted in approximately a fivefold increase in annual energy and capacity savings. By the end of 1991, the utilities' total investments during the 1987–1991 period had resulted in the installation of approximately 350 MW of DSM capacity in Massachu-

Table 4-15. Massachusetts Utilities' Annual DSM Spending and Savings, 1987–1991

Year	DSM Expenditures ($ million)	Operating Revenue ($ million)	Expenditures as Percent of Revenue	Incremental Installed MWH[a]	Incremental Installed MW[a]	Cumulative Installed MW
1987	$ 17.8	$2,923	0.6%	52,837	46	69
1988	$ 30.2	$3,020	1.0%	143,061	72	98
1989	$ 55.6	$3,291	1.7%	238,792	122	190
1990	$117.7	$3,490	3.4%	322,088	179	274
1991	$174.2	$3,701	4.7%	389,470	188	346

Source: All data supplied by utilities. 1991 data estimated in most cases.

Notes: Figures include data from BECo, COM/Electric (except for cumulative MW), MECo, and WMECo. Data from FG&E, Eastern, and Nantucket are not included.

[a] Incremental installed MW and MWH represent annualized numbers (that is, if all measures were installed on January 1 of the year).

setts. (See Appendix 1 for data on the individual utilities between 1987 and 1991.)

The increase in spending and projected savings that has occurred since the collaboratives' inception is real and measurable, and the increases in projected future expenditures and savings also appear significant. However, the credit that the DSM collaboratives deserve for these accomplishments is more often debated. Even without the collaboratives, all of the utilities' DSM efforts would undoubtedly have increased—perhaps substantially. For over half a decade prior to the collaboratives, the Massachusetts DPU had been increasing its pressure on the utilities directly through its rate orders to accelerate and deepen their DSM efforts. Penalizing BECo on its rate of return, in large part for inadequately pursuing DSM, was perhaps the most extreme example of the commission's willingness to spur the utilities into action. Other companies were also receiving harsh words and increasing directives from the DPU with respect to DSM. With the DPU's initiation of a DSM inquiry within its integrated resource management rulemaking proceeding just prior to the initiation of the collaboratives, the DPU was likely to increase its pressure on the utilities to pursue DSM more aggressively.

Yet, despite the DPU's willingness to pursue a fairly interventionist course of action in support of DSM, the utilities' DSM programs would probably not have developed as far or as fast absent the collaborative process. Everyone interviewed for this case, including the former commissioners, concurred with this observation. For instance, even after several years of increasingly critical orders by the DPU on DSM issues, between 1987 and 1988 the Massachusetts utilities continued to increase their commitments to DSM, but at a much slower rate than after the collaboratives were in full swing.[100]

Given the limited resources and expertise at the DPU, it would have been extremely difficult, if not impossible, for the DPU to step in and micromanage the utilities in a way that would guarantee that they implement the DPU's policy objectives. As former commissioner Tierney points out, the collaboratives deserve significant credit for jump-starting the companies' DSM efforts:

> If there were no collaboratives, even if we wanted to push DSM, we simply didn't have enough staff to do so. Therefore the process would have been much slower with the company making proposals, then the intervenors attacking them, then the commission deciding, and then going through the entire process again and again. I think that without the collaborative there would have been a lot

less DSM, and that the DSM that was done would not have been as comprehensive. (Tierney interview)

Lastly, some literature implies an alternative hypothesis: namely, that the utilities' new-found ability to earn positive financial incentives on their DSM investments (for example, shared savings) deserves credit for recent enhancements to the utilities' DSM efforts (Nadel et al. 1992). This issue needs sorting out, since in both of the individual utility collaboratives in which financial incentives occurred (that is, NEES and WMECo), they were awarded in the context of DSM collaboratives.

The financial incentive mechanism should be seen largely as an innovation of the collaboratives themselves, since it emerged for the first time in the collaborative between NEES and CLF.[101] Also, without the collaboratives to help sort out the issue of when performance should be considered "exemplary," the Massachusetts DPU would probably not have been forthcoming with financial incentives, which were controversial both inside and outside the DPU. Moreover, neither NEES nor WMECo were granted financial incentives until after they had agreed to extensive program design changes and the acceleration of program implementation. BECo and COM/Electric's efforts give further evidence that the collaborative processes, not just the new-found financial incentives, were behind the utilities' increased willingness to increase their DSM investments. These efforts were comparable to NEES's and WMECo's in most respects, although they did not initially request, or receive, positive financial incentives.[102]

Program Design

The DSM-related experience and knowledge of the Massachusetts utilities and NUPs were augmented by the hiring of consultants with extensive experience in running DSM programs. This guaranteed that the collaboratives had access to the best available information when designing DSM programs. Comprehensive and generally innovative program designs emerged as a result of this technical expertise in conjunction with the political agendas of the various participants in the collaborative processes. Innovative features of the programs included (1) detailed market segmentation and target marketing; (2) the concept of direct investment in DSM (that is, utilities paying up to their avoided cost of new supply to purchase DSM resources); (3) an emphasis on capturing lost-opportunity resources (for example, new construction and equipment replacement) and avoiding cream skimming (for example, not installing suboptimal levels of insulation or doing only lighting retrofits when other measures are also cost-effective); (4) detailed monitoring and evaluation plans to, among other things, try to measure actual savings; and (5) creating mechanisms to link utility profits directly to DSM performance.

Most likely the DPU would not have had any more success pushing the utilities to adopt these innovative program design elements than it had had in trying to accelerate program implementation. In fact, the DPU was largely hamstrung with respect to program design issues without the collaboratives. Although the DPU could react to program details that it was asked to review, it would have had greater difficulty predesigning programs on its own in sufficient detail to direct the utilities to undertake specific efforts. The DPU had tried this approach to program design with mixed success in the pre-DSM-collaborative era when it had ordered the utilities to pilot-test performance-contracting programs (that is, pay customers and third-party energy service companies for DSM, generally on a predetermined cents-per-kWh basis).

At best, absent the collaboratives, the program detailing would have been subject to extensive litigation. Instead, despite some modifications ordered during each company's preapproval cases, the DPU enthusiastically endorsed the program designs worked out by the utilities and the NUPs in the collaboratives. Moreover, almost all the programs are in the field instead of tied up in potentially endless litigation.

Though still evolving, most collaboratively designed programs have resulted in higher than expected levels of participation. Furthermore, the program designs are recognized nationally as state of the art, and the participants of the collaboratives have been key presenters at every major conference on DSM since the collaboratives began.

Resolving Policy Issues

The collaboratives successfully resolved a multitude of technical issues necessary for the design of DSM programs and the implementation of the DPU's DSM-related policies. However, they have not been nearly as successful in resolving related underlying policy issues. For instance, during Phase I, attempts to reach agreement on an appropriate cost-effectiveness test and on cost-recovery issues were extremely contentious and polarized. Difficulties arose both between the utilities and the NUPs, and between the individual NUPs, especially on cost-recovery issues.

Although the DPU order issued in the midst of the Phase I joint-utility collaborative (Mass. D.P.U. 86-36-F [1988d]) effectively broke the impasse on many of the bigger policy questions, some that remained unanswered or that required a level of detailing beyond the

DPU's order continued to elude consensus right through the end of Phase I, into Phase II and beyond. The DPU's DSM preapproval orders, issued at the conclusion of Phase II and Phase III, continued to resolve critical underlying policy disputes between the parties on the appropriate cost-effectiveness test, customer incentives, program scale, and cost-recovery issues, to name a few.

The parties' inability to agree to an environmental externality methodology through a separate minicollaborative, encouraged by the DPU, is another example of the collaboratives' difficulty in resolving critical policy issues. Finally, the utilities considered the issue of whether electric companies should include fuel substitution measures within their DSM programs so politically sensitive that they would not allow it to be discussed even in the collaboratives. As a consequence of the collaboratives' inability to resolve the environmental externality and fuel substitution issues, as well as a host of other DSM-related policy issues, many of those issues were subsequently decided by the DPU through further adjudicatory proceedings.

The DSM collaboratives may not have done a great job resolving underlying policy issues that often touched on important distributional issues and philosophic underpinnings. However, their attempts were not necessarily unheeded. Debates on cost-effectiveness testing and even environmental externalities highlighted important technical information and clarified parties' interests and positions. By the time these policy issues were presented to the DPU for resolution, they were much more finely honed than they might have been without the benefit of the debates during the collaboratives. This focusing helped the DPU make more informed (and therefore hopefully more practical) decisions.

Process Evaluation

One major difference between traditional settlement and the DSM collaboratives is that the collaboratives began prior to any specific adjudicatory proceeding, and not after discovery, hearings, or the filing of legal briefs, as is usually the case in traditional adjudicatory settlements in rate cases. By focusing on consensus building during the prefiling rather than the postfiling period, the parties had a greater potential for process-related savings. More importantly, since the parties' positions were not yet publicly staked out, as they usually are in traditional adjudication (that is, filing of testimony early on, and briefs after hearings), there was more flexibility to explore creative settlements that better satisfied everyone's interests.

The use of these prefiling settlement processes appeared particularly well suited for the prospective nature of formulating the utilities' DSM programs. Historic facts were not really at issue here. Instead, the immediate focus was to formulate the best strategy for procuring cost-effective DSM resources in the future.

Both Phase I of the joint-utility collaborative and the NEES collaborative began with a joint fact-finding effort in which the parties developed a technical data base and explored program design options. This venture was particularly important because it pulled together the technical information that was essential for ultimately shaping the program designs. It also allowed parties to create program design options without having to make final decisions about funding or incentive levels, which were reserved for Phase II. Finally, the joint fact-finding effort gave these traditional adversaries an opportunity to begin to build interpersonal relationships and trust where little had previously existed.

Another important and unique feature of the DSM collaborative process was the funding provided by utilities for the NUPs to secure their own independent technical expertise. As discussed earlier, $5.4 million was spent to this end through late 1993 in Massachusetts. The outside experts provided state-of-the-art technical knowledge for the collaboratives, particularly in the early phases, in which information about the experience of other programs from across the country was critical. Whereas in traditional adjudication technical knowledge is often used as a weapon, in the collaboratives the experience and recommendations of the outside consultants were readily shared and often served as a starting point for further negotiations.

Moreover, the funding for outside experts allowed the NUPs, which had a political interest in the utilities' DSM efforts but varying degrees of technical expertise, to participate more effectively in the collaborative processes. In this regard, the funding of outside experts helped to further empower the NUPs.

Despite these extensive resources, several of the individual utility collaboratives suffered because the NUPs and their consultants were spread too thin. The parties acknowledged that this problem was at least partially responsible for the tensions that arose around WMECo's first preapproval filing, and COM/Electric specifically mentioned it as a major frustration. The problem was in part due to the consultants' being so overcommitted that they could not deliver technical work products in a timely fashion. There were also bottlenecks within the NUPs' respective organizations in the form of members who took a long time to review documents and reach decisions.

Of course, there were also instances in which the utilities themselves proved to be the laggards. Still, the collaboratives might have benefited from increased resources, particularly to help fund the NUPs' own internal staffing needs. However, the NUPs consider it problematic to secure money from the utilities (and hence from the ratepayers) for internal staffing purposes (the only exception being when CLF secured money from BECo to retain an attorney), and the utilities might consider such funding comparable to intervenor funding, which they have always opposed. This poses a hurdle to sustaining ongoing collaborative efforts—particularly when the same NUPs are involved in more than one effort simultaneously.

Traditional settlement processes often must contend with all the intervenors in the case. In contrast, the participants in these voluntary collaboratives were self-selected. Despite the presence of four NUPs in each of the collaboratives (except for the NEES collaborative, which included only CLF), all were structured more or less as two-party negotiations, with the NUPs acting as a coalition—hiring a single NUP coordinator and a single set of consultants. This structure was possible because of the NUPs' common interest in seeing more aggressive DSM programs implemented as soon as possible. Other typical intervenors, such as industrial consumers, were not viewed as allies by the NUPs and were not invited to participate.

This selectivity worked well for the parties in the short run, allowing them to stay focused and often to reach creative agreements on complex matters in a relatively short time. However, the failure to directly embrace all interested parties within the collaboratives resulted in subsequent intervention by nonparticipants and contentious litigation before the DPU in every case. Still, it is not apparent that less exclusivity in these collaboratives would have automatically improved the end results. The Oak Ridge National Laboratory study on DSM collaboratives, for instance, found that some collaboratives that were more inclusive did quite well (for example, the California collaborative, with fifteen parties covering the full spectrum of stakeholders, still reached substantial consensus), whereas others had serious problems (for example, the New York State Electric and Gas Corporation collaborative, which included industrial intervenors that were not supportive of developing utility DSM programs) (Raab and Schweitzer 1992).

The process would have needed a different structure if additional parties had been included in the joint-utility collaborative, since it is unlikely that they would have been compatible with the NUPs. A single NUP coordinator or set of consultants might not have sufficed.

It is worth reiterating that the DPU staff also did not participate in any of the DSM collaboratives in Massachusetts, either as a full party or even as an observer, whereas in many other states, PUC advocacy staffs often actively participate and PUC advisory staffs occasionally observe (Raab and Schweitzer 1992). Massachusetts did not at the time have an advocacy staff, and the commission determined that its advisory staff should not participate even as observers.[103] The DPU's absence from the process resulted in some collaborative agreements that were ultimately rejected by the DPU and some stalemates within the collaboratives themselves, particularly on policy-related issues, that might have been avoided.

Greater access to the DPU staff and commissioners either on a formal or informal basis might have succeeded in clarifying past decisions and revealing current perspectives so that the consensus-building process did not get bogged down or unnecessarily polarized. The DPU attempted to provide such access with some success when it held a facilitated informal session on DSM ratemaking issues. More technical sessions on a regular basis, at least with the DPU staff, might have been appropriate and useful.

The DPU might also have been able to play a greater mediatory role on policy issues by hearing policy disputes and issuing interim rulings. Alternatively, the collaboratives might have benefited from the services of an outside mediator to help participants resolve policy disputes, or even to help the processes accommodate a broader range of interested parties. However, as discussed in Chapter 6, any such changes, particularly with respect to greater DPU involvement, must be done with an eye to ex parte and other legal restrictions.

To the extent that DSM collaboratives occur prior to a utility's filing, they do not preclude the use of more traditional settlement processes between the time when the programs are filed and the time when a PUC order is issued. In this respect, prefiling settlement processes not only supplement traditional adjudication but can supplement traditional settlement processes as well. This scenario is exactly what occurred in both Rhode Island and New Hampshire, where the DSM agreements between NEES and CLF were settled with the advocacy staffs of the PUCs and other intervenors after the collaborative filings. In the third phase of the COM/Electric collaborative, a diverse group of parties were able to reach a settlement after the collaborative had broken down and an extremely vitriolic, contested-case proceeding had ensued. In this way, the prefiling settlement process expands both the points of opportunities for settlement and the span of time during which a settlement can be forged.

A final distinguishing characteristic of the DSM collaborative processes studied here is that many are ongoing. In contrast to traditional settlement procedures, which rarely last more than several months, the NEES, BECo, and WMECo collaboratives have all continued for over five years. Although the collaboratives have operated in phases, with discrete products delivered at the end of each phase (for example, filing at the DPU), and although there have been brief hiatuses from time to time (for example, several months), these processes have been ongoing. These rather unprecedented relationships have for the most part been extremely fruitful in developing programs, and then in jointly reviewing monitoring and evaluation results and in refining the programs as necessary (that is, in accordance with evaluation and monitoring data and changing circumstances, such as the downturn in the New England economy). Even as these collaboratives continue to mature, however, it is not clear whether they will continue indefinitely.

SUMMARY

This chapter has evaluated two attempts to introduce supplemental consensus-building processes in traditional adjudicatory proceedings. The first was a settlement process at the end of extremely contentious litigation associated with expenditures made by Boston Edison Company during a thirty-two-month outage at its Pilgrim nuclear power plant. The second entailed a collaborative process between utilities and several nonutility parties to prospectively design comprehensive demand-side management programs during negotiations that lasted over several years.

The analyses presented here indicate that consensus building can enhance the legitimacy of adjudicatory proceedings, largely by giving stakeholders an opportunity to design remedies and plans that better satisfy their own interests. In the Pilgrim case, the mere fact that traditional adversaries were able to reach a consensus after one of the most contentious adjudicatory proceedings imaginable suggests this possibility. PUC approval, lack of appeals, and several other factors bear this out despite several noteworthy problems. The effect that the DSM collaboratives had on the legitimacy of their adjudicatory proceedings, while also positive, was somewhat more difficult to characterize definitively because it involved many subcollaboratives that fluctuated between consensus building and fractious litigation for several years.

Both cases also provide strong evidence that consensus building can improve the practicality of final remedies and future plans in adjudicatory proceedings. Parties creatively resolved thorny issues in the Pilgrim settlement by tying BECo's cost recovery to the future performance of the plant (including operational, health, and safety factors) and by having the company deliver $75 million of DSM in lieu of refunding replacement power monies paid by ratepayers. The remedies were attractive to the DPU but probably would not have arisen from formal adjudications.

In the DSM collaboratives, over $5 million were spent to hire consultants from across the country to bring state-of-the-art information into the negotiations. The collaboratives have in turn produced DSM efforts for Massachusetts utilities with many nationally recognized program design innovations. Again, these practical plans probably would not have emerged from traditional litigation at any time in the near future.

However, the consensus-building processes have been relatively resource-intensive. The Pilgrim settlement required an entire summer of negotiations among the parties and occurred after virtually all the litigation was completed. The DSM collaboratives have required enormous investments of time and money over several years. Yet, despite these collaborative efforts, the DSM agreements were still all litigated before the DPU. I conclude that short-term process-related resource savings are not guaranteed in adjudicatory settlements. However, long-term net benefits appear to be positive and significant compared with traditional adjudication, once the actual improvements to the remedies and plans are factored into the analyses.

Chapter 5

Rulemaking

The preceding chapter focused on the use of consensus building in PUC adjudicatory matters. The current chapter first differentiates agency rulemaking from adjudication and traces the history of agency rulemaking from its introduction at the federal level in 1946 through the present, highlighting the shortcomings of traditional agency rulemaking and introducing the promise of alternative, consensus-based rulemaking processes. Two case studies then illustrate the use of consensus-building processes in agency rulemaking. The first case analyzes the use of facilitated technical sessions in developing integrated resource management rules in Massachusetts. The second examines the negotiated settlement process used to develop resource bidding policies in New Jersey.

Differentiating Agency Rulemaking from Adjudication

Decisions in agency adjudications, though often considered precedential, are not formally binding on persons who are not parties to the case. Rules, on the other hand, legally apply to all parties under an agency's jurisdiction. Theoretically, agencies use rulemaking to act proactively by formulating policies that are applied prospectively, whereas they use adjudications to apply (and necessarily interpret) preexisting rules to individual cases retrospectively. Because of this important distinction, rules are generally more appropriate for resolving industrywide policies.

The courts have historically afforded agencies much latitude in choosing to resolve policy matters through either process.[1] However, over the past decade, all branches of government have increasingly expressed a preference for rulemaking in creating broad policies. Still, agencies frequently use adjudication for these purposes (Breyer 1982, Burns 1988, Shapiro 1965, Strauss 1989).

Agency rulemaking also differs procedurally from adjudication in theory. The procedural differences stem from the basic premise that agency adjudications are "quasi-judicial," whereas rulemaking is essentially a legislative function. In the former, agencies must make every effort to act as an impartial judge; in the latter, neutrality is neither assumed nor expected. In adjudications, the agency is required to make decisions based on the facts in a particular case as presented by the parties. In rulemaking, agencies are generally less restricted by courtlike, due process constraints. As such, requirements for agencies to build a detailed record, to justify their final decision, and to avoid ex parte communications are supposedly more relaxed.

In practice, however, many of the procedural distinctions between agency rulemaking and adjudication have been blurred by both the courts and the legislatures. Courtlike restrictions have been layered onto the rulemaking process over time, resulting in its increased judicialization (Harter 1982, Strauss 1989). Still, agencies do not appear to be any more capable of resolving complex issues now than they were before. Moreover, judicialization may actually be aggravating an already adversarial process just when agencies are being forced to resolve increasingly more technical and contentious issues. In the midst of these dilemmas, negotiated rulemaking and other supplemental consensus-based options are now being successfully used to address some of the shortcomings of more traditional approaches to rulemaking and policy formation.

The Evolution of Agency Rulemaking at the Federal Level

In 1938, James Landis, then dean of Harvard Law School and formerly one of the first commissioners on the Securities and Exchange Commission, published a seminal book entitled *The Administrative Process*. In it he criticized agencies' use of adjudication and proposed that they be allowed to promulgate rules (Burns 1988, McCraw 1984). Landis argued that agencies needed to be able to formulate policies to pursue their mandates separate from adjudicatory proceedings:

> For that [administrative] process to be successful in a particular field, it is imperative that controversies be decided as "rightly" as possible, independently of the formal record the parties themselves produce. The ultimate test of the administrative [process] is the policy that it formulates; not the fairness as between the parties of the disposition of a controversy on a record of their making. (Landis 1938, pp. 38–39)

Landis's persuasive call was instrumental in the passage of the federal Administrative Procedures Act (APA) in 1946 (McCraw 1984).

Besides codifying existing adjudicatory procedures used by agencies, the APA created rulemaking procedures allowing federal agencies to promulgate rules. Known as informal or "notice-and-comment" rulemaking,[2] these procedures required agencies to (1) give notice of a proposed rulemaking in the *Federal Register*, (2) provide interested parties with an opportunity to participate in the process via written comments, and (3) publish a final rule, generally thirty days before it is to go into effect.[3] The requirements for informal rulemaking were extremely permissive and did not even direct agencies to conduct hearings except when mandated by Congress under special statutes and in specific circumstances, or when agencies decided to do so on their own.

The same year that the federal APA was adopted (1946), the National Conference of Commissioners on Uniform State Laws promulgated a Model State Administrative Procedures Act (MSAPA) that was virtually a carbon copy. Adoption of the Model State APA is voluntary; however, almost every state has either copied it verbatim or with minor changes (Bonfield 1986, Burns 1988, Davis 1972).

Although the APA's rulemaking requirements directed agencies to offer the public a chance to participate in the process, the new laws approached the agencies as "expert guardians" and relied heavily on their knowledge and experience (Harter 1982). Since the advent of agency rulemaking in 1946, administrative rulemaking has accelerated greatly—perhaps far beyond the original expectation of its architects. One need only look at the explosion of administrative rules on health, safety, and the environment that cropped up beginning in the 1970s to understand this trend. At the same time, Congress and the courts have tried to make agencies more accountable and to provide even greater opportunities for public participation. However, they have tried to bolster the legitimacy of the rulemaking process by layering additional procedural requirements on the scant rulemaking requirements found in the original APA.

Congress, for example, in passing the Freedom of Information Act in 1969 and the Government in Sunshine Act in 1976, altered rulemaking practices by respectively bringing much of the internal documentation related to agency rulemaking and more of the decision-making process itself into public view (Strauss 1989). It also tried to increase agency accountability by passing the Federal Advisory Committee Act of 1976, which placed restrictions on the ad hoc committees often used by agencies to help develop policies and rules (Harter 1982). Finally, Congress has increasingly required administrative agencies to promulgate rules implementing numerous new statutes using procedures that are stricter than those required by the APA.[4]

For the federal courts' part, several significant cases have contributed to the refinement of the procedures that govern agency rulemaking. Beginning in 1971 in Overton Park, Inc. v. Volpe, the U.S. Supreme Court required agencies to conduct thorough, probing, and careful reviews that would enable the courts "to see what major issues of policy were ventilated by the informal proceedings and why the Agency reacted to them as they did."[5] This case contributed to administrative agencies increasingly embracing "paper hearing" procedures, whereby an agency would carefully document all the information it used in reaching a decision and would respond to important comments made by interested parties (Strauss 1989). In 1977, in Home Box Office v. FCC,[6] a lower court appeared to interpret the Overton decision to (1) extend strict ex parte restrictions to rulemaking procedures (that is, make it impermissible for regulators to have private, off-the-record conversations with interested persons, as is typical for legislators) and (2) allow an opportunity for adversarial comment (that is, allow interested parties to cross-examine each other in courtlike fashion) (id.).

The courts later receded from some of the specific suggestions made in Home Box Office. In fact, in Vermont Yankee Nuclear Power Corp. v. Natural Resources Defense Council, Inc. in 1978, the U.S. Supreme Court unanimously decided to forbid the lower courts to require agencies to follow more stringent procedures than those included in the APA.[7] However, although the sweep of the Vermont Yankee decision is often debated, today's administrative rulemaking process has undeniably adopted more of the trappings of adjudicatory proceedings than was originally envisioned in 1946 when the APA was first promulgated. Current law does not require strict ex parte rules, adversarial hearings, or an exhaustive record that includes everything an agency knows or has heard. However, agencies are required to develop elaborate public records that include all the documents received during the rulemaking process and to respond to all comments made (Strauss 1989).

The current administrative process is often referred to as "hybrid rulemaking" to reflect the gradual judicialization (that is, formalization) of the informal notice-and-comment process resulting from the actions taken by Congress and the courts (Harter 1982, Susskind and McMahon 1985). Philip Harter, in his ground-breaking article "Negotiated Regulations: A Cure for Malaise" (1982), observes that many of these rulemaking requirements are appropriate given the significant impact of rules on our society. However, he argues that the requirements have contributed to a "malaise" whereby "parties complain about the time, expense and legitimacy of the administrative decisions reached through the hybrid process" (id., p. 6). Harter maintains that agencies are no more capable of resolving what are essentially political questions in a seemingly legitimate way than they were prior to the judicialization. Susskind and Morgan go somewhat further in claiming that increased judicialization may paradoxically be aggravating the malaise:

> We are facing something of a paradox. Many of the steps taken to enhance the legitimacy of decisionmaking have caused substantial delay and inefficiency—undermining the very credibility they were meant to enhance. (Susskind and Morgan 1986b, p. 24)

The rulemaking process itself has become more adversarial, and the appeal rate of agency decisions has increased dramatically. For example, William Ruckelshaus, former federal Environmental Protection Agency (EPA) administrator, claims that in the early 1980s more than 80 percent of EPA's rules were appealed and approximately 30 percent were changed as a result of litigation (Susskind and McMahon 1985). Four of every five EPA decisions continue to be appealed in the 1990s, according to EPA's current administrator, William Reilly (M. Wald 1991). This situation is not unique, though the appeal rate of rules varies among federal agencies (Harter interview, Schuck and Elliott 1990).[8]

It is important to point out, however, that although the judicialization of the rulemaking process may be increasing, it is not the root cause of the crises of legitimacy that the process is currently experiencing. At the heart of the crises is the growing inability of agencies, and the public generally, to resolve increasingly more technical and controversial issues. In this respect, overreliance on agency "expertise" seems neither feasible nor prudent. At the same time, Congress and the courts have attempted in the past two decades to transform agencies as they make rules from experts into "umpires," albeit active ones, and to guarantee the public greater influence on the rules that emerge from the process. Nonetheless, these attempts appear to be failing (Harter 1982, Susskind and McMahon 1985). Susskind and McMahon describe the dilemma:

> If all regulations had a clearly determinable factual basis, arguments about the exercise of agency discretion would be moot. Agencies, however, must also make policy choices in situations where either the desired facts are not available or the "facts" are contested. In such instances, the agency exercises considerable discretion as it interprets inconsistent facts, balances various and often competing interests, and ultimately makes subjective policy choices with very real economic and political ramifications. In this

context, an agency can expect opposition to almost every rule it develops. (Susskind and McMahon 1985, p. 135)

Alternative Rulemaking Procedures

In "Negotiating Regulations," Harter proposes to cure the malaise by introducing an alternative rulemaking procedure based on negotiations between interested parties, including the agency:

> Thus, an alternative, more direct way to make [agencies'] inherently political decisions would be to adapt the legislative process itself to the development of regulations. Such a process would enable representatives of the competing interests, including the relevant agency itself, to thrash out a consensus on the policy instead of making a pitch to the umpire. A form of negotiation among the affected parties by a proposed rule would be such a process. (Harter 1982, pp. 28–29)

Although Harter was not the first to suggest the possibility of improving agency rulemaking through negotiations,[9] he was the first to thoroughly detail what such a process might look like.

Harter's proposal, often referred to as "reg-neg" ("negotiated regulations"),[10] contains the essential steps shown in Table 5-1. Harter's and Susskind and McMahon's works contain other important recommendations on specific details of negotiated rulemaking (for example, the use of mediation and the creation of a resource pool to fund participants and outside experts); however, Table 5-1 represents the major stepping stones of the process (Harter 1982, Susskind and McMahon 1985). Consultation with the Office of Management and Budget (OMB) is the only step missing from the table with respect to federal negotiated rulemaking. Given OMB's substantial powers to oversee agency decision making for cost-effectiveness and other purposes, OMB is supposed to be consulted early and often in a negotiated rulemaking process (EPA 1991, Pritzker interview).[11]

What is of critical importance is that the process has been designed to supplement the traditional rulemaking procedure, rather than replace it. The negotiation process is used essentially in formulating an agency's proposed rule. Once this rule is developed, the rulemaking process takes its normal "notice-and-comment" course. As such, the addition of negotiation at the outset is not inconsistent with the APA's rulemaking requirements, which are virtually silent on how agencies develop their initial proposed rules. If all interested parties were involved in the settlement, comments on the proposed rule (that is, the settlement) should be minimal. In theory, this type of process should

Table 5-1. Steps in Negotiated Rulemaking

1. An outside convenor, selected by the agency, helps assess whether a rule is appropriate for negotiation (that is, whether there is a reasonable likelihood of achieving consensus) and identifies and helps solicit representative stakeholders.
2. If the rule is considered appropriate for negotiation and parties are willing to participate, an agency gives notice in the Federal Register of its intention to negotiate a particular rule.
3. Once final participants are selected, negotiations commence. Agency staff participate as full parties. The process works by consensus.
4. If and when consensus is reached, the agency publishes the consensus rule as the agency's proposed rule in the Federal Register.
5. Comments are received, and the agency publishes the final rules in the Federal Register, either without change or with minor revisions, at least thirty days before the rules take effect. (If the comments reveal major flaws, an agency may choose to send the rules back to the original negotiating group or develop a new proposed rule of its own.)
6. After the final rules are published, interested persons (outside of those who negotiated the rule) can appeal to the courts during a specified time period.

Source: Based on Harter 1982, Susskind and McMahon 1985.

result in rules that have much broader acceptance and are, therefore, more legitimate. As such, appeals should be minimized and the rules implemented as designed rather than resisted at every turn. Also, the literature claims that the negotiated rulemaking process should be more efficient—saving time and money for the parties and the agency itself (Harter 1982, Susskind and McMahon 1985). Finally, the rules should be more practical to the degree that the less adversarial process can produce better information and more realistic remedies.

Even if consensus is not reached, proponents claim that the process of negotiation can improve rulemaking. Susskind and McMahon explain why:

> In some respects, negotiated rulemaking cannot fail. At the very least, conflicts can be clarified, data shared, and differences aired in a constructive way. Even if full consensus is not achieved, the negotiations process may still have narrowed the issues in dispute. (Susskind and McMahon 1985, p. 159)

Since Harter's article in 1982, at least eight federal departments and agencies have used negotiated rulemaking.[12] The EPA, for example, completed at least ten reg-negs through the end of 1991—the most of any federal agency (EPA 1991, Pritzker interview). Of the ten, five reached a complete consensus, and three others reached agreement among most of the participants—an agreement mirrored in EPA's final rules (EPA 1991).[13] However, even when a full consensus was not reached, the process significantly helped shape EPA's final rules (Pritzker 1990).

Only two of EPA's rules that went through the reg-neg process were appealed, although neither on procedural grounds, and the courts upheld EPA's decisions in both instances (Pritzker interview). Still, despite the courts' support for reg-negs thus far, there has been some concern in the literature with respect to how well reg-negs will fare in the courts over time (P. Wald 1985).[14] However, many argue that the process itself should obviate the necessity of the courts taking a "hard look" at the results (Harter 1986, Sturm 1991, Susskind and McMahon 1985).

A complete evaluation of the federal experience with reg-neg is beyond the scope of this inquiry. However, it is worth noting that lead staff at the EPA and others consider the reg-neg process successful in creatively resolving thorny issues in a way that has added to the practicality of the rules and helped to better legitimize both the process and the results (Fiorino 1988, Fiorino and Kirtz 1985, Pritzker 1990, Susskind and McMahon 1985). It is also worth reiterating at this juncture that on November 29, 1990, President Bush signed into law the Negotiated Rulemaking Act (Public Law 101-648), which encourages federal agencies to pursue negotiated rulemaking whenever possible and details the rulemaking process to be followed.[15] The passage of this act is testimonial to the positive impression that negotiated rulemaking has made on federal agencies, Congress, and the administration to date.

Before turning briefly to state PUC rulemaking practices and the introduction of the cases, I must again emphasize that reg-neg is not the only supplement to traditional rulemaking procedures that can begin to address the malaise of current rulemaking practices described by Harter and others. Negotiated rulemaking is perhaps the most visible and celebrated consensus-building technique on the federal level. However, it stands at the top of a pyramid of other supplemental consensus-building procedures. Such procedures include policy dialogues, advisory committees, workshops, round table discussions, and technical sessions. All of these alternatives serve to provide parties, including the agency staffs, with the potential for greater understanding of issues, proposals, and the interests and perspectives of others. They also provide opportunities for consensus building, although reg-neg is perhaps the most formal and aggressive in this regard. As such, all of these techniques have the potential to make rules both more practical and more legitimate.

State PUC Rulemaking

Under American federalism, each state regulates its own administrative procedures. As mentioned previously, the National Conference of Commissioners on Uniform State Laws adopted a Model State Administrative Procedures Act (MSAPA) in 1946 to provide states with the opportunity to implement the federal APA procedures at the state level. The National Conference updated those procedures in 1961 and again in 1981.

According to a study by the National Regulatory Research Institute (NRRI) in 1988, over 80 percent of the states have adopted some version of the MSAPA (Burns 1988).[16] However, the same study found that PUCs in only about half the states are actually required to comply with the MSAPA. The remaining PUCs either have received an explicit exemption from their state's APA, or their state never adopted the MSAPA in the first place (id.).[17] These facts are not necessarily of major significance since all PUCs, even those that are exempted from their state's APA, have rulemaking rules that rarely deviate much from the federal APA requirements.

Of greater significance is the NRRI report's finding that state PUCs do not regularly use rulemaking proceedings to make major industrywide policy decisions. Although the incidence varies from state to state, apparently many PUCs still tend to set industrywide policy by precedent through adjudicatory proceedings (id.).[18] For example, even the Massachusetts PUC, which initiated several significant rulemaking proceedings during the 1980s (discussed later in this chapter), chose to revisit its environmental externality policies and to explore creating fuel substitution policies (that is, requiring electric utilities to pay for their customers to substitute gas and other fuels for electricity as a DSM measure) through adjudicatory proceedings (Mass. D.P.U. 91-131 [1992b] and Mass. D.P.U. 90-261-A, respectively). Over the past decade, as mentioned in Chapter 4, the DPU has initiated only two rulemaking proceedings on electricity issues (Yoshimura interview).

The reasons why state PUCs appear to be embracing rulemaking more slowly than federal agencies are not completely clear. This difference is probably connected to a greater procedural inertia at state PUCs, caused by a longer history than most other state and federal agencies—and one that, until recently, has been exclusively focused on adjudicatory proceedings. Nonetheless, many PUCs have begun to promulgate rules on issues of major structural and regulatory import, such as least-cost integrated planning, resource bidding, DSM incentives, preapproval ratemaking, environmental "adders," avoided-cost calculations, and marginal cost pricing.

Rulemaking will begin consuming an increasing proportion of PUCs' dockets as the industry and its regulatory environment continue to change rapidly. For the most part, this is happening voluntarily as PUCs recognize the virtues of trying to resolve inherently subjective public policy disputes through rulemaking rather than adjudication. However, state legislatures, administrations, and even the courts are increasingly pressuring state PUCs to pursue industrywide policies through rules, as is happening at the federal level.

When state PUCs do make rules, they have often experienced many of the same criticisms as federal agencies. The rulemaking proceedings are often time consuming and contentious. The only notable difference between PUC and other state agency rulemaking and federal agency rulemaking is that state rules appear to be appealed less frequently. Though I have no hard data to confirm this observation as fact, those experts I queried on this subject during my interviews concurred with this observation (Burns, Harter, Miragliotta, Oppenheim, and Pritzker interviews). The less frequent appeal rate makes some intuitive sense. First, each federal rule has a greater impact on national interest groups than have state rules. Second, appeals are more affordable at the federal level relative to the resources of those interest groups. Finally, the success rates of appeals at the state level, where courts may have historically shown greater deference to agency decision making, may be lower.

A lower appeal frequency does not necessarily imply that state PUCs, or state agencies in general, are somehow more competent rulemakers and that the rules are ultimately more practical and palatable. However, to the extent that parties, particularly the regulators themselves, are motivated to experiment with consensus-building techniques as a means of avoiding lengthy appeals, that motivation may be somewhat diminished at the state level. Yet, appeals are not uncommon on the state level and may grow as PUCs and other state agencies rely more on rulemaking and the rules become more sweeping, controversial, or both. More importantly, as mentioned previously, high appeal rates are just one impetus among many for trying to improve rulemaking practices.

Introduction to the Case Studies

The following case studies explore what benefits, if any, consensus-building processes, including negotiated rulemaking, can add to traditional rulemaking at state PUCs. The first case shows how the development of integrated resource management rules in Massachusetts successfully used a structured technical session process over several years with the assistance of outside facilitation. The second case examines the formation of New Jersey's bidding policies through a negotiated settlement process that resembled a reg-neg process in many respects.

IRM RULEMAKING IN MASSACHUSETTS

Between 1988 and 1990, the Massachusetts Department of Public Utilities (DPU) and the Energy Facilities Siting Council (EFSC) made use of an innovative rulemaking process to develop rules that greatly affect the way electric utilities plan for and procure resources. Known as integrated resource management (IRM) rules, these had two overarching objectives. First, that electric utilities conduct a solicitation process approximately every other year to procure resources to meet their power needs. Second, that both supply- and demand-side resources, regardless of ownership (that is, utility or nonutility), be considered under one consistent, competitive solicitation framework.

The process used to develop these rules differed from a more traditional notice-and-comment rulemaking process by including a series of ten technical sessions hosted by the agencies (eight by the DPU and two by the EFSC) over two years. These sessions were attended by more than 130 people from seventy-one organizations and by staff from both agencies. Independent facilitators were used in all the sessions.

The value of these consensus-building processes may be judged by whether they allowed for greater public participation and ultimately improved the final rules themselves. The evidence shows that the sessions helped make the rules both more practical and more legitimate even though no consensus was ever sought or achieved. They also helped improve the regulatory climate with positive benefits beyond the IRM rules themselves.

This case study rests on several methods. First, I was one of the lead staff at the DPU responsible for the development of the IRM rules and the design of the supplemental technical session process. As such, I was a participant-observer throughout the external public hearing and technical session process as well as the internal DPU process of drafting the actual orders and rules. In addition to direct observation, I had the benefit of a long paper trail, including both public documents and confidential internal memoranda. Also, after each of the two rounds of technical sessions, I administered a detailed evaluation form to the participants to solicit their feedback on the strengths and weaknesses of the sessions (see Appendix 2 for evaluation form and data compilation). This case write-up includes the results of fifty-three completed surveys after the first round of sessions and forty-one completed surveys after the second. Finally, I conducted face-to-face, structured interviews with fourteen of the participants in the rulemaking process, as shown in Table 5-2.

Background

Prior to proposing actual rules, both federal and state administrative agencies often undertake generic investigations or inquiries during which questions are posed to the public on a particular issue and information is gathered through hearings, written comments, or both. The IRM rulemaking process grew out of such a generic investigation. However, the original intent of the investigation, which was initiated in February 1986 on the Department of Public Utilities' own motion, was to examine an important but much narrower question regarding the appropriate pricing and ratemaking treatment to be afforded new, utility-owned electric generating facilities.

This narrower ratemaking investigation followed on the heels of the DPU's issuance of a proposed rule in a prior investigation. That proposed rule contemplated requiring electric utilities to conduct an annual competitive bidding process to implement the federal Public Utilities Regulatory Policy Act (PURPA) by procuring electricity from Qualifying Facilities (QFs).[19] The QF rule (220 CMR 8.00), finally adopted in August 1986 (Mass. D.P.U. 84-276-B [1986a]), constituted the first statewide PURPA-related rule in the nation to rely on bidding.[20] The key innovation was its attempt to stimulate a QF market while harnessing competitive forces to set a market price for power. This approach was an attempt to stimulate the market by guaranteeing QFs long-term contracts at or below each utility's full avoided cost of power while avoiding the expensive problems of oversubscription that California utilities had experienced.[21]

The generic investigation undertaken in 1986 in Massachusetts to look at the ratemaking treatment for utility-owned and -operated resources was in part an attempt by the Massachusetts commission, chaired by Paul Levy, to examine whether the concept of market-based pricing from the QF regulations could somehow be infused into the traditional cost-of-service ratemaking process typically applied to utility investments.[22] As this generic investigation commenced, three important things were happening. First, in the face of a vibrant New England economy, forecasters were predicting significant increased

Table 5-2. Interviews for Massachusetts IRM Rules

Utilities

Al Destribats	Vice-President for Planning, New England Electric System
Robert Fratto	Manager of Demand Program Administration, COM/Electric
Richard Hahn	Vice-President for Marketing, BECo

Government

Mary Beth Gentleman	Attorney, private law firm (former Assistant Secretary for Policy, Division of Energy Resources)
Jerrold Oppenheim	Assistant Attorney General, Massachusetts Attorney General's Office
Robert Shapiro	General Counsel, Department of Public Utilities (former Executive Director, Energy Facilities Siting Council)
Robert Werlin	Attorney, private law firm (former Commissioner and Chair, Department of Public Utilities)

Third-Party Providers

Stephen Cowell	President, Conservation Services Group, Inc.
Sherif Fam	Manager of Regulatory Affairs, Thermo-Energy Systems Corporation (former President, New England Cogeneration Association)
Rolly Rouse	President, Conservation Conversions, Inc. (former Chief Operating Officer, Citizens Conservation Corporation)

Environmental and Consumer Groups

Armond Cohen	Senior Attorney, CLF
Alan Nogee	Energy Program Director, MASSPIRG

Other

David O'Connor	Executive Director, Massachusetts Office of Dispute Resolution (facilitator for technical session process)
Harvey Salgo	Manager Least Cost Utility Planning, TELLUS Institute (represented the Division of Energy Resources in the IRM proceedings)

Note: Positions and affiliations are as of the time of the interviews.

power needs for the foreseeable future (New England Governors' Conference 1986). Second, in the wake of major cost overruns on several new utility-owned generating facilities (most notably nuclear power plants), coupled with substantial cost-recovery disallowances by state regulators, utilities were reluctant to build new facilities. Third, even absent disallowances (or the threat of disallowances), utility investments in several large, costly construction projects (for example, Seabrook 1 and 2, Millstone 3, and Pilgrim 2) left them in a weak financial condition, making it extremely difficult to attract additional capital to finance future construction projects.

With the 1984 addition of a "used and useful" standard in Massachusetts to the existing prudence review, utilities and others were maintaining that the regulatory promise of cost recovery for their investments had been broken (Kalt et al. 1987). Under the "prudent, used, and useful" standard, utilities could only recover a return *of* prudently incurred investments and a return *on* investments prudently incurred and economically useful. To be economically useful, the power was required to still be "useful" (that is, cost-effective) and actually "used" (that is, operational), regardless of whether it was projected to be economic and needed when the decision to construct the plant was initially made.

The commission perceived that a lack of a vibrant QF market, coupled with the utilities' reluctance or inability to undertake new power plant construction, threatened to leave the region short on power, faced with rising power costs as utilities purchased expensive power elsewhere, or both. Having resolved the QF situation to their satisfaction (at least in theory), the commission turned their attention to ratemaking issues associated with utility resources. However, during the early phases of the generic ratemaking investigation, many participants filed comments emphasizing that the commission should *also* consider other alternatives to new utility-owned supply-side investments. Most notably, they suggested the need to look at demand-side management (DSM) opportunities and purchases from independent power producers (IPPs), including QFs,[23] and stressed the need to integrate all demand and supply options under one comprehensive regulatory framework (see Mass. D.P.U. 86-36-B [1987b]).

Recognizing the validity of these comments, a new commission chaired by Bernice McIntyre[24] decided to broaden the investigation:

> The Department finds . . . that it should consider in this docket ways in which the regulatory structure can encourage electric utilities to consider on a systematic, equitable, and integrated basis all supply and demand options and to implement those measures that

will result in providing reliable service in a cost-effective manner. (Mass. D.P.U. 86-36-B [1987b])

Although this order added the issues of integrated resource planning and procurement to the more traditional issues of ratemaking that the DPU was already considering, the department elected to pursue the two sets of issues in two parallel tracks. The primary reason for this decision was to accomplish the more immediate task of ratemaking quickly while allowing more time to resolve the thornier and newer issue of resource selection. Eventually the DPU employed a more innovative process to develop rules for integrated resource planning but chose to use a traditional process to form the ratemaking preapproval rules for utility-generated new power sources.

The Traditional Process (Formation of Preapproval Rules)

When the investigation into the ratemaking treatment for new utility-owned generation commenced in February 1986, the DPU described its intentions as follows:

> This proceeding has been structured as a generic rulemaking case so as *to allow a full exchange of ideas*, unencumbered by specific project circumstances, on the wide range of issues pertaining to the impact of various ratemaking alternatives on utility investment [emphasis added]. (Mass. D.P.U. 86-36 [1986c], p. 2)

As mentioned, the DPU wished to explore possible alternatives to its "prudent, used, and useful" standard, which many considered too onerous and potentially inconsistent with the more market-based pricing embodied in the QF regulations.

The procedures the DPU used to pose questions, solicit input, and formulate regulations essentially followed the traditional notice-and-comment rulemaking process as illustrated in Table 5-3. This process generally typifies the way administrative agencies such as state PUCs traditionally conduct rulemaking processes. However, it includes several steps that go beyond the minimal standards required by the federal Administrative Procedures Act (APA) and the APA requirements adopted by most states. First, it is legally permissible to initiate a rulemaking process with proposed rules (step 5) rather than with a fact-finding investigation. Second, the issuance of an interim order (step 3) that digests what has already been submitted and asks for further information is not necessarily typical. Rather, regulators often propose actual rules directly after an initial fact-finding process. Lastly, although hearings are usually held as a matter of course, they are gener-

156 — Chapter Five

Table 5-3. Preapproval Rulemaking Steps	
Step 1:	Announce opening of investigation; pose questions (Mass. D.P.U. 86-36, February 1986 [1986c])
Step 2:	Hold formal hearings; receive written comments
Step 3:	Issue interim order that discusses comments received; review options; pose additional questions; request further comments (Mass. D.P.U. 86-36-A, April 1987 [1987a])
Step 4:	Receive written comments
Step 5:	Issue proposed rules; request comments (Mass. D.P.U. 86-36-C, May 1988 [1988a])
Step 6:	Hold formal hearings; receive written comments
Step 7:	Issue final rules (Mass. D.P.U. 86-36-E, October 1988 [1988c])

ally not required unless an interested party specifically requests them. The DPU, for instance, accepted written comments after issuing its interim order but did not hold a second round of hearings prior to issuing proposed rules.

The initial order opening the investigation was a concise statement of the problem(s) the DPU believed needed to be addressed (Mass. D.P.U. 86-36 [1986c]). After receiving comments and holding hearings, the DPU issued an interim order that discussed several alternatives for addressing the problems and expressed its inclination to pursue a "preapproval" approach (Mass. D.P.U. 86-36-A [1987a]). Under a preapproval cost-recovery system, the utilities and the ratepayers would sign a contract prior to plant construction for a certain amount of power at a given price. In addition to guaranteeing a market for the power, the DPU—and through the contract, the ratepayers—would agree not to second-guess the decision to build the plant through future proceedings. In return, the utilities would agree on a cost-recovery cap on construction costs and a linkage of actual recovery to the operating performance of the new plant. Different risks would be borne by ratepayers and utility shareholders. After receiving written comments on the interim order, the DPU decided to split the inquiry into separate proceedings for ratemaking and resource selection (Mass. D.P.U. 86-36-B [1987b]).

In the interim order, additional questions were posed and comments requested from everyone except the utilities, who were actually ordered to file responsive comments (id.). After receiving comments, but without holding hearings, the DPU issued proposed rules based on the preapproval concept (Mass. D.P.U. 86-36-C [1988a]). These rules would apply both to new and existing utility-owned supply resources in which expenditures were anticipated to (1) exceed $250/kW, (2) extend the life of the plant, or (3) expand the capacity of the plant (Mass. D.P.U. 86-36-C [1988a], p. 103). The DPU further proposed that the risks associated with various changes unanticipated at the time of signing the preapproval contract be divided between the utility and its ratepayers, as shown in Table 5-4. According to the order accompanying the proposed rules, the preapproval cost recovery policy became effective as of May 12, 1988—the day the proposed rules were issued but prior to their final adoption.

After the proposed rules were issued, a single public hearing was held to "accept comments." Four parties testified: the Attorney General; the Division of Energy Resources (DOER—known as the Executive Office of Energy Resources [EOER] until late 1989); and the two largest utilities, Boston Edison Company and Massachusetts Electric Company (MECo—the Massachusetts retail company of New England Electric System [NEES]). Seven additional parties provided written comments. Of the total eleven parties—a modest number for rules of such import—only one commenter, the Massachusetts Public Interest Research Group (MASSPIRG), was not representing a utility, state agency, or legislator. Although the final rules (220 CMR 9.00) clarified some issues and established a preapproval review time of eight

---

Table 5-4. Division of Risks in Proposed Preapproval Ratemaking Rules

Risks Shouldered by Utilities

1. Construction costs (including inflation)
2. Operation and maintenance costs
3. Unforeseen government regulation (e.g., environmental, safety, and health)
4. Plant performance
5. Cost of capital

Risks Shouldered by Ratepayers

1. Decreased demand
2. Fuel price volatility
3. Decreased cost of alternative energy resources

Source: Based on Mass. D.P.U. 86-36-C (1988a).

months, no other substantive changes were made from the proposed rules despite continued criticism (Mass. D.P.U. 86-36-E [1988c]).

The proposed preapproval rules represent a significant substantive departure from traditional ratemaking practices, and with their adoption Massachusetts headed into territory uncharted by other state PUCs. Though receiving general support from many parties, the rules have become increasingly controversial since they were adopted.[25]

Despite the few embellishments to the minimal legal rulemaking requirements used to formulate the preapproval rules, the process remained fairly traditional. I note several potential shortcomings: First, although the DPU initiated the rulemaking by claiming that the purpose was "to exchange ideas," the exchange remained extremely formal, with the DPU issuing orders and posing questions and commenters responding. Although both the DPU's and participants' positions were given some room to evolve through an iterative process of orders and comments, no real dialogue ever occurred. Questioning of the participants on the record by the commissioners and staff during the formal hearings did not really constitute a dialogue. Certainly any discussions that may have occurred were bilateral (that is, between the DPU and a single participant), and no free-flowing discussion between the DPU and the interested parties, or among the parties, occurred. Even the formal questioning was limited since no hearings were held between the interim order and the proposed rules. Furthermore, given the importance of the rules, a surprisingly limited number of parties, including only one public interest group, participated in the rulemaking process.

No real effort was made in the preapproval rulemaking to build consensus on either the main thrust of the rules or specific implementation details. Although informal comments are permitted in rulemaking (that is, interested parties speaking directly to staff or commissioners is allowed), my interviews and my own observations show that little of this occurred.[26] Given that (1) the commission delivered its final decision to implement a preapproval approach in the proposed rules rather than in the final rules and (2) virtually none of the detailing changed between the proposed regulations and the final regulations despite numerous critical comments, the commission apparently made up its mind by the time proposed rules were promulgated.

Most of those interviewed on the IRM case who also participated in the preapproval rulemaking maintained that the preapproval rules could have benefited from infusing technical sessions or other consensus-building supplements into the rulemaking process. They suggested that such processes could have helped in conceptualizing the overall framework as well as in fleshing out the details[27] and that such supplemental sessions might have clarified several issues that are being litigated in recent cases involving the application of the preapproval rules (for example, the case involving Boston Edison Company's Edgar Station).

The IRM Rulemaking Process

The process used to develop the IRM regulations is shown in Table 5-5.

The process included several significant modifications to the more traditional rulemaking process used to develop the preapproval rules. First, rather than moving directly to formal comments and hearings after issuing an interim order, the DPU sponsored four half-day technical sessions to discuss the proposed regulatory framework with interested parties (step 4). Second, after holding formal hearings and issuing proposed rules, the DPU again sponsored four half-day technical sessions, this time to discuss the proposed rules with interested parties (step 7). Lastly, although both the preapproval and the IRM rulemaking process issued interim orders that are not generally required in rulemaking proceedings, the IRM interim order went further than the preapproval order by including a detailed description of a potential new regulatory framework that it wished to use as a starting text for further discussion and comment (step 3, Mass. D.P.U. 86-36-F [1988d]).

Table 5-5. Massachusetts IRM Rulemaking Steps

Step 1: Announce opening of investigation; pose questions (Mass. D.P.U. 86-36-B, November 1987 [1987b])

Step 2: Six (plus) days of formal hearings; receive written comments (December 1987–June 1988)

Step 3: Issue order including some final DSM policies and proposal for IRM structure; pose questions on IRM proposal (Mass. D.P.U. 86-36-F, November 1988 [1988d])

Step 4: Four half-day technical sessions (December 1988–February 1989)

Step 5: Three days of formal hearings; receive written comments (February–March 1989)

Step 6: Issue proposed rules; request comments (Mass. D.P.U. 86-36-G, December 1989 [1989b])

Step 7: Four half-day technical sessions (January 1990)

Step 8: Four days of formal hearings; receive written comments (March–May 1990)

Step 9: Issue final rules (220 CMR 10.00; Mass. D.P.U. 89-239, August 1990 [1990b])

The IRM Proposal

Prior to the issuance of the interim order (Mass. D.P.U. 86-36-F [1988d]) in November 1988 (step 3), the DPU held over a half dozen days of formal hearings on energy planning, competitive bidding, and DSM issues. Many of the parties sponsored expert witnesses from across the United States to enter a broad range of information and experience into the record. DOER, which had been instrumental in formulating the DPU's QF regulations, presented a detailed proposal for IRM rules for the DPU's consideration. The DPU concurred with many of DOER's proposals but differed with others, most notably on the role of the utility in a new regulatory structure (DOER did not want the host utility to participate in an all-resource bidding process, whereas the DPU was more inclined to allow that). The DPU therefore decided to issue its own proposals.

The DPU attempted to address three primary objectives with its proposed regulatory framework. First, it wanted to see all resources—demand and supply, as well as utility- and nonutility-owned resources—better integrated in utility resource decision making. Second, it wanted to build on its QF regulations and proposed preapproval regulations by fostering greater competition for electricity resources and market-based pricing. Together these first two objectives are often called attempts "to level the playing field" between utility supply-side resources and other resource options. Lastly, the DPU wanted to further expand the criteria on which resources were selected by more formally including factors other than direct cost, most notably environmental externalities.

The DPU's proposed regulatory structure contained four phases, delineated in Mass. D.P.U. 86-36-F (1988d) and abstracted in Table 5-6.

Under this proposed new regulatory structure, each utility would conduct an all-resource solicitation every other year, and the entire process from the initial filing in Phase I to the approval of individual contracts in Phase IV—was slated to last seventeen months. Despite staggering the utilities' solicitations to facilitate reviews, the DPU specified that meeting this ambitious schedule would necessitate securing additional staff resources.

It is worth mentioning at this juncture that the DPU's proposed regulatory structure represented a significant departure from the prevailing modes of resource decision making and regulation used across the country. First, whereas most utilities that engaged in what is often called least-cost integrated planning (or integrated resource planning) in other jurisdictions focused on a "planning" model, the DPU's proposed approach focused more on a "market-driven" model. Both ap-

Table 5-6. Four Phases of Proposed IRM Structure

Phase I

- The utility submits to the DPU and EFSC for review and approval its (1) demand forecast, (2) inventory of committed resources (existing and planned), (3) technically feasible uncommitted DSM resources, (4) potentially viable plant life extension, and (5) an all-resource RFP (request for proposals) solicitation proposal.

Phase II

- The utility issues its approved all-resource RFP solicitation, receives bids from third parties, submits bids itself, ranks all the projects, selects a final portfolio of projects, and submits it to the DPU as its integrated resource plan for review and approval.

Phase III

- The DPU reviews the integrated resource plan to make sure that the utility properly applied the approved RFP criteria and that there was no self-dealing (that is, the utility unfairly favoring its own projects). The DPU also conducts a preapproval investigation regarding the cost-recovery terms of any utility project in the final mix.

Phase IV

- The utility negotiates final contracts with resource providers and submits them to the DPU for review and approval.

Source: Abstracted from Mass. D.P.U. 86-36-F (1988d).

proaches begin similarly with a determination of need based on projections of demand and committed resources. However, the "planning" model relies on the utility to identify a combination of specific or generic project types that could best meet the projected need. The identification and procurement of resources, while often rigorously conducted under the "planning" model, is somewhat ad hoc as it relies on a utility's skills in identifying alternatives. The Northwest Power Planning Council and the utilities in Wisconsin have been leaders in applying this approach. In contrast, the DPU proposed to use a "market-based" all-resource bidding process as a means of identifying and procuring needed resources.

Second, the DPU's proposed all-resource solicitation process also differed from bidding processes that utilities were implementing in other states. Although utilities in other states were beginning to expand their QF bidding process to include bids from independent power producers (IPPs) and demand-side management (DSM) providers (for example, Central Maine Power and several New York and New Jersey utilities), no other state was proposing that utilities participate in their own solicitation processes. Concerned that a true least-cost portfolio could not be achieved unless utility resources competed head-to-head with the resources of third-party suppliers, the DPU's proposed structure allowed utilities to participate in their own solicitation. In fact, the DPU's proposal actually required the utility to bid a portfolio of projects that would cover the entire need, based on the utility's "obligation to serve," just in case better projects did not emerge from the solicitation process.

In addition to the proposed IRM structure, the interim order also included policy statements and findings with respect to DSM. Table 5-7 outlines the major DSM policies enunciated in Mass. D.P.U. 86-36-F (1988d). Unlike the proposed IRM structure, which would eventually be reformulated, first into proposed and then final rules, the DSM policies were adopted as DPU policy as of the issuance of the order on November 30, 1988.[28]

The Decision to Use Technical Sessions

As discussed, the commission could legally have simply issued proposed IRM rules, taken public comment, and then issued final regulations. Instead, they chose to issue an interim order that contained a description of a potential new regulatory framework and to hold technical sessions prior to receiving formal comments. Both decisions stemmed from the same basic objective—to provide parties with a greater opportunity to participate in and contribute to the process of formulating the regulations. In addition, the DPU hoped that increasing the public's input into the decision would result in greater public acceptance of the rules that resulted.

The interim order (Mass. D.P.U. 86-36-F [1988d]) represented the commission's disposition at the time, based largely on the evidence in the proceeding thus far. However, the commission was well aware that it was proposing a major restructuring of the industry that needed substantial public review and debate. The DPU sought feedback on all aspects of its proposal, which clearly contained many unresolved, or partially resolved, issues. Specifically, it sought input on the issues that represented the greatest changes to the existing regulatory structure and which it correctly suspected would engender the greatest controversy. These issues included

1. whether utilities should participate in their own solicitations.
2. how much flexibility utilities should have in selecting resources once they are identified (that is, whether they should adhere to

Table 5-7. DSM Policies in D.P.U. 86-36-F

1. Utilities must use a "societal" cost-effectiveness test when evaluating resource decisions including DSM. Such a test must include environmental externalities and, for DSM, any additional costs and benefits to the customers.[a]
2. Utility DSM programs must attempt to capture all potential lost opportunities, avoid cream skimming, and pay particular attention to hard-to-reach sectors (e.g., rental housing, small commercial businesses).[b]
3. Utilities must file an annual status report on their DSM programs with the DPU.[c]
4. Large utility DSM programs are eligible for preapproval under the preapproval rules developed for utility supply-side resources.
5. Utilities have the option to either expense their DSM expenditures or amortize them with a return. Utilities can also apply for compensation for any unforeseen revenue loss between rate cases as a result of their DSM programs.[d]

Source: Abstracted from Mass. D.P.U. 86-36-F (1988d).

[a] The order specifically rejected the "no-losers" test, which would limit utility investment in DSM to the difference between a utility's marginal avoided cost and average rates. The "societal" test requires utilities to pay up to the utility's full avoided cost plus any costs associated with environmental damages for DSM resources. However, although the DPU required utilities to include environmental externalities in their cost-effectiveness screening, it did not provide formulas or numbers to do so. Instead, the order urged interested parties to work together to develop a proposal (Mass. D.P.U. 86-36-F [1988d]).

[b] "Lost opportunities" can result from the failure to capture cost-effective DSM savings at the time when it is most practical and inexpensive to do so—for example, when a building is first constructed or when a customer replaces mechanical equipment. "Cream skimming" is the act of installing only those DSM measures with the highest benefit/cost ratio, without capturing all other cost-effective DSM. Cream skimming can often lead to lost opportunities since it may be uneconomic to return to a customer's premises at a later date. "Hard-to-reach sectors," such as low-income customers, generally have greater market barriers that hinder their participation in DSM programs.

[c] The annual DSM filing format was issued several months later by staff after conducting two half-day informal technical sessions with the utilities and other interested parties to work through the DPU's proposed format. The process was successful at developing common definitions for the terms and smoothing out many, but not all, of the rough edges in the filing format.

[d] In Massachusetts, Mass. D.P.U. 86-36-F (1988d) gave utilities the clear option of selecting "expense treatment" for their DSM investment, wherein they recoup their investments essentially in the year they are incurred, but without return. Alternatively they can select "amortization treatment," wherein they recoup only a portion of their expenses each year, plus a return on the unamortized balance. Utilities can also recoup any lost revenue that may occur when DSM decreases energy sales below the anticipated sales used to determine rates in the prior rate case. It can therefore erode expected revenue and serve as a disincentive to the aggressive pursuit of DSM by utilities. It is an important historical note that additional positive financial incentives, such as shared savings, were not mentioned in the order nor widely discussed at the time. Additional financial incentives were first approved by the DPU in Mass. D.P.U. 89-194/195 (1990a) in the DSM preapproval case for MECo.

a strict self-scoring system or be allowed to pick and choose according to a more subjective evaluation).
3. whether demand-side resources and supply-side resources should be integrated into a single solicitation, and if so, how.
4. whether existing and planned resources should be considered committed, or whether they should be eligible for replacement through the IRM process.
5. whether utilities should be allowed to procure any resources outside of an IRM solicitation process.
6. whether the seventeen-month time frame for the process was workable (that is, short enough so that projects would not be stale, but long enough to allow for adequate review).
7. how environmental externalities associated with electric generation should be valued and included in IRM.
8. how public involvement in the IRM process itself could be enhanced.

Later in the proceeding, the DPU would also query participants regarding whether utilities needed additional financial incentives to better guarantee their diligent pursuit of IRM objectives.[29] In addition to all of these broad policy questions, the interim order also included many specific questions on implementation details.

The commission explored a range of options with staff to enhance public involvement in the IRM rulemaking process and decided to pursue a highly structured technical session process. Bernice McIntyre, chair of the commission, described their goals in adding technical sessions to the traditional rulemaking process in her opening remarks at the first technical session in December 1988:

> Our decision not to proceed immediately with proposed regulations, and to use facilitated technical sessions is an attempt to give all of you maximum input into these crucial regulations. We hope that we can accomplish several objectives during these sessions: First, we want to make sure that all of you fully understand the regulatory framework that we have outlined in Mass. D.P.U. 86-36-F. This includes both the details of the most recent Order, and the rationale behind all aspects of our proposed regulatory framework. Second, we want to hear from all of you about the parts of our proposed regulatory framework that you support and those parts that you do not. Third, we would like to examine—together—any suggestions you may have for improving the proposal. Lastly, we expect that the formal public hearings that will begin shortly after these technical sessions conclude, will be even

more focused and productive than usual as a result of our efforts here.

Several points regarding the commission's decision to use technical sessions need to be underscored. First, although technical sessions had been used at the DPU on prior issues, the ones proposed here were significantly more ambitious in many respects, most notably their number and size and their use of outside facilitation. Second, although the commission hoped to accomplish much during the sessions, they were viewed as supplemental enhancements to the formal hearing and subsequent comment process. Lastly, although the commission hoped that the sessions would reveal areas of general agreement and disagreement with respect to its proposed rules, it did not view them as a formal attempt to reach consensus among the parties.

At the staff's suggestion, the commission considered more active consensus-building processes, such as negotiated rulemaking, but rejected them in favor of a technical session process. Former commissioner Robert Werlin explained during our interview that the commission was skeptical that a consensus could emerge from a negotiated rulemaking given the complexity and controversial nature of the proposed IRM structure and was afraid that if one did emerge, it might be unacceptable to them.

The Technical Sessions

Altogether, ten half-day technical sessions were used in the course of finalizing the IRM rules for both the DPU and the EFSC.[30] Four were held between December 1988 and February 1989 to consider the proposed regulatory framework described in the interim order (Mass. D.P.U. 86-36-F [1988d]). An additional four were held in January 1990 to consider the DPU's actual proposed regulations (Mass. D.P.U. 86-36-G [1989b]). Finally, the EFSC hosted two sessions in August 1990 to consider its proposed regulations covering its portion of the IRM structure (that is, the approval of the demand forecast, committed resources, and resource need) (EFSC 90-RM-100 [1990]). Since the DPU's rulemaking is the focus of this case study, the following discussion of the technical sessions exclusively examines the eight sessions hosted by the DPU, unless otherwise noted.

Structural Overview

The DPU's technical sessions differed somewhat between the first and the second round. During the first round, the participants spent most of their time in three groups of twenty-five to thirty participants. Each participating organization was invited to send two representatives, and the DPU staff preselected the small groups with an eye to balancing the different interests within each of them. Each group included a DPU staffperson and a professional facilitator from outside the DPU. On the first day, the groups brainstormed on the strengths and weaknesses of the DPU's IRM proposal. The entire group usually assembled at the beginning and end of each day to share information and ideas. The agendas for the remaining three sessions were based on the first day's discussions. Although the commissioners opened the first session and returned at the end of the fourth, they were not present throughout.

The second round of technical sessions, which occurred after the DPU issued actual proposed rules, did not use small groups. Instead, a single representative from each organization sat around one enormous table during all four sessions, and one facilitator was used. DPU and EFSC staff actively participated in the second round, although the commissioners were not present. The agendas were essentially preset in the invitation letters mailed with the proposed rules, although some changes occurred in the course of the sessions.

The change in structure between the first round of technical sessions and the second underscored the slightly different purpose contemplated for each. The first round was clearly a time for participants to familiarize themselves with the DPU's proposal and the interests and perspectives of other parties. It was also a time when the commission was most interested in soliciting alternatives to its proposals. As such, small-group brainstorming worked best to provide each individual with both maximum exposure and input. In the second round, the DPU and the facilitator believed that less time was needed for parties to understand the proposed rules or the interests and perspectives of others since much groundwork had been laid in the first round of sessions. At the same time, although the commission was still not seeking a formal consensus from the group, it did hope to clearly identify areas of convergence and divergence, and to solicit any suggestions for fine-tuning the proposed regulations. It was determined that one group with representatives from the interested parties better served this final focusing process than three smaller groups.

Participation

Approximately 85 people, not including the DPU or EFSC staffs or the facilitators, attended one or more of the technical sessions in the first round. A majority of the participants attended all four of them. In the second round, following the issuance of the proposed rules, despite the fact that only one representative from each organization was al-

Table 5-8. IRM Technical Sessions Participants

Type	Number	Percent
Utilities	11	15%
Government	7	10%
Nonutility providers		
Supply-side	25	35%
Demand-side	8	11%
Environmental and consumer groups	5	7%
Other [a]	15	21%
TOTAL	71	99% [b]

[a] "Other" includes consulting firms, law firms, private citizens, and academics.
[b] Does not equal 100% because of rounding.

lowed around the table (alternates were invited to sit outside the circle), approximately 110 people attended at least one of the sessions. Again these participants did not include the DPU or EFSC staff. Table 5-8 lists the participating organizations by type and shows that seventy-one organizations attended at least one of the eight technical sessions (130 people altogether).

The seventy-one organizations greatly exceeded the eleven organizations that participated in the preapproval rulemaking that had immediately preceded the IRM process. Two factors of seemingly equal importance account for this. First, the preapproval rules directly apply only to utility-owned resources. Even though the rules could greatly influence a utility's inclination to build its own resources instead of buying from third-party providers, the earlier rulemaking attracted only a handful of nonutility parties and no one from the development community. In contrast, the potentially sweeping impact on energy planning and procurement practices in Massachusetts of the IRM rules was obvious to everyone from the outset.

Second, as many of the interviewees mentioned, the technical sessions were a far more inviting and accessible process than the formal notice-and-comment process, particularly for organizations that do not regularly appear before the DPU. Whereas in the formal process, parties are merely given notice regarding the existence of hearings, the DPU actually sent letters to individuals, directly inviting the groups concerned to the technical sessions.

Also, the technical sessions were conducted in a significantly different atmosphere from the normal hearing room process. The sessions took place away from the DPU's windowless hearing room with its uncomfortable wooden pews facing the elevated bench where the commission and staff preside. Instead, the sessions were held in an old mansion owned by the Boston Adult Education Center in the Back Bay section of Boston. People sat around one large table or met in small groups. The DPU staff, which generally had little informal contact with interested parties because of ex parte rules, participated in all the sessions.[31] Finally, the presence of facilitators and occasionally the commissioners differentiated the sessions from the normal course of affairs.

As Table 5-8 illustrates, a broad spectrum of interested parties attended the sessions. Reflecting the sentiment of the vast majority of those interviewed, Steve Cowell, president of Conservation Services Group, Inc., described the attendance as follows: "Everyone who was anything in energy in Massachusetts attended the technical sessions. It was an extremely well-endowed group" (Cowell interview).

Despite the diverse participation, some of those interviewed lamented that more consumer groups (for example, low-income, small commercial, and large commercial and industrial) were not more directly represented, although they were indirectly represented through several state agencies, citizen groups, and law firms. In addition, several of the environmental and consumer groups interviewed mentioned that they felt at a disadvantage, in part because of the overwhelming number of utilities and supply-side developers in attendance (over 50 percent) and in part because their own limited resources curtailed their ability to fully participate. Despite these legitimate concerns, which hint at ways to improve subsequent rulemaking processes, it is important to stress here that the technical sessions used in the IRM rules represented a significant broadening of public participation compared with prior rulemaking and adjudicatory proceedings before the DPU.

Role of Staff and Commission

DPU staff took an active part in the technical sessions. During the first four sessions, a technical staff member was in each of the three small groups. In the last four sessions, the three technical staff members joined the other participants around the large table.[32] Their role was twofold. First, in both the small groups and the large group, staff acted as interpreters for the DPU, continuously describing to participants the DPU's proposals and, perhaps more importantly, the reasoning behind them. Second, staff acted as emissaries from the sessions to the commission, bringing criticisms, observations, and recommendations back to them after each session.

Staff opened most discussions with a brief presentation describing the DPU's proposals and posing one or more pointed questions to the group. Throughout the discussions, the technical staff clarified issues, reacted to suggestions, and assisted the facilitator in keeping the discussions focused on relevant issues.

All of those interviewed felt that the staff's participation was essential to the success of the process for both of the reasons described above. The evaluation forms completed by participants after each round rated the effectiveness of staff's serving as a technical resource extremely high (a mean of 5.1 out of 6 in both years). Of equal importance to staff's technical contribution during the sessions, however, was the exposure they gained to the concerns of the participants and the real complexities of the business side of resource development. This was invaluable to their subsequent efforts to assist the commission in formulating rules that were more practical and more responsive to the diverse interests.

The commission's direct participation in the technical sessions was rather limited. The commissioners initiated the first session with a brief statement followed by an opportunity for participants to question them on the proposed regulatory structure—a reversal of the normal course of affairs, in which the commission questions parties from the bench. The commission then returned at the end of the fourth session to hear comments first-hand and to discuss the issues raised by the participants. The commissioners did not attend the second set of sessions but did participate in the EFSC's two technical sessions.

Although some commissioners had more interest than others in participating directly in the technical sessions, they ultimately decided that the potential benefits of their regular attendance did not justify the potential of stifling the free-flowing dialogue. Most of those interviewed concurred that the commission's limited participation in the technical sessions was appropriate. Some, however, felt that the process would have benefited from greater access to the commissioners on the one hand, and greater exposure of the commission to their views on the other.

Facilitation

The commission found staff's argument for outside facilitation compelling and made arrangements with Massachusetts Mediation Service (which has since changed its name to the Office of Dispute Resolution) to secure facilitation services.[33] David O'Connor, the executive director of that office, was the lead facilitator throughout both the DPU and EFSC technical sessions. To facilitate the other two small group sessions in the first round of sessions, the DPU hired John McGlennon and Peter Schneider of ERM-McGlennon, Inc., both of whom had experience mediating negotiated rulemaking processes sponsored by the EPA.

Given the large number of participants and complexity of the issues being discussed, facilitation was necessary to keep the sessions focused. Outside facilitation also freed staff to participate in the substantive discussions. In addition, the facilitators brought a level of expertise to the role that PUC staff do not generally possess.

In the formal evaluations after both rounds of technical sessions, participants claimed that the facilitators managed the sessions effectively (a mean of 4.9 and 5.2 in 1989 and 1990, respectively). The follow-up interviews revealed overall enthusiasm for the use of facilitation in general, and David O'Connor's performance specifically. Although some wished that he had more technical expertise, others felt that his level of technical expertise was adequate for acting as a facilitator and that he also was able to make some insightful and useful substantive suggestions. With respect to consensus building, some felt that O'Connor's natural inclination to push for consensus from his mediation work seemed inappropriate at times and actually hindered the free flow of ideas. In contrast, others felt that they would have liked to see him push for consensus more aggressively.

Substantive Results of the Technical Sessions

As Table 5-9 reveals, much ground was covered during the two rounds of technical sessions, and the breadth was consistent with the broad scope of the emerging IRM rules themselves. The first round focused on the major theoretical and policy questions. The second revisited some of the issues but generally focused on critical implementation details. This evolution is not surprising as the proposed rules confirmed many of the commission's predispositions hinted at in the interim order (for example, the need to include the host utility in the solicitation process). The second round also addressed environmental externalities and ratemaking issues in response to significant concerns raised by the DPU in the order accompanying the proposed regulations (Mass. D.P.U. 86-36-G [1989b]).

The substantive discussions in the sessions were generally quite animated. However, although there was sufficient time to get a strong flavor of the issues, including the range and intensity of participants'

Table 5-9. Substantive Agenda of the Technical Sessions

Sessions After Interim Order (Mass. D.P.U. 86-36-F)

First session	(12/21/88)	Strengths and weaknesses of proposed structure
Second session	(1/4/89)	Role of utilities in the solicitation process
Third session	(1/18/89)	Integrating demand and supply resources
Fourth session	(2/1/89)	Intergovernmental coordination, timeline, and transition rules

Sessions After Proposed Rules (Mass. D.P.U. 86-36-G)

First session	(1/3/90)	Balancing flexibility and reviewability (utility projects, self-scoring, negotiation, optimization)
Second session	(1/10/90)	Other structural issues (resource selection criteria, prefiling settlement process, committed resources, acquiring resources outside IRM)
Third session	(1/17/90)	Environmental externalities
Fourth session	(1/24/90)	Transition rules and ratemaking treatment

Note: EFSC also held two technical sessions in August 1990 pertaining to its own proposed rules. The first session, on August 8, covered demand forecasting and the prefiling settlement process. The second session, on August 16, covered committed resources, planned resources, and resource need.

interests, there was insufficient time to explore or revisit issues in any depth. It is not surprising that 45 percent of the postsession survey respondents in 1989 and 27 percent in 1990 claimed that there was "too little" time allotted to the technical sessions, and that many of those interviewed lamented not having enough time to explore issues further. In contrast, less than 10 percent each time felt that "too much" time was spent.

Convergence of Opinion

The technical sessions were not a formal consensus-seeking process. No votes were ever taken, nor was consensus otherwise rigorously tested. Nonetheless, surprising areas of agreement were uncovered, and parties who had differed significantly found their opinions converging during the discussions. This convergence was noted by staff and facilitators during the course of the sessions and was reflected in the participants' testimony and comments during the formal steps in

Table 5-10. Areas of Convergence of Opinion During the Technical Sessions

1. Support for the overall principles of increasing competition and better integrating all resources.
2. Support for inclusion of a prefiling settlement phase preceding a utility's initial filing.
3. Support for utility negotiations with providers after the initial ranking of projects.
4. Support for a utility making its final resource selections on the basis of an analysis of its optimal portfolio of resources.
5. Preference for an environmental externality method that focused on impacts rather than on technologies.
6. Recognition of the need for increased coordination between the DPU and the EFSC in overseeing IRM and acceptance of the need for increased staffing at the two agencies to implement IRM.

the rulemaking. Finally, it was verified in the interviews. Table 5-10 highlights six areas of substantial convergence of opinion by participants that were first revealed during the technical sessions.

First, as noted in the table, although the notion of supporting the overall principles of increased competition and resource integration is fairly popular today, only a few years prior to the technical sessions, many of the participants argued against pursuing DSM and QF resources in a serious manner. The general acceptance and approval of these concepts by all the participants in the sessions, despite disagreements on how to accomplish these goals, is not trivial.

Second, the DPU suggested the inclusion of an eleven-week prefiling settlement process at the front end of the IRM regulations, during which interested parties could get together with the utility to try to settle its demand forecast, committed resources, need for power, and RFP criteria for the first time in its proposed rules (Mass. D.P.U. 86-36-G [1989b]). The proposal grew in part out of general discussions during the first round of technical sessions and formal comments regarding the need to streamline the process, and in part out of the DPU's increasing appreciation of the potential for greater use of consensus-building activities in implementing its policies in light of current rate case settlements, the DSM collaboratives, and the technical sessions themselves. With the exception of MASSPIRG, which feared that a prefiling settlement process might further disadvantage resource-constrained public interest groups, everyone was supportive of the concept. However, most parties were rather skeptical that wholesale settlement could be achieved given the short time frame and the complexity of the issues. They did believe, however, that a process could narrow subsequent litigation and better prepare utilities and intervenors alike.

Third and fourth, the technical sessions revealed participants' virtual unanimity as to providing utilities greater flexibility in selecting the final mix of resources in the IRM process by allowing them to renegotiate project details with developers and to base their final selection on an optimized portfolio analysis. These changes marked a significant departure from the QF regulations in force at the time, which required the awarding of contracts on the basis of a strict self-scoring ranking system. Everyone supported greater flexibility than the existing QF regulations afforded. However, participants differed about where to draw appropriate boundaries around a utility's ability to deviate from the original project ranking through negotiation and optimization, given markedly different concerns with respect to utility self-dealing. To a certain degree, parties' support for added flexibility can be traced to persuasive arguments made during the technical sessions by MECo about the success of its negotiation approach to acquiring QF power,[34] and by the Energy Lab at MIT with respect to the need to optimize the resource mix by basing final selection on a portfolio analysis approach using a production-costing model.[35]

Fifth, participants expressed a surprising amount of agreement during the sessions that including environmental externalities in IRM was reasonable. Even more surprising was participants' unanimous rejection of a simplified technology-based approach to environmental externalities proposed in Mass. D.P.U. 86-36-G (1989b). Instead of adding a fixed amount to the cost of electricity based on the technology used to generate it (for example, one level of environmental adder to coal-fired power and another level to gas-fired power), participants preferred to calculate the environmental adder on the basis of the impacts created by the emissions (for example, one adder per pound of SO_x and another adder per pound of NO_x). Although participants disagreed on how to derive such an impact-based approach (that is, whether monetization was necessary and whether the cost of control represented an adequate proxy for damage costs), they all clearly favored using a more complex and disaggregated one.

Last, everyone agreed that the IRM process would benefit if the DPU and EFSC's reviews were better coordinated. Parties also accepted the need for both agencies to increase their staff to implement IRM—regardless of its ultimate form. Proof of the participants' support for increased staffing and agency funding came after the technical sessions ended but prior to the issuing of the final regulations. At that point, and in the midst of major budget cuts for virtually all other state agencies, the governor signed a bill providing the DPU and the EFSC with approximately $1 million per year to increase their staffs to implement IRM.[36]

Ongoing Controversies

Convergence on some issues during the technical sessions definitely occurred, as described in the preceding section. However, other issues remained controversial and divisive. Table 5-11 highlights several issues in which substantial disagreement persisted.

First, as noted in the table, despite the theoretical appeal of allowing the utilities to compete head-to-head with other providers in an all-resource solicitation, participants such as DOER and the Attorney General remained unconvinced that adequate protection could be mustered against self-dealing. Second, the utilities and some of the developers voiced strong opposition to exposing their existing and planned resources to possible displacement through the solicitation process. They felt this way even if those units were not part of the least-cost mix, and even if they would be financially compensated. Third, although parties generally agreed on including externalities as part of the RFP evaluation criteria and rejected a simplified approach based on technology, they strongly disagreed about what constituted adequate impact-based methods and values. One group—led by DOER, environmentalists, DSM providers, and Boston Gas Company—proposed higher externality values than any other state had adopted to

---

Table 5-11. Issues in Which Substantial Disagreement Persisted

1. Whether utilities should be permitted to participate in their own solicitation processes.
2. Whether existing or planned resources should be considered eligible for displacement through the solicitation process, or whether they should be considered committed resources.
3. Whether environmental externalities needed to be monetized to be included in the solicitation criteria, and if so, whether using the cost-of-control technology was the appropriate approach.
4. Whether DSM bidding should be included, excluded, or phased into an all-resource solicitation process.
5. Whether the initial ranking of resources should be based strictly on a self-scoring system.
6. Whether the DPU's proposed seventeen-month timeline was appropriate.

date, basing their values on the cost of pollution control. The electric utilities, on the other hand, wanted to use a weighting and ranking approach and recommended much lower externality values. The disagreement between these two camps was not new, as the parties had reached the same impasse during an attempted collaborative process on the subject undertaken at the DPU's encouragement between April and June of 1989.

Fourth, the DSM energy service companies (ESCOs) were pushing hard for a fully integrated demand- and supply-side solicitation process. Meanwhile, the electric utilities and all four nonutility parties that were engaged in a collaborative process to design comprehensive DSM programs for the utilities (DOER, the Attorney General, CLF, and MASSPIRG) argued for providing the nascent utility DSM programs with a "safe harbor" from competition for the near future. The utilities and nonutility parties involved in the DSM collaboratives claimed that an all-resource solicitation could undo their efforts in launching comprehensive DSM programs for each utility and result in paying too much for DSM and in cream skimming (that is, getting the most cost-effective DSM, but leaving other cost-effective DSM untouched). The ESCOs countered that all-resource bidding did not necessarily lead to expensive DSM or cream skimming, but that the "safe harbor" proposal would effectively reduce competition and shut them out of the market by locking up all the DSM technical potential in the utility programs (Raab 1990).

Fifth, many participants maintained that the initial ranking should be based on a strict self-scoring formula, even though almost everyone was willing to provide the utilities a certain degree of flexibility in selecting an optimized final resource mix, provided it did not result in self-dealing. Others argued against using a strict self-scoring approach in favor of an approach that gave the utilities greater flexibility in the initial ranking as well. Last, developers and utilities generally kept pushing for a tighter timeline to avoid the problem of projects becoming stale, whereas intervenors like the Attorney General and MASSPIRG kept arguing that they needed more time for review and potential litigation than the current proposal allowed.

Despite the fact that there were still many issues involving major disagreements at the end of the technical sessions, the groups had reasonably aired the substantive issues. As a result, everyone came to understand the opposing perspectives more clearly, as well as the complex tradeoffs associated with changing any one aspect of the rules. As Harvey Salgo, formerly of TELLUS Institute and representing DOER during the sessions, observed in our interview, "The most striking, and perhaps the only real, consensus reached during the technical sessions was a shared appreciation for the complexity of the issues." As will be seen, a greater understanding of this complexity by the staff and the participants contributed to both more palatable and more practical rules and to a more successful rulemaking process generally.

Formal Rulemaking Process and Final Rules

At the end of the first round of technical sessions, comments were filed, and three days of formal hearings were held. Nine months after the comments were received, the DPU issued proposed rules, in December 1989. After the second round of technical sessions was held in January 1990, four days of hearings were held in March and April 1990, during which twenty interested parties testified. Written comments were received from thirty-two interested parties in May. Final rules were issued in August. At both rounds of hearings, the commission heard all the testimony and questioned the commenters directly.

For both the proposed and final rules, staff met often with the commission to help forge a rule that was responsive to the issues and concerns raised during the technical sessions, formal hearings, and comments and that all three commissioners could support. Extensive meetings were also held between the DPU and the EFSC during these periods to work through coordination issues and to assist each other in the development of the two agencies' respective rules.

Many of the technical session participants interviewed said that their formal comments were much more informed and focused as a result of the technical sessions. Former commissioner Robert Werlin, a recipient of those comments, concurred:

> The technical sessions were extremely helpful in providing us with better comments. The sessions provided an iterative process that successfully funneled the comments. Proposals that we were getting in the formal comments were already compromises. As such, we got a much better glimpse of the middle ground A traditional rulemaking would've been much more positional, and we would have had to pull teeth in the hearings to try and separate the parties' underlying interests from their positions. (Werlin interview)

It is my observation that staff found it much easier to understand the comments and immediately identify any changes in perspective or new ideas after having discussed all the issues and heard the parties' interests expressed during the technical sessions.

The DPU and EFSC did an enormous amount of work crafting both the proposed and final rules. They attempted to find the right balance between what often felt like disparate goals of stimulating competition, maintaining utility discretion, taking a societal perspective, and guaranteeing adequate reviewability. The issues discussed in the previous section, regardless of whether there was a convergence of opinion, could not be considered in isolation as they are all interdependent pieces of the IRM framework. Changing one piece of the puzzle often required rethinking numerous other pieces—if not the entire structure.

When convergence was revealed during the technical sessions and formal hearings, the final rules incorporated it in every case, despite the fact that the DPU was legally free to do otherwise. When there was no convergence, difficult policy choices were made by the commission after careful consideration of the record established over the course of both the informal technical session process and the formal hearings and comments. In every case, the DPU understood the ramifications of its decisions much better than it would have without the benefit of the technical session process. Table 5-12 highlights the major changes and refinements to the IRM structure as they appear in the final rules (Mass. D.P.U. 89-239 [1990b]) in contrast to the original proposals of the interim order (Mass. D.P.U. 86-36-F [1988d]) (delineated in Table 5-6).

Evaluating the Success of the IRM Rulemaking Process

Evaluating the success of the facilitated technical session process used in formulating Massachusetts IRM rules vis-à-vis traditional notice-and-comment rulemaking requires a comparative analysis of the process-related resources, the perceived legitimacy of both the process and the final results, and the practicality of the rules themselves.

Process-Related Resource Savings

The DPU's eight technical sessions cost the DPU approximately $15,000 to hire the facilitators, rent the elegant but inexpensive meeting rooms at the Boston Adult Education Center, and provide refreshments at each session. Massachusetts Mediation Service contributed limited additional funds and services from its own budget to the facilitation pool for the first round of technical sessions. The two rounds of technical sessions required approximately six hundred person-days (a little more than two full-time person-years) of time, assuming an average of seventy-five people attended eight DPU-sponsored technical sessions for a full day for each session (that is, attendance, travel, preparation, and debriefing).

Notably, the vast majority of participants (that is, over 90 percent

Table 5-12. Major Changes and Refinements in the Final IRM Rules

Prefiling Settlement Process (11 Weeks)
- The DPU adds an eleven-week prefiling settlement process to the front end of the process to help educate interested parties with respect to a utility's Phase I filing and parties' interests and concerns, to settle issues when possible, and to better focus subsequent litigation. Process must begin with a technical session.[a]

Phase I (5 Months)
- In addition to filing its demand forecast, inventories of committed resources and uncommitted DSM resources, and an all-resource RFP solicitation proposal, the utility must submit detailed descriptions of each of the projects it intends to propose as its response to its own RFP. This requirement, which the DPU included as a means of diminishing concerns of self-dealing, does not, however, include the project price, which the utility must submit concurrent with the other bids.
- Utilities must include in their RFP selection criteria environmental adders based on impacts (rather than technologies). The DPU adopts specific adders submitted by DOER and Boston Gas and based on cost of control. (These adders represent the highest values adopted by any PUC in the country at the time [see Appendix 3].)
- The DPU reduces the possibility of considering existing and planned resources as uncommitted (that is, decreases eligibility for displacement through the solicitation process) except in extraordinary circumstances.
- The DPU and EFSC require joint filing instead of two separate ones.[b] Filings will be considered approved as submitted if the DPU cannot complete its review in the time allotted.

Phase II (7 Months)
- Utilities must allow for DSM bidding but are permitted to use either a combined or separate solicitation process. DPU-preapproved utility DSM programs have status as committed resources and are protected in the near term.
- The DPU makes a rigid self-scoring system optional for the initial ranking of projects but requires weights for each broad category of criteria (for example, utilities will evaluate diversity, price) and an explicit qualitative description of how each criterion will be evaluated.
- Utilities may deviate from the rank order of bid resources (actually the re-ranked order after negotiations) on the basis of an optimized portfolio analysis of different groupings of projects in conjunction with their existing and planned resource mix.
- Utilities must negotiate with projects representing 130 percent of need in rank order to improve the projects. The DPU gives utilities the option to negotiate with additional projects.

Table 5-12. *(continued)*

Phase III (3 Months)

- No major changes. DPU still reviews final resource mix to make sure that the utility properly selected resources according to the approved criteria (with modifications based on optimizing the entire portfolio) and that there was no self-dealing. The only modification is the decision to move the preapproval process of successful utility resources to Phase IV, which is the time that all other projects are negotiating final contracts.

Phase IV (5 Months)

- No additional changes besides inclusion of utility preapproval process. Utilities negotiate final contracts with award group and seek approvals from the DPU.

Other Highlights

- *Overall timeline:* The DPU changes the overall timeline of the process from seventeen months as originally proposed to twenty months (not including the prefiling settlement process).
- *Transition rules:* The DPU orders utilities to expand the QF bidding process to include IPPs (but not DSM) and to apply environmental externality adders in any bid process or DSM program design during the transition period to IRM.
- *Incentive ratemaking:* DPU approves the use of incentive ratemaking for utility DSM programs, as well as for the purchasing of nonutility resources (both supply- and demand-side) but defers specifics to case-by-case basis.

Source: Based on Mass. D.P.U. 86-36-F (1988d) and Mass. D.P.U. 89-239 (1990b).

[a] Discussions and positions taken by parties during the course of settlement negotiations will not be admissible or subject to discovery during any adjudicatory proceeding, although facts disclosed during the process are discoverable. Any settlement, partial settlement, or contested settlement reached by the parties will be filed with the DPU and the EFSC as a component of the company's initial filing (980 CMR 12.03 [4]).

[b] EFSC findings on the adequacy of a utility's demand forecast, committed resources, resource need, and resource potential will be adopted by the DPU and reflected in its review of the utility's solicitation proposal.

in both rounds) claimed in the postsession evaluations that the amount of time allotted to the technical sessions was "just right" or "too little," with a distinct minority claiming that "too much" time was spent in technical sessions (see Appendix 2). This evaluation represents at least an informal, "first-cut" indication by the participants that the benefits of the time and effort they dedicated to the technical sessions outweighed the costs.

Although the cost side of the equation is relatively straightforward, estimating the gross and net benefits (that is, benefits minus costs) is more complicated. In many respects, the formal portions of the rulemaking process proceeded in virtually the same way as they would have without the technical sessions in terms of holding hearings, filing comments, and writing the orders and rules. In fact, without the technical sessions, the DPU probably would have skipped the interim policy piece (Mass. D.P.U. 86-36-F [1988d]) and issued proposed rules directly. Also, the time-consuming and expensive processes of adjudicatory proceedings—issuing discovery, allowing parties to cross-examine one another, and writing briefs—are not typical in rulemaking and therefore cannot be counted as savings here (despite the assumptions to the contrary of many of those interviewed). However, as numerous interviewees pointed out, the formal testimony and written comments were more finely focused than they would have been without the technical sessions, and this in turn facilitated the commission's decision making and the drafting of the rules and orders. Since parties proceeded to write lengthy comments, and the DPU wrote detailed orders, any savings that may have occurred in this regard were probably small.

It is also true that the IRM rules were not appealed to the state Supreme Judicial Court (SJC) and that the technical sessions may have contributed to parties' greater acceptance of the final rules. However, as discussed in the first part of this chapter, although appeal of administrative rules is fairly common in federal agencies, such appeals are much rarer at the state level. According to Jerrold Oppenheim, assistant attorney general in Massachusetts, "parties would generally be hesitant to appeal new rules here because they are well aware of the SJC's inclination to defer judgment on technical issues to administrative agencies, thus making a successful appeal of a rule such as IRM unlikely" (Oppenheim interview). Therefore, the avoidance of the cost of an appeal should probably not be credited to the technical sessions. In any case, appeals of this sort are usually made on fairly narrow grounds and, although requiring some resources to prepare briefs and argue before the SJC, are not nearly as resource-intensive as a fully litigated case.

Another process-related benefit could be claimed if the technical sessions contributed to a better understanding and acceptance of the rules and improved compliance while reducing costly future litigation associated with implementation. Although it is certainly too early to evaluate this issue, it is worth noting that the first utility to go through the IRM process, MECo, settled the case with a wide range of intervenors prior to the beginning of litigation.[37]

On balance, it is not clear that the technical sessions saved any resources related to the rulemaking process itself, although they may save process-related resources in the long run. However, in addition to the process-related costs and benefits described above, as discussed in Chapter 3, it is also critical to assess whether the regulations themselves are better because of the supplemental process. If so, the net benefits to society are likely to be substantial given the relatively insignificant costs described above. In separate interviews, both Robert Werlin, then commissioner and former chair of the DPU, and Robert Shapiro, then executive director of the EFSC, expressed their firm belief that because the sessions improved the final rules, their inclusion in the rulemaking process was a definite net societal gain.

Legitimacy

The addition of technical sessions and the decision to issue an interim order prior to releasing proposed rules enhanced the legitimacy of the traditional rulemaking process and made the final rules more palatable to the public. The mere fact that the process elicited the active involvement of more participants, representing a larger number and broader spectrum of society than any prior proceeding before the DPU (over 130 people from seventy-one organizations), suggests this possibility. However, the critical advantage of adding the technical sessions to the traditional process was that the technical sessions provided the participants with a better forum for (1) understanding what was being proposed, (2) hearing the interests of other participants, (3) exploring the strengths and weaknesses of various alternative proposals, and (4) having an opportunity to try to persuade others to adopt their viewpoint. As Robert Fratto of COM/Electric explains, the sense of having been better heard because of the technical sessions added to the acceptability of the rules.

> The rules represented major policies that affect the entire way that utilities operate. However, the rules were much more palatable to a wider audience because more people had a real opportunity to provide input through the technical sessions, and the DPU was generally responsive to that input. (Fratto interview)

Consensus was not actively sought during the technical sessions. However, whenever a convergence of perspectives did emerge, it appeared in the final regulations. This convergence of opinion could not have emerged as strongly from the formal notice-and-comment process. First, convergence happened only at the tail end of lengthy discussions of particular issues (for example, the issue of increased flexibility to negotiate and optimize). Second, in the formal process, parties tend to focus their comments almost exclusively on the issues of greatest concern to them, often completely omitting certain issues. The technical sessions ferreted out opinions on a broader range of issues than would likely have emerged in the formal process. Lastly, the technical sessions allowed the participants and the DPU staff to observe the range and intensity of comments in a way that was far more compressed in both time and space, and thus easier to understand, than in a formal process that is spread over days of hearings and mountains of written comments. As Rolly Rouse, former chief operating officer of Citizens Conservation Corporation, aptly observed, "The technical sessions allowed everyone to see the entire picture all at once, thus avoiding the blind-person-and-the-elephant syndrome" (Rouse interview).

The ability to see the whole picture at once allowed some convergence of opinion and allowed the staff to propose alternatives to the commission, which, it believed, would better address the participants' diverse interests. The incorporation of any emerging consensus from the technical sessions and formal comments further legitimized the process.

Even in areas in which differing perspectives were sustained throughout the technical session process and formal comments, participants still had a greater understanding of the opposing arguments and a respect for the commission's difficult decisions than if no technical sessions had been used. This heightened sensitivity also added to the enhanced legitimacy of the final rules. Richard Hahn, vice-president at Boston Edison Company, describes this phenomenon, which many of those interviewed also mentioned:

> If nothing else, the technical sessions gave me a higher comfort level with the final regulations. I had a better understanding of the diversity of interests and a greater appreciation of the difficult tradeoffs the commission had to grapple with. (Hahn interview)

In the areas in which major substantive disagreements persisted, the commission made the final decisions. Though every issue had clear winners and losers, no single interest group considered itself to be a winner or loser on all issues. When asked to rank the DPU's balancing of the diversity and intensity of interests expressed during the technical sessions and formal comments on a scale of 1 to 10, ten of the twelve participants I interviewed thought the commission did extremely well, scoring it in a range of 6.5 to 9. Only two parties did not concur—giving the effort a 3. However, their reasoning perhaps suggests the commission did better than the low scores imply. Both could not give the DPU a higher rating because they felt they had lost on two of their most important issues. However, although both were somewhat disappointed at the DPU's decision to let utilities bid in their own solicitation process, one was incredulous that the commission did not further shorten the timeline of the process, whereas the other was equally incredulous that the timeline was not lengthened—both felt changing the timeline as they proposed would have better balanced the interests! Others were hard-pressed to suggest ways that could have better balanced the interests of stakeholders.

Better balancing of interests in a rulemaking process in which all interests are represented should lead to better rules. However, the key point to notice here is the overall perception that the final rules were fairly balanced despite continued controversy over many of the specific details. This phenomenon supports the argument that the technical sessions enhanced the legitimacy and acceptability of the final rules and the process itself.

Several interviewees claimed that the resolution of one issue may have somewhat compromised the legitimacy of the IRM rulemaking process: the DPU's decision to include the largest environmental externality adders adopted by any state in the nation. Al Destribats, former vice-president at NEES, for instance, stated:

> On a subject as complicated as environmental externalities, we needed much more discussion and expert opinion than the technical sessions and hearings allowed. It was basically handled too quickly and bothered a lot of people here at the Company. (Destribats interview)

On the one hand, it is tempting to dismiss this claim by pointing to the following facts: (1) the DPU had put parties on notice of its intent to include externalities two years before the final rules in its Mass. D.P.U. 86-36-F order (1988d) and had in fact requested proposals; (2) an involved environmental externality collaborative process including all the utilities and many nonutility parties failed to reach consensus; (3) one entire technical session and much of the formal hearings were focused on externality alternatives; (4) the DPU specifically solicited supplemental comments on the adders it ultimately adopted prior to their adoption; and (5) the commission acknowledged that the values were preliminary and that alternative values could be established in future cases. However, the opposing facts that the specific adders adopted (1) were not in the proposed rules, (2) surfaced relatively late in the process (that is, during the penultimate technical session and final hearings), and (3) represented essentially the largest numbers proposed rather than any type of compromise lend credence to the criticism that the externality portion of the final rules was not as thoroughly mulled-over as most other portions.

In the end, although the process used to adopt the externality adders probably did not violate legal due process requirements, it may have compromised the gains in legitimacy that the technical sessions generally seemed to offer. Further analysis and discussion of the externality adders might have changed the final numbers, made the adopted numbers more palatable, or both. However, when a new commission reexamined the adders through an involved and expensive adjudicatory proceeding, they decided to leave them essentially unchanged.[38]

Practicality

The technical sessions contributed significantly to making the final rules more practical than originally proposed. Former EFSC executive director Robert Shapiro explains:

> In addition to better understanding how each issue affected different groups, I also could understand "real-world concerns" much better than I had previously experienced in formal proceedings. As a result, I believe the final regulations of both agencies are far more "practical" than they would have otherwise been. (Shapiro interview)

Former DPU chair Robert Werlin concurs, noting that "originally, we inadvertently had things in our proposal that would have caused problems and which we may have missed without the technical sessions" (Werlin interview).

At least two factors contributed to the technical sessions' ability to infuse greater practicality into the rules. First, the process itself attracted business concerns, such as supply-side developers and DSM providers, to participate in the rulemaking in a way that the formal process by itself may have precluded. The time commitment to attend the technical sessions was far smaller than that needed to become an intervenor in a formal proceeding. In addition, the format was more accessible: participants could show up, drink coffee, eat muffins, and discuss the issues instead of having to prepare legalistic comments. As Mary Beth Gentleman, former assistant secretary of energy policy for the Commonwealth (currently representing cogenerators and DSM providers in private law practice) pointed out in our interview, the mere presence of these business folks added a critical "reality check" to the entire process. Second, throughout the course of the technical sessions, the practical concerns regarding project selection, timing, and financing issues were amplified in a way that is unlikely to have emerged from the hearings and written comments alone.

The feedback from the technical sessions and subsequent comments convinced the DPU and the EFSC to retreat in several areas they considered theoretically appealing, because they recognized that the solutions were untenable from a practical viewpoint. The most striking example of this was the two agencies' decision not to subject existing and planned units to displacement in the all-resource solicitation process. Both agencies believed strongly that an integrated planning framework should optimize the entire resource mix, not just incremental new resources. However, as a practical matter, they were convinced, largely through the technical sessions, that the rather limited opportunity for displacement (that is, it is unlikely that operating plants could be displaced by unbuilt plants except when operating costs or environmental impacts of an existing plant are substantial) did not justify either the substantial work involved in putting every resource through the solicitation process each time or the potentially chilling effect that this would have on utilities and developers with respect to financing their projects.[39]

The technical sessions assisted the DPU in translating theory into practice on other issues, such as a retreat from self-scoring in favor of greater utility flexibility in selecting resources. Similarly, DPU gave in and forewent a fully integrated solicitation that would have subjected all supply- and demand-side resources (including the utilities' DSM programs) to compete head-to-head with the same evaluation criteria. Finally, in response to constant admonishments during the technical sessions to streamline the process and enhance interagency coordination, the DPU did make several changes to improve coordination and to better the chances for everyone to meet the ambitious timeline. Such enhancements included: (1) the addition of a prefiling settlement process, (2) the change from separate filings at each agency to a single joint filing, (3) self-imposed deadlines for the agencies to issue orders or the filings would be considered approved as submitted, and (4) a process whereby each agency agreed to incorporate the findings of the other agency into its own proceedings. In addition, the timeline for the process was stretched from seventeen to twenty months. Few actors wanted it lengthened, but it was considered more feasible for them to comply with this more realistic schedule.

Process Evaluation

The IRM rulemaking process differed from traditional rulemaking procedures in at least two important respects. First, rather than issuing proposed rules early in the rulemaking process, the DPU issued an interim order that described a potential new regulatory structure and requested public comment on every aspect of its proposal. Second, rather than moving directly to formal comments and hearings after issuing the interim order and again after issuing proposed rules, the

DPU sponsored a series of technical sessions. Both innovations were attempts to enhance public input into the rulemaking process.

The DPU held eight technical sessions over the course of the rulemaking process (two additional sessions were hosted by the EFSC in finalizing its portion of the rules). More than 130 individuals (not including DPU or EFSC staff) representing seventy-one different organizations, agencies, and private interests attended at least one of the DPU's technical sessions. Most of the seventy-one participating entities were represented at all of the sessions.

The number and diversity of participants was impressive and critical to the success of the process. All of the major players on electricity issues in Massachusetts were present. The process may have further benefited by including additional stakeholders, such as local governments or other ratepayer groups (for example, residential, small commercial, and industrial). However, the DPU would have needed to actively recruit these groups since they did not show up on their own and many of them are not regular parties before the DPU.

Holding the technical sessions away from the DPU hearing rooms in an informal setting was another important ingredient to the success of the technical sessions. This helped to more clearly differentiate the process from traditional proceedings. It also provided a more relaxed atmosphere to explore the issues and each other's underlying interests.

The sessions began after the DPU proposed an IRM structure in a policy order (Mass. D.P.U. 86-36-F [1988d]) but prior to the DPU issuing actual proposed rules. The existence of an actual proposed structure served as an important starting text and helped focus discussions. By not beginning with proposed regulations, the DPU sent an important signal that it sought public input. The process might have benefited from some technical sessions even prior to the DPU's issuance of its policy framework, although the approach taken marked a substantial improvement over traditional notice-and-comment rulemaking.

DPU staff actively participated in all the sessions. Their role was threefold. First, they represented the commission's perspective within the group. Second, they served as technical resources for the group. Third, they served as a two-way conduit between the sessions and the commission. All these roles were essential. Their presence helped inform the sessions and keep them focused on what the commission needed. More importantly, the ideas gleaned from the sessions were immediately used to help the DPU reshape its proposals. The sessions would have been much less useful and productive without the staff's presence, as both the surveys and the interviews confirmed.

The commissioners, however, decided not to maintain an ongoing presence at the sessions, although they did attend small parts of two of the DPU's sessions and both EFSC-sponsored sessions. More direct involvement by the commissioners might have been useful and appropriate to explain their proposals and for them to hear the participants' interests and opinions first-hand. However, with respect to exploring alternative proposals and building consensus, on balance, the commissioners' presence might have dampened the free-flowing dialogue that occurred. Most of those interviewed concurred with this observation.

The use of facilitation was well received by the participants and at the commission and was considered by everyone to be an essential ingredient to the success of the technical sessions themselves. The facilitators' level of technical expertise and lack of a more aggressive consensus-building posture were appropriate given their role as defined by the DPU. A more aggressive consensus-seeking process might have required more of a mediatory role and possibly more substantive knowledge of the issues.

Although the process resulted in substantial convergence of opinion on many issues, it stopped short of actively seeking consensus. The benefit of using technical sessions instead of a more aggressive, consensus-seeking process such as negotiated rulemaking was that it allowed many more people to have direct input in the process. It also allowed for ongoing brainstorming throughout the sessions. The disadvantage of not pushing for consensus was that many issues were not resolved by the group, and the discussions remained at the broad policy level. There was neither the time nor the inclination to develop detailed implementation mechanisms or resolve the actual wording of the rules.

A more active consensus-seeking process, perhaps only in the second round of technical sessions, might have been appropriate and achievable. Using a negotiated rulemaking approach would have necessitated a more substantial resource commitment by participants and the DPU. It might also have required limiting participation to a representative subgroup and perhaps securing mediation services. However, if such an approach further enhanced both the legitimacy and practicality of the rulemaking process and the final rules, it probably would have been worth the effort.

THE NEW JERSEY BIDDING SETTLEMENT

In late 1987, the New Jersey Board of Public Utilities (BPU) initiated an innovative settlement process to develop policies for electric utility resource procurement practices. These policies were to cover resources from alternative power producers (APPs), including Qualifying Facilities (QFs), non-QFs, independent power producers (IPPs), and demand-side management (DSM) resources. The process used to develop these policies differed from a more traditional notice-and-comment rulemaking in its use of settlement negotiations before the board formulated a set of policies. It differs from the Massachusetts IRM technical sessions described in the preceding case study in that the New Jersey negotiations actively sought consensus among the participants, whereas the effort in Massachusetts stopped short of this objective, focusing solely on education and open discussion.

In the end, eleven of the thirteen parties representing a broad spectrum of interests signed a fifty-two-page comprehensive set of all-resource bidding policies after half a year of negotiations. However, although the board did embrace the settlement without change, it decided not to go through a formal rulemaking process. That decision was appealed by three separate entities. The appeals were ultimately dropped, and the settlement went into effect.

The success of infusing a settlement process at the front end of a policy-making or rulemaking process hinges on whether doing so enhances public participation and improves the final policies or rules. The evidence shows that the use of a settlement process made the final New Jersey bidding policies more practical in many respects while enhancing the legitimacy of the process. However, other factors, such as the decision not to formalize the settlement in rules and various implementation-related issues, have threatened to compromise some of these gains.

The presentation of this case draws on a wide range of primary documentation, such as board orders, written comments, agendas, correspondence, staff reports, and internal board memos. It also benefits from several secondary sources, including comparative studies that analyzed New Jersey's bidding system and an article written by one of the participants to the settlement that appeared in *Public Utilities Fortnightly* (Walker 1989).

In addition, the story and conclusions are bolstered by lengthy telephone interviews with representatives of eight of the thirteen participating members of the settlement process. Those eight were a representative cross-section of the stakeholders in the negotiations (for example, two of the four utilities and two of the four QFs) and included representatives from both of the nonsignatories. In addition, four other individuals who did not participate in the settlement process were interviewed and provided invaluable background information on the rulemaking requirements in New Jersey and on how the implementation of New Jersey's bidding process compares with other experiences in the country. A list of all those interviewed is shown in Table 5-13.

Background

The bidding settlement approved by the board in 1988 was a direct outgrowth of the BPU's policies for QFs adopted in 1981 to implement the federal Public Utilities Regulatory Policies Act of 1978 (PURPA) (NJ B.P.U. 8010-687 [1981]). The BPU's 1981 policies established guidelines for determining the rates that QFs were entitled to be paid for delivering electricity to the utilities, as well as a series of related

Table 5-13. Interviews for New Jersey Bidding Settlement

Utilities

Dennis Baldassari	Vice-President of Rates, Materials, and Services, Jersey Central Power & Light Company
Harold Borden	Senior Vice-President for External Affairs, Public Service Electric and Gas Company

Government

Michael Ambrosio	Chief, Electric Division, Bureau of Rates and Tariffs, Board of Public Utilities
Joe Bowring	Chief Economist, Division of Rate Counsel, Department of Public Advocate
William Potter	Partner, private law firm (former Special Counsel, Division of Energy, Department of Commerce and Economic Development)

Alternative Power Producers and Industrial Consumers

Harry Kociencki	Director of Corporate Energy Administration and Operation, Hoffman-LaRoche, Inc. (represented large industrial consumers)
Robert McNair	Chairman and President, COGEN Technologies, Inc.
Michael Walker	Attorney, private law firm (represented small power production interests)

Other

Charles Goldman	Staff scientist, Lawrence Berkeley Laboratory
Edward Kahn	Group leader, Utility Planning and Policy, Lawrence Berkeley Laboratory
Jim McGuire	Attorney, Division of Rate Counsel, Department of Public Advocate (former Director, Department of Public Advocate, Center for Public Dispute Resolution)
Anthony Miragliotta	Assistant Director of Rules and Publications, New Jersey Office of Administrative Law

Note: Positions and affiliations are as of the date of the interviews.

issues (that is, interconnection costs, standby rates, backup rates, and safety requirements). These QF policies were rulelike in their scope and content. However, they were formulated after a contested adjudicatory proceeding rather than a formal rulemaking.

In an effort to enhance QF development in New Jersey, the BPU actually required utilities to pay 10 percent more than the utility's projected avoided energy cost although PURPA only requires that QFs be paid up to a utility's full avoided cost (that is, cost of the next available electricity supply option).[40]

> The Board is of the opinion that QF energy has a value in excess of the PJM [Pennsylvania, New Jersey, Maryland Power Pool] billing rate and that a figure of 10% above the billing rate is a reasonable and appropriate measure which reflects the excess value. We further believe that the setting of avoided energy cost at 10% above the PJM billing rate will help to adequately promote cogeneration and small power production in New Jersey and, at the same time, will yield long term benefits to utility ratepayers. (NJ B.P.U. 8010-687 [1981], p. 3)

In 1983, the board issued an order of clarification, which stated that all QF projects, not just those of 1 MW or less, as some had previously interpreted the 1981 order, were entitled to receive these prices (NJ B.P.U. 8010-687 [1983]). The 1983 order also explained that QFs were entitled to receive levelized payments for their electricity instead of prices that escalated over time. This levelization, which allowed for the front loading of payments to QFs, was considered essential for nurturing the nascent QF industry.

Only a few contracts with small QFs were signed in New Jersey through 1985, despite the fact that many essential ingredients necessary for a vibrant QF market were in place (for example, the BPU's generous pricing and levelization requirements, a sizable need for power by the utilities, and a large industrial base that provided numerous potential cogeneration sites). According to Michael Ambrosio, chief of the Bureau of Rates at the BPU, the primary reason for the inactivity was the protracted negotiations between the QFs and the utilities over contract details (Ambrosio interview).

In 1985, Jersey Central Power and Light Company (Jersey Central) became the first electric utility in the state to extend a standard-offer long-term contract for QFs over 1 MW. Previously such a contract had been available only for small QFs. The contract, which was guaranteed to QFs on a first-come, first-served basis at the pricing terms required by the BPU, was an immediate hit with the QFs, compared with the preexisting negotiation process. Jersey Central's first

200 MW block was oversubscribed almost immediately (NJ BPU 1987, p. 15).

Both Jersey Central and Atlantic Electric reached settlements with BPU staff that effectively institutionalized the standard-offer approach by 1987. Subsequently, QF development in New Jersey began to flourish. By the end of 1987, the board had approved 600 MW of QF contracts, and an additional 1,500 MW were in the pipeline (that is, in the final negotiating and signing stage or under review by the board). A study conducted by Lawrence Berkeley Laboratory identified New Jersey as one of four states (along with California, Texas, and Maine) with "significant levels of QF development" during that time (E. Kahn et al. 1989). Still, the other two utilities in New Jersey—Public Service Electricity and Gas (PSE&G) and Rockland Electric (RECo)—which did not have standard-offer contracts, signed up relatively few QFs during the mid-1980s.

In May 1987, the BPU released a staff report entitled "An Assessment of Cogeneration and Small Production Policy in New Jersey 1981–1986" (NJ BPU 1987). The report was required as part of the five-year review of New Jersey's QF policies as mandated in the original 1981 order. The BPU issued a cover letter with the report requesting public comments on it and related BPU policies:

> The Board welcomes your comments on staff's report and is interested in hearing your views on any other ratemaking and regulatory issues related to cogeneration and small power production in New Jersey.

In its report and during the hearings in September 1987, BPU staff maintained that QF development was finally taking off in New Jersey after the advent of standard-offer contracting and that the BPU should "stay the course" with respect to its existing policies (Gabel 1987, p. 2). Staff did, however, make two recommendations. One was to remove the 10 percent bonus to QFs from the avoided-energy-cost calculation, which they saw as no longer necessary to jump-start the QF industry. The other was to include additional protection against potential utility self-dealing (that is, the utilities contracting with their own QF affiliates).[41] Staff adamantly rejected the notion of replacing the standard-offer contracting approach with a bidding system, as several New Jersey utilities were suggesting:

> The concept of auctions or bidding systems should be rejected by the Board as an approach which will limit the growth of economic QF development in the State by slowing down the signing of contracts and giving the utilities an unfair, uncompetitive market advantage over QFs. (NJ BPU 1987, p. 40)

The other nonutility parties (NUPs) that provided comments on the staff's report and the BPU's QF policies seemed generally to align with the staff's call for "staying the course." All the NUPs, including the QFs, the Public Advocate, the state Division of Energy, and the industrial users, wanted to see the continuation of a standard-offer approach with prices set close to full avoided cost. The QFs and industrial users (who were cogenerators themselves), wanted to maintain the 10 percent bonus, whereas the others did not.

The utilities, however, were dissatisfied with the emerging standard-offer process and wanted to see major changes. Harold Borden, senior vice-president for external affairs at PSE&G, explains:

> PURPA and the board's orders implementing it were unleashing a lot more cogeneration than we had anticipated. While we had some need to purchase QFs, we were concerned that we would have to buy more than we needed at prices that we considered too high. (Borden interview)

During the hearings, both PSE&G and Jersey Central offered testimony calling for the board to scrap the standard-offer approach and initiate a bidding process. The utilities viewed a bidding process as a way to provide themselves with greater flexibility in selecting QFs (that is, it would no longer be a first-come, first-served process) while driving down the price they had to pay below full avoided cost to a competitive market price.[42]

Settlement Process

The procedural context in which the board received comments and held hearings was unclear at the time. Specifically, it was not obvious whether a contested case, a rulemaking, or some other procedure would follow public comment. Without clarifying this important issue, but after hearing testimony and receiving comments, the board determined that many valid arguments had been made on both sides of the bidding-versus-standard-offer debate. Subsequently, the board directed its staff to convene settlement discussions with other interested parties rather than move directly into litigation or rulemaking (Ambrosio interview).

On December 4, 1987, Steven Gabel, then director of the Electric Division at the BPU, sent a letter inviting interested parties to a conference to discuss the possibility of settlement. He justified his request as follows: "It is our opinion that the commonality of interest in the development of cost effective generation sources is sufficient to make settlement a reasonable possibility." Although BPU staff often settled adjudicatory proceedings, such as rate cases, this constituted their first attempt to settle a case involving large policy issues outside the context of a contested proceeding.

Approximately one hundred people showed up at the initial conference. The staff suggested a settlement working group of eleven interested parties, including themselves, and gave those present an hour to select representatives. According to interviews conducted for this book, everyone agreed on the negotiating representatives and decided to allow the cogenerators to have three representatives instead of one—supposedly to account for the diversity of interests they represented. Table 5-14 shows the make-up of the final thirteen representatives to the settlement group.

The only representatives from consumer groups were the Public Advocate and the industrial users (who apparently were more interested in their role as cogenerators than in their role as ratepayers). No environmental groups were present. According to those interviewed, no other environmental or consumer groups were active in New Jersey at the time, although several mentioned that in hindsight at least the state Department of Environmental Protection should have been recruited.

All interested parties were invited to attend the meetings, although only representatives of the settlement group were permitted to sit at the table. Several other groups, such as the Clean Coal Developers, regularly attended the negotiating sessions. Commencing officially in early January 1988, biweekly negotiating sessions were held through July 1988, when most of the parties reached an agreement. Toward the end of the negotiations, participants began meeting more frequently—up to several times per week. All negotiating sessions were held in a conference room at the BPU's offices.

The New Jersey bidding settlement process did not use an outside

Table 5-14. Representatives to the New Jersey Bidding Settlement Group

Board staff
Cogenerators (three representatives)
Department of Public Advocate, Division of Rate Counsel
Department of Commerce, Division of Energy
Independent power producers
Industrial energy users
Small power producers
Utilities (four representatives)

facilitator. Instead, the BPU staff set the agendas, convened the meetings, and as the process progressed, drafted each iteration of the settlement document. According to those interviewed, the tremendous amount of power that this granted the staff was not surprising given staff's preexisting clout with the board. Staff's clout appears to have been a combination of staff members' individual skills[43] and the structure of the agency itself vis-à-vis staff's relationship to the board.

Unlike most other state PUCs, the New Jersey BPU is one of the only ones in which the staff can act in both an advocacy and advisory capacity on the same case. Most other states have either no advocacy staff at the PUC, a permanent separation between advocacy and advisory staffs (sometimes with the advocacy staff housed in another agency altogether), or a case-by-case separation of advisory and advocacy staff. The fact that the parties in New Jersey know that after staff negotiates a case as an advocate, they can often advise the board on the outcome gives the staff more power than is typically enjoyed by advocacy staffs across the country (that is, where there is more formal separation between the advocacy staff and the board or commission). Couple this structure with a long history of the board's heavy deference to staff judgment on most issues, as the interviews revealed, and you have a fairly formidable staff. Given this influence, the staff's decision early on to switch their support from a "stay the course" approach, which continued to rely on standard-offer contracts, to a bidding system created quite a stir in the negotiations. The staff's reasoning for what interviewees viewed as a sudden change was explained by Michael Ambrosio:

> We changed our mind on the standard-offer-versus-bidding debate because we saw that with certain protections, we could use a bidding process to prioritize projects and set price without squeezing out cogenerators. We realized that we couldn't close our eyes to the fact that bidding was being used throughout the country with apparent success, nor to the fact that getting the utilities to agree on a standard-offer contract approach was unlikely. At the same time, if we didn't get the concessions we were looking for on the utilities' original bidding proposals, we would've returned to a standard-offer approach. (Ambrosio interview)

From the utilities' perspective, as Dennis Baldassari, vice-president of rates, materials, and service at Jersey Central, explained: "The group didn't convene meaningful discussions until staff said that they were willing to move toward a bidding system" (Baldassari interview). However, all NUPs interviewed felt that once the staff announced this change, the NUPs' influence on the outcome of the negotiations plummeted—while the utilities' power soared. Some NUPs felt that they were forced to "concede turf on every point." Others, particularly the Public Advocate, felt that they were virtually ignored (Bowring interview).

Despite the NUPs' perceptions, intensive negotiations continued for half a year. By mutual agreement, the original March 31 completion deadline was extended for four months. During the negotiations, the original two-page settlement proposal ballooned into the fifty-two-page settlement that was ultimately signed by eleven of the thirteen representatives in July (industrial users and the Public Advocate ultimately did not sign). The decision to shift from a standard-offer approach to a bidding paradigm was essentially a *fait accompli* once the staff aligned with the utilities. However, the details of such a system were by no means settled early on and engendered intensive debate and compromise.

During the negotiations, many creative compromises surfaced that might not have emerged through a traditional rulemaking. Other issues remained controversial and somewhat acrimonious.

The Settlement

The final settlement signed by eleven of the thirteen parties represented a detailed set of bidding guidelines and policies that defined a whole new way of procuring nonutility power in New Jersey. Table 5-15 highlights the settlement's major components.

Comparison with Massachusetts IRM Rules

The settlement reached by the New Jersey parties is no less comprehensive or complex than the Massachusetts IRM rules described in the previous case. But although the two approaches to utility energy planning and procurement practices are similar, they are also significantly different. A brief comparison between the New Jersey settlement and Massachusetts IRM rules offers insight into the substance of the New Jersey settlement.

First, by including IPP power and DSM resources, both the New Jersey settlement and the IRM rules in Massachusetts expanded the bidding process that had been used by numerous utilities throughout the United States during the mid-1980s to secure QF resources.[44] However, even though the Massachusetts rules require utilities to participate in their own solicitations and the New Jersey settlement forbids utilities from directly participating and bans affiliates for at least three years, these contrary requirements are each hotly contested in their respective states.

Table 5-15. Major Components of the New Jersey Bidding Settlement

1. All electric utilities must conduct bids concurrently on an annual basis whenever power need is projected (first round assumed to take longer).

2. All QFs, conservation projects greater than 400 kW, and IPPs (at a utility's option) are eligible to respond.

3. Utilities may not participate in their own bids. Utility subsidiaries may not participate for at least the first three years.

4. Utilities will rank projects using a system consisting of three parts: (1) economic factors, which cannot be more than 55 percent of total weight; (2) project status and viability, which cannot be less than 25 percent of total weight; and (3) noneconomic factors (e.g., fuel type, location, environmental benefits), which cannot be less than 20 percent of scoring weight.

5. Prior to release, utilities will submit requests for proposals (RFPs) to the board and interested parties. BPU staff settles any objections raised by commenters (that is, staff represents commenters and its own position) and utility. If objections cannot be settled, or commenters do not agree with settlement, the board hears complaints at its own discretion.

6. Bidders must surpass numerous minimum thresholds regarding site control, fuel supply, thermal sales, permit identification and scheduling, milestone schedule, and so forth.

7. If a bidder makes the award group in two or more utility solicitations, each utility has the option to bid against the other by offering to sweeten a bidder's original bid.

8. The board reviews individual contracts but does not formally examine the entire award group. There is no deadline for contract review and approval by the board (two to six months expected).

9. Utilities must establish a liquidated damage fund into which developers put money at certain times and risk losing a portion of the money whenever milestones are missed. A security deposit is required if there is substantial front loading of payments to APPs (that is, greater than 20 percent of forecast avoided cost for oil/gas plants, and 35 percent for renewable and solid fuels).

10. Several nonbidding options exist: (1) utilities must continue to offer short-run tariffed rates for QFs for energy-only; (2) each utility must set aside a five-year block of power (ranging from 25 MW [RECo] to 200 MW [PSE&G]) for small projects under 10 MW to receive long-term contracts at full avoided-cost rates; and (3) for three years, utilities must sign long-run contracts with qualifying resource recovery facilities at full avoided cost (after three years, new facilities must bid).

11. Utilities must provide wheeling to in-state QFs on an average-cost basis. Utilities may provide wheeling for IPPs but may not practice self-wheeling (that is, from one industrial facility to another).

Table 5-15. *(continued)*
12. Utility bid process and all resulting power purchase contracts approved by the board are deemed reasonable and prudent (unless discovered that utility has financial interest in facility).
13. Utilities must calculate their avoided costs over a twenty-five-year period by using the differential revenue requirement method rather than the PJM method required by the 1981 board order.
14. The policies expire after five years from date of board approval unless renewed.

Second, the project selection process in New Jersey relies on self-scoring and is probably less flexible but easier to review than the Massachusetts process. The utilities in New Jersey are allowed less latitude to negotiate with projects and less opportunity to reoptimize the final mix of projects to mesh with existing and planned resources.

Third, at least on paper, the New Jersey bidding cycle is more frequent (for example, every year instead of every two to three years), and each bid, from submittal of a request for proposals (RFP) to signed contract, is slated to be completed within one year, rather than eighteen months as in Massachusetts. Fourth, the New Jersey settlement has a less formalized public review process but greater involvement from BPU staff than the Massachusetts proposal for both the review of the initial RFP and the final award group.

Fifth, although the New Jersey settlement changed the way utilities calculate avoided cost, the Massachusetts rules virtually eliminated avoided-cost calculations altogether. Sixth, although the Massachusetts rules call for the inclusion of a liquidated damage fund and security when there is front loading, the New Jersey settlement includes more detailed formulas for doing so. Lastly, although the New Jersey bidding criteria require looking at environmental externalities, the Massachusetts rules lay out a detailed set of externality "adders."

Compromise and Creativity

The New Jersey bidding settlement included several noteworthy features that highlight the potential benefits of a negotiated approach to policy formation. The first is the way the settlement balanced the need to provide financial protection to ratepayers against failure of an APP to come on-line in a timely fashion (or at all, for that matter) with the need to encourage APP development. Again, as a benchmark that is fairly typical in the country, the IRM rules in Massachusetts require all successful bidders to pay a fixed fee of $15 per kW into an in-service security account within thirty days from contract signing. If the project comes on-line as scheduled, the money is returned to the developer. If it is delayed, the utility retains a percentage of the money based on a straight-line formula (the utility retains the entire fund if the project fails). In contrast, New Jersey's liquidated damages fund is far more detailed, as shown in Table 5-16.

The primary difference between the two remedies is that the New Jersey approach, although involving a slightly greater amount (that is, $1.8 million for a 100 MW APP instead of $1.5 million), steps up payments into the fund to coincide with meeting each successive milestone instead of requiring a flat deposit at the outset. This innovation is an acknowledgment that at certain junctures, the developer is willing to put up more money as the project becomes more real, whereas less potential damage is done to a utility and its ratepayers if a project fails early on. New Jersey's liquidated damages fund also differentiates between coal, which is much more capital-intensive and more difficult to permit than other fuels, and keys penalties to missed milestones.

All of those interviewed in New Jersey concurred that the degree of specificity and the resultant practicality of the liquidated damage

Table 5-16. New Jersey's Liquidated Damage Fund for APP Developer

LIQUIDATED DAMAGE FUND

Milestone	Coal Project	Other Projects	Amount Forfeited if Milestone Missed
Bid accepted by utility	$ 2/kW	$ 4/kW	na
Environmental permit filed	$ 2/kW	$ 2/kW	$1/kW
Environmental permit received	$ 5/kW	$ 3/kW	$2/kW
Financial commitment received	$ 2/kW	$ 2/kW	$1/kW
Construction commences	$ 7/kW	$ 7/kW	$4/kW
TOTAL	$18/kW	$18/kW	

Source: NJ B.P.U. 8010-687B (1988a).

fund would not have surfaced in a traditional rulemaking. Michael Ambrosio explains:

> No one would have suggested this approach in a rulemaking. The focus would have been on what bottom-line amount to require for liquidated damages. Extreme positions would have been taken, and the board would have picked a number. Meanwhile, it took us three to four entire sessions to negotiate this solution. During the course of those negotiations we not only realized how complex the issue was, but more importantly, we eventually realized that there was actually a way to structure it that could satisfy both the utilities and the developers. While we still went back and forth on the actual numbers, in the end, it was a lot easier once we agreed on the principles. Everyone appeared satisfied with this part of the settlement when it was completed. (Ambrosio interview)

Two other features of the settlement were identified during the interviews as examples of creative and detailed approaches that are unlikely to have surfaced in traditional proceedings. The first is the security provisions that protect the utility and its ratepayers from the risks of providing front-loaded, levelized payments to APPs. Under the settlement, security is only required when front loading is forecast to exceed the utility's avoided cost by 20 percent for oil and gas projects and 35 percent for solid fuel and renewable projects (NJ B.P.U. 8010-687B [1988a], pp. 16–17). The second issue is the scoring system, which not only specifies an array of factors that must be evaluated for each bid but limits the weights that the utilities can give each of the three major scoring categories (for example, economic factors must be less than or equal to 55 percent of the score, project status and viability factors must be greater than or equal to 25 percent, and other noneconomic factors must be greater than or equal to 20 percent) (id., p. 13).

In both cases, participants in the settlement process spent several entire days negotiating these issues—much more time than a traditional rulemaking process would ever allow. More importantly, by allowing for a full airing of the issues during the settlement discussions, the group was able to craft solutions that everyone could live with (even the nonsignatories expressed support for these elements). This outcome would have been unlikely if the board had determined these elements on its own after brief exposure to everyone's positions through written comments, and hearings, if any.

Dissent and Discontent

The New Jersey bidding settlement included a high degree of consensus among the parties on most issues. However, there was also a certain amount of dissent and discontent. As mentioned, two of the thirteen parties to the negotiations, the Public Advocate and the industrial users, did not sign the final stipulation of settlement. In fact, several people informed me that the Division of Energy signed the final settlement at the last moment, against the advice of its staff, and after "substantial arm twisting."[45] The cogenerators signed the final agreement. However, they were basically dissatisfied with the overall thrust of the settlement (particularly the movement towards bidding) and many of the details, according to Robert McNair, president and CEO of COGEN Technologies and one of the three representatives of the Cogeneration Interest Group. In hindsight, McNair claimed that he should not have signed but should have taken the cogenerators' concerns directly before the board, despite a de facto moratorium on signing new QF contracts during negotiations that pressured cogenerators to settle the case. In addition, many cogenerators were reluctant to bite the hand that had been feeding them (McNair interview).

Several issues were central to much of the dissent and discontent over the final settlement. The Public Advocate and Division of Energy remained opposed to involvement of a utility or a utility subsidiary in its own bidding process. Although a compromise was reached to delay involvement of utility subsidiaries for at least three years, apparently this deferral was not sufficient to allay the fears of the two organizations (Bowring and Potter interviews). They also remained bothered by the amount of discretion that the settlement seemed to leave the utilities in defining the amount of power they would solicit through the bidding process (that is, the bid block) versus the power that the utility could still pursue outside the bidding process by building its own projects and through other purchases from outside its service territory. As William Potter, who represented the Division of Energy throughout most of the negotiations, explained, the division feared that the bidding policies would "create QF ghettos" that would not be properly integrated with the utilities' entire resource mix (Potter interview). The BPU staff intended to minimize this potential ghettoization by taking a lead role in the review of proposals for utility projects and any additional solicitations for APP bids.

This intention, however, apparently raised a series of process-related concerns for the Public Advocate and the Division of Energy. The settlement, instead of automatically providing the opportunity for interested parties to litigate a utility's RFP proposal, gives the BPU staff the opportunity to settle with the utility any of its objections plus those raised by parties in written comments (NJ B.P.U. 8010-687B [1988a], p. 40). If no settlement is reached, or parties remain disgruntled, the board *may* choose to hear the case.

For both the Public Advocate and the Division of Energy, giving BPU staff the authority to essentially represent the entire public interest, at least initially in the review process, raised questions of due process and of competing jurisdictions (Bowring and Potter interviews). The Public Advocate maintained that its job was to represent ratepayers before the board, and the Energy Office maintained that its job was to review utility energy planning decisions. Both agencies apparently felt that the preeminent role of the BPU staff in future reviews was not appropriate[46] and that parties' right to put on a contested case should not be compromised.[47]

As mentioned, the NUPs, except for the BPU staff, were less than enthusiastic about embracing a bidding framework, and the APPs (including the industrial users) were upset about an apparent erosion in the price they would receive for future power. In addition, the industrial users were dissatisfied because they could not convince any of the other parties to let them wheel power from one industrial site to another via the utility grid (that is, "self-wheeling"). Finally, the inclusion of DSM in the bidding process, which occurred at the Division of Energy's insistence within the last few weeks of negotiations, by all accounts was not adequately specified in the final settlement, leaving many unanswered questions. The parties I interviewed were not fundamentally opposed to DSM bidding. However, most would have preferred to defer discussion on the subject until a subsequent "Phase II" negotiation.

Postsettlement Process

Several days after the settlement was signed, the board released it for public comment. To the chagrin of the industrial users, neither the settlement document nor the request for comments mentioned that two parties to the negotiations had not signed (nor the reasons for their dissent). Also, although the board referred to the settlement as containing new "guidelines and procedures," the board's intentions regarding New Jersey's formal rulemaking requirements were still not clear. Under New Jersey's Rules for Agency Rulemaking, if the board intended to adopt the settlement as a rule, it needed to publish the settlement in the *New Jersey Register* as a board-proposed rule, receive comments, hold a hearing if requested and deemed necessary, address the written and oral comments, and publish a final rule in the *New Jersey Register* that reflected the public comment (N.J.A.C. 1:30).

Despite receiving comments from twelve parties, including the Public Advocate and several developers and large users—most of whom were critical of various aspects of the settlement—the board decided not to hold hearings on the settlement. The board also decided to adopt the settlement as BPU policy without going through a formal rulemaking process. According to Michael Ambrosio of the BPU staff, this decision engendered substantial debate within the BPU, on both legal and strategic grounds (Ambrosio interview).[48] In the end, according to Ambrosio, the Electric Division staff's desire for greater future flexibility won out:

> Staff's primary interest was not to take a procedural short-cut on the adoption of the bidding policies themselves; rather, we wanted the ability to fine-tune the policies while they were being implemented without going through a six-month rulemaking process for each minor change. As such, we viewed a board order as providing us with much more flexibility than a formal rule. (Ambrosio interview)

On August 24, 1988, the board adopted the settlement, and an order to that effect was issued in late September (NJ B.P.U. 8010-687B [1988b]). In the order, the board praised both the settlement process and the results:

> The Board believes that the Stipulation of Settlement was fairly negotiated, will impart substantial benefits to ratepayers over the term of the Settlement and will lead to the efficient development of future supplies of capacity and energy. The *new* policy should enhance the level of ratepayer benefit from APP development, improve the environment for APP investment and development by maintaining an ongoing, known market with adequate protection and will improve the system planning process of the utilities. (Id., p. 8; emphasis added)

The same day that the board voted to adopt the settlement, William Potter, former negotiator for the Division of Energy and then representing Clean Coal, filed a notice of appeal with the superior court, appellate division. The next day he filed a "Motion for a Stay and for Reconsideration" at the BPU (Potter 1988). Potter claimed that the board had truncated the public participation for no apparent reason and that the end result was a set of policies that were "neither fish nor fowl" since the board had followed neither a rulemaking process nor a contested case proceeding (Potter 1988, Potter interview). His motion to the board elaborates further:

> What the Board cannot do, absent serious risk of judicial review, is to proceed to conclude this docket through *ad hoc* procedures of its own. . . . It is not enough to consider the Stipulation as neither a rule nor a contested case but rather as a mere "policy statement"

or validation of a "contract" entered into by private parties. . . . If characterized as a "policy decision," the Stipulation becomes a rule-making according to the A.P.A. . . . If characterized as an order concluding a contested case, no stipulation which has not been signed by all parties or where interested parties object . . . can be approved in a summary manner. (Potter 1988)

The Cogeneration and Independent Power Coalition of America, Inc. (CIPCA) and the Public Advocate also filed motions for rehearing and reconsideration regarding the board's failure to follow requisite rulemaking procedures. In addition, the Public Advocate's motion protested the process included in the settlement for reviewing the RFPs of individual utilities and the resultant contracts. As discussed in the previous section, the Public Advocate had some serious reservation about the wisdom and the legality of the proposed review procedures.

In the written order issued on September 28, 1988, the board rejected the parties' claims that its approval of the settlement violated New Jersey law and found that its actions were "consistent with proper administrative procedures . . . and are not inconsistent with our statutory authority" (NJ B.P.U. 8010-687B [1988b], p. 7). The board explains in the order that it provided adequate notice and a full opportunity for parties to provide feedback throughout the hearing, settlement, and comment stages (id.). On October 19, 1988, and March 22, 1989, the board denied the motions for rehearing and reconsideration filed by Clean Coal and CIPCA, respectively.

On September 13, 1989, the Public Advocate withdrew the last remaining appeal regarding the board's decision-making processes associated with the adoption and implementation of the settlement. According to Joe Bowring, chief economist at the Public Advocate, the Public Advocate withdrew its appeal as a quid pro quo for the board's order of clarification issued on August 9, 1989, which effectively guaranteed them participation in the ongoing review of utilities' bidding RFPs (Bowring interview). With all the appeals withdrawn, the court never heard or ruled on these procedural issues.

Implementation Experience

It is too early to gauge the success of the new policies with any certainty. Table 5-17 summarizes the initial bidding experience. Only a few bid cycles have actually been completed, and no IPPs were on-line by mid-1993. In large part because of the economic downturn, less bidding than expected has occurred. However, some DSM resources secured after the first bidding cycle are in place (Ambrosio in-

204 — Chapter Five

Table 5-17. New Jersey Bidding Experience 1988-1992

Utility	Start Date[a]	Completion Date[b]	Bid Size	Response[c]	Signed[c]
JCP&L	1988	Dec. 1989	270 MW	768 MW (712/56)	261 MW (235/26)
PSE&G	1988	Dec. 1989	200 MW	700 MW (654/47)	257 MW (210/47)
Atlantic[d]	na				
Rockland[e]	1988	Dec. 1989	200 MW	1412 MW (1395/17)	212 MW (195/17)
PSE&G	1992		85 MW		
JCP&L	1992		150 MW		

Source: Michael Ambrosio, New Jersey Board of Public Utilities.

[a] Start date = when RFPs submitted for approval.

[b] Completion date = when award group named.

[c] Numbers in parentheses = split between supply- and demand-side resources respectively.

[d] Atlantic Electric has not gone out to bid because no power need is projected through 2000.

[e] The Rockland bid was combined with the Orange and Rockland bid in New York through an RFP that was approved in both states. Most of the power (approximately two-thirds) was assigned to O&R in New York.

terview). Still, several facts and observations are worth noting at this juncture.

Utilities have not conducted annual bids as originally anticipated—in part because of the tight timeline proposed in the settlement, which was probably unrealistically short, and in part because of a perceived reduction in the need for APP power by the utilities. Part of this drop in demand can be attributed to the depressed Northeast economy and is not heavily contested; however, the portion that stems from utilities continuing to pursue power options outside of the bidding process is controversial. For instance, Jersey Central decided not to go out to bid for APP power but rather to pursue a 500 MW purchase power arrangement through its holding company, General Public Utilities.[49] Meanwhile, Atlantic Electric sought a certificate of need to construct its own 220 MW generating facility if necessary to meet its customers' demand, and PSE&G pursued major repowerings and expansion at two of its facilities equivalent to over 900 MW.[50]

The utilities' decisions to aggressively pursue electricity options outside the bidding process rubs salt in the NUPs' old wounds. During the settlement negotiations, the NUPs argued that utilities should not have the flexibility to circumvent the bidding process at will by seeking power through other avenues. All the NUPs interviewed said that their biggest fears are being realized in this regard, because utilities have kept the size of the bidding block small. The situation puts the BPU in the precarious position of having to make sure that a utility could not have done better by purchasing APP power through a bidding solicitation than by building it or contracting for it with other utilities. NUPs give the BPU staff high marks for trying to devise such a test but nonetheless see their interests being harmed in the process. Some of the NUPs also said they had difficulty getting access to the utility's submittals (including block size, avoided costs, and the RFP) in a timely fashion and that they were able to have little meaningful influence on the BPU's review process, which, as mentioned previously, is spearheaded by the BPU staff in accordance with the settlement and order of clarification (Potter and Walker interviews).

A second observation, based on interviews and Table 5-17, is that the responses to the bids have been relatively smaller (approximately 3:1 for PSE&G and Jersey Central combined) than responses to comparable integrated demand and supply bids by utilities outside of New Jersey, where bid responses have averaged 9:1 (Goldman and Busch 1991). Several possible explanations may account for these phenomena. First, with the advent of bidding, power plant development is not as profitable for APP developers in New Jersey as before, and some may have refocused their efforts on greener pastures. This reduced profitability is in part due to the removal of the generous incentives offered prior to bidding (that is, the PJM rate plus 10 percent, plus the capacity deficiency charge). Many of the best steam host sites in New Jersey may already have had cogenerators installed during the successful standard-offer contracting process (Ambrosio interview).

However, Michael Walker, who represented the small power producers, claims the volume of bids has been low, mainly because utilities are suppressing their avoided costs (thereby reducing the ceiling price available to developers) by inappropriately applying the avoided-cost methodology that was agreed to in the settlement (Walker interview). Walker believes that this is occurring largely because the settlement provided insufficient detail on how utilities were to make these calculations.[51]

Robert McNair of COGEN Technologies, Inc., one of the biggest APP developers in New Jersey, agrees with Walker's assessment (McNair interview). Even though he signed the settlement, he recently decided not to participate in the New Jersey bidding process because of the low prices and small block sizes.[52]

Although the BPU staff's primary motivation for adopting the settlement through a board order instead of a formal rulemaking was to provide the board with flexibility, they have not invoked that privilege often. In fact, the only changes to the approved settlement have been a lengthening of time for the bidding cycles and an extension of the ban on utility affiliate participation in the bidding process. In both cases, the changes were made by stipulation between the BPU staff and the utilities. Other interested parties, including the other participants to the settlement itself, were provided an opportunity to submit written comments to the board, but only after the stipulation was reached. The changes were not too controversial substantively. However, the fact that staff stipulated only with the utilities, and provided only limited opportunity for input generally, aggravated those who already feared that the amendment process was unclear at best and possibly illegal (Bowring and Walker interviews).

Finally, adoption of a rule in 1991 on DSM resource planning and ratemaking incentives is relevant to the bidding case study both substantively and procedurally (N.J.A.C. 14:12). Among other provisions, the DSM rules effectively reduced the importance of DSM bidding by encouraging a greater role for utility DSM programs and by allowing utilities to offer ESCOs a standard-offer contract in lieu of including DSM in concurrent APP bids. Michael Walker believes that the adoption of this DSM rule was a "blatant disregard of the bidding settlement" because it compromised the inclusion of bidding as the settlement required (Walker interview). Michael Ambrosio of the BPU staff, however, argues that the DSM rules do not undermine the settlement but merely attempt to clarify important issues glossed over in the bidding settlement (Ambrosio interview).

On a procedural level, it is notable that the DSM policies were adopted as rules, in compliance with New Jersey's rulemaking requirements. According to Michael Ambrosio, the board decided to pursue a rulemaking in this instance because it was chastised by the courts on several occasions for not following rulemaking procedures. It also wanted to address the wishes of the then-new administration under Governor James Florio, which put all agencies on notice of its preference for pursuing rulemaking rather than adjudication whenever possible.

The board chose not to use a settlement process in the DSM rulemaking because of its perception that the issues could not readily be settled.[53] Instead, the staff convened six roundtable discussions over the course of two years and numerous smaller focus groups. The roundtables were similar to the technical sessions used in Massachusetts during the formation of the IRM rules in the sense that they brought interested parties together to discuss the BPU's proposals and explore alternatives.[54] Both the staff and the other roundtable participants I spoke with considered the sessions informative and productive. However, they found the bidding settlement process to be more intense, but ultimately more productive, regardless of what they thought of the respective final policies.[55]

Future Revisions

The bidding settlement expired in 1993—five years after the date of the board's approval.[56] The expiration provides the BPU and stakeholders with an opportunity to change the policies. In July 1993, a board-appointed advisory council on electricity planning and procurement, composed of thirty-eight individuals representing nineteen different organizations (and including BPU staff and a commissioner), concluded its year-long review and negotiations and issued a final report, *Recommendations for an Enhanced Electric Utility Planning and Procurement Process* (Armenti et al. 1993). This diverse group, including many of the participants in the original bidding settlement negotiations, all agreed that the board should commence a rulemaking proceeding to develop comprehensive integrated resource planning (IRP) requirements for the utilities. However, the advisory council had already reached consensus on many aspects of such requirements, including the frequency of filings, the basic steps in IRP, the reliance on the existing DSM rules for the time being, and the need for public participation—recommending that a broad-based collaborative IRP working group be permanently established.

Still, they did not reach agreement on many of the controversial issues that arose during the formation and implementation of the bidding policies related to how supply-side resources will be selected and paid for. These issues were left for the board to decide, most likely through a formal rulemaking procedure (Ambrosio interview). Notably, the advisory council recommended that IRP working group reconvene to collaborate on a draft of any proposed rules (Armenti et al. 1993).

Evaluating the Success of the New Jersey Bidding Settlement

The overall success of the New Jersey bidding settlement should be evaluated by examining whether, in comparison to more traditional policy development and rulemaking proceedings, this settlement saved process-related resources; enhanced the legitimacy of the traditional process and the final results; and improved the practicality of the final policies.

Process-Related Resource Savings

The New Jersey bidding settlement negotiations were labor-intensive. Representatives from thirteen organizations met biweekly over a six-month period—meeting more frequently toward the end. One member of the group, Robert McNair, a cogeneration developer, flew in from Texas for every meeting.

The process-related benefits of the settlement are difficult to assess since the appropriate benchmark process is not obvious. The policies were never adopted through a formal rulemaking or even through an adjudicatory process. The settlement process was probably much more resource-intensive than a de minimis notice-and-comment rulemaking process. However, the resources invested might not appear so large if the alternative to the settlement were to thrash out the policies through a more involved rulemaking process (for example, with several rounds of rule proposals, comments, and perhaps even technical sessions) or a lengthy adjudicatory process.

The board's adoption of the settlement without subjecting it to a formal proceeding or making any changes resulted in the filing of several appeals with the state's supreme court. Although the appeals were ultimately withdrawn, if they had been pressed (particularly if the board had been ordered to conduct an entire formal proceeding), the settlement process itself might have precipitated some additional costs that a formal process might have avoided (that is, traditional rulemaking outcomes are not routinely appealed to the courts at the state level).

It is still early to tell whether the settlement will produce process-related savings. On the one hand, implementation of the bidding policies appears to have progressed as agreed in the settlement, with several possible exceptions (discussed in the following sections). When problems arose, the BPU staff settled them fairly expeditiously with the utilities. On the other hand, these settlements engendered some discontent and potential future challenges by the NUPs, who felt unduly excluded.

All things considered, it does not appear that the settlement saved process-related resources in the short run. However, the benefits caused by improving both the legitimacy and the practicality of the policies themselves may outweigh these short-run costs.

Legitimacy

Despite numerous problems, on balance, the settlement process enhanced the legitimacy of the traditional policymaking process in New Jersey. The final settlement appears to have better satisfied the interests of most, if not all, of the participants than if the issues had been resolved through traditional proceedings. A convincing example of this assertion can be found by examining the interests and positions of the BPU staff. The staff's primary interests were to avoid utility self-dealing, eliminate excessive payments to APPs without dampening the market, and increase their ability to oversee utility activity in this area generally. Meanwhile, the staff's original position prior to the settlement was to "stay the course" by retaining the standard-offer contracting approach. Their decision during the settlement negotiations to switch to a bidding framework if certain checks and balances were included represented a major reversal of their position and had a profound effect on the outcome of the settlement. If the resolution of these issues had remained in the traditional process, it is unlikely that the staff would have changed their position because they would not have undergone the give-and-take that was part of the intensive settlement negotiations. Ironically, given staff's clout with the board, their original position probably would have been adopted. But according to Michael Ambrosio, that scenario would have resulted in an outcome that BPU staff now realize would not have served their own interests as well as the final settlement (Ambrosio interview).

The enhanced legitimacy of the policy-formation process produced by the addition of the settlement process is underscored by the fact that eleven of the thirteen participating groups, representing a broad spectrum of interests, signed the final settlement. That settlement was approved by the board without change, and though three appeals were filed (primarily on procedural rather than substantive grounds), they were all withdrawn prior to being acted upon.

It can be argued that although the settlement generally enhanced the legitimacy of the process, the refusal of two parties to sign the agreement and the discontent of some of those who did sign undermined the legitimacy of the accord. However, most of the dissent and discontent were over major structural issues, such as whether a bidding framework was better than a standard-offer framework or what the appropriate role of utility generation in a competitive marketplace should be. It is true that the settlement did not adequately resolve these issues to everyone's satisfaction. However, it is not clear that the dissatisfied parties would have preferred the outcome of a traditional rulemaking absent the settlement process.

The consensus of those interviewed was that including supplemental settlement negotiations is preferable to a traditional rulemaking process alone. This opinion was true even of those who did not sign the settlement or were otherwise discontented. One example is Harry Kociencki, who represented the large industrial consumers, including the New Jersey Pharmaceutical and Food Energy Users Group and did not sign the settlement. He explains:

> The settlement process gives people the opportunity to truly be heard and to negotiate. Despite the fact that we didn't do so well in the settlement process, I prefer to be in that type of forum than delegated a slot in a hearing. . . . Although many of my primary interests (for example, self-wheeling and maintaining generous short-term, energy-only rates) were not satisfied, I felt the overall settlement did a fair job balancing the diverse interests at the table. (Kociencki interview)

Joe Bowring of the Public Advocate, the other nonsignatory, also stated a preference for including a settlement process:

> I prefer the inclusion of a settlement process in rulemaking to rulemaking alone. Although we did not ultimately sign the bidding settlement, there were definitely changes to the settlement that addressed some of our interests because we were involved. This was not the case in the subsequent DSM rulemaking, where there was no settlement process; we had no channel for meaningful input, and we were not satisfied with the outcome. (Bowring interview)

However, although the inclusion of the settlement process helped to better legitimize the overall policy formation process, several other factors detracted from that sense of enhanced legitimacy. First, many of the participants were surprised and annoyed by the fact that the board chose not to formalize the settlement in a rulemaking process, as appears to be required by the New Jersey Rules for Agency Rulemaking. Three separate appeals on this issue were filed in the courts. Although the appeals were ultimately withdrawn for various reasons unconnected to the veracity of the allegations themselves, the issue continues to undermine the perceived legitimacy of the entire process.

Predicting court rulings with any certainty is always difficult. However, Anthony Miragliotta, assistant director of rules and publications in the New Jersey Office of Administrative Law, concurred that the court probably would have concluded that the board should have followed rulemaking procedures.[57] However, even if the board had followed New Jersey's rulemaking procedures after the settlement had been reached, perhaps subjecting it to greater public scrutiny, the final rules might not have differed substantively from the settlement. This conclusion is reasonable because (1) the settlement had broad representation and involved extensive debate; (2) the board, after hearing the substantive concerns raised by disgruntled participants and other interested parties, still chose to adopt the settlement as proposed; and (3) since the courts provide administrative agencies more latitude on substantive issues than procedural ones, they probably would not have ordered substantive changes if the board had not been inclined to do so.

However, by not subjecting the settlement to a formal rulemaking process, the board eroded some of the perceived legitimacy of the policies that the settlement process itself helped to bolster. Also, because the settlement is not codified in rules, the policies are more legally vulnerable to challenge, change, and even wholesale board reversal. Ironically, New Jersey is the only state that I have found with negotiated rulemaking provisions in its rulemaking regulations.[58] However, BPU staff were unaware of the negotiated rulemaking provisions, which were codified in 1986 (Ambrosio interview).[59]

A second feature of the settlement process and final results that may have compromised the perceived legitimacy are the provisions in the settlement allowing BPU staff to spearhead the review of utility-bidding RFPs and resulting contracts. By providing staff with substantial leverage, these implementation review procedures supposedly streamline the process. However, deterring involvement of other interested parties seems antithetical at best to opening the public involvement process, as the bidding settlement process ostensibly sought to engender. At worst, this arrangement may violate due process rights, as the Public Advocate's office maintained in its appeal.

Lastly, the legitimacy of the settlement process has been called into question by those who believe that the utilities did not implement the settlement in good faith. In particular, some of the NUPs interviewed (both signatories and nonsignatories) pointed to utilities' methods of determining their bid blocks and calculating their avoided costs. Allegedly, the utilities took advantage of the ambiguities in the settlement to reduce both the block sizes and the avoided costs in ways that significantly diminished the importance of APP power and, by implication, the settlement itself. Although the utilities may not have violated the letter of the settlement, some of the NUPs feel that the spirit of the settlement was compromised.

Practicality

The New Jersey bidding settlement attained a degree of implementation savvy on many issues that almost certainly would not have surfaced through a traditional rulemaking process. Everyone interviewed agreed with this conclusion, even those who did not sign the final settlement or who signed despite being somewhat dissatisfied with the overall direction of the new policies (that is, a bidding approach instead of standard offer).

The liquidated damages mechanism, which set up an insurance fund to provide compensation to the utility and its ratepayers if projects fail to meet certain milestones or to come on-line, is a good example of the practicality of much of the final settlement. It appears to have been a workable solution embodying a creative balancing of the needs of the developers, utilities, and the public. This particular aspect of the settlement took three to four all-day sessions to negotiate.

All those interviewed agreed that this positive solution to a thorny problem would not have surfaced through a traditional rulemaking process. In a traditional rulemaking, the board would probably just have taken testimony and then selected a single dollar/kW figure somewhere in the middle of the range argued by the parties. The rich texturing embedded in the milestones with their differentiated payment schedules would have been lost.

To the extent that the liquidated damages fund better reflects the tradeoffs in the marketplace, the settlement can be credited for having infused greater practicality into the policies than might have occurred through a traditional rulemaking. Other areas that were settled after lengthy negotiations and the airing of different perspectives, such as the security provisions for front loading and the RFP scoring system, also appear more practical because of the settlement process.

However, not every issue contained in the settlement received as much attention or detail. Two examples are the method for determining the highest price that can be paid to a prospective bidder (that is, the price cap, which is based on a utility's avoided cost) and the method for determining the bidding block size. In the case of the bid price cap, the settlement required abandoning the old method and using a differential revenue requirements approach but did little to specify this approach.[60] In the case of defining the bidding block, the utilities were required to bid out any incremental load, but the settlement only listed factors the utilities must consider in determining such load. It did not specify how to make the tradeoffs between APP power and a utility's own construction plans or outside power purchases (NJ B.P.U. 8010-687B [1988a], pp. 8–9).

In both cases, the ambiguity in the settlement provided substantial discretion to the utilities, and this was the source of much discontent among the NUPs (including those that signed the settlement). Some interviewees claimed that the lack of specificity was due to a lack of time. Others claimed it was a strategic decision to preserve as much flexibility for the utilities as possible. It is also possible that parties did not recognize the potential problems associated with such ambiguity. Clearly, these issues could have been better fleshed out in the settlement itself.

A skeptic might argue that the scrutiny of a formal rulemaking process would have better resolved issues such as the methods for determining the bid ceiling price and bid block size. A formal rulemaking, for instance, might have forced the board to address these ambiguities definitively. However, it is even more likely that a formal process would have made less headway producing practical solutions than the settlement did.

Process Evaluation

The use of a settlement process to resolve policy issues of this scope and complexity was unique and innovative. It constituted a more aggressive attempt at consensus seeking than the technical session process used to formulate the IRM rules in Massachusetts. The New Jersey settlement also resolved many complex issues that the Massachusetts Department of Public Utilities did not believe could be settled when it decided to pursue technical sessions (for example, whether utilities should be allowed to bid in their own solicitation).

The New Jersey bidding settlement process benefited from its reliance on a core negotiating group. The thirteen representatives of a broad spectrum of interested parties were selected by their peers. This representative approach kept the group to a manageable number (over one hundred people showed up to the original meeting) and allowed the parties to proceed expeditiously. However, efforts were not made to solicit input from interest groups that did not normally appear before the board at that time (for example, environmental groups and agencies). Also, it appears that some of the individuals did not confer regularly with those they purported to represent.

The settlement process effectively used the drafting of the settlement language itself as a focal point of the negotiations. Beginning with a two-page, single-text proposal formulated by the BPU staff, six months and many drafts later, eleven of the thirteen parties signed off on a fifty-two-page settlement document. Concentrating on the specific language of the policies helped keep participants grounded in crafting a tangible and workable product. It also forced them to resolve most issues at a level of detail rarely entertained in formal rulemaking proceedings. Such detail was not even attempted in the technical sessions used in Massachusetts during the development of its IRM rules.

BPU staff chaired the meetings, drafted the text of the emerging settlement, and also actively participated as a full party. This gave them substantial control in guiding the process to meet their needs and undoubtedly played a pivotal role in brokering the final settlement between the utilities, developers, and themselves. However, the Public Advocate, the industrial intervenors, and even the Division of Energy (which somewhat reluctantly signed the final settlement) felt shut out of the process. Several parties protested the settlement before the board, filed appeals to the courts, and remonstrated against various events during the implementation phase as a result of their discontent with the original process and its results.

It is possible that the process could have been improved if staff had not tried to play a dual role as both an active party and a facilitator (or, more accurately, a mediator). A professional third-party neutral might have helped parties find ways to bring everyone into the final settlement and to resolve some issues that were left ambiguous.

The process also seemed to suffer because of a lack of clarity regarding where the settlement would fit within the traditional regulatory structure. Most parties assumed the settlement would be adopted as BPU rules. When it was not, numerous appeals were filed. Although the appeals were withdrawn for various reasons, the courts probably would have required the board to put the policies developed in the settlement through a formal rulemaking process.

Although the board did not adopt the bidding settlement as a rule, but as a policy, they could have easily transformed the settlement into a formal rule. The board needed only to publish the settlement in the *New Jersey Register* as their own proposed rule and then to put the final rule in the *Register* after addressing any comments received.[61] If the board had done so, this case would have provided a true example of a negotiated rulemaking, similar to the "reg-negs" conducted by the EPA. However, even without having gone through a formal rulemaking process, the New Jersey bidding settlement still constitutes a major innovation as one of the only examples in recent U.S. electric utility regulatory history in which rulelike policies that apply across the industry have been formulated through a settlement process.

SUMMARY

This chapter has evaluated two attempts to introduce supplemental consensus-building processes in traditional rulemaking proceedings. The first used structured technical sessions with outside facilitators to develop integrated resource management (IRM) rules in Massachusetts. The second used a negotiated settlement process to develop resource bidding policies for the state of New Jersey.

Together, the cases show the potential for improving the legitimacy of PUC rulemaking with consensus-building techniques. The IRM case shows that legitimization can occur in the absence of formal consensus seeking, whereas the New Jersey case shows that it can occur even when a complete consensus is not reached. Legitimacy was enhanced in both cases—not because everyone loved the final rules and policies, which many did not, but because overall, stakeholders preferred the process. They also took more direct responsibility for crafting the ultimate rules and policies and came to better understand and appreciate the difficult tradeoffs that needed to be made. However, both cases also showed how legitimacy can be undermined when some stakeholders are not accommodated or when the regulators make hasty decisions.

The processes also reached a surprising amount of agreement on structural issues and implementation details. Specific agreements were more formally accomplished in New Jersey's settlement process than in the technical session process in Massachusetts, but they occurred in both locations. Overall, these agreements produced practical improvements to the rules and policies that were unlikely to have emerged through the traditional processes.

The consensus-building processes were relatively resource-intensive. The Massachusetts IRM technical sessions required approximately one hundred people to invest an additional ten days of time over a two-year period. The New Jersey settlement required a biweekly commitment from representatives of thirteen organizations over six months. Concurrent savings in the traditional processes are less clear-cut but are probably small, if any. However, long-term net benefits factoring in the improvements to the actual policies and rules appear to be positive compared with traditional rulemaking processes.

Chapter 6

Improving Electric Utility Regulation: Cultivating Consensus

Society currently faces major controversies regarding the regulation of electric utilities. The infusion of consensus-building processes into electric utility regulation can improve the resolution of these complex, and often contentious, disputes. Although settlements in electric utility regulatory cases are not uncommon today, use of consensus building can be expanded and improved. The end of this chapter provides numerous recommendations on the design of consensus-building supplements to traditional regulatory processes for public utility commissions (PUCs), utilities, and others to consider.

Challenges Facing Society on Electricity Issues

The days are over when electricity issues were relatively noncontroversial and utilities were routinely left alone to run their businesses as they saw fit. Since the rise in electric rates in the early 1970s, utility decision making has been constantly challenged by the public and by regulators. Intervention by outside groups in utility ratemaking and other adjudicatory proceedings, and interventionism by the regulators themselves, are now commonplace. Stakeholders also regularly participate in contentious rulemaking proceedings to consider sweeping changes in electric utility planning, management, and cost-recovery practices.

The contention over electric utility-related disputes often goes to the core of how utilities select and manage energy resources. For instance, although stakeholders agree that from a societal perspective, demand-side management (DSM) resources should be aggressively pursued whenever they cost less than new supply, they disagree about the appropriate role of the utility in purchasing them and delivering DSM services. This debate has intensified recently as some intervenors and regulators have called for utilities to include customer fuel substitution measures in their DSM programs, and others have called for slowing down utility DSM expenditures to curb short-term rate increases. The decisions about how utilities should recover the costs of DSM programs have also been controversial.

Similar conflicts have arisen regarding the appropriate role of utilities in providing supply-side resources. Despite a growing trend to open up the generation market to competition from nonutility generators, stakeholders continue to debate about how far and how fast this should be done. Moreover, they have extensive disagreements about the design of various mechanisms, most notably bidding systems, to encourage competition.

Environmental concerns also promise to remain controversial and challenging. Siting electricity-producing facilities of virtually any size or fuel type is extremely difficult. Recently, regulators and other intervenors have tried to require utilities to consider potential environmental impacts alongside the direct costs of electricity when selecting resources and deciding how to operate them. As expected, these attempts have engendered substantial debate.

Proceedings to change the ratemaking system itself and to realign the incentives for utilities to pursue "least-cost" energy options through market-based pricing, shared-savings incentives, and decoupling sales from profits often stir controversy. Meanwhile, as the cost of electricity continues to rise, utilities and intervenors spend countless hours litigating how those increases should be allocated between customers and utilities, among customer classes, and between current and future generations.

Finally, federal and state entities and states themselves have significant interjurisdictional conflicts on electricity issues. The areas of conflict include the resource decisions made by multistate holding companies, transmission access and pricing, utility mergers, authority over certain Qualifying Facility issues, and environmental issues.

Together these issues represent major challenges for society. Most of these challenges are likely to continue to intensify for the foreseeable future, and new challenges will surely arise. The electric utility industry and its regulatory environment are clearly at a number of complex, controversial, and critically important crossroads.

Shortcomings of Current Regulatory Approaches: Interventionism Revisited

With the increase in intervention before PUCs in the early 1970s, regulators assumed a more active stance than they had in the past. Tentatively at first, many regulators began to use their new-found interventionism to spearhead numerous campaigns to change utility ratemaking and resource planning practices (Barkovitch 1989). Marginal cost pricing in New York, aggressive DSM programs in California, and substantial nuclear plant-related disallowances associated with "prudent, used, and useful" tests in several states are all examples of this interventionism.

Yet, beginning in the late 1970s and throughout the 1980s, problems with PUC interventionism, and with the remedies produced after contested case proceedings more generally, began to surface. For instance, despite continued public support, California utilities did not sustain their aggressive DSM programs once PUC attention was diverted elsewhere. In Massachusetts, regulators and others feared that large nuclear plant cost disallowances under the DPU's "prudent, used, and useful" test had scared utilities away from building new generation at a time when it might be needed. These two examples suggest that interventionism alone can lead to remedies that are not considered legitimate or practical by stakeholders and can cause unintended or undesirable results.[1]

PUC interventionism is not likely to fare any better in the 1990s and beyond. Most of the contentious issues of the 1980s are still with us, and new issues that promise to be even more complex and contentious will probably emerge. Moreover, with increasing options for many customers (particularly large industrial customers) to buy alternative energy supplies, self-generate, or cut consumption through DSM, the utilities' monopoly on the distribution of electricity services is weakening. This, in turn, partially undercuts the ability of regulators and other interested parties to push their own agendas (for example, environmental considerations or aggressive DSM programs) because doing so might increase rates and further aggravate the by-passing of the utility system by customers (which could, in turn, aggravate rate increases on captive customers) (Barkovitch 1989, Stalon and Lock 1990). Therefore, when by-pass concerns are real and potentially substantial, interventionism may necessarily be tempered.

Meanwhile, utilities repeatedly must tangle with consumer and environmental intervenors with respect to almost any action they wish to take, whereas environmental and consumer interests often conclude that despite winning many battles before state PUCs, they are losing the war. They can often stop what they consider unacceptable utility decisions but can rarely precipitate more attractive options in their place. Litigation is usually resource-intensive and acrimonious, and regulators are forced to make decisions that often leave all parties dissatisfied. Appeals to the courts and resistance to implementing remedies ordered by PUCs are common.

Finally, the opening up of traditional utility generation to nonutility generators and to DSM resources has made utilities (and hence ratepayers) much more dependent on others for providing resources than ever before. This growing interdependence renders interventionism relatively ineffective unless accompanied by substantial consensus building. Remedies designed by PUCs alone in complex and controversial cases may be doomed for failure. Although this prediction may be more accurate when prospective issues and plans are the focus of attention (for example, a utility's future DSM programs), it is relevant for cases concerning past actions as well.

Benefits of Supplemental Consensus-Building Processes

A wide range of consensus-building mechanisms—such as technical sessions, advisory committees, case settlements, prospective collaboratives, and negotiated rulemaking processes—can supplement traditional adjudicatory and rulemaking procedures. As the case studies in Chapters 4 and 5 revealed, such approaches can improve traditional adjudicatory and rulemaking proceedings in several ways. First, when long-time adversaries reach consensus in an adjudicatory or rulemaking proceeding, and that consensus is approved by the PUC (and upheld in the courts if appealed), the legitimacy of both the process and the results are generally enhanced. The settlements in the Pilgrim nuclear outage case and the DSM collaboratives satisfied the interests of the participants and the regulators (who did not participate in the settlement) better than contested case proceedings usually do. Even in the New Jersey bidding case, in which not all the parties joined the final settlement, the parties agreed that the settlement process represented an improvement over the traditional process (that is, parties who did not sign the final settlement believed their interests would not have been any better served through a contested-case proceeding or rulemaking alone).

The second major finding from the cases in Chapters 4 and 5 is that consensus building can also enhance the practicality of remedies, plans, and policies in ways that should improve implementation and reap greater benefits for society. Several noteworthy illustrations from the cases include (1) tying BECo's cost recovery to Pilgrim's performance, (2) detailed insurance-related provisions in the New Jersey bidding settlement, and (3) various program design innovations and financial incentives in the DSM collaboratives.

At least four positive attributes of consensus building account for these substantive improvements:
- The best technical information was sought and shared, instead of being selectively pursued and used as a weapon, as in traditional contested cases.
- The parties' own concerns and experience were more directly reflected in the proposed solutions.
- The parties were able to reach beyond the confines of precedent and other potential legal restrictions that a PUC might have faced to find more workable and efficient solutions that better met their needs.
- The parties could work out their solutions at a level of technical detail that would be extremely difficult, if not impossible, in a contested-case or rulemaking proceeding.

Even when a formal consensus is not actively sought, as in the integrated resource management (IRM) rulemaking case in Massachusetts, a facilitated technical session process helped identify areas of convergence and numerous practical improvements to the proposed rules. Where disagreements on issues persisted, the informal sessions still focused the controversies in ways that greatly assisted the Massachusetts Department of Public Utilities (DPU) in its decision making. Although not everyone was completely satisfied by the final rules, virtually everyone found the technical sessions invaluable. No interviewees believed their interests would have been better satisfied without them.

The last major finding is that, contrary to conventional wisdom, resources associated with the processes themselves are not necessarily saved in the short run. Consensus building usually requires extensive time and expense from participants compared with the resources that would be expended in the traditional processes. Even the IRM technical sessions, which were the least resource-intensive of the four cases, still required participation in ten additional days of technical sessions without compensatory reductions in the traditional hearing-and-comment process.

However, stakeholders should realize process-related resource savings over a longer time horizon from avoided appeals, reduced future litigation, and greater implementation compliance. More importantly, when the long-term potential benefits of more legitimate and practical PUC decisions are considered, net benefits to society can be substantial even if the cost of the process increases.

Cultivating Consensus

Barbara Barkovitch concludes in her book on the utility industry that regulatory interventionism will not end but will shift its focus in significant ways over the next decade (Barkovitch 1989). Specifically, she predicts that regulators will focus on areas that minimize utility revenue requirements (in order to protect customers who have no bypass options) but will shy away from areas that shift costs and benefits among customer groups and between current and future generations (that is, cost allocation and rate design) (id.). But PUCs cannot live up to their responsibilities while running from a significant subset of the issues at hand. Controversies that cannot be settled well through regulatory intervention must be addressed in other ways. Furthermore, even in areas in which PUCs might want to continue intervening actively, that intervention will gain only limited success unless it is accompanied by consensus building—as seen above.

A paradigm shift is therefore necessary. PUCs must seek to improve utility regulation by cultivating consensus among interested parties. In areas in which PUCs still retain considerable leverage, supplemental consensus building can help earn greater legitimacy for their decisions while producing practical improvements that may not surface otherwise. In areas in which PUCs' authority has been weakened by industry restructuring and other factors, or where rules and policies are being formulated in new areas, consensus building seems imperative. Regulators can no more go it alone in today's complex and controversial environment than can utilities. As Philip Harter said, when administrative agencies, such as state PUCs, embrace consensus-building processes, these processes should be seen as a "positive means of resolving important issues, not as a second-best alternative to the real thing" (Harter 1987).

This paradigm shift must extend beyond PUCs. Utilities and other intervenors must also change their modus operandi by seeking to augment rulemaking and adjudication with the addition of consensus-building supplements. Although these processes are not new to electric utility regulation in most states, their use can be improved and expanded.

However, since PUCs are the gatekeepers of the formal regulatory avenues, it is both appropriate and necessary for PUCs to play an active role in shaping these processes. PUCs can help cultivate consensus on policy matters by sponsoring policy dialogues or technical sessions or by initiating formal negotiated rulemaking proceedings. In adjudicatory proceedings, PUCs can hold prefiling conferences and postfiling technical sessions. PUCs can also encourage parties to settle issues. Finally, PUCs can promulgate settlement guidelines, rules, or both.

Yet a PUC's role in cultivating consensus should not be confused with that of mediators, whose job is to help parties better satisfy their interests, but who are not supposed to bring their own substantive agenda to the negotiations. PUCs have both quasi-judicial and quasi-legislative responsibilities and are therefore in many ways parties as well as final arbitrators (unless, of course, appeals are filed with the courts). Even in adjudicatory proceedings, in which they are required to act as neutral judges, most PUCs have either internal or external advocacy staffs who are given full-party status and often indirectly represent the PUC's interests in the proceedings.[2] Given this dual role, PUCs should take a leadership role in initiating and structuring consensus-building processes while also participating in them to the extent allowed by their quasi-judicial responsibilities and staff resources.

Principles for Designing Consensus-Building Processes to Improve Electric Utility Regulation

From my analysis of the cases presented earlier in this book, the dispute resolution literature, and my personal experience, I have derived eight principles for designing consensus-building processes to improve electric utility regulation. These principles, listed in Table 6-1, are not meant to represent formal rules or guidelines for settlement negotiations. Instead, these are issues that PUCs and others who design such rules or guidelines, or who design consensus-building processes in specific instances, should consider. Although not exhaustive, these

---

Table 6-1. Eight Principles for Consensus Building in Electric Utility Regulation

1. Initiate consensus building as early as possible.
2. Include all stakeholders.
3. Secure direct involvement of the PUC whenever possible.
4. Provide adequate resources.
5. Do not exclude contentious or sensitive issues from consensus-building efforts.
6. Consider assisted negotiation.
7. Structure consensus-building processes to supplement traditional adjudicatory and rulemaking procedures.
8. Modify traditional procedures to better accommodate consensus-building opportunities.

are the main ingredients necessary to improve traditional adjudicatory and rulemaking proceedings. Improving regulatory processes does not by itself guarantee better regulation. However, it represents a critical step in that direction.

Initiate Consensus Building as Early as Possible

Consensus-building processes should be initiated as early as possible to expand the opportunities for stakeholders to reach consensus and to influence the utilities' and, ultimately, the regulators' decisions. The earlier consensus building begins, the greater the chance of saving resources that would be expended on traditional proceedings.

In adjudicatory proceedings, consensus-building processes can occur even before a utility files a rate case or resource plan. This approach was used quite successfully in the DSM collaborative cases. In rulemaking proceedings, consensus building can be initiated prior to the release of proposed rules. In the development of IRM rules in Massachusetts, the first round of technical sessions occurred prior to the release of proposed rules but after the DPU released a policy paper that served as a starting text for interested parties. The settlement negotiations in the New Jersey bidding policy case also occurred prior to any formal rulemaking or adjudicatory proceeding.

The early beginning of consensus building does not necessarily mean that discussions start off by focusing on a possible settlement; indeed, that would often be counterproductive. Formal consensus seeking may often need to wait until sufficient information has been revealed for parties to better understand the issues and to better assess the relative strength of their respective cases (that is, if the PUC were to decide the case without settlement). Workshops, technical sessions, and other joint fact-finding processes can help establish facts and identify potential remedies and thus can productively precede formal settlement discussions.

Given the complexity of the Pilgrim outage case, it is unlikely that settlement discussions either prior to BECo's filing its case, or even early in the proceedings, would have been particularly productive. However, other consensus-building supplements, such as technical sessions, should have allowed parties to establish the information necessary to begin settlement discussions in less than the ninety days required to hear the case. Moreover, technical sessions may have done a better job revealing the parties' underlying interests and building trust than the contested proceedings—which appeared to do just the opposite. The DSM collaborative cases and the New Jersey bidding case also included some joint fact finding in the early stages of their negotiations.

Include All Stakeholders

Participants should strive to include the full spectrum of stakeholders in consensus-building processes. The broader the support for a negotiated remedy, plan, or policy, the less likely it will be challenged before the PUC or in the courts. Also, when legitimate stakeholders are excluded, the possibility increases that practical improvements may be overlooked that would have rendered the final resolution both more implementable and more efficient.

In adjudicatory proceedings, settlements are generally restricted to only those parties that have formally intervened in a case. It is therefore important to encourage and support broad representation in adjudicatory proceedings from the start.[3] However, when broader participation in adjudicatory proceedings has not occurred, parties can still try to bring those interests into a consensus-building process indirectly through such mechanisms as advisory boards. The Pilgrim outage settlement suffered substantial criticism from local citizen groups that might have been tempered had the participants more directly addressed their interests. As part of their job, third-party mediators can bring the concerns of unrepresented interests into the process (mediation is discussed in more detail under a later principle).

In prospective collaborative processes and rulemaking proceedings, parties have much more flexibility to embrace all stakeholders and should do so as much as possible. No automatic ceiling on the number of parties that can be accommodated in a consensus-building process exists; rather, it depends on the particulars of the situation and the structure of the process itself. The facilitated technical sessions used in the IRM rulemaking in Massachusetts were open to all interested parties (although parties were asked to send no more than two representatives per organization), and as many as one hundred people actively participated in some of the sessions.[4]

To facilitate settlement discussions or negotiated rulemaking proceedings, it may be necessary for stakeholders to work with a subgroup of interested parties to attain a manageable group. If a subgroup is necessary, parties should make sure it is representative of the larger group, and that formal linkages between representatives and their cohorts are established. The New Jersey bidding settlement applied this approach fairly successfully—using a self-selection process within interest groups to pare down the one hundred parties that showed up at the initial meeting to thirteen representatives.

Phasing negotiations is another potential way to include all interested parties when the number of parties is large or the interests are considered too divergent to be accommodated at one time. Under a phased approach, a core group of participants attempts to settle among themselves and then negotiate with the remaining interested parties. To a degree, the DSM collaboratives studied here used this phased approach. However, all of the collaboratives resulted in substantial litigation before the DPU by parties that were not part of the initial core group. The collaboratives might have ultimately benefited from the inclusion of these other interested parties from the start. A phased approach may therefore generally represent only a second-best option to either direct involvement of all interested parties or a representative approach.

Secure Direct Involvement of the PUC Wherever Possible

PUC staff, and possibly even the commissioners, should participate in consensus-building processes wherever permissible and appropriate to do so. This can provide an opportunity for the PUC's own interests to be better reflected in any settlement that may emerge from the process. It also provides an excellent opportunity for the PUC's representatives to explore technical issues and gain insight into the underlying interests of the various parties in ways that formal proceedings generally cannot.

Staff Involvement

When the goal of a particular supplemental consensus-building process is not actual settlement (as in workshops, technical sessions, and policy dialogues), it is appropriate and, I would argue, necessary for PUC staff to participate. As was shown in the IRM rulemaking case, the staff's involvement in the technical sessions was critical to their success and the success of the entire rulemaking process. Not only were staff able to make invaluable contributions to the sessions by interpreting the DPU's proposals and the reasoning behind them, but the sessions helped to educate the staff and the commission (primarily through the staff's role as emissary but also through improved comments in the formal proceedings).

It is also permissible and advisable for a representative of a PUC's advocacy staff to be a party to the development of an actual adjudicatory settlement or negotiated rule. The simplest way for staff to participate in these processes is for them to sign any negotiated agreement in a way that binds the advocacy staff, but not the commission.[5] The settlement must then be reviewed and endorsed by the commission itself, after an opportunity for public comment.[6] This approach was taken in the New Jersey bidding case, in which the policies settled by the BPU's staff were circulated for comment prior to the board's adoption.

When PUCs have advocacy staffs, they should play an active role in settlement discussions. However, in both the Pilgrim settlement and the DSM collaborative cases, staff from the Massachusetts DPU did not participate directly in the settlement processes. As an advisory staff to the commission, they had to preserve their ability to advise the commission on the cases. Particularly in the DSM collaborative cases, staff's absence from the settlement processes caused some shortcomings in the final agreements from the DPU's perspective. These might have been avoided had the DPU had an advocacy staff that could have participated in the collaboratives.[7]

Unlike the situation in adjudicatory proceedings, in which the advocacy staff is forbidden from conferring directly with a commission, it would be permissible and advisable in rulemaking negotiations for the staff to confer with their commissioners throughout the settlement negotiations. However, if a PUC's open meeting laws forbid commissioners from congregating in a closed executive session, such conferences may either have to take place during public meetings, or with the staff meeting with individual commissioners.

Commissioners' Involvement

The direct participation of commissioners in supplemental consensus-building forums other than formal settlement discussions is usually legal in rulemaking proceedings, and possibly even in adjudicatory proceedings if precautions are taken not to violate ex parte rules.[8] However, although commissioners' direct involvement is advantageous for some reasons, their presence can have a chilling effect on the exploration of parties' interests and the development of even rudimentary consensual agreements. Parties often are either inhibited or overly positional before commissioners—generally much more so than before the PUC staff. During the IRM technical sessions in Massachusetts, the commission decided to appear only at the beginning of the first technical session to answer questions, and at the end of the last session to get feedback. On balance, commissioners' direct involvement in consensus-building processes, even when settlement is not part of the immediate agenda, should be used selectively and with caution (particularly in adjudicatory proceedings).

Commissioners cannot, in any state that I am aware of, directly participate as a party in actual settlement negotiations in adjudicatory proceedings. It does appear legally permissible, however, for commissioners to directly participate in negotiated rulemaking proceedings. But despite several possible advantages to the inclusion of commissioners in negotiated rulemaking (such as the benefit of a particular commissioner's substantive knowledge or the added sense of importance given the negotiations by the participation of commissioners), there are several significant drawbacks. First, since commissions have to be free to make the final decision on a rule after receiving formal comments (including comments from those not present at the settlement negotiations or simply not in agreement with the negotiated rules), direct participation in the settlement process may unnecessarily compromise the appearance of fairness.[9] The effect may run even deeper than mere appearances: if commissioners participate in forming a consensus, they might be less open to criticism from outside the process. If the settlement group left out a particular constituency, then part of the public could be disenfranchised. Second, a commissioner's participation only makes sense if the entire commission intends to formally ratify a settlement prior to signing, since binding one commissioner to a settlement has no real meaning. Third, as discussed previously, commissioners' direct presence in the negotiations may have a chilling effect on creative problem solving. Lastly, commissioners may have less expertise on the subject matter for a particular rulemaking than their staff. Direct participation by commissioners in negotiated rulemaking proceedings is therefore not generally advisable, although there may be instances in which their participation is appropriate and workable.

However, even if commissioners do not directly participate in adjudicatory or rulemaking settlement negotiations, every effort should be made to communicate their interests and concerns to the participants. Obviously, prior orders on related questions can be the first place to look for commissioners' concerns and views. In addition, much can be accomplished through their staff. But commissioners can also communicate more directly. In rulemaking proceedings, in which they have more procedural flexibility than in adjudications, commissioners can hold periodic policy dialogues with all stakeholders to discuss various issues. In adjudicatory proceedings, commissioners can meet with interested parties prior to a utility's filing to discuss PUC policies and possible issues that may arise in a forthcoming case. Also, when a commission issues an order opening a docket on a case, it can identify issues it believes are important for the parties to address. Commissioners can also hold discussions on the record about issues they would like to see addressed in a settlement. Similarly, when a settlement is first proposed, commissioners can issue an order delineating issues they believe must be addressed for them to fully consider the final settlement.[10]

Provide Adequate Resources

Consensus building can require participants to devote a substantial commitment of time and financial resources. Securing adequate resources can often be problematic—particularly for nonutility parties (NUPs). Although they can probably participate in occasional technical sessions, NUPs may require financial assistance for more intensive and protracted efforts, such as proactive collaboratives, negotiated rulemaking proceedings, and other complicated settlement negotiations. PUCs may also need more resources to participate effectively.[11]

Utilities (and therefore indirectly ratepayers) are the most logical source for such funding. Consensus-building processes are voluntarily pursued as a means of better satisfying everyone's interests (including those of the utilities). Thus, utilities should not consider financial assistance as equivalent to intervenor funding and should not oppose it automatically. In the Massachusetts DSM collaboratives, the utilities voluntarily provided over $5 million during ongoing negotiations for the NUPs to secure outside supplemental technical expertise. The outside consultants served as a critical resource, not just for the NUPs, but for the utilities, too. Without the funding, the collaboratives would have been much less fruitful and might not have been possible at all.

However, even in the DSM collaboratives, the NUPs did not receive resources to help defer costs associated with their own in-house and extensive participation in the processes. They did not request such funding because several feared it would not sit well with their constituents; it would probably have been rejected by the utilities in any case. Without the funding, the processes suffered somewhat. The NUPs spread themselves too thin and appeared unresponsive at times. In the other cases studied in this book, NUPs received no supplemental funding (either for in-house staff or outside experts), although all the cases may have benefited from funding (for example, for additional joint fact finding).

Future consensus-building efforts must address this potential constraint. If direct funding from utilities is not forthcoming, PUCs and intervenors should explore other avenues. One possible approach would be to establish a general consensus-building fund that is replenished with small, but regular assessments on utility bills and administered by the PUC or some other appropriate entity (for example, in Massachusetts the State Office of Dispute Resolution would be a possible alternative). PUCs must carefully determine eligibility requirements for distributing funding so that expenditures are not excessive and are allocated fairly among legitimate stakeholders. Other sources of funding, such as foundations, may be appropriate for start-up or unique processes but are probably unreliable for repeated and ongoing efforts.[12]

Do Not Exclude Contentious or Sensitive Issues from Consensus-Building Efforts

All issues, regardless of how contentious or potentially sensitive, should be considered for inclusion in consensus-building efforts. Even issues that seem intractable may prove soluble when parties focus on underlying interests. One of the reasons that the Massachusetts commission pursued a technical session process instead of a negotiated rulemaking was its belief that the parties would never agree on whether utilities should bid in their own solicitation processes. However, in the New Jersey bidding settlement, parties were able to agree to keep utilities and their affiliates out for at least three years. In the DSM collaboratives in Massachusetts, parties decided that fuel substitution was too controversial to settle and chose to exclude it from the processes and litigate it before the DPU (where it is still not resolved). In contrast, DSM collaboratives in Vermont included fuel substitution issues. Despite substantial contentiousness, the Vermont parties eventually settled most of the fuel substitution issues as part of comprehensive DSM agreements.

Excluding particular issues a priori can unnecessarily erode fertile ground on which parties can make trades on a broader range of issues that may ultimately benefit all of them. Parties retain veto power in a consensual process, and a PUC can reject settlements it does not find to be in the public interest, so neither parties nor commissioners should feel threatened by inclusion of particularly controversial issues.

Some PUCs, however, either forbid parties to settle certain issues, such as cost allocation and rate design, or dissuade them from doing so because they fear participants may dump costs on unrepresented parties. But if efforts are made to include all stakeholders in negotiations, or the PUC staff look out for the interests of parties who are not at the table, such restrictions seem unnecessary and counterproductive—particularly since the PUC itself gets a chance to review every settlement. The New York Public Service Commission recently withdrew its own proposed ban on negotiating rate design and rate of return issues after being persuaded that their exclusion could stifle rate case settlements.

Parties may wish to delay negotiations, particularly on certain contentious issues, until a later phase so that they can agree on other issues (thus building positive momentum) without sacrificing opportunities for mutual gains in the near term. As discussed in the next section, parties may also want to consider using mediators or settlement judges to assist with particularly contentious disputes.

Even if parties do not reach consensus on difficult issues, consensus-building efforts can help to inform the debate while narrowing its scope, thereby facilitating the decision-making process for PUCs. Such was the case with a minicollaborative effort on environmental externalities in Massachusetts, which did not end in consensus but did help crystallize the issues for the DPU.[13]

Consider Assisted Negotiation

Participants in a consensus-building process should consider whether facilitation or mediation services can be beneficial in their particular circumstances. Facilitation can help parties by allowing a neutral third party (or parties) to take responsibility for the myriad of details necessary to make such processes work smoothly (for example, arranging meetings, compiling minutes)—details that can sap energy from participants' involvement in the substantive negotiations. More importantly, facilitators can help moderate discussions and make sure they remain focused and on schedule. Mediation generally includes all of the functions of facilitation but brings with it a more intense involvement by the neutral party in the substance of the case. Mediators often work with individual participants outside the larger group meetings and generally take a more active role in helping parties shape actual agreements. Neither facilitators nor mediators impose solutions on participants; instead parties must agree to any consensus that emerges from an assisted negotiation. Any resultant settlements meanwhile must still withstand the scrutiny of the PUC, and the courts if appealed.[14]

Adversarial parties do not always need outside assistance to reach agreements in consensus-based processes. The Pilgrim outage case is an example of an extremely creative settlement among parties with a long history of animosity without the use of outside assistance. Settlements in electric utility cases have historically not relied on third-party assistance, but this tendency has slowly been changing in recent years.[15]

Still, assistance could be beneficial in many circumstances, such as in cases involving heated controversy or numerous parties. For instance, it is unlikely that the technical sessions the Massachusetts DPU used in formulating its IRM regulations would have been as successful without the use of experienced outside facilitators. Given that as many as one hundred parties showed up at some of the sessions, it is hard to imagine how the technical staff of the DPU could have both managed the process and actively participated in the discussions.

The dispute resolution literature concludes that mediation can be beneficial for resolving the types of public disputes encountered in electric utility regulation (Harter 1987, Susskind and Cruikshank 1987). None of my case studies included a third-party mediator. However, both the New Jersey bidding settlement process and the DSM collaborative processes might have benefited from mediation because numerous issues remained unresolved at the end of those settlements, despite the many accomplishments attained there. Mediation could have been beneficial throughout the processes, or just for particularly difficult parts.

If parties in a particular dispute decide to secure outside assistance, they must make at least three important decisions. First, they need to decide if they are looking for facilitation or mediation services. For technical sessions and other processes in which the goal is to create a dialogue, a facilitator may be sufficient. A mediator is probably preferable for adjudicatory settlements, proactive collaboratives, and negotiated rulemaking proceedings in which a consensus is actively sought.

Second, parties must decide whether they want to secure an outside professional facilitator or mediator or to use a settlement judge (or other staffperson) from within the PUC itself. As long as any individual selected (1) is perceived as neutral by the participants, (2) has adequate skills and experience in providing facilitation or mediation assistance, and (3) has sufficient technical expertise if called on to mediate, an inside or outside neutral can be used.[16] If inside settlement judges are used, however, they should be different from the individuals who preside over the formal cases. Whether inside or outside assistance is sought, participants should be involved in the identification and selection of the facilitator or mediator as much as possible.[17]

Third, parties must decide who will pay for the facilitation or mediation services. As is the case with the provision of resources to intervenors, utilities (and therefore probably ratepayers) should be the primary source. However, other state and private funding options can also be pursued.

Structure Consensus-Building Processes to Supplement Traditional Adjudicatory and Rulemaking Procedures

Consensus-building processes must be structured to supplement—not supplant—traditional adjudicatory and rulemaking processes. PUCs cannot delegate their decision-making authority and must make the final decisions on adjudicatory settlements and negotiated rules before they can take effect. Consensus-building processes must also be careful not to violate preexisting regulatory and statutory requirements with respect to ex parte contacts, open-meeting laws, and other applicable matters.

On a practical level, if a settlement is reached either in an adjudicatory or rulemaking proceeding, parties must have an opportunity to comment prior to a final PUC ruling. When adjudicatory settlements are contested, parties may need the opportunity to conduct cross-examination and to file written (and possibly oral) comments. All of the DSM collaboratives in Massachusetts have necessitated extensive hearings, although the Pilgrim outage settlement, which had unanimous support, did not.

After a settlement in a negotiated rulemaking, PUCs must, at a minimum, put the settlement out for public comment as proposed rules. However, if the settlement is not unanimous or some parties were not part of the negotiations, the PUC should solicit comments and hold hearings prior to releasing the negotiated settlement as its proposed rule.

However helpful a consensus of the litigants may be, it does not ensure that the PUC will accept it—unlike the situation in civil cases before the court system. In making its final decision with respect to a settlement, a PUC must also independently determine that the settlement is in the public interest. PUCs should require participants to file documentation that could support such a determination. Supporting evidence should include both factual background information and testimony from parties supporting the settlement (or contesting it if there are any nonsignatories). The earlier in a formal proceeding that a settlement occurs (for example, before the close of hearings, or even prior to a utility filing), the more critical the supplemental information becomes, since little or no formal record will have been previously established.

When parties use technical sessions or other processes in which settlement is not the primary focus, mechanisms are needed to feed the valuable information that emerges directly into the formal proceedings. This can be done by entering documents produced during the informal negotiating process (or a verbal summation by one or more party) directly into the record. PUCs should afford all parties an opportunity to explore this material further in the formal proceedings.

Modify Traditional Procedures to Better Accommodate Consensus-Building Opportunities

Traditional adjudicatory and rulemaking processes can be modified, or in some cases merely clarified, to provide a more conducive environment for consensus building. For instance, rather than rejecting settlements outright or even making substantial modifications unilaterally, PUCs should send settlements they cannot accept back to the parties for further work. If time constraints do not allow for renegotiation, parties should at least be given the opportunity to comment on any modifications or rejections proposed by the PUC prior to final adoption. As discussed above, commissions should also communicate their interests and concerns to participants in a consensus-building process as early and directly as possible.

PUCs must seek ways to provide adequate time for consensus building. A perennial problem with settlements in rate case proceedings is that states often have a fixed suspension period (for example, six months), after which the rates are approved as originally proposed if no decision is issued by the PUC. Obviously, this provides substantial pressure on participants and the PUC for settlements to occur quickly and for the formal litigation process to stay on schedule. Litigants can agree to extend suspension periods in many states (or in some cases by unilateral action by a utility). More research is needed to determine how PUCs can stop the litigation clock when settlement discussions appear promising.

PUCs can also foster consensus building by clearly and proactively developing policies that protect the participants' rights. For instance, PUCs should make clear that matters discussed in the course of settlement procedures (for example, admissions, concessions, or offers to settle) are not subject to discovery, or admissible in any hearing unless all parties agree. PUCs might require that all parties in a proceeding receive notice when settlement negotiations are beginning. Although parties must ultimately be allowed to settle with whomever they please (after weighing the cost and benefits of leaving out any particular party), all legitimate stakeholders should be invited to participate in settlement discussions. This requirement should not, however, preclude subgroups either from meeting prior to the beginning of actual settlement negotiations for exploratory discussions or from caucusing during the course of settlement negotiations.[18] When settlement discussions begin prior to a docketed case, and hence parties have not formally identified themselves, notice should be provided to all potentially interested parties, including those who have intervened in a utility's last few cases.

PUC policies on settlement and other consensus-based processes should be institutionalized through the adoption of guidelines, rules, or both. Currently only few states have done this, although the Staff Subcommittee on Administrative Law Judges of the National Association of Regulatory Utility Commissioners (NARUC) adopted model settlement guidelines in 1991 for states to consider.[19] There are two important reasons why states should formalize their settlement procedures and policies. First, it makes the policies explicit, so everyone is playing by the same rules. Second, it elevates consensus-building processes, such as settlement, to a stature comparable to traditional adjudication and rulemaking procedures, which have enjoyed clearly articulated guidelines, rules, or both for some time.

Parting Comment: One State's Evolution

When I first began working at the Massachusetts Department of Public Utilities in 1988, consensus-building processes were not used extensively. Although the commission had encouraged and approved many rate case settlements, the DPU did not have settlement guidelines or an in-house advocacy staff to participate in settlement discussions. Also, technical sessions were rarely initiated by the DPU. When the commissioners were approached by me and others about using more alternative dispute resolution mechanisms, although not hostile to the notion, they expressed numerous concerns about the delegation of their authority, the appropriateness of staff participation, and the use of outside facilitation.

Over the course of my three-year tenure at the DPU, I witnessed many substantial changes in this area. Much of the initiative for change came from utilities and intervenors outside the DPU, through such creative settlements as the one forged in the Pilgrim outage case, and through the formation of the innovative DSM collaboratives. Some of the innovation, however, came from within the DPU. In particular, the successful use of facilitated technical sessions in conjunction with the formation of the DPU's new IRM regulations helped allay many of the commissioners' fears about using supplemental consensus-building techniques. It also pointed at new possibilities for future applications. By the time I left the DPU in 1991, the IRM rules had been finalized (and even included a required prefiling settlement process),[20] technical sessions were commonplace, settlement guidelines had been issued for settling water cases, and an advocacy staff charged with representing the DPU in settlement negotiations had been created and had even settled its first few cases.

In some ways, the Massachusetts DPU's recent embrace of consensus-building processes represents a spiraling back to the regulatory approach pioneered by Charles Adams at the Massachusetts Railroad Commission in the 1870s. Adams believed that regulators should cultivate consensus while still pushing forward their own agendas (McCraw 1984). Adams's use of consensus building was in part philosophic and in part a result of not having the authority to order the railroad companies to do what he wanted. The Massachusetts DPU's use of consensus building represents a recognition that, despite the DPU's extensive powers to intervene in utility matters, interventionism without consensus building in this complicated and ever-changing world of electric utility regulation faces a high risk of failure.

The Massachusetts DPU, along with the utilities and other intervenors that appear before it, are not alone in this realization. Consensus building has a major role to play in the evolution of electric utility regulation. Settlements, DSM collaboratives, and other consensus-building processes are springing up with increasing frequency across the country. I hope that these case study analyses, theoretical discussions, and recommendations will help guide those efforts.

Appendix 1. DSM Expenditures and Estimated Savings of Massachusetts Utilities, 1987–1991

	Year	DSM Expenditures ($ Million)	Operation Revenue ($ Million)	Expenditures as Percent of Revenue	Incremental Installed MWh	Incremental Installed MW	Cumulative Installed MW
Boston Ediston Company (BECo)	1987	$ 5.2	$1,181	0.4%	14,022	23	23
	1988	$ 7.3	$1,203	0.6%	27,284	37	41
	1989	$13.8	$1,269	1.1%	50,911	80	91
	1990	$29.5	$1,259	2.3%	105,940	120	134
	1991	$40.4	$1,259	3.2%	93,887	120	147
COM/Electric	1987	$ 0.8	$ 361	0.2%	1,524	0.1	23
	1988	$ 1.5	$ 359	0.4%	41,187	na	na
	1989	$ 6.3	$ 441	1.4%	84,942	na	na
	1990	$25.2	$ 465	5.4%	81,870	17	na
	1991	$27.8	$ 465	6.0%	107,745	17	na
Massachusetts Electric Company (MECo)	1987	$ 9.4	$1,086	0.9%	21,393	21	21
	1988	$18.4	$1,140	1.6%	65,417	33	54
	1989	$31.0	$1,232	2.5%	92,196	40	94
	1990	$53.4	$1,391	3.8%	110,257	38	131
	1991	$90.0	$1,559	5.8%	134,738	51	182
Western Massachusetts Electric Company (WMECo)	1987	$ 2.4	$ 295	0.8%	15,898	2	2
	1988	$ 3.0	$ 318	0.9%	9,173	2	3
	1989	$ 4.5	$ 349	1.3%	10,743	2	5
	1990	$ 9.6	$ 375	2.6%	24,021	4	9
	1991	$16.0	$ 418	3.8%	53,100	8	17

Note: All numbers were provided by the utilities. 1991 numbers are estimated in most cases. MECo assumed to equal 75 percent of NEES DSM expenditures.

Appendix 2. Evaluation of the Massachusetts DPU's IRM Technical Sessions, 1989 and 1990

The following table shows the tabulation of responses to surveys designed and administered by the Massachusetts DPU staff and the facilitator at the conclusion of the 1989 and 1990 IRM technical sessions. The evaluation form used in the surveys follows the table.

	Year	Ineffective 1	2	3	4	5	Very Effective 6	Mean
How effective were the technical sessions in furthering your understanding of DPU proposals?	1989	0%	11%	9%	30%	45%	5%	4.4
	1990	0%	2%	5%	17%	56%	20%	4.9
eliciting alternatives to DPU proposals?	1989	2%	4%	17%	30%	35%	13%	4.4
	1990	0%	7%	27%	44%	20%	2%	3.8
improving your understanding of others' perspectives?	1989	0%	0%	0%	26%	49%	25%	5.0
	1990	0%	0%	7%	15%	56%	22%	4.9
How effective were outside facilitator(s) in managing sessions?	1989	0%	0%	14%	22%	25%	39%	4.9
	1990	0%	0%	2%	17%	34%	46%	5.2
DPU staff in serving as a technical resource?	1989	2%	2%	2%	13%	42%	38%	5.1
	1990	0%	0%	2%	12%	56%	29%	5.1

How would you evaluate the amount of time alloted to the technical session?

	Too Little	Too Much	Just Right
1989	45%	6%	49%
1990	27%	10%	63%

If you attended both 1989 and 1990 technical sessions, compare 1990 to 1989: [a]

Less Successful	Same	More Successful
9%	36%	55%

Note: Sample size for 1989 = 53; for 1990 = 41.
[a] Twenty-two participants attended both 1989 and 1990 sessions.

Appendix 2. Technical Session Evaluation Form
(continued)

THE COMMONWEALTH OF MASSACHUSETTS
DEPARTMENT OF PUBLIC UTILITIES

D.P.U. 86-36
Technical Session Evaluation Form

	Ineffective					Very Effective

1. How effective were the technical sessions in furthering *your understanding of the Department's regulatory framework* as proposed in D.P.U. 86-36-F?   1   2   3   4   5   6

2. How effective were the technical sessions in *eliciting alternatives* to elements of the Department's proposed regulatory framework?   1   2   3   4   5   6

3. How effective were the technical sessions in improving *your understanding of other parties' perspectives* on all resource solicitations and least-cost planning in general?   1   2   3   4   5   6

4. What aspects of the Department's proposals in 86-36-F do you think should not be changed? (Please list.)

　_____

5. What aspects of the Department's proposal should definitely be changed? (Please list.)

　_____

6. What did you like most about the technical sessions? (Please list.)

　_____

7. What did you like least about the technical sessions? (Please list.)

　_____

8. The Department chose to use outside facilitators to manage the technical sessions. How effective were the facilitators in carrying out this role?   1   2   3   4   5   6

9. The Department assigned staff to serve as a resource in each small group. How effective were the staff in carrying out this role?   1   2   3   4   5   6

Appendix 3. Summary of Environmental Externality Values to Be Used by Massachusetts Utilities in Evaluating the Emissions of Energy Resource Options (1989 $)

	$/ton	$/lb
Nitrogen oxides (NO_x)		
Ambient air quality	$ 6,500	$ 3.25
Greenhouse	—	—
TOTAL	$ 6,500	$ 3.25
Sulfur oxides (SO_x)	$ 1,500	$ 0.75
Volatile organic compounds	$ 5,300	$ 2.65
Total suspended particulates	$ 4,000	$ 2.00
Carbon monoxide (CO)		
Ambient air quality	$ 820	$ 0.41
Greenhouse	$ 50	$ 0.02
TOTAL	$ 870	$ 0.43
Carbon dioxide (CO_2)	$ 22	$ 0.011
Methane (CH_4)	$ 220	$ 0.11
Nitrous oxide (N_2O)	$ 3,960	$ 1.98

Source: Mass. D.P.U. 89-239 (1990b), p.85.

Endnotes

Chapter One

1. In actuality, only fourteen states call the agency with authority over electric utility rates the "Public Utility Commission." Twenty-five states (including Washington, D.C.) call such agencies the "Public Service Commission," and twelve states call them something entirely different (for example, "Public Utility Board," "Service Board," or "Department of Public Utilities"). However, *PUC* is the most commonly used term in the literature, and it is used throughout this book to refer to all of the above.

2. Since 1992, I have helped represent the staff of the Rhode Island Public Utilities Commission in demand-side management collaborative negotiations with two utilities and various intervenor groups. From September 1992 through June 1993, I mediated an intensive environmental externality rulemaking for the Vermont Public Service Board. In 1993, I facilitated the technical review of NARUC's draft gas integrated-resource-planning handbook by its diverse steering committee, and in 1994, I designed and facilitated an all-day retreat of the Centerior energy demand-side management collaborative in Ohio. Finally, I have instructed hundreds of regulators, utilities, and intervenors on using dispute resolution techniques during more than half a dozen national trainings and have written extensively on the subject.

Chapter Two

1. The executive committee of the federation included such diverse membership as Samuel Insul of Commonwealth Electric; John Mitchell, president of the United Mine Workers; and Louis Brandeis, then a lawyer in Boston and a future Supreme Court Justice (D. Anderson 1981).

2. The governors included Charles Hughes (New York), Robert La Folette (Wisconsin), Hiram Johnson (California), and Woodrow Wilson (New Jersey) (D. Anderson 1981).

3. Federal regulation of electric utilities did not commence until the 1920s and 1930s, when utility holding companies merged utilities in different states and utility activities (that is, wheeling power over the transmission and distribution system) crossed state lines (Barkovitch 1989).

4. In several U.S. Supreme Court cases between the 1890s and mid-1920s, the Court appeared fairly protective of utility management discretion. Since the mid-1920s, the Court has upheld commissions' rights to regulate utility operating and other costs. The Court has also placed the burden of proof for establish-

ing the reasonableness of expenditures with the utility rather than with the commission (Barkovitch 1989).

5. The one exception occurred when the utility holding company structure collapsed during the Great Depression. As a result of this collapse, increased federal oversight of the corporate structure of utilities was instituted through the newly formed Securities Exchange Commission. Political fallout also refueled the debate over the issue of public versus private power and resulted in the formation of the Bonneville Power Administration, the Tennessee Valley Authority, and the Rural Electrification Administration by the federal government (E. Kahn 1988).

6. Steadily declining marginal costs should have allowed regulators to reduce rates more regularly while still maintaining utilities' expected rates of return. However, since utilities' rates were based on their historic costs, there was no great incentive for them to come in for rate cases, in contrast to when marginal costs were increasing.

7. See pages 4–7 of Hirsh's book *Technology and Transformation in the American Electric Utility Industry* (1989) for some excellent graphs depicting these trends.

8. Hirsh defines technological stasis as the cessation of technological advances in an industrial process. He argues that stasis comprises more than a hardware problem—representing in addition a condition that occurs within a social system of engineers, business managers, regulators, financiers, and the general public.

9. Barkovitch points out that although the fuel and financing cost increases the utilities faced during this period were not necessarily of their own making, their inability to respond to the changes—instead of continuing to construct large, expensive, capital-intensive facilities—was problematic. She also points to their resistance to environmental regulation, new technologies, and new rate designs as evidence of an "obliviousness" to the changes required of them by new circumstances (Barkovitch 1989).

10. The choices facing the industry were perhaps most eloquently and influentially stated in a 1976 *Foreign Affairs* article by Amory Lovins, entitled "Energy Strategy: The Road Not Taken?" In this article, Lovins suggested that the nation must choose between a "hard" and "soft" (that is, sustainable) energy path. Although there is greater acceptance today that both these paths will remain fixtures on the energy landscape for the foreseeable future, beginning in the mid-1970s the political debate was more sharply focused on trying to choose between these allegedly mutually exclusive paradigms.

11. Alfred Kahn had detailed his thoughts on marginal cost pricing in *The Economics of Regulation: Principles and Institutions*, which was first published in 1970 and remains to this day one of the primary textbooks on regulatory economics.

12. The CPUC also ordered a residential appliance program, a conservation voltage reduction program for the distribution system, and several commercial and industrial programs (Barkovitch 1989).

13. For example, in the early 1980s, the CPUC adopted a decoupling mechanism known as ERAM (Electric Revenue Adjustment Mechanism), which guaranteed utility revenues regardless of reduced sales from DSM or other factors. It also tried to have utilities design programs to avoid raising the rates of nonparticipants, even though such programs could jeopardize capturing all DSM that was cheaper than new supply.

14. Jerry Brown openly espoused the philosophy of "appropriate technology" and brandished E. F. Schumacher's book *Small Is Beautiful* during his campaign.

15. Kahn quotes an unpublished study by Lewis Perl of National Economic Research Associates (White Plains, N.Y.). Joskow also claims that utilities were disallowed tens of billions of dollars, allegedly accounting for 20 percent of nuclear investments (Joskow 1989).

16. Former FERC commissioner Charles Stalon points out that increased prudence reviews were in part due to the fear that raised rates would escalate the amount of bypass (that is, customers self-generating or fuel substituting), causing even more pressure on rates (Stalon and Lock 1990).

17. When Congress authorized the Northwest Power Planning Council (which oversees the Bonneville Power Planning Administration) in 1980, it required the council to provide conservation with a 10 percent cost bonus when comparing it with other resources, largely on environmental grounds. Until 1992, Wisconsin provided all nonfossil fuel-fired resources (including conservation) with a 15 percent credit. At that time, Wisconsin switched to emissions cost adders for greenhouse gases only. Vermont provides conservation with a 15 percent advantage over other resources (5 percent based on lower externalities and 10 percent based on lower risk). In 1993, Vermont was considering alternative approaches, including emission-reduction targets.

18. The federal Clean Air Act Amendments of 1990 may reduce the impetus for state PUCs to attempt to further internalize externalities associated with certain pollutants, such as sulfur dioxide, because by setting up a market trading system and effectively pricing the externality, it can be argued that most, if not all, of the externality has been internalized. However, for other pollutants, such as carbon dioxide, state PUC efforts may actually increase in anticipation of future federal laws in this area.

19. A more subtle variation of this approach, known as the "nonparticipant" or "no-losers" cost-effectiveness test, has been advocated by some who maintain that it is fine for the utility to pay up to its full avoided cost for DSM as long as most of the cost is recovered directly from participants (Cicchetti and Hogan 1988, Katz 1989). Many have argued that this is simply the "no-losers" test wolf in sheep's clothing (Lovins and Hirst 1989).

20. Although Moskovitz et al. maintain that DSM investment in 1990 was slightly less than $2 billion, continued escalation of expenditures since then should easily put the total price tag for 1992 above $2 billion.

21. Although 3 percent of the total electricity generated was produced by industry

in 1978, the year that PURPA passed, it was all used exclusively to meet all or part of its own electricity needs and was not sold to the utilities (Joskow 1989).

22. As of May 1991, eleven states had bidding rules; eight allowed bidding but had no rules; six were developing rules; eleven were currently considering or would consider bidding in the future; and fifteen were not currently interested (Robertson 1991). As of February 1992, ninety requests for proposals had been let by utilities and government agencies for 22,000 MWs, with 190,000 MWs being bid, and 12,500 MWs being awarded so far (Robertson 1992).

23. In Mississippi Power & Light Co. v. Moore (108 S.Ct. 2428 [1988]), the state upheld FERC's position that states may not review the prudence of FERC's allocation of costs among holding company subsidiaries. This decision raised concerns among state PUCs that their broader authority to review utilities' power planning and acquisition decisions in comparison to other possibly less costly alternatives that had been established in another court case—Pike County & Light Co. v. Pennsylvania Utility Commission (77 Pa. Commw. 268, 465 A.2d 735 [1983])—could be in jeopardy (Stalon and Lock 1990).

24. The reforms to PUCHA propose opening up competition by, in part, allowing unregulated utility subsidiaries to compete with other QFs and IPPs.

25. California and several other states have had a more limited decoupling mechanism for some time.

Chapter Three

1. Numerous references to literature describing this history are provided in an article by Frederick Anderson published in the *Duke Law Journal* in April 1985. See footnote 235 on page 325 of that article.

2. Prior to Fisher and Ury's book, other works touched on many of the ideas embodied in *Getting to YES*. See, for example, Schelling 1960, Schuck 1979, Walton and McKersie 1965.

3. Figure 3-1 shows only a two-party dispute. Although graphically more difficult to show, a similar model would also apply to multiparty disputes.

4. Raiffa's book provides probably the best discussion of the theory of integrative bargaining from an economic and mathematical perspective. In the book Raiffa claims, "We act like a zero-sum society, when in reality there is a lot of non-zero-sum fat to be skimmed off to everyone's mutual advantage" (Raiffa 1982, p. 310).

5. See Harter's "Negotiating Regulations: A Cure for Malaise" (1982) for a detailed discussion of negotiated rulemaking. Also see his "Points on a Continuum: Dispute Resolution Procedures and the Administrative Process" (1987). Although Harter's work does not directly discuss state PUC regulation and, in fact, is almost exclusively focused on federal agencies, it provides an excellent discussion of the opportunities for ADR in administrative agencies and how to address some of the concerns raised by others.

6. See Susskind and Cruikshank's *Breaking the Impasse: Consensual Approaches*

to *Resolving Public Disputes* (1987), for an analysis of ADR in resolving public disputes and the potential for improving ADR through assisted negotiation (for example, mediation). Susskind and McMahon's article "The Theory and Practice of Negotiated Rulemaking" (1985) is an important addition to Harter's article on negotiated rulemaking. Susskind and Morgan's article "Improving Negotiation in the Regulatory Process" (1986b) specifically addresses the potential for ADR in electric utility regulation. See numerous other articles by Susskind listed in the Bibliography.

7. Although Douglas Amy's book *The Politics of Environmental Mediation* (1987) is focused more specifically on the shortcomings of environmental mediation vis-à-vis its handling of preexisting power imbalances, the critique is extended to ADR generally.

8. Intervention before PUCs, particularly in litigated cases, can be extremely costly and time consuming. To the degree that interested parties cannot afford to intervene, it can be argued that the initial distribution of resources places a real barrier to the parties' participation, rendering them effectively powerless. For this reason, intervenor funding is offered in some states (that is, payment of intervention costs by utilities of select third-party intervenors) and has been an ongoing debate in many others.

9. Other ideas put forward by Raiffa (1982) and Lax and Sebenius (1986) include mediation, focusing on single-text negotiation, and postsettlement settlements, to name only a few.

10. The NYPSC was apparently concerned that rate design settlements could place undue burden on the rates of customers not party to the negotiations. However, the NYPSC was persuaded that the staff's participation combined with the NYPSC's own ultimate authority to reject a settlement were adequate protection, and that preclusion of settlements on rate design issues might unnecessarily restrict potential overall settlements (Elwood interview).

11. Although the Palo Verde nuclear power plant is located in Arizona, the El Paso Electric Company, a provider of electricity in cities in southern New Mexico, was part owner.

12. Based on the attendance lists for these two trainings, the distribution of participants was 35 percent utility executives and senior managers; 34 percent PUC commissioners and senior staff; 16 percent public advocates; and 15 percent others (industrial consumers, consultants, academics, and so forth). The first training, in Boston, was co-taught by Susskind, Richard Cowart (chair of the Vermont PSB), James Richardson (University of New Mexico), and Eric Van Loon (Endispute, Inc.). The second training, in Florida, was taught by Susskind, Cowart, Richardson, and me.

13. These trainings were conducted at NARUC's National Conference of Environmental Externalities in Jackson Hole, Wyoming (October 1–3, 1990); NARUC's Third National Integrated Resource Planning Conference in Santa Fe, New Mexico (April 8–10, 1991); and Lawrence Berkeley Laboratory's Advanced Least-Cost Utility Planning seminars for senior PUC staff in Berke-

248 — Chapter Three Notes

ley, California (January 1990 and June 1991). All of these trainings, which I conducted myself, included the use of a simulated consensus-building exercise and discussions of using ADR in electric utility regulation. The combined attendance at the four events totaled over one hundred.

14. For example, a five-day training by Lawrence Susskind and Max Bazerman (Northwestern University) at MIT each year always attracts numerous people involved in electric utility affairs. Similarly, seminars led by Roger Fisher have also been attended by utility representatives, regulators, and intervenors. In 1991, David O'Connor, director of the Massachusetts Office of Dispute Resolution, and I conducted a two-day training on ADR for over twenty-five staff from the Massachusetts Department of Public Utilities and the Energy Facilities Siting Council. I also trained over twenty regulators, utilities, and intervenors on using ADR to formulate externality policies in British Columbia in June 1993. Undoubtedly other ADR-related trainings have also taken place.

15. The forum article contained the answers from regulators to two questions on dispute resolution: (1) Does adversarial advocacy still make sense today for state utility commissions when so much of the caseload seems to be changing from simple dispute resolution to policy making? (2) What experiments have you tried (or thought of trying) for alternative dispute resolution or formulation of policy?

16. In contrast, advisory staffs can discuss cases with commissioners but do not take part in the cases as parties.

17. In fact, only California and New York have been identified as having comprehensive settlement guidelines or rules. Two separate, informal surveys conducted by the staff of the New York PSC and by NARUC's Staff Subcommittee on Administrative Law Judges in 1990 and 1991, respectively, confirmed this surprising finding.

18. The Negotiated Rulemaking Act of 1990 (Public Law 101-648, November 29) establishes a framework for conducting negotiated rulemaking but does not require its use. Agencies planning to use negotiated rulemaking must give public notice. An agency representative must participate but may not chair the negotiations. Meetings are chaired by a neutral facilitator or mediator. If the committee reaches consensus on a proposed rule, it is submitted to the agency to consider adopting as its proposed rule. Agencies may pay expenses of committee members who are needed for the process but who do not have adequate resources.

19. The settlement was reached with Dayton Power and Light. The cases with Cincinnati Gas and Electric and with Columbus Southern Power were not settled.

20. The letter was signed by thirteen parties representing the majority of participants and a comprehensive cross-section of interest groups. Several parties did not sign the letter simply because they were not comfortable encouraging the board to resort to this process again without knowing the specifics of the case (Russell interview). These nonsigning parties otherwise supported the assertions in the letter regarding the overall benefits of the externality mediation.

21. Although focusing on settlements in the judiciary rather than on those that occur in the administrative process, Carrie Menkel-Meadow concludes in an article published in the *UCLA Law Review* in 1985 that contrary to popular belief, empirical studies have not confirmed that settlement conferences, arbitration, and mediation decrease delay of case-processing time or promote judicial efficiency. She goes on, however, to advocate ADR for improving the quality of dispute resolution, which she claims is a far more important reason anyway (Menkel-Meadow 1985).

22. A PUC decision is appealed directly to the state supreme judicial court in most, if not all, states. Appeals of decisions by the state supreme courts go directly to the U.S. Supreme Court.

23. I base this observation and the observation in the previous sentence on my discussions with PUC commissioners and senior staff in approximately a dozen states.

24. Breyer claims, "The present law of judicial review of administrative decision making . . . contains an important anomaly. The law requires the courts to defer often and strongly to agency judgments about matters of law, but it also sometimes suggests that courts conduct independent in-depth reviews of agency judgments about matters of policy" (Breyer 1987, p. 68). Although Breyer's work refers specifically to federal case law, state laws—although probably different from state to state—undoubtedly reflect similar tensions.

25. It is misleading to conclude that PUC approval of a consensus (and for that matter any PUC decision sustained by the court) is a sufficient barometer of substantive success. PUCs (and ultimately the courts if their opinion is solicited) are required only to make sure that settlements fall within a reasonable range of substantive outcomes that may have emerged from a contested case. PUCs do not generally require that settlements constitute substantive improvement over the likely range of outcomes from traditional procedures.

26. Raiffa's approach not only is useful in analyzing unrealized joint gains but can also be applied to better understanding what gains were already realized. Hence the approach advocated by Raiffa is useful for assessing the movement from a relativist baseline as well.

27. It is worth noting that if "simplicity and continuity" were substituted for "wisdom," Susskind and Cruikshank's list of evaluative objectives would be identical to the Massachusetts Department of Public Utilities' criteria for evaluating rate structures (Keegan 1986).

28. The following section draws heavily on a paper entitled "When Should a Collaborative DSM Process Be Considered Successful?" which I prepared for the Fifth National DSM Conference (Raab 1991).

29. In an article in the June 1991 *Georgetown Law Journal* entitled "A Normative Theory of Public Law Remedies," Susan Sturm makes a compelling argument that the courts can enhance the legitimacy of the development of remedial priorities and plans by relying on a deliberative model centered on the consensus-based negotiations of the disputant parties themselves. This argument, and

many others made in this excellent piece, which is focused on the courts rather than on administrative agencies, often parallels many of the arguments made in this book (for example, she argues (1) against limiting application of the socalled deliberative model a priori, (2) for the need to look at both the process and the results, and (3) for the possibility that such an approach may increase short-run process-related resources).

Chapter Four

1. In reality, commissioners in states with open-meeting laws often confer with each other indirectly through their staffs outside public meetings.

2. Although technically the federal Administrative Procedures Act (discussed in detail in Chapter 5) classifies ratemaking as formal rulemaking, as opposed to adjudication or informal (notice-and-comment) rulemaking, which is how agencies almost always make rules, there is little if any procedural difference between formal rulemaking and formal adjudication in the APA (Breyer and Stewart 1979). More importantly, on the state level, where PUCs follow state laws rather than the federal APA, PUC ratemaking is virtually always considered to be an adjudicatory proceeding.

3. Although rate case structures and adjudicatory structures may vary slightly from state to state, or case to case, Table 4-1 provides the general structure. Any differences are relatively insignificant (for example, a utility might file its testimony with its initial filing rather than after discovery).

4. Rates are typically set by dividing the costs incurred in a single year—adjusted for known and measurable changes and for a return to stockholders—by the anticipated sales of electricity in order to obtain a rate per unit. Even states that compute rates for a future year base their projections on a historic test year.

5. Historically, forward-looking cases were limited to financing cases that approved the issuance of long-term equity or debt to finance a major project or retire old debt and replace it with new debt at lower rates.

6. This number does not include data from seven states that had not reported back to NARUC prior to publication of the cited sources. If the rate cases from these states were included, the numbers would definitely be higher.

7. These numbers actually represent the cases from only half the states. The other states did not provide information on this question in NARUC's annual survey. The actual numbers therefore might be twice as large.

8. The high number of general rate cases in 1982 (seven) is somewhat of an anomaly and may be explained by the fact that 1982 was the transition year from a Republican to a Democrat as governor. It is possible that utilities believed they had a better chance of getting a substantial rate increase approved under the existing PUC than under an unknown future one (Massachusetts differs from virtually all other states in that commissioners' terms are coterminous with that of the governor rather than staggered). However, the cases in 1982

were much less complex and controversial than cases today, and the PUC orders were extremely short by today's standards.

9. Again, only half the states provided information at this level of detail. As such, the real number of cases may be twice as many.

10. Although the average rate case takes 8.6 months, the range is 4 months to 30 months, with a standard deviation of 4.0 months. (These numbers were calculated from data in Bauer 1991, pp. 946–950.) Many states have adopted deadlines for reviewing rate cases. In Massachusetts, for example, the commission must issue an order within six months, or the utility's request is automatically granted.

11. The long length of orders in cases not settled by the parties represents a significant change even from the early 1980s. In Massachusetts, for example, orders in 1982 averaged less than 50 pages, whereas today they average over 250 pages.

12. In a response to a question posed to PUC commissioners from thirteen states by *Public Utilities Fortnightly* about the appropriateness of the adjudicatory process for policy making, most identified many of the overall shortcomings of adjudication that I have described at length. See endnote 15 in Chapter 3 for additional information on the *PUF* piece.

13. The twenty-two states reported thirty-nine appeals (twelve states reported appeals; ten reported none). (Compiled from Bauer 1991, pp. 22–161.)

14. The average time of an appeal was 14.3 months, compared with 8.6 months for a typical rate case. The range of time to resolve an appeal between 1985 and 1990 was 4 months to 30 months. The standard deviation is 6.9 months. (Compiled from Bauer 1991, pp. 946–950.)

15. This amount was to grow to $1.6 billion in 1963 dollars before the FPC was able to catch up (Freeman 1965).

16. The states were California, Massachusetts, New Hampshire, New Jersey, New York, Rhode Island, and Vermont.

17. This percentage was derived by comparing the number of settlements with the number of major cases docketed during this period (that is, fifty-four from 1981–1989). According to Ron Elwood of the New York PSC's Consumer Services Division, who supplied the raw data, the figures should be considered only rough approximations because of some data-tracking inaccuracies, timing differences between when cases were docketed versus when they were settled, differences between major cases and minor settlements, and so forth.

18. According to Henry Yoshimura, director of the Massachusetts DPU's Electric Power Division, who compiled the data, in Massachusetts there were ten settlements out of seventy-one major cases.

19. The reason for the New York commission's reluctance to encourage rate design settlements was a fear that it would be too easy for participants to unfairly pass costs on to rate classes that were not parties to the settlement. However, in the final version of New York's new settlement guidelines and rules adopted in

252 — Chapter Four Notes

February 1992, the preclusion of rate design settlements present in earlier drafts was removed (Elwood interview).

20. In the process of revising its settlement guidelines, New York did a survey of the states to identify other models and found settlement guidelines only in California and at FERC (Elwood interview). Also, prior to formulating its model settlement guidelines, NARUC conducted a search for other models but turned up nothing more than the New York survey had (Marland interview).

21. Virtually identical settlement guidelines were first drafted by NARUC in May 1989, but they were not finally adopted and widely circulated until May 1991.

22. The focus of the cases in this chapter is primarily on adjudicatory settlement. The other consensus-building activities explored in Chapter 3 (for example, technical sessions), which are less rigorous in terms of consensus seeking, are only touched on here but are discussed more fully in Chapters 5 and 6.

23. DOER was called the Executive Office of Energy Resources until late 1989. The name DOER is used throughout this case and the other two Massachusetts cases in this book.

24. The Massachusetts DPU has traditionally interpreted Massachusetts's open-meeting law (Chapter 30) to allow the DPU to deliberate on and decide rate cases in closed-door executive sessions. Internal memos leading up to such decisions as well as discussions among commissioners and staff during these sessions are considered confidential and not for disclosure. Although it is conceivable that some of these internal memos could be obtained through the Freedom of Information Act, without making a formal request (which would certainly be challenged by the DPU), those documents are not available for direct quotation by present or former DPU staff.

25. A study by the Massachusetts Department of Public Health found that people who lived within ten miles of Pilgrim between 1972 and 1979 were four times more likely to develop adult leukemia than residents from elsewhere in twenty-two communities near the plant. However, direct causality to Pilgrim has not been substantiated and continues to be contested, particularly by BECo (*Boston Globe*, October 10, 1990).

26. Exhibit AG-4 in Mass. D.P.U. 88-28 (1989a). NRC letter to BECo president Francis Staszesky, January 16, 1982.

27. Although there is ongoing dispute with respect to the similarities between Chernobyl and plants resembling Pilgrim, the heightened concern in the United States regarding reactors like Pilgrim is undeniable. In June 1986, for instance, Harold Denton, NRC's top safety official, publicly stated that General Electric's Mark I nuclear containment—the design used at Pilgrim and twenty-four other U.S. plants—had "something like a 90 percent probability" of failure in a severe accident (Nogee and Brach 1988, quoting *Inside N.R.C.*, June 9, 1986).

28. Stephen Sweeney remained as chief executive officer until 1989. Reportedly, Sweeney left only after Reznicek threatened to leave if he was not promoted as

promised and after former senator Paul Tsongas, who was on BECo's board of directors, intervened on Reznicek's behalf (*Boston Globe*, February 15, 1992).

29. The NRC ultimately rejected MASSPIRG's "show cause" petition, and the courts refused to reverse that rejection. However, the petition received a great deal of press attention and was the subject of several congressional hearings (Shimshak interview).

30. It is worth noting that Pilgrim's original price tag was between $200 and $250 million in 1972, when it first came on-line. Although in real 1986 dollars this is certainly equivalent to more than $500 million, the outage capital and operation and maintenance costs are substantial and may have exceeded the original cost of the plant.

31. Massachusetts, like many other states, uses a fuel charge to pass the fuel and purchased power costs associated with power generation—regardless of whether they go up or down—directly to ratepayers. Although the fuel charges are adjusted quarterly, the hearings associated with the adjustments are generally perfunctory, and the pass-through is virtually guaranteed. In Pilgrim's case, BECo had been allowed to pass through the replacement power costs, subject to future refund.

32. An independent study conducted by the Nielsen-Wurster Group and funded by BECo concluded that forty-one days of the outage could have been avoided. This translated into approximately $7.6 million of replacement power costs, which BECo decided not to seek recovery on (or rather, not to retain, since the company had already collected it). However, BECo maintained that it did "not believe all forty-one days were avoidable" (letter from BECo's deputy general counsel, Douglas Horan, to the DPU on September 15, 1988).

33. The Pilgrim-related items included (1) a return on $332 million of capital expenditures at Pilgrim ($221 million spent during the outage and $111 million of capital improvements made prior to the outage but after the previous rate case had been filed in December 1985) and (2) $101 million of incremental operation and maintenance costs (that is, the O&M expenditures that were more than the expected test-year levels established in the prior rate case), which BECo proposed amortizing over five years.

34. Although there were other intervenors in the cases, DOER and the Attorney General were the only parties who sponsored testimony and, along with MASSPIRG, were the only parties who actively participated in the cases.

35. After leaving the DPU, Commissioner Tierney became the secretary of environmental affairs for the Commonwealth of Massachusetts and was subsequently selected by President Clinton to be the Assistant Secretary for Policy, Planning, and Program Evaluation at the Department of Energy.

36. In Massachusetts, DPU staff at the time served only as advisors to the commission. Staff did not act as advocates, unlike the situation in many other states, where the advocacy staff put on a case in much the same way as other parties did. Instead, technical staff would sit on the bench with a hearing officer and

question the witnesses for the DPU. In 1992 this arrangement changed, and the DPU now uses staff also as advocates in certain cases.

37. The results indicated that in order to be economic, Pilgrim would need to operate at a capacity factor greater than 60 percent, when measured from the end of the outage, and at greater than 68 percent if measured from the beginning of the outage. The historic capacity factor was 57 percent.

38. The new rules required that any capital investments over $250/kW be subject to preapproval. BECo's $332 million investment probably exceeded that threshold.

39. According to Alan Nogee, prior to Reznicek's call to Shannon, MASSPIRG and BECo had engaged in exploratory discussions regarding the possibility of settling the case. Although these discussions occurred with senior managers within BECo, they did not involve the senior executives. Everyone interviewed agreed that the official starting point of the settlement discussions began with Reznicek's call to Shannon (Nogee interview).

40. Mike Meyer, a consultant to DOER, also participated in all the negotiations. Donna Sorgi, director of the Regulated Division of the Attorney General's Office at the time, attended settlement meetings on occasion and briefed Attorney General James Shannon weekly on the negotiations (Dean interview).

41. The results were Shimshak, 7; May, 7–8; Nogee, 7.5; and Dean, 8. All commented that they considered these rankings extremely high, and both Nogee and Dean mentioned that anything higher than an 8 would be unrealistic, if not impossible.

42. In the other two cases, both plants still had to comply with state and federal health and safety requirements, but their economic recovery was not directly linked to their performance as in BECo's case.

43. The second year included a refueling outage that BECo claims accounts for the drop in capacity factor (May interview).

44. Mechanisms such as California's Electric Revenue Adjustment Mechanism (ERAM) attempt to hold a utility's revenue collection constant regardless of whether sales increase or decrease because of unanticipated factors.

45. For example, the parties debated the proper way to handle administrative costs for over two years. The utility argued that administrative costs should be assigned to each measure prior to screening, whereas the NUPs argued that administrative costs should be included only when screening the cost-effectiveness of the entire program, rather than for each measure.

46. The financial incentives included both a lost-revenue adjustment mechanism and a positive financial bonus for successful DSM implementation. The former compensates utilities for any revenue losses associated with reduced sales resulting from DSM programs that were unanticipated in the prior rate case. The latter refers to financial bonuses (or shared savings) given to a utility above reimbursement for direct expenditures on DSM or lost revenue.

47. On April 15, 1992, after the three-year stay-out provision of the Pilgrim settlement expired, BECo did file for a rate increase of approximately 7 percent.

48. All interviews were face to face except those with Besser, Burrington, Chaisson, Pastuszek, Watts, and White, which were done by phone. Chaisson, Cohen, and Werlin were interviewed on two separate occasions—once for the NEES collaborative and once for the joint-utility collaborative and subsequent individual utility subcollaboratives.

49. In the ORNL study, the NEES and joint-utility collaboratives were researched and described separately, but here they have been combined into one case. All the work on the two original cases was done by the author.

50. My tenure at the DPU began in May 1988 as a senior economist and ended in January 1991 as the assistant director of the Electric Power Division. In January 1989, I became the lead staffperson responsible for DSM.

51. In June 1987, the DPU severely chastised WMECo for its lackluster DSM efforts (Mass. D.P.U. 86-280-A [1987c]).

52. D.P.U. 86-36 ultimately resulted not only in new resource "preapproval" regulations, but also in DSM cost-recovery and ratemaking rules, an environmental externality methodology, and a new all-resource bidding process. The formation of these rules is discussed in detail in the integrated resource management rule case study in Chapter 5.

53. Though not formal members of NEEPC, representatives of the Attorney General and DOER attended many of the coalition's meetings and supported the process.

54. The expansion and bifurcation of the generic investigation was largely in response to a request by the Attorney General, DOER, CLF, and other members of NEEPC.

55. The panel of experts included Nancy Benner (Portland Energy Conservation, Inc.); Joseph Chaisson and Armond Cohen (CLF); Paul Chernick (PLC, Inc.); Stephen Cowell (Conservation Services Group, Inc.); Thomas Foley (Northwest Power Planning Council); H. Gil Peach (Pacific Power & Light); and Arthur Rosenfeld (Lawrence Berkeley Laboratory). The experts were sponsored by CLF, MASSPIRG, and seven other members of NEEPC and were funded by DOER.

56. CLF had been an active participant in the initial litigated case and the subsequent DSM collaborative in Connecticut.

57. Cagnetta had lead responsibility in NU's participation in the DSM collaborative in Connecticut as well. It is also notable that Cagnetta had previously taken a course on "principled negotiation" from Roger Fisher, author of *Getting to YES*. See Chapter 3 for discussion of nexus between dispute resolution literature and electric utility consensus-building experiments.

58. NEES also has retail companies in New Hampshire (Granite State Electric Company, with 5 percent of retail sales) and Rhode Island (Narragansett Electric Company, with 20 percent of retail sales). Although this case study attempts to analyze the entire collaborative between NEES and CLF, it emphasizes the

experience of the collaborative results in the Massachusetts regulatory process—the primary focus of this case.

59. Sentinel Energy Services Company, which was involved in residential performance contracting, sent the DPU a letter protesting the exclusive nature of the collaborative. The NUPs decided not to expand the process, but the parties held a meeting with sixteen people representing nine ESCOs and energy consulting firms to review the programs being developed and to solicit recommendations. The DPU did not order the parties to expand their membership, primarily because it considered the process voluntary.

60. The DPU had never previously allowed the funding of intervenors in rate cases or other proceedings and did not believe that it had the authority to do so, despite frequent requests by intervenors to allow such funding.

61. The order was silent on the NEES collaborative, which the DPU was never asked to approve.

62. In Mass. D.P.U. 86-36-D (1988b), the DPU issued the following directives: (1) programs should be implemented as soon as they are ready (that is, utilities should not wait until the following summer after Phase II); (2) parties should address other hard-to-reach sectors (besides low-income), including (a) rental housing, (b) small commercial establishments, and (c) public buildings and facilities, to "spread the direct benefits" of DSM; (3) all interested parties should be directly or indirectly invited to participate in the process; (4) parties should not come to the commission to resolve collaborative disputes on a regular basis; (5) utilities should consider the $385,000 for the NUPs' experts allowable as a legitimate DSM development cost; and (6) parties should focus on program design and implementation issues rather than on policy issues.

63. With respect to the appropriate cost-effectiveness test, the debates included (a) whether a utility revenue minimization test or a societal test should be utilized; (b) how, if at all, environmental externalities should be internalized; and (c) how, if at all, DSM measures and DSM programs that include bundles of measures should be evaluated differently. With respect to cost recovery, the debates included (a) whether utilities should expense or amortize their DSM investments; (b) whether utilities should be entitled to any lost sales revenue associated with the pursuit of DSM; and (c) whether any additional incentives beyond recovery of direct costs and lost revenues were justified.

64. In the end, the Phase I program designs did not use any cost-effectiveness test to screen the program designs—leaving that level of detail for Phase II (Mass. Collaborative Parties 1988, p. 4).

65. With respect to cost-effectiveness testing, the order required that utilities use a societal test that includes both customer and utility costs as well as environmental costs and any other significant nonenergy costs and benefits (Mass. D.P.U. 86-36-F [1988d], pp. 19–24). With respect to cost recovery, the order indicated its willingness to entertain proposals either to expense or amortize direct DSM expenditures, as well as proposals to recover lost revenue (id., pp. 31–36). The order further indicated that substantial DSM programs could be

submitted for "preapproval" just as supply resources could (that is, utilities could commit to providing DSM at a certain price in exchange for the DPU's essentially finding the programs "prudent" and "used and useful" prior to construction rather than through reviews conducted after a new resource was on-line, as was traditionally done in Massachusetts and most other states) (id.). The order did not grant the utilities any additional incentives, such as shared savings.

66. CLF did, however, push fuel substitution in its collaboratives with utilities in Vermont from the start. Largely because of the controversy on that issue, those collaboratives were extremely contentious and slow moving, although they eventually settled the fuel substitution issue with all the utilities (Raab and Schweitzer 1992). Meanwhile, as of this writing, the fuel substitution docket remains open in Massachusetts, ever since Boston Gas intervened in NEES's DSM preapproval case in 1991 and over twenty additional parties followed suit.

67. On August 31, 1990, absent a consensus, the DPU issued its final rules in its ongoing D.P.U. 86-36 investigation. In the order, the DPU adopted a series of environmental adders for different pollutants recommended by DOER, which were the highest adopted values by any state at the time (Mass. D.P.U. 89-239 [1990b], pp. 51–85). These adders represent a cost per unit of pollutant released into the environment. These costs are added to the direct cash costs of a power source in computing its cost-effectiveness for purposes of resource planning.

68. The DPU staff's concerns included (a) making sure the cost-effectiveness tests were consistent with those outlined in Mass. D.P.U. 86-36-F (1988d); (b) addressing all hard-to-reach sectors, including rental housing in one- to four-unit structures and institutional facilities; (c) avoiding lost opportunities and cream skimming (the letter warned against using the proposed appliance labeling program); and (d) retaining performance contracting as an option.

69. David O'Connor, executive director of the Massachusetts Office of Dispute Resolution (then called Massachusetts Mediation Service), provided facilitation. At the time, O'Connor was also facilitating a series of technical sessions for the DPU in its integrated resource management rulemaking process. His role, and the use of outside neutrals, is discussed in detail in the DPU rulemaking case in Chapter 5.

70. Although both Eastern and Nantucket began Phase II collaboratives and ultimately achieved some consensus among the parties, these collaboratives, involving smaller utilities, never had much momentum, and each eventually withered away. The Eastern and Nantucket collaboratives are therefore not pursued further in this case study.

71. The NEES incentive proposal was actually a two-part incentive. The first part rewarded the utility for each kWh saved at a fixed price (a maximizing incentive), whereas the second part rewarded the utility with a percentage of the difference between NEES's avoided cost and the cost of DSM (an efficiency or shared-savings incentive). In theory, the maximizing incentive was to guarantee

that the utility pursue all cost-effective DSM (that is, less than NEES's avoided cost) and not just the cheapest DSM, whereas the efficiency incentive rewarded the company for delivering its programs as efficiently as possible.

72. WMECo proposed using the model-based statistical sampling (MBSS) technique. In the MBSS technique, the error ratio is used in place of the more familiar coefficient of variation of the target variable. The advantage of the MBSS technique, according to WMECo, is that it allows sample size to be reduced substantially below that in conventional sampling techniques.

73. MASSPIRG and DOER did not intervene in the case, and all the NUPs, including the Attorney General, let CLF represent their interests on most issues in the case. However, the DPU did solicit the testimony of all the NUPs (even those not formally in the case) on WMECo's programs.

74. Specifically, the industrial intervenors (Kimberly-Clark Corp., Meade Corp., and Monsanto Co.) argued that provisions in the Large Commercial and Industrial program violated antitrust law by precluding self-generation as a precondition for participating in the company's DSM programs (Mass. D.P.U. 89-260 [1990d]).

75. CLF challenged only one aspect of COM/Electric's proposal—the sole sourcing of audits in the Electric Heat program.

76. The increases were caused by a combination of factors, including (1) increasing costs for Commonwealth Electric combined with its not having had a rate case since 1982, (2) the elimination of discounted electricity prices for space heating customers, (3) the movement to marginal cost-based pricing generally, and (4) a dramatic increase in the fuel charge almost immediately after the rate increase went into effect.

77. COM/Electric maintained that because of all the controversy over its rates, it would not be wise to push for incentives or even lost revenue at that time (Zajac interview).

78. MECo, NEES's Massachusetts retail company and the only other utility in Massachusetts of comparable size, essentially volunteered to have its DSM programs regulated by the Commonwealth instead of by FERC. Also, the collaborative with NEES involved only CLF.

79. Under Massachusetts's unique preapproval rules, originally designed for major supply-side investments, utilities could have their resources approved prior to construction as opposed to afterwards. However, preapproval requires that the resource be anticipated to be cost-effective and that cost recovery be tied to performance (Mass. D.P.U. 86-36-E [1988c] and 86-36-F [1988d]).

80. The DPU clarified and refined its cost-effectiveness screening criteria in the orders in these preapproval cases, which addressed for the first time free riders (people who would have installed a particular DSM measure in the absence of any utility program); free drivers (people who install a measure without taking part in the program, yet heard about it as a result of the program's existence); and administrative costs. As a result, most of the controversy that continued to

surround the DPU's cost-effectiveness screening criteria in the collaboratives was resolved. However, in the process, some of the programs that had previously appeared cost-effective were no longer deemed to be so, and vice versa.

81. The DPU approved the programs for one year instead of on an indefinite basis, as other PUCs had done. The DPU made this decision in part because NEES, the first utility through the process, requested only a one-year approval and in part because the DPU desired to continue to keep the utilities' DSM programs on a short leash.

82. The DPU concluded in making its cost allocation decision that "fairness dictates that customers who are prohibited from participating in a program because their class has not been offered that program should not have to see their bills rise to pay for it" (Mass. D.P.U. 89-194/195 [1990a], p. 212). This decision hinges on the important question (discussed in Chapter 3) of whether DSM is a resource, a customer service, or both. If one views DSM purely as a resource, it should be allocated as NEES proposed. However, if DSM is viewed solely as a customer service, it should probably be allocated directly back to the participating customer, as Cicchetti and Hogan and others have proposed (Cicchetti and Hogan 1988). Ironically, despite a long history of the utilities in Massachusetts viewing DSM primarily as a customer service and the DPU arguing that DSM was a resource, the DPU's final decision cuts a middle course between the two approaches. Al Destribats of NEES, in our interview, acknowledged that his company later concluded that the DPU's cost allocation decision was a wise one that served the interests of NEES's Massachusetts customers, as well as NEES's own interests, better than the company's original proposal.

83. In actuality, the savings must only be measured for the first two years. Lifetime savings, which is what the incentive payments are based on, are calculated by multiplying the annual measured savings by prespecified measure lives for each measure. It should also be noted that NEES and CLF volunteered to use after-the-fact measurement in Massachusetts in the course of the hearings after sensing the DPU's interest from staff questions and knowing about the interest of the Attorney General (Hicks interview).

84. A good example of this reaction came with the DPU's rejection of an appliance labeling program that all the parties had agreed on in all three cases. The DPU was not convinced that the program was cost-effective. More importantly, the DPU thought that a rebate program might be more effective and ordered the companies to reevaluate their programs—to all the participants' chagrin.

85. According to this study, only two other utilities spent more than NEES on DSM as a percentage of revenue in 1991 (Seattle City Light spent $15 million, which represented 6.2 percent of revenue, and Sacramento Municipal Utility District spent $42 million, representing 6.4 percent of revenue). Only two other utilities spent more than NEES in absolute dollars, although neither spent more as a percentage of revenue (Southern Cal Edison spent $108 million, representing 1.4 percent of revenue, and Pacific Gas & Electric spent $154 million, representing 1.7 percent of revenue).

86. NEES's preapproval filings in Massachusetts also represented a consensus, but only between the company and CLF. As discussed, in the 1990 case the Attorney General intervened against parts of NEES's preapproval request.

87. Mort Zajac of COM/Electric maintained that the NUPs would constantly want to renegotiate issues that had been agreed to after they were revisited in the BECo collaborative, which he maintained absorbed most of the NUPs' focus.

88. The four programs were (1) Residential Hot Water/General Use; (2) Residential Electric Heat; (3) Direct Investment (for small/medium commercial and industrial customers, nonprofit organizations, and other nonresidential customers that lease); and (4) Customized Rebate (for larger commercial and industrial customers and schools).

89. CLF justified its punitive request on the basis that the company had proved it was incapable of running successful DSM programs and had no plans to carry out the DPU's policies of pursuing all cost-effective DSM opportunities from its customers (CLF 1990). CLF also asked the DPU to order COM/Electric to develop and implement various programs not part of its proposed portfolio (for example, new construction), to develop detailed evaluation and monitoring plans, and to change its cost-effectiveness screening tool (id.).

90. For instance, COM/Electric argued it gained a much higher absolute participation in both its Small Commercial and Industrial program and its Electric Heat program than any other utility in Massachusetts in 1990 (despite its relatively small size). It also argued that it had spent more money on its overall DSM effort in 1990, when measured as a percent of revenue, than any other utility in Massachusetts.

91. BECo argued that even if it pursued and acquired all the cost-effective DSM opportunities as agreed to in the collaborative, it still needed Edgar. The Attorney General, MASSPIRG, and CLF contended, among other things, that the collaborative agreement only covered five years and that more DSM should be available, making the plant virtually unnecessary for the foreseeable future.

92. The DPU's directives in this regard included (1) approving the increase in rebate levels for NEES's Energy Initiative and Design 2000 programs; (2) putting NEES on notice that its Small Commercial and Industrial program must include nonlighting measures in 1992 to be considered for approval; (3) ordering NEES to increase expenditures in Massachusetts for its Home Energy Management (residential load management) program from $2.9 to $4.5 million; (4) ordering NEES to go systemwide with its Residential Lighting program in 1991, and to offer compact fluorescent lights with electronic ballasts in 1992 unless the company could prove they would be detrimental to the system; (5) requiring quarterly tracking of company performance with respect to residential programs because of poor performance in 1990 (that is, residential expenditures were down 45 percent from budget, whereas commercial and industrial expenditures increased 15 percent from budget); and (6) ordering NEES to study and implement all cost-effective voltage reduction opportunities on the system.

93. The DPU ordered NEES to include evaluation and monitoring costs and any

projected bonus in the cost-effectiveness analysis of each program in Massachusetts. It also directed NEES to use the DPU's externality numbers from Mass. D.P.U. 89-239 (1990b).

94. It is also possible that the complete change in commissioners and the senior DPU staff responsible for DSM immediately after the Phase III NEES order (and hence also after the previous WMECo DSM order) also played a role. The new leadership at the DPU may be willing to provide more deference to settlements on DSM and other issues than the prior commission and staff.

95. The settlement also included the Energy Consortium and the city of Worcester. The settlement largely accepted the filing as submitted and did not require any major modifications to program design or budget. In a rather unique approach to settlement, two of the DPU advisory staff who cross-examined the witnesses changed roles and became advocates in order to settle the case after the close of hearings.

96. This litigation apparently cost CLF over $100,000 for its own staff time and for purchasing the services of outside expert witnesses (Coakley interview).

97. In Monsanto Co. v. Department of Public Utilities, the Massachusetts Supreme Judicial Court concurred with the DPU's conclusion that "the program design submitted by the Company appears to be consistent with the clearly articulated and affirmatively expressed policies of the Department" and that therefore neither state nor federal antitrust acts were violated (412 Mass. 25 [1992]).

98. Henry Yoshimura, then-director of the Electric Power Division at the DPU, does not recall there ever being another appeal on a DSM-related decision in the eight years that he had been with the DPU (Yoshimura interview).

99. The symbolism of the former chair of the DPU and BECo's CEO writing an article together must be noted as nothing less than impressive given the long history of confrontation between the two entities.

100. For example, there was only a $2 million, 25 percent increase in DSM expenditures by Massachusetts utilities between 1987 and 1988, as opposed to the doubling that occurred between 1988 and 1989, and the redoubling that occurred between 1989 and 1990.

101. Prior to the NEES proposal, the shared-savings concept was discussed only theoretically in the literature (see Moskovitz 1989).

102. Both COM/Electric and BECo were constrained from applying for financial incentives by factors essentially external to their respective collaboratives. For COM/Electric, it was the threat of a ratepayer revolt that precluded the company from asking for any more cost recovery than absolutely necessary. It is possible that COM/Electric's recent backpedaling of its DSM commitments may in part be due to the lack of adequate financial incentives. For BECo, it was the constraint of the Pilgrim settlement that provided that the first $75 million of the company's DSM expenditures be paid by its stockholders at no cost to the ratepayers. BECo immediately requested a lost-revenue adjustment and posi-

tive financial incentives on its incremental investment from the DPU (with the NUPs' support) once the $75 million was exceeded.

103. The commission's decision was in part based on their concern that staff could not fit the collaboratives into their preexisting workload and in part based on legal concerns that participation even as observers might violate ex parte rules (since the utilities would eventually request approval through adjudicatory proceedings).

Chapter Five

1. SEC v. Chenery Corp., 332 U.S. 194, 198, 203 (1947).

2. Notice-and-comment rulemaking is otherwise known as "informal" rulemaking to distinguish it from "formal" rulemaking, which was also discussed in the APA. Informal rulemaking is the norm among most agencies and is the only type of rulemaking referred to here. Formal rulemaking occurs when Congress requires a special set of formal rulemaking procedures in a particular application (Pritzker and Dalton, 1990, p. 49).

3. Section 553 of the Administrative Procedures Act of 1946 (5 U.S.C. §§551–559).

4. See note 18 in Harter's "Negotiating Regulations" (1982). Here he cites numerous statutes in which Congress has required stricter procedures than those required by the EPA, including the National Highway Traffic Safety Act of 1976, the Consumer Product Safety Act of 1976, and the Toxic Substances Control Act, also of 1976.

5. Overton Park, Inc. v. Volpe, 401 U.S. 402 (1971).

6. Home Box Office v. FCC, 567 F.2d 9 (D.C. Cir. 1977).

7. Vermont Yankee Nuclear Power Corp. v. Natural Resources Defense Council, Inc., 435 U.S. 519 (1978).

8. Harter observed during our phone interview that rules from certain federal agencies such as the FDA and FAA are appealed less often than rules from EPA, DOT, and OSHA.

9. In notes 157 and 158 of "Negotiated Rulemaking," Harter cites several earlier works (Dunlop 1975, Reich 1981, Schuck 1979, Stewart 1981) that contain references to the possibility of alternative rulemaking procedures, including negotiations. See also two articles by Henry J. Perritt, Jr. (1986 and 1987) for additional discussion of the evolution of negotiated rulemaking.

10. The term *reg-neg* is a bit of a misnomer since it refers only to negotiated rulemaking, whereas *regulation* is made up of rulemaking, adjudication, and other regulatory functions. Perhaps *rule-neg* would have been a more appropriate coinage.

11. Although OMB has not been a direct participant in negotiated rulemaking thus far, the lead agency is supposed to work closely with OMB throughout the process. In EPA's guidelines for contractors, it claims OMB must be consulted prior to the negotiations regarding the appropriateness of the subject and the

recommended committee members. OMB must then receive all documents throughout the negotiations and be briefed on an ongoing basis. OMB attendance is encouraged.

12. The federal departments and agencies that have attempted negotiated rulemaking include the Department of Transportation, the Environmental Protection Agency, the Department of Labor, the Department of the Interior, the Federal Trade Commission, the Nuclear Regulatory Commission, the Department of Education, and the Department of the Interior (Pritzker and Dalton 1990, pp. 327–343).

13. The five reg-negs that reached consensus were (1) Nonconformance Penalties under Section 206 (G) of the Clean Air Act (1985) (for manufacturers of heavy-duty engines that do not meet EPA standards); (2) Emergency Pesticide Exemptions under Section 18 of the Federal Insecticide, Fungicide, and Rodenticide Act (1986); (3) New Source Performance Standards for Woodburning Stoves (1988); (4) Fugitive Emissions from Equipment Leaks (1991); and (5) Oxygenated and Reformulated Fuels (1991). The other reg-negs in which most parties agreed and EPA's final rules were close to that agreement included (1) Resource Conservation and Recovery Act Permit Modifications (1988); (2) Asbestos-Containing Materials in Schools (1987); and (3) Underground Injection of Hazardous Wastes. Two other reg-negs did not end in consensus rules, and no rules have been promulgated by EPA: (1) Worker Protection Standards for Agricultural Pesticides; and (2) Recycling of Lead Batteries.

14. Wald argues that "negotiation typically does not eliminate court involvement altogether; instead it changes the nature and scope of the judicial role" (P. Wald 1985, p. 17). Specifically, she argues that judges will need to decide thorny issues, such as the development of legal standards for identifying relevant interest groups, assessing the extent of their participation, and checking up on the negotiating "process" itself.

15. See Chapter 3, endnote 18, for a fuller discussion of the Negotiated Rulemaking Act.

16. Of the thirty-seven states that responded to the survey, five claimed the state had not adopted the MSAPA, and two were uncertain (Burns 1988, pp. 3–4).

17. According to my interview with Robert Burns of NRRI, PUC exemptions from state APA requirements appear driven by a PUC's desire to be relieved from the APA's adjudicatory requirements, rather than from its rulemaking requirements. Exemptions are usually granted as a way of grandfathering PUC rate-setting rules that generally existed before the APA, and in recognition of some of the unique characteristics of rate setting compared with other forms of adjudication.

18. In addition to the NRRI study, many of those I queried on this point during my interviews concurred (Burns, Harter, Miragliotta, Oppenheim, Pritzker interviews).

19. The Public Utilities Regulatory Policy Act was signed into federal law in 1978.

It requires that utilities buy power from Qualifying Facilities, which are defined as electricity generators that are under 80 MW and use renewable resources or as cogenerators of any size or fuel type that meet certain efficiency requirements.

20. Central Maine Power voluntarily implemented a QF bidding system for several years, but bidding was not used by other Maine utilities nor required by the PUC.

21. California utilities suffered from both oversubscription (that is, more power than was needed) and undue expense—particularly in the face of falling world oil prices and reduced demand growth (Wiggins et al. 1988).

22. Beginning in the early 1980s, the Levy Commission, which included commissioners Robert Keegan and Bernice McIntyre, as well as chair Paul Levy (all three appointed by Governor Dukakis), also pushed utilities to implement marginal cost pricing.

23. Independent power producers (IPPs) represent all supply-side generation that is not built by a utility for its own use. Though IPPs are generally owned by non-utility entities, there is no legal prohibition against utility or utility subsidiary ownership of IPPs, although FERC often frowns on affiliated transactions. IPPs use all technologies and fuel types. Qualifying Facilities (QFs) are a subset of IPPs that is defined in federal law per note 19 above.

24. Paul Levy left to head the Massachusetts Water Resources Authority. Robert Werlin, former general counsel at the DPU, took Chairwoman McIntyre's commission seat. Several months later, Robert Keegan left and was replaced by Susan Tierney, then executive director of the Energy Facilities Siting Council. After Governor Weld came into office at the end of 1990, all new commissioners were appointed (Massachusetts is one of the only states that does not have staggered commission terms). Susan Tierney was made secretary of environmental affairs, and commissioners McIntyre and Werlin joined private consulting and law firms respectively. Subsequently, President Clinton appointed Tierney as assistant secretary of energy in charge of energy policy, planning, and program evaluation at the U.S. Department of Energy.

25. Boston Edison Company's Edgar preapproval request has resulted in contentious litigation with many parties. At the center of the litigation is whether Edgar is needed and whether it represents the least-cost option.

26. I believe that the lack of informal comments was largely due to the fact that both the parties and the DPU spent most of their time operating in an adjudicatory mode with strict restrictions against ex parte communications. As a result, the commission and staff did not encourage informal dialogue, nor did many of the participants pursue this avenue.

27. It is notable that the rules were formulated almost entirely by the commission and the general counsel without the assistance of the DPU's technical staff. Staff was only brought in after the fact-finding hearings were closed.

28. These policies were of immediate assistance to the electric utilities and four

nonutility parties that were engaged in a collaborative process to design comprehensive DSM programs for the utilities. The DPU's policies helped overcome an impasse in the collaborative negotiations over the appropriate cost-effectiveness test and ratemaking treatment for DSM resources. The collaborative DSM process is described in detail in Chapter 4.

29. Specifically, the order accompanying the proposed regulations asked if incentives were needed to better guarantee utility enthusiasm for purchasing supply- and demand-side resources from third-party providers, since under the existing ratemaking system there was only a strict dollar-for-dollar pass-through to ratepayers with no additional return (Mass. D.P.U. 86-36-G [1989b]). The order also requested comments on whether utilities needed positive financial incentives in addition to the other options (that is, expensing, amortizing, preapproving, and lost-revenue compensation).

30. The technical sessions all began at 8:30 in the morning and ended at 1:00 in the afternoon.

31. During adjudications, which comprise the vast majority of DPU proceedings, commissioners and technical advisory staff are not allowed to have off-the-record discussions with litigants. Although some states have advocacy staffs that act as full parties and are permitted to discuss issues with parties during adjudications, the Massachusetts DPU had only advisory staff at the time.

32. Representing the DPU were (1) Henry Yoshimura, assistant director of the Electric Power Division (EPD) at the first session and becoming the EPD's director by the last one; (2) myself, a senior economist at the EPD at the first session, becoming the assistant director prior to the issuance of the final rules; (3) Susan Coakley, also a senior economist at the EPD, present for the first four technical sessions before leaving to help coordinate the Massachusetts DSM collaboratives for the nonutility parties; and (4) Tim Woolf, also a senior economist at the EPD, who participated in the second round of technical sessions after leaving DOER, where he had spearheaded that agency's earlier participation in the DPU's IRM proceedings. In addition, other DPU staff participated in the technical sessions as scribes and in other administrative roles.

33. Massachusetts is one of six states with a state-sponsored office of dispute resolution. The other states are Hawaii, Minnesota, New Jersey, Ohio, and Oregon (Pritzker and Dalton 1990, O'Connor interview).

34. In 1986 the DPU approved an exemption from the QF regulations for MECo so that it could pursue a negotiation approach. MECo filed an annual report with the DPU comparing its negotiation-based results with the bidding approach used by utilities in Massachusetts and elsewhere. MECo's relative success was shared with participants during the technical sessions.

35. MIT Energy Lab was working with interested parties throughout New England in modeling various scenarios. Their findings were described during the technical sessions, and many participants were involved in MIT's research effort.

36. Governor Dukakis signed into law (Chapter 150) a bill providing DPU and EFSC $620,00 and $430,000 per year, respectively, to implement IRM. Although the

monies to fund IRM staffing were to come directly from utility assessments and developer contributions and therefore would not directly affect the state budget (Mass. D.P.U. 90-278 [1990e]), the public perception of these agencies' enrichment in the wake of the collapse of the "Massachusetts Miracle" (the booming Massachusetts economy, which began to falter during Dukakis's presidential campaign) was not taken lightly by anyone. The support of the utilities, which probably had the political power to delay, if not undermine, the funding legislation, without their even seeing the final rules speaks to the support of increasing the staffing of the two agencies generally, and perhaps support for an IRM-type process specifically.

37. Many factors contributed to the settlement, including a projection of little or no need for power and the uncertainty of the DPU's jurisdiction over a utility that is part of a regional holding company. However, this does not detract from the fact that a creative settlement was reached with many parties representing quite disparate interests. Even MASSPIRG's Alan Nogee, who provided the most substantive criticism of the notion of a prefiling settlement process during the technical sessions (and continues to maintain that the process disadvantages resource-poor public interest groups), but who participated in the settlement, claimed in our interview that it was "creative and reasonable." Although Nogee and several other parties did not sign the final settlement, they did not oppose it. The case was a joint MECo/New England Power Company IRM filing, and the two agencies issued a joint order (EFSC 91-24/Mass. D.P.U. 91-114 [1991]).

38. On November 10, 1992, the Massachusetts DPU issued D.P.U. 91-131 (1992b), which reaffirmed the originally adopted approach and the actual numbers that emerged from it. However, the order also allows utilities to use emissions offsets to reduce compliance costs in certain instances. Thus three new commissioners appointed by a Republican governor upheld the original order made by a commission of Democrat Michael Dukakis's appointees.

39. Though the issue of committed resources was discussed at length at the DPU's technical sessions, it was also discussed at the EFSC's technical sessions, which were attended by the DPU commissioners.

40. The avoided-energy component in the New Jersey system was to be determined by adding 10 percent to a utility's PJM (Pennsylvania, New Jersey, Maryland Power Pool) billing rate—the rate charged to member utilities by the power pool to which New Jersey electric companies belong—projected over time. The avoided-capacity component was the PJM deficiency charge for capacity (that is, the cost of buying additional capacity from the pool, which is the average cost to a PJM member of a combustion turbine).

41. A dispute between BPU staff and Atlantic Electric over the utility's award of a contract to a subsidiary was eventually settled. Staff had also lost a dispute with Public Service Electric and Gas on self-dealing (that is, the board did not find that self-dealing had occurred).

42. In contrast to the utilities' call for bidding in New Jersey, which in large part was to better control what they perceived as runaway QF development, the call

for bidding in Massachusetts several years earlier came from the commission and the state Energy Office as a way to stimulate QF development.

43. Staff representatives included Steve Gabel, director of the Electric Division; Robert Chilton, chief of the Bureau of Rates and Tariffs in the Electric Division; and Michael Ambrosio, chief engineer of the Electric Division. All three had been with the BPU for some time, Gabel since before 1980, and all received substantial praise for their intelligence and their savvy from all those interviewed.

44. Although IPP participation is at the utility's option in New Jersey, IPPs have been allowed into all of the bidding cycles thus far. On the other hand, whereas DSM bidding for large projects or programs is allowed outright in New Jersey according to the settlement, in Massachusetts's IRM rules it is allowed only when it does not conflict with an existing utility DSM program.

45. Several people told me in no uncertain terms that the Division of Energy, until literally hours before the end, was not intending to sign the settlement. Apparently, significant pressure was brought to bear on them, although no one was sure (or willing to tell) whether the pressure came from within state government, from the utilities, or both.

46. Turf battles between the BPU and both the Public Advocate and the Division of Energy were intense at the time of the settlement discussions for numerous reasons, many of which were beyond the scope of this bidding settlement process.

47. Some of the due process concerns were (1) parties' need to file comments prior to discovery and cross-examination, (2) the inability of parties to try to settle their concerns directly with the utility, and (3) great discretion on the part of the board and staff in determining if and when to adjudicate a utility's RFP. It should be noted that similar due process concerns were raised with respect to the review of the winning bidders.

48. The debate on whether to pursue rulemaking and the apparent last-minute decision made by the board is evidenced by the written speech delivered by board president Christine Todd Whitman on the morning of the board's adoption and circulated to interested parties. In the speech, the words "for publication in the *New Jersey Register*" were deleted after the words "I recommend that it [the settlement] be approved."

49. Apparently GPU is planning to purchase 500 MW for Jersey Central from Duquesne Power—350 MW of system capacity and energy and 150 MW interest in the existing Phillips coal plant.

50. Atlantic plans to build the 250 MW facility only if some of the APP power on which Atlantic is relying fails to materialize. However, this is still indicative of tensions between meeting incremental load with a utility's own resources or going back to the marketplace in a subsequent bid. PSE&G plans to replace and expand two of its facilities—one in Bergen County and the other at Burlington.

51. For instance, Walker points out that there are many variables in the calculations, which should be the same across all utilities, but none were ever speci-

fied. He further points out that some utilities inappropriately considered unprocured resources as committed. This effectively decreases the size of the resource block and reduces avoided costs.

52. McNair built a 600 MW cogeneration facility at EXXON in PSE&G's service territory but sold the power across the Hudson River (via an underwater cable built by his company) to Con Edison at prices significantly higher than he could have procured through the bidding process in New Jersey (McNair interview).

53. According to Michael Ambrosio, the plumbers' union was up in arms over the utilities' running DSM programs, which union members believed would detract from their business. Apparently at every meeting in which DSM was discussed, many vocal plumbers (sometimes in the hundreds) showed up and protested. The BPU did not think that settlement discussion would be productive in that environment (Ambrosio interview).

54. The roundtables and the technical sessions differed in that the Massachusetts IRM technical sessions used outside facilitation, were more highly structured, and apparently made a greater effort to guarantee that all stakeholders participated.

55. An interesting postscript to the DSM rules is that they too were appealed by the Public Advocate on procedural grounds. However, according to Joe Bowring, the appeal was not based on the rulemaking process, but on the implementation process, which the Public Advocate is again claiming will compromise due process (Bowring interview).

56. Although the five-year expiration clause was part of the settlement, it is worth noting that even if the settlement had been adopted as a formal rule, it would have expired at the end of five years, as is required of all administrative rules under New Jersey law.

57. This assertion was based on his observation of the court's treatment of similar cases (Miragliotta interview).

58. Although the Administrative Council of the United States in its *Negotiated Rulemaking Sourcebook* (Pritzker and Dalton 1990) also claims that Minnesota has negotiated rulemaking provisions, Roger Williams, director of the Minnesota Office of Dispute Resolution, maintained during a phone interview that that was not the case. However, other states' rulemaking regulations would generally permit negotiated, settlement-type procedures for developing proposed rules as long as the rule then goes through the same rulemaking procedures afforded a rule developed through more traditional means (that is, the commission develops a proposed rule on its own, perhaps after hearings, comments, or even technical sessions). New Jersey's rules actually set up a voluntary structure for negotiating a rule (N.J.A.C. 1:30–3.5).

59. The fact that staff were not aware of the "negotiating a rule" provisions is not surprising, since Anthony Miragliotta reported that though many agencies have inquired about the provisions, none have followed the procedures. Under the voluntary procedures, the Office of Administrative Law (OAL), at an agency's

request, acts as a convenor and facilitator to the negotiations. The negotiations are limited to ten parties, who attempt to complete the negotiations in ten days (longer if by mutual consent). If a settlement is reached, the agency reviews it to determine if it wants to propose the rules. If it does, the formal rulemaking procedure is followed from then on. The voluntary use of the OAL does not preclude agencies from pursuing other types of settlement approaches, such as the one followed by the BPU, to develop proposed rules.

60. The settlement provides only the following rather skimpy guidance:

    The avoided costs will reflect the difference between: (i) the utility's best supply plan developed without additional APP capacity, and (ii) the utility's best supply plan changed to reflect, at zero cost, the "Avoided Cost Block." These supply plans should include the level of QF capacity commitments which are currently expected to be placed in service, but should not include previously contracted-for capacity which is unlikely to develop (NJ B.P.U. 8010-687B [1988a], pp. 11–12).

61. The board would also have been required to acknowledge and respond to all comments received on the proposed rule, regardless of whether it incorporated their suggestions into the final rules. If the board had gone the rulemaking route, as it probably should have, it might also have needed to change some of the language of the settlement to make it more rulelike.

Chapter Six

1. Another good example of interventionism run amiss is the problem with California utilities' oversubscription to relatively expensive power from Qualifying Facilities because of long-term standard-offer contracts required by the PUC in the 1980s.

2. I note a broad array of arrangements between PUCs and their advocacy staffs—ranging from complete and constant separation, to staff members' rotating between advisory and advocacy roles. Obviously the closer the staff are to the commission on a regular basis, the greater the likelihood that the staff will understand and try to represent the commission's interests in settlement negotiations.

3. One way to encourage broader representation is to make funding available to support the intervention of outside parties that would not otherwise have the resources to participate. Such an approach has often met with substantial resistance by many utilities and PUCs and must be taken carefully to avoid subsidizing parties who would intervene even without support and also to avoid eliciting intervention from parties who do not have a genuine interest in the case but are encouraged merely by the availability of intervenors' support.

4. In the first round of four technical sessions, three smaller facilitated groups were interspersed with larger plenary meetings to provide all parties a chance to discuss their views. In the second round of four sessions, only one group was used, with one representative from each organization sitting around a large table while alternates sat in an outer circle.

5. This could be more difficult at PUCs that do not have advocacy staffs. Staffs that normally act only in an advisory capacity (that is, do not put on a case during adjudications) may need additional authority from their commissions to negotiate and bind themselves to a settlement.

6. In an adjudicatory proceeding, comments are generally limited to participants in the formal proceedings. In rulemaking proceedings, PUCs are not so restricted and must, in fact, solicit comments from the broader public.

7. After these cases, when the Massachusetts DPU hired additional staff to implement its IRM rules, a rotating advocacy staff was established (that is, the same staffperson may serve as an advocate on one case and an advisor on another).

8. Ex parte rules that preclude commissioners from interacting with parties off the record in adjudications generally do not apply in rulemaking. In rulemaking proceedings, despite increasing judicialization, commissioners still have the flexibility to act in a legislative mode and to discuss issues freely. Even if ex parte restrictions do extend to PUC rulemaking proceedings in some states, the types of forums discussed here, in which all interested parties are invited to attend, should be permissible.

9. Although commissioners do not have to maintain impartiality as in adjudicatory proceedings, they still need to maintain a certain degree of independence, which direct participation in a settlement—as opposed to technical sessions—could appear to compromise.

10. These recommendations and others were recently included in New York PSC's "Opinion, Order and Resolution Adopting Settlement Procedures and Guidelines" (NY PSC 1992). The New York order also points out that if commissioners disagree on issues, dissenting opinions can also be offered to participants.

11. Some PUCs can shift staff workloads to accommodate additional involvement in consensus-building processes, whereas others will need new resources. The ease of acquiring new resources will vary from state to state. The settlement of the NEES-CLF collaborative with the Rhode Island PUC included a provision that NEES provide the advocacy staff with an additional $25,000 per year so that they could hire the necessary expertise to participate in future collaborative efforts.

12. Funding for participation of environmental and consumer groups in many DSM collaboratives across the country has often come from foundations, such as the Pew Memorial Trust. This funding, while having substantial impact for those groups on DSM issues, is not available for a wider range of intervenor groups or for a broad range of contested-case or rulemaking issues.

13. In some ways, all the IRM technical sessions served this function of informing and focusing issues for the DPU. In other ways, the DPU's decision to use a technical session process instead of a negotiated rulemaking process conveyed a sense that the DPU either did not believe that the issues could be (or perhaps more accurately—should be) settled. In contrast, the New Jersey bidding policies, which covered the same territory as did the IRM rules in many respects, did rely on a full-blown settlement process.

14. See Susskind and Cruikshank's *Breaking the Impasse: Consensual Approaches to Resolving Public Disputes* (1987) for a detailed discussion of the advantages of using assisted negotiation and the differences between various approaches. Susskind and Cruikshank also discuss nonbinding arbitration as another option to facilitation and mediation, but one which has had little field testing in resolving public disputes. As such, it is only flagged here as an area for further investigation and consideration.

15. FERC historically used settlement judges in only 10 to 20 percent, and NY in less than 10 percent, of all cases settled. Outside mediators were rarely used. But as discussed in Chapter 3, the use of both inside and outside third-party neutrals has been increasing somewhat in recent years.

16. Some might argue that PUC settlement judges should not be considered neutrals. Others might argue that it is unlikely that outside, professional neutrals would have the substantive knowledge necessary to effectively mediate a contested electric utility dispute. However, I believe it depends on the particulars of the dispute and the individuals being considered.

17. In technical sessions or rulemaking proceedings with large numbers of participants, it may be impractical to get all parties together and in accord on the need for a neutral, let alone the identification and selection of one. In such circumstances, it might be appropriate for the PUC itself to select an individual or individuals that meet the three criteria outlined in the text. However, if participants have strong objections to the selection, PUCs should be willing to find acceptable alternatives.

18. The confidentiality and notice recommendations draw heavily from the New York Public Service Commission's new settlement rules and guidelines (NY PSC 1992). However, one of their requirements appears unwise and overly restrictive. It prohibits utilities from caucusing with individual nonutility parties unless they first give notice to all the other parties and provide them with an opportunity to attend. The broader settlement process, along with the PUCs' ultimate oversight, should provide sufficient protection against potential abuses.

19. California, New York, and Maine were identified as having formally adopted settlement policies. Massachusetts has settlement guidelines only for water cases. Although more states may have such guidelines, at least two other surveys (one by the New York PSC and one by NARUC, both in 1991) and my informal inquiries have not identified any as of this writing. NARUC's model settlement guidelines were issued in April 1991.

20. The final IRM rules in Massachusetts (D.P.U. 89-239 [1990b]) require that a utility (1) circulate a draft IRM filing several months prior to the actual filing date, (2) host at least one technical session to review the document with all interested parties, and (3) enter into settlement discussions with interested parties.

References and Bibliography

Allen, Scott. 1991. "Pilgrim Performance Earns High Marks." *Patriot Ledger*. November 27, pp. 1, 16.

Ambrosio, Michael. 1987. "Testimony Before the New Jersey Board of Public Utilities on Cogeneration and Small Power Production Contracting Reliability and Related Issues." September.

Amy, Douglas. 1987. *The Politics of Environmental Mediation*. New York: Columbia University Press.

Anderson, Douglas. 1981. *Regulatory Politics and Electric Utilities: A Case Study in Political Economy*. Boston: Auburn House Publishing.

Anderson, Frederick. 1985. "Negotiation and Informal Agency Action: The Case of Superfund." *Duke Law Journal* (2): 261–380.

Anderson, John. 1991. *Summary of ELCON's Position on Integrated Least Cost Resource Planning*. Washington, D.C.: ELCON.

Armenti, Carmen, et al. 1993. *Recommendations for Enhanced Electric Utility Planning and Procurement Process*. Report of the Advisory Council on Electricity Planning and Procurement. New Jersey Board of Regulatory Commissioners. July.

Atlantic Electric et al. 1988. *New Jersey's Electric Energy Future: Issues and Challenges*. September.

Bacow, Lawrence, and Michael Wheeler. 1984. *Environmental Dispute Resolution*. New York: Plenum.

Barkovitch, Barbara. 1989. *Regulatory Interventionism in the Utility Industry: Fairness, Efficiency, and the Pursuit of Energy Conservation*. New York: Quorum Books.

Bauer, Karen, ed. 1991. 1990 *Annual Report on Utility and Carrier Regulation*. Washington, D.C.: National Association of Regulatory Utility Commissioners.

Bazerman, Max. 1987. "Getting to Yes Six Years Later." *National Institute for Dispute Resolution Forum*. May.

Bergmann, David. 1992. "ADR in Major Ratemaking Proceedings: Cautions and Concerns (A Doubter's Almanac)." Paper presented at the Fifth Annual Conference on Electricity Law and Regulation, American Bar Association, Section of Natural Resources, Energy, and Environmental Law, Denver, Colorado, March 12–13.

Bernow, Stephen, Bruce Biewald, and Donald Marron. 1991. "Full-

Cost Dispatch: Incorporating Environmental Externalities in Electric System Operation." *Electricity Journal*, March, pp. 20–33.
Bingham, Gail, et al. 1987. "Applying Alternative Dispute Resolution to Government Litigation and Enforcement Cases." *Administrative Law Journal* (American University) 1 (2): 527–551.
Bonfield, Arthur E. 1982. "State Law in the Teaching of Administrative Law: A Critical Analysis of the Status Quo." *Texas Law Review* 61: 95–137.
———. 1986. "The Federal APA and State Administrative Law." *Virginia Law Review* 72: 297–336.
Boston Edison Company (BECo). 1990. Pilgrim Analysis. Submitted as Exhibit BE5, in Energy Facilities Siting Council EFSC 90-12/12A, Vol. 4. May 1.
Boston Edison Company (BECo) et al. 1989. Settlement Agreement in D.P.U. 88-28/88-48/89-100. October. (Pilgrim-related general rate case and outage investigation.)
———. 1990. *The Power of Service Excellence: Energy Conservation for the 90's.* (Results of the Phase II collaboration on conservation programs.)
Boucher, Thomas, and Mike Weedall. 1991. "The Collaborative Planning Process: One Utility's Experience." In *Proceedings of the Fifth National DSM Conference: Building on Experience* (Boston, July 30–August 1).
Breyer, Stephen. 1982. *Regulation and Its Reform.* Cambridge: Harvard University Press.
———. 1987. "Judicial Review of Questions of Law and Policy." In *New Perspectives on Institutions and Policies*, edited by Elizabeth Bailey. Cambridge: MIT Press.
Breyer, Stephen, and Richard Stewart. 1979. *Administrative Law and Regulatory Policy.* Boston: Little, Brown.
Browne, Gerald. 1991. "A Utility View of Externalities: Evolution, Not Revolution." *Electricity Journal*, March, pp. 34–39.
Burnett, Larry B. 1990. "The Collaborative Process in Strategic Energy Planning." *Strategic Planning for Energy and the Environment* (Fall): 35–40.
Burns, Robert. 1988. *Administrative Procedures for Proactive Regulation.* Columbus, Ohio: National Regulatory Research Institute.
Bush, George. 1990. "Statement Upon Signing S.303." (Negotiated Rulemaking Act.) *Weekly Compilations of Presidential Documents.* December 3.
California Collaborative. 1990. *An Energy Efficiency Blueprint for California* (with appendixes). Report of the Statewide Collaborative Process to the California Public Utilities Commission. January.

Calwell, Chris, and Ralph Cavanagh. 1989. *The Decline of Conservation at California Utilities: Causes, Costs, and Remedies.* San Francisco: Natural Resources Defense Council.

Cavanagh, Ralph. 1988. "Responsible Power Marketing in an Increasingly Competitive Era." *Yale Journal on Regulation* (5): 331.

Center for Public Resources, Inc. (CPR). 1993. *Negotiated Settlement of Utility Regulatory Proceedings: Recommended Practices.* New York: CPR.

Chernick, Paul, and Emily Caverhill. 1992. "Rebuttal Testimony of Boston Gas Company." In Mass. D.P.U. 91-131.

Chouteau, Chris. 1991. "The California Collaborative: A Way Out." In *Proceedings of the Fifth National DSM Conference: Building on Experience* (Boston, July 30–August 1), 136–139.

Cicchetti, Charles, and William Hogan. 1988. *Including Unbundled Demand Side Options in Electric Utility Bidding Systems.* E-88-07. Cambridge: Harvard University, Energy and Environmental Policy Center. August.

Cohen, Armond, and Joseph Chaisson. 1987. *Power to Spare: A Plan for Increasing New England's Competitiveness Through Energy Efficiency.* Boston: New England Energy Policy Council. July.

———. 1990. "Least-Cost Doing: Lessons from the New England Collaborative." In *Proceedings of the ACEEE 1990 Summer Study on Energy Efficiency in Buildings*, 5.29–5.33. Washington, D.C.: American Council for an Energy-Efficient Economy.

Cohen, Armond, and Michael W. Townsley. 1990. "Perspectives on Collaboration as Replacement for Confrontation." *Public Utilities Fortnightly* 125 (5): 9–13.

Cohen, Sam, et al. 1990. "Environmental Externalities: What State Regulators Are Doing." *Electricity Journal*, July, pp. 24–30, 35.

Conservation Law Foundation. 1990. Initial letter brief in Mass. D.P.U. 89-260. (WMECo's DSM preapproval case.)

———. 1991. Brief in Mass. D.P.U. 91-80, Phase II-A. (COM/Electric's DSM preapproval case.)

Costello, Kenneth. 1987. "Ten Myths of Energy Conservation." *Public Utilities Fortnightly* 119 (6): 19–22.

Cowan, William, and Stewart Boschwitz. 1985. "Alternatives to Administrative Litigation in the Utility Regulation Areas." Paper presented at the Eighth Annual Convention of the National Conference of Regulatory Attorneys, Hartford, Connecticut, May 12–15.

Cowell, Stephen. 1990. "Collaborative Design of the DSM Power Plant." In *Proceedings of the ACEEE 1990 Summer Study on Energy Efficiency in Buildings*, 5.51–5.59. Washington, D.C.: American Council for an Energy-Efficient Economy.

Davis, Kenneth C. 1972. *Administrative Law Text*. 3d. ed. St. Paul Publishing.
Dean, George. 1989. Cover letter to Massachusetts DPU accompanying Pilgrim settlement (agreement in Mass. D.P.U. 88-28/88-48/89-100). October 3. (Highlights key elements of settlement.)
Destribats, Allen, and R. Rosenblum. 1992. *DSM Incentives: What Type of Cheese and How Much?* Synergic Resources Corporation. March.
Duane, Timothy. 1989. "The Risk-Adjusted Cost Evaluation of Electric Resource Alternatives." Ph.D. diss., Stanford University.
Dunlop, John. 1975. "The Limits of Legal Compulsion." In O.S.H. Rep. (BNA) 884, 886. November 12.
Ellis, William. 1989. "The Collaborative Process in Utility Resource Planning." *Public Utilities Fortnightly* 123 (13): 9–12.
Endispute, Inc. 1991. *The Alternative Dispute Resolution (ADR) Process in the Zimmer Electric Rates Cases: A Report to the Public Utilities Commission of Ohio*. December. Boston: Endispute.
Environmental Protection Agency (EPA). 1991. "Negotiated Rulemaking at the Environmental Protection Agency." In Dispute Resolution Support Services Contract Orientation Materials (Section T). October. Washington, D.C.: USEPA.
Federal Energy Regulatory Commission (FERC). "Settlement Rules." Sections 385-601 through 385-604.
Finnigan, Richard. 1984. "The Use of Mediation and Negotiation Techniques in the Utility Rates Cases as an Alternative to the Contested Case Model." In *Proceedings of the Fourth NARUC Biennial Regulatory Information Conference* (September 5–7, Columbus, Ohio), 1293–1341. Washington, D.C.: NARUC.
Fiorino, Daniel. 1988. "Regulatory Negotiation as a Policy Process." *Public Administrative Review* 48: 764.
Fiorino, Daniel, and Chris Kirtz. 1985. "Breaking Down the Walls: Negotiated Rulemaking at EPA." *Temple Environmental Law and Technology Journal* 4: 29.
Fisher, Roger. 1983. "Negotiating Power." *American Behavioral Scientist* 27 (2): 149.
―――. 1984. "Comments on James White's Comments on *Getting to YES*." *Journal of Legal Education* 34 (1): 120–124.
―――. 1985. "Beyond YES." *Negotiation Journal* 1 (1): 67–70.
Fisher, Roger, and William Ury. 1981. *Getting to YES: Negotiating Agreement Without Giving In*. Boston: Houghton Mifflin.
Fisher, Roger, et al. 1991. *Getting to YES: Negotiating Agreement Without Giving In*. 2d ed. New York: Penguin Books.
Fiss, Owen. 1984. "Against Settlement." *Yale Law Journal* 93: 1073.

———. 1985. "Out of Eden." *Yale Law Journal* 94: 1669.
Flavin, Christopher. 1987. *Reassessing Nuclear Power: The Fallout from Chernobyl*. Worldwatch Institute Paper No. 75. March. Washington, D.C.: Worldwatch.
Forester, John, and David Stitzel. 1989. "Beyond Neutrality: The Possibilities of Activist Mediation in Public Sector Conflicts." *Negotiation Journal* 5 (3): 251–264.
Franklin, James. 1990a. "Edison to Invest $213 Million to Conserve." *Boston Globe*, March 14, pp. 17, 20.
———. 1990b. "Leukemia Link to Pilgrim Plan Found for 1972–1979." *Boston Globe*, October 10, pp. 1, 62.
Freeman, S. David. 1965. "Administrative Reform of FPC Natural Gas Regulation." *Public Utilities Fortnightly*, February 18, pp. 34–40.
Gabel, Steven. 1987. "Testimony Before the New Jersey Board of Public Utilities on Cogeneration and Small Power Production Policy." September.
Gerber, Abraham. 1988. "Questions for Regulators in a Competitive Electric Utility Environment." *Public Utilities Fortnightly*, July 21, pp. 11–15.
Goldman, Charles A., and John Busch. 1991. "Review of Utility Demand-Side Bidding Programs." In *Proceedings of the Fifth National DSM Conference: Building on Experience* (Boston, July 30–August 1), pp. 321–328.
Goldman, Charles A., and David R. Wolcott. 1990. "Demand-Side Bidding: Assessing Current Experience." In *Proceedings of the ACEEE 1990 Summer Study on Energy Efficiency in Buildings*, 8.53–8.68. Washington, D.C.: American Council for an Energy-Efficient Economy.
Gray, Barbara. 1989. *Collaborating: Finding Common Ground on Multiparty Problems*. San Francisco: Jossey-Bass.
Hall, Mary (moderator). 1983. "The Negotiated Rate Case: An Alternative to the Adversarial Process." In *Proceedings of the Ninth Annual NARUC Convention* (November 16), pp. 253–271.
Hamrin, Jan. 1989. "Non-utility Power and the Reliability Issue." *Electricity Journal*, June, pp. 14–27.
Harter, Philip. 1982. "Negotiating Regulations: A Cure for Malaise." *Georgetown Law Journal* 71: 1–113.
———. 1984. "Regulatory Negotiation: The Experience So Far." *Resolve* (Washington, D.C.: Conservation Foundation). Winter.
———. 1986. "The Role of the Courts in Reg-Neg: A Response to Judge Wald." *Columbia Journal of Environmental Law* 11: 51.
———. 1987. "Points on a Continuum: Dispute Resolution Proce-

dures and the Administrative Process." *Administrative Law Journal* (American University) 1 (1): 141–211.
Hempling, Scott. 1990. "Preserving Fair Competition: The Case for PUCHA." *Electricity Journal,* January/February, pp. 51–63.
Hesse, Martha. 1989. "A New Era in Energy Regulation." *Public Utilities Fortnightly* 123 (6): 18–21.
Hicks, Elizabeth G. 1990. "Conservation for Profit and Program Evaluation in a Collaborative Planning Process." In *Proceedings of the ACEEE 1990 Summer Study on Energy Efficiency in Buildings*, 6.47–6.51. Washington, D.C.: American Council for an Energy-Efficient Economy.
Hirsh, Richard. 1989. *Technology and Transformation in the American Electric Utility Industry*. Cambridge, England: Cambridge University Press.
Honeyman, Christopher. 1990. "On Evaluating Mediators." *Negotiation Journal* 6 (1): 23–36.
Joseph, Daniel, and Michelle Gilbert. 1990. "Breaking the Settlement Ice: The Use of Settlement Judges in Administrative Proceedings." *Administrative Law Journal* (American University) 3 (3): 571–600.
Joskow, Paul. 1974. "Inflation and Environmental Concern: Structural Change in the Process of Public Utility Price Regulation." *Journal of Law and Economics* 17 (2): 291–328.
———. 1988. "Testimony Before the Subcommittee on Energy and Power, U.S. House Committee on Energy and Commerce." March 31.
———. 1989. "Regulatory Failure, Regulatory Reform, and Structural Change in the Electrical Power Industry." In *Brookings Papers: Microeconomics*, 125–208. Washington, D.C.: Brookings Institute.
———. 1991. "Dealing with Environmental Externalities: Let's Do It Right?" Paper presented at the Harvard Northeast Electric Utility Executive Conference, Killington, Vermont, October 17–18.
Joskow, Paul, and Richard Schmalensee. 1986. "Incentive Regulation for Electric Utilities." *Yale Journal on Regulation* 4 (1): 1–49.
Kahn, Alfred. 1970/1988. *The Economics of Regulation: Principles and Institutions*. Cambridge: MIT Press.
———. 1990. "Deregulation: Looking Backward and Looking Forward." *Yale Journal on Regulation* 7: 325–354.
———. 1991. "Environmentalists Hijack the Utility Regulators." *Wall Street Journal*, August 7, A10.
Kahn, Edward. 1988/1991. *Electric Utility Planning and Regulation*. Washington, D.C.: American Council for an Energy-Efficient Economy.

———. 1990. "Structural Evolution in the Electric Utility Industry." *Public Utilities Fortnightly* 125 (1): 9–17.

Kahn, Edward, Charles A. Goldman, Steven Stoft, and Douglas Berman. 1989. *Evaluation Methods in Competitive Bidding for Electric Power*. LBL-26924. Lawrence Berkeley Laboratory. June.

Kalt, Joseph, Henry Lee, and Herman Leonard. 1987. *Re-establishing the Regulatory Bargain in the Electric Utility Industry*. E-87-02. Cambridge: Energy and Environmental Policy Center, Harvard University. March.

Katz, Myron. 1989. "Utility Conservation Incentives: Everyone Wins." *Electricity Journal*, October, pp. 26–35.

Keegan, Robert. 1986. "Putting Together the Major Components of a Rate Case." Massachusetts Department of Public Utilities.

Kilmarx, M., and P. Wallis. 1991. "DSM LCP: Least-Cost Planning Comes to Demand-Side Management." *DSM Quarterly*. Fall.

Kolbe, Lawrence, and William Tye. 1991. "The Duquesne Opinion: How Much 'Hope' Is There for Investors in Regulated Firms?" *Yale Journal on Regulation* 8: 113.

Krasner, Jeffrey. 1989. "DPU Approves Edison's Landmark Pilgrim Pact." *Boston Herald*, November 1, p. 32.

Krause, Florentine, John Busch, and Jonathan Koomey. 1991. *Incorporating Global Warming Risks in Power Sector Planning: A Case Study of the New England Region*. LBL-30797. Lawrence Berkeley Laboratory. May.

Landis, James. 1938. *Administrative Process*. New Haven: Yale University Press.

———. 1960. "Report on Regulatory Agencies to the President-Elect [Kennedy]." U.S. Congress. Senate Committee on the Judiciary. 86th Cong. 2d sess. Washington, D.C.: Government Printing Office.

Lax, David, and James Sebenius. 1986. *The Manager as Negotiator*. Free Press Publishers.

Lehr, Ronald. 1990. "Regulatory Negotiations." *Public Utilities Fortnightly* 126 (6): 20–25.

Lovins, Amory. 1976. "Energy Strategy: The Road Not Taken?" *Foreign Affairs* 55: 65.

Lovins, Amory, and Lynde Gilliam. 1986. Invited Comments on Kenneth Costello's article "Should Utilities Promote Energy Conservation." *Electric Potential*, March/April, pp. 3–13.

Lovins, Amory, and Eric Hirst. 1989. "The Great Demand-Side Debate Rages On: Open Letters Challenge Harvard's Bidding Proposal." *Electricity Journal*, March, pp. 34–43.

McCarthy, William. 1985. "The Role of Power and Principle in *Getting to YES*." *Negotiation Journal* 1 (1): 59–66.

McCraw, Thomas. 1984. *Prophets of Regulation*. Cambridge: Belknap Press of Harvard University.

McCreary, Scott T., Deborah Kolb, and Lawrence Susskind. 1990. *An Assessment of Negotiation and Collaborative Problem Solving at the Environmental Defense Fund and the Natural Resource Defense Council*. Prepared for the William and Flora Hewlett Foundation. December.

McIntyre, Bernice, and Bernard Reznicek. 1992. "Collaborative Approaches to Conservation." *Public Utilities Fortnightly* 129 (5): 16–19.

McKibben, Gordon. 1989. "DPU Curbs Edison Rates for 3 Years." *Boston Globe*, November 1, pp. 67, 69.

Maine PUC. 1991. "Environmental and Economic Impacts: A Review and Analysis of Its Role in Maine Energy Policy." Report to the 115th Maine Legislature Joint Standing Committee on Utilities. May.

Massachusetts Collaborative Parties. 1988. Phase I DSM Report. December.

Massachusetts Department of Public Utilities. 1986a. D.P.U. 84-276-B. August. (Issues Qualifying Facility bidding rule, 220 CMR 8.00.)

———. 1986b. D.P.U. 85-271-A/86-266-A. June. (Chastises BECo's management with respect to its energy planning and DSM activities and lowers BECo's rate of return.)

———. 1986c. D.P.U. 86-36. February. (Opens rulemaking on ratemaking treatment for new utility-owned generation.)

———. 1987a. D.P.U. 86-36-A. April. (Issues interim order on ratemaking treatment for utility-owned resources.)

———. 1987b. D.P.U. 86-36-B. November. (Announces bifurcation of 86-36 process into integrated resource planning and ratemaking dockets.)

———. 1987c. D.P.U. 86-280-A. June. (Chastises WMECo for its DSM performance.)

———. 1988a. D.P.U. 86-36-C. May. (Proposes rules on ratemaking treatment for utility-owned resources.)

———. 1988b. D.P.U. 86-36-D. August. (Approves DSM collaborative and discusses DPU expectations.)

———. 1988c. D.P.U. 86-36-E. October. (Adopts performance-based preapproval ratemaking for new supply-side resources and major investments in existing plants.)

———. 1988d. D.P.U. 86-36-F. November. (Defines DSM cost-effectiveness tests and allowable DSM cost recovery. Proposes new in-

tegrated resource management process based on all-resource solicitation.)
———. 1988e. D.P.U. 87-169. (Investigates brownouts. Reiterates utilities' obligations to pursue DSM.)
———. 1989a. D.P.U. 88-28/88-48/89-100. October. (Approves Pilgrim settlement.)
———. 1989b. D.P.U. 86-36-G. December. (Issues proposed integrated resource management rules.)
———. 1990a. D.P.U. 89-194/195. March. (Preapproves MECo's DSM programs.)
———. 1990b. D.P.U. 89-239. August. (Final rule—establishes all-resource bidding process and adopts specific environmental externality method.)
———. 1990c. D.P.U. 89-242/246/247. July. (Preapproves COM/Electric's DSM programs.)
———. 1990d. D.P.U. 89-260. June. (Preapproves WMECo's DSM programs.)
———. 1990e. D.P.U. 90-278. November. (Institutes funding mechanism for IRM staffing.)
———. 1991a. D.P.U. 89-261. January. (Preapproves MECo's DSM programs.)
———. 1991b. D.P.U. 91-205. December. (Approves MECo's DSM programs for 1992.)
———. 1992a. D.P.U. 91-80. Phase II-A. January. (Information request, COM/Electric's DSM preapproval case.)
———. 1992b. D.P.U. 91-131. November. (Reaffirms DPU's approach to environmental externalities and specific values; adds offset provisions.)
Menkel-Meadow, Carrie. 1985. "For and Against Settlement: Uses and Abuses of the Mandatory Settlement Conference." *UCLA Law Review* 33: 485–514.
Millhauser, Marguerite, Charles Pon, Jr., Laurie Bayles, and Diane Stockton. 1987. *Sourcebook: Federal Agency Use of Alternative Dispute Resolution*. Washington, D.C.: Administrative Conference of the United States.
Moskovitz, David. 1989. *Profits and Progress Through Least-Cost Planning*. Washington, D.C.: National Association of Regulatory Utility Commissioners (NARUC). November.
Moskovitz, David, and Gary Swofford. 1991. "Decoupling Sales and Profits: An Incentive Approach That Works." *Electricity Journal*, July, pp. 46–53.
Moskovitz, David, Steven M. Nadel, and Howard Geller. 1991. *Increasing the Efficiency of Electricity Production and Use: Barri-

ers and Strategies. Washington, D.C.: American Council for an Energy-Efficient Economy. November.

Nadel, Steven M., Michael W. Reid, and David R. Wolcott, eds. 1992. *Regulatory Incentives for Demand-Side Management*. Washington, D.C.: American Council for an Energy-Efficient Economy.

Naill, Roger, and Sharon Belanger. 1989. "Impacts of Deregulation on U.S. Electric Utilities." *Public Utilities Fortnightly* 124 (8): 24–31.

National Association of Regulatory Utility Commissioners (NARUC). 1990. *Proceedings of the NARUC National Conference on Environmental Externalities* (Jackson Hole, Wyoming, October 1–3). Washington, D.C.: NARUC.

———. 1991. *NARUC Staff Subcommittee on Administrative Law Judges Draft Model Settlement Guidelines*. NARUC 14-1991, pp. 14–20. April 8. Washington, D.C.: NARUC.

New England Electric System (NEES) and Conservation Law Foundation (CLF). 1989. *Strategic Energy Efficiency Investment for the 1990's: A Collaborative Project*. January.

New England Energy Policy Council. 1987. *Power to Spare: A Plan for Increasing New England's Competitiveness Through Energy Efficiency*. Boston. June.

New England Governors' Conference, Inc. 1986. *A Plan for Meeting New England's Electricity Needs: Final Report of the New England Governors' Conference, Inc.'s Assessment of New England's Electricity Situation*. Governors' Report. Boston.

New Jersey Board of Public Utilities (BPU). 1981. B.P.U. 8010-687. Decision and Order. "In the Matter of the Consideration and Determination of Cogeneration and Small Power Production Standards Pursuant to the Public Utility Regulatory Policies Act of 1978." October. (Requires utilities to pay QFs 10 percent more than avoided costs.)

———. 1983. B.P.U. 8010-687. Order of Clarification. December. (Clarifies that QF rules apply to all QFs.)

———. 1987. "An Assessment of Cogeneration and Small Production Policy in New Jersey." Staff report. May.

———. 1988a. B.P.U. 8010-687B. Stipulation of Settlement. July.

———. 1988b. B.P.U. 8010-687B. Decision and Order. September. (Adopts settlement.)

———. 1989a. B.P.U. 8010-687B. Order Denying Motion for Rehearing and Reconsideration. April.

———. 1989b. B.P.U. 8010-687B. Order of Clarification. August.

New Jersey Board of Regulatory Commissioners. 1991. "Demand Side Resources Planning Rules." N.J.A.C. 14:12. November 4. *New Jersey Register*.

New Jersey Office of Administrative Law. 1986. "Rules for Agency Rulemaking." N.J.A.C. 1:30. March 3. *New Jersey Register.*
New York Public Service Commission. 1989. Opinion No. 89-7: "Opinion and Order Establishing Guidelines for Bidding Program." April. (Includes externality method.)
———. 1990a. Opinion No. 90-14. April. (Rejects settlement plan in New York Telephone Company case for telephone service rate moratorium.)
———. 1990b. "Settlement Tracking Sheets." (Compiled by PSC staff and supplied to author by Ron Elwood.)
———. 1992. Opinion No. 92-2. "Opinion, Order and Resolution Adopting Settlement Procedures and Guidelines." March.
New York Times. Editorial. 1991. "Cleaner Air, by Consensus." August 27, p. A22.
Nogee, Alan. 1987. *Nuclear Lemon: Ratepayer Savings from Retiring the Pilgrim Nuclear Power Plant.* Boston: Massachusetts Public Interest Research Group (MASSPIRG). November.
———. 1990. "Comments of MASSPIRG to the NRC on Economic Performance Incentive Regulation for Nuclear Power Plants." Boston: Massachusetts Public Interest Research Group (MASSPIRG). December.
Nogee, Alan, and William Brach. 1988. *Whitewash: Painting Over Management Problems at the Pilgrim Nuclear Plant* (1986–1988). Boston: Massachusetts Public Interest Research Group (MASSPIRG). October.
Northwest Power Planning Council. 1983. *Northwest Conservation and Electric Power Plan.* Vol. 1. April.
———. 1988. "The Role for Conservation in Least-Cost Planning." June. (Comments submitted to the U.S. House Committee on Energy and Power in DSM bidding hearings.)
Nuclear Regulatory Commission (NRC). 1986. Confirmatory Action Letter to BECo. CAL-86-10. April 12.
———. 1987. NUREG-1256. Incentive Regulation of Nuclear Power Plants by State Public Utility Commissions. Vol. 1. December.
———. 1990. "NRC Policy Statement on Nuclear Plant Economic Performance Incentive Programs." *Federal Register.* Vol. 55, No. 208. October 26 at 434231.
Nye, David. 1990. *Electrifying America: Social Meanings of a New Technology.* Cambridge: MIT Press.
O'Leary, Marilyn. 1986. "Negotiated Settlements in Utility Regulation." *Public Utilities Fortnightly*, August 21, pp. 11–14.
Pace University Center for Environmental Legal Studies. 1990. *Environmental Costs of Electricity.* New York: Oceana Publications.

Perritt, Henry J., Jr. 1986. "Negotiated Rulemaking Before Federal Agencies: Evaluation of Recommendations by the Administrative Conference." *Georgetown Law Journal* 74: 1625.

———. 1987. "Administrative ADR: Development of Negotiated Rule-making and Other Processes." *Pepperdine Law Review*.

Petrulis, Robert. 1985. "NRRI Report: Commissions Use Negotiated Settlements to Expedite Regulatory Process." *NRRI Quarterly Bulletin* 6 (4): 379–390.

Potter, R. William. 1988. "Motion for a Stay and for Reconsideration in Docket No. 8010-687B." New Jersey Board of Public Utilities. August 25.

Pritzker, David. 1990. "Working Together for Better Regulations." *Natural Resources and the Environment* 5 (4).

Pritzker, David, and Deborah Dalton. 1990. *Negotiated Rulemaking Sourcebook*. Washington, D.C.: Administrative Conference of the United States, Office of the Chairman.

Public Utilities Fortnightly. 1990. "The Forum: Question 2: Dispute Resolution." 126 (10): 28–36.

Raab, Jonathan. 1989a. "Consensus Building in Electric Utility Rate-making." Unpublished paper. May.

———. 1989b. "Should Consensus Approaches to Demand-Side Planning and Integrated Resource Management Be Required?" In *Proceedings of the ECNE National Conference on Utility DSM Programs: Demand-Side Management: Partnerships in Planning* (Boston, November 16–17). Electric Power Research Institute.

———. 1990. "Is There Room for Integrated Demand-Side Bidding?" In *Proceedings of the ACEEE 1990 Summer Study on Energy Efficiency in Buildings*, 8.223–8.230. Washington, D.C.: American Council for an Energy-Efficient Economy.

———. 1991. "When Should a DSM Collaborative Process Be Considered Successful?" In *Proceedings of the Fifth National DSM Conference: Building on Experience* (Boston, July 30–August 1), 129–136.

———. 1993. "Why Include Externalities?" *Maine Policy Review* 2 (1): 1–6.

Raab, Jonathan, and Richard Cowart. 1992. "Fuel Switching in Vermont: Pragmatic Answers to Ideological Issues." In *Proceedings of the Fourth National NARUC Conference on Integrated Resource Planning* (Burlington, Vt., September 13–16). Washington, D.C.: NARUC.

Raab, Jonathan, and Martin Schweitzer. 1992. *Public Involvement in Integrated Resource Planning: A Study of Demand-Side Manage-*

ment Collaboratives. ORNL/CON-344. Oak Ridge National Laboratory. February.

Raab, Jonathan, et al. 1994. "Reinvigorating Demand-Side Management in California." *Journal of Corporate Environmental Strategy* 1 (3): 13–22.

Raiffa, Howard. 1982. *The Art and Science of Negotiation.* Cambridge: Belknap Press of Harvard University.

RCG/Hagler, Bailly, Inc. 1992. "Profile VI: Independent Power Market, 1992 Status and Trends."

Reich, Robert. 1981. "Rethinking Regulation: Negotiation as an Alternative to Traditional Rulemaking." *Harvard Law Review* 94: 1871.

Richardson, James. 1991. "Overcoming Obstacles to Negotiating Rates and Regulations in the Electric Utility Industry." *Negotiation Journal* 7 (1): 41–53.

Robertson, Hope. 1991. *Current Competition* (newsletter of the National Independent Energy Producers Association, Stockton, N.J.) 2 (5).

———. 1992. *Current Competition* 3 (8).

Roe, David. 1984. *Dynamos and Virgins.* New York: Random House.

Rowe, John. 1990. "Making Conservation Pay: The NEES Experience." *Electricity Journal,* December, pp. 18–25.

Ruff, Larry. 1988. "Utility Conservation Programs: When Are They Really Least Cost?" In *Proceedings of the NARUC National Conference on Least-Cost Utility Planning* (Aspen, Colorado, April 10–13). Washington, D.C.: NARUC.

Schelling, Thomas. 1960. *A Strategy of Conflict.* Cambridge: Harvard University.

Schuck, Peter. 1979. "Litigation, Bargaining, and Regulation." *Regulation: AEI Journal of Government and Society,* July/August, 26–34.

Schuck, Peter, and Donald E. Elliott. 1990. "To the Chevron Station: An Empirical Study of Federal Administrative Law." *Duke Law Journal* (5): 984–1061.

Schultz, Don, and Joe Eto. 1991. "Waiting for Godot." *Electricity Journal,* March, pp. 13–19.

Schweitzer, Martin, and Jonathan Raab. 1992. "Do Collaboratives Really Work?" *Electricity Journal,* November, pp. 47–57.

Shapiro, David L. 1965. "The Choice of Rulemaking or Adjudication in the Development of Administrative Policy." *Harvard Law Review* 78 (5): 921–972.

Stalon, Charles, and Reinier Lock. 1990. "State-Federal Relations in the Economic Regulation of Energy." *Yale Journal on Regulation* 7: 427–475.

Steinmeier, William. 1990. "Where Theory Meets Reality: The Case

Against PUCHA 'Reform.'" *Electricity Journal*, January/February, pp. 40–50.

Stewart, Richard. 1981. "Regulation, Innovation, and Administrative Law: A Conceptual Framework." *California Law Review* 69: 1256.

Stone, Deborah. 1988. *Policy Paradox and Political Reason*. Glenview, Ill.: Scott, Foresman.

Strauss, Peter. 1989. *An Introduction to Administrative Justice in the United States*. Carolina Academic Press.

Sturm, Susan. 1991. "A Normative Theory of Public Law Remedies." *Georgetown Law Journal* 79: 1357.

Susskind, Lawrence. 1981. "Environmental Mediation and the Accountability Problem." *Vermont Law Review* 6 (1): 1–47.

———. 1985. "Mediating Public Disputes: A Response to the Skeptics." *Negotiation Journal* 1 (2): 117–120.

Susskind, Lawrence, and Jeffrey Cruikshank. 1987. *Breaking the Impasse: Consensual Approaches to Resolving Public Disputes*. New York: Basic Books.

Susskind, Lawrence, and Gerard McMahon. 1985. "The Theory and Practice of Negotiated Rulemaking." *Yale Journal on Regulation* 3 (1): 133–165.

Susskind, Lawrence, and Allen Morgan. 1986a. "The Uses of Mediation in Electric Utility Regulatory Negotiation: The Results of Three Demonstrations." Report prepared for the Edison Electric Institute, Washington, D.C.

———. 1986b. "Improving Negotiation in the Regulatory Process." *Electric Perspectives* (Edison Electric Institute), Spring, pp. 22–31.

Susskind, Lawrence, and Connie Ozawa. 1985. "Mediating Public Disputes: Obstacles and Possibilities." *Journal of Social Issues* 41 (2): 145–159.

Technical Development Corporation. 1987. *Evaluation of the Edison Electric Institute Demonstration Project on Principled Negotiation*. Washington, D.C.: Edison Electric Institute.

Tierney, Susan. 1989. "A Fun List of Issues Affecting the Role of QFs and IPPs in Utilities' Least-Cost Plans." Paper presented at NARUC's Second National Conference on Least-Cost Utility Planning, Charleston, South Carolina, September 12.

———. 1990. "Using Existing Tools to Pry Open Transmission: A New England Proposal." *Electricity Journal*, April, pp. 24–28, 33–39.

Trebing, Harry. 1967a. "A Critique of the Planning Function in Regulation." *Public Utilities Fortnightly*, March 16, pp. 21–30.

———. 1967b. "Toward Improved Regulatory Planning." *Public Utilities Fortnightly*, March 30, pp. 15–24.

———. 1981. "Equity, Efficiency, and the Viability of Public Utility Regulation." In *Applications of Economic Principles in Public Utility Industries*, edited by Werner Sichel and Thomas Gies. Ann Arbor: University of Michigan, Graduate School of Business.

Tye, Larry. 1992. "Tsongas Explains Nuclear Plant Role." *Boston Globe*, February 14, 15.

U.S. Department of Energy. 1991. *Monthly Energy Review*. DOE/EIA–0035(91/03). Washington D.C. March.

U.S. General Accounting Office (USGAO). 1990. *Electricity Supply: The Effects of Competitive Power Purchases Are Not Yet Certain*. GAO/RCED-90-182. Washington, D.C.: USGAO.

Vermont parties. 1993. Letter to Vermont Public Service Board Chairman Richard Cowart on externality rulemaking. Signed by thirteen parties (nonutility and utility). July 21.

Vermont Public Service Board. 1989–1991. Docket Nos. 5270, 5270-CV-1, 5270-CV-2, 5270-CV-3. "Investigation into Least-Cost Investments, Energy Efficiency, Conservation and Management of Demand for Energy." (Various orders in filing related to CV collaborative.)

———. 1990. Docket No. 5270. "Least-Cost Investments, Energy Efficiency, Conservation and Management of Demand for Energy." April.

Vince, Clinton, et al. 1990. "Regional Regulation of Multistate Holding Companies: A Model for Readjusting the Federal-State Boundary." *Electricity Journal*, December, pp. 56–66.

Wald, Mathew. 1991. "U.S. Agencies Use Negotiations to Preempt Lawsuits over Rules." *New York Times*, September 23, A1, B10.

Wald, Patricia. 1985. "Negotiation of Environmental Disputes: A New Role for the Courts?" *Columbia Journal of Environmental Law* 10 (1).

———. 1991. "The 'New Administrative Law'—With the Same Old Judges in It?" *Duke Law Journal* (3): 647–670.

Wall, Bruce J., and Thomas M. Griffin. 1990. "Connecticut's Collaborative Process Experience: Utility Conservation and Load Management for Electrically Heated New Residential Construction." In *Proceedings of the ACEEE 1990 Summer Study on Energy Efficiency in Buildings*, 5.201–5.208. Washington, D.C.: American Council for an Energy-Efficient Economy.

Walker, Michael. 1989. "New Jersey's Competitive Bidding System: An Attempt at a Balanced Energy Supply Policy." *Public Utilities Fortnightly*, February 16, pp. 34–39.

Walton, Richard, and Robert McKersie. 1965. *A Behavioral Theory of Labor Relations*. McGraw-Hill.

Washington Post. Editorial. 1991. "Creeping Reg-Neg." August 24, p. A26.

White, James. 1984. "The Pros and Cons of Getting to Yes." *Journal of Legal Education* 34 (1): 115–120.

Whitman, Christine Todd. 1988. "Comments on the Cogeneration and Small Power Production Settlement." New Jersey Board of Public Utilities. August 24.

Wiggins, Lyna L., Timothy P. Duane, and Allen L. Brown. 1988. "Diversification in Energy Production." In *California Policy Choices*, Vol. 4, edited by John Kirlin and Donald Winkler. Los Angeles: University of Southern California, School of Public Administration.

Williams, Stephen F. 1975. " 'Hybrid Rulemaking' Under the Administrative Procedures Act: A Legal and Empirical Analysis." *University of Chicago Law Review* 42 (3): 401–456.

Wisconsin PSC. 1989. Findings of Fact, Conclusions of Law and Order, Advance Plan 5. Docket No. 05-EP-5. April 6.

Zajac, Edward. 1978. *Fairness or Efficiency: An Introduction to Public Utility Pricing*. Cambridge: Ballinger Publishing.

Interviews

Interviews were conducted between September 1991 and January 1994. Positions and affiliations are as of the time of the interviews.

Pilgrim Settlement (Chapter 4)

Brian Abbanat	Chief Engineer, Electric Power Division, Massachusetts Department of Public Utilities
George Dean	Director of Regulated Industries Division, Massachusetts Attorney General's Office
Thomas May	Executive Vice-President, Boston Edison Company
Alan Nogee	Energy Program Director, MASSPIRG
Rachel Shimshak	Director of Policy and Planning, Massachusetts Division of Energy Resources
Robert Werlin	Attorney, private law firm; former Commissioner and Chair, Massachusetts Department of Public Utilities

DSM Collaboratives (Chapter 4)

Utilities

John Cagnetta	Senior Vice-President for Corporate Planning and Regulatory Relations, Northeast Utilities
Al Destribats	Vice-President for Planning, NEES
Peter Flynn	Director of Conservation and Load Management, NEES
L. Carl Gustin	Senior Vice-President for Customer Savings, Marketing, and Corporate Relations, Boston Edison Company
Elizabeth Hicks	Director of Demand Planning, NEES
Kathleen Kelly	Manager of Evaluation and Monitoring, Boston Edison Company
Lydia Pastuszek	President of Granite State Electric Company (former Director of Demand Planning), NEES
John Rowe	President and CEO, NEES
Richard Sergel	Treasurer (former Director of Rates), NEES
Earle Taylor	Director of Conservation and Load Management, Northeast Utilities

Ben Tucker	Technical Assistant to L. Carl Gustin, Boston Edison Company
Wendy Watts	Director of Conservation, Nantucket Electric Company
Carol White	Supervisor of Demand-Side Planning and Evaluation, EUA Services Corporation
Mort Zajac	Manager of Demand Program Administration, COM/Electric

Nonutility Parties

Steve Burrington	Attorney, CLF
Joseph Chaisson	Consultant, lead coordinator of NUP consultants
Susan Coakley	Consultant, coordinator of NUP consultants for Boston Edison Company, COM/Electric, and EUA collaboratives (former staff Massachusetts Department of Public Utilities)
Armond Cohen	Senior Attorney, CLF
Stephen Cowell	President (former lead residential consultant), Conservation Services Group, Inc.
Douglas Foy	Executive Director, CLF
Alan Nogee	Energy Program Director, MASSPIRG
Jerrold Oppenheim	Assistant Attorney General, Massachusetts Attorney General
Rachel Shimshak	Director of Policy and Planning, Massachusetts Division of Energy Resources

Regulators

Janet Besser	Manager of Energy Planning, New Hampshire Public Utilities Commission
Mary Kilmarx	Director of Energy Policy and Planning, Rhode Island Public Utilities Commission
Susan Tierney	Secretary for Environmental Affairs (former Commissioner, Massachusetts Department of Public Utilities)
Robert Werlin	Attorney, private law firm (former Commissioner and Chair, Massachusetts Department of Public Utilities)

Other Intervenors

| Andrew Newman | Attorney for lighting retailers and large industrial consumers |

Massachusetts IRM Rules (Chapter 5)

Utilities

Al Destribats	Vice-President for Planning, NEES
Robert Fratto	Manager of Demand Program Administration, COM/Electric
Richard Hahn	Vice-President for Marketing, Boston Edison Company

Government

Mary Beth Gentleman	Attorney, private law firm (former Assistant Secretary for Policy, Massachusetts Division of Energy Resources)
Jerrold Oppenheim	Assistant Attorney General, Massachusetts Attorney General's Office
Robert Shapiro	General Counsel, Massachusetts Department of Public Utilities (former Executive Director, Energy Facilities Siting Council)
Robert Werlin	Attorney, private law firm (former Commissioner and Chair, Department of Public Utilities)

Third-Party Providers

Stephen Cowell	President, Conservation Services Group, Inc.
Sherif Fam	Manager of Regulatory Affairs, Thermo-Energy Systems Corporation (former President, New England Cogeneration Association)
Rolly Rouse	President, Conservation Conversions, Inc. (former Chief Operating Officer, Citizens Conservation Corporation)

Environmental and Consumers Groups

Armond Cohen	Senior Attorney, CLF
Alan Nogee	Energy Program Director, MASSPIRG

Other

David O'Connor	Executive Director, Massachusetts Office of Dispute Resolution (facilitator for technical session process)
Harvey Salgo	Manager Least Cost Utility Planning, TELLUS Institute (represented Massachusetts Division of Energy Resources in the IRM proceedings)

New Jersey Bidding Settlement (Chapter 5)

Utilities

Dennis Baldassari	Vice-President of Rates, Materials, and Services, Jersey Central Power & Light Company
Harold Borden	Senior Vice-President for External Affairs, Public Service Electric and Gas Company

Government

Michael Ambrosio	Chief, Electric Division, Bureau of Rates and Tariffs, New Jersey Board of Public Utilities
Joe Bowring	Chief Economist, Division of Rate Counsel, New Jersey Department of Public Advocate
William Potter	Partner, private law firm (former Special Counsel, Division of Energy, New Jersey Department of Commerce and Economic Development)

Alternative Power Producers and Industrial Consumers

Harry Kociencki	Director of Corporate Energy Administration and Operation, Hoffman-LaRoche, Inc. (represented large industrial consumers)
Robert McNair	Chairman and President, COGEN Technologies, Inc.
Michael Walker	Attorney, private law firm (represented small power production interests)

Other

Charles Goldman	Staff scientist, Lawrence Berkeley Laboratory
Edward Kahn	Group leader, Utility Planning and Policy, Lawrence Berkeley Laboratory
Jim McGuire	Attorney, Division of Rate Counsel, New Jersey Department of Public Advocate (former Director, Department of Public Advocate, Center for Public Dispute Resolution)
Anthony Miragliotta	Assistant Director of Rules and Publications, New Jersey Office of Administrative Law

Supplemental Interviews

Robert Burns*	Attorney, National Regulatory Research Institute
John Crary	Deputy General Counsel, New York Public Service Commission

Michael Dworkin*	General Counsel, Vermont Public Service Board
Ron Elwood*	Associate Policy and Compliance Analyst, Consumer Services Division, New York Public Service Commission
Philip Harter	Private attorney
John McGlennon	President, ERM-McGlennon, Inc.
Melissa Marland	Chief Administrative Law Judge, West Virginia Public Service Commission
William Olmstead	Executive Director, Administrative Council of the United States (former Associate General Counsel at the Nuclear Regulatory Commission)
Susan Orenstein	Director of Mediation and Training, RESOLVE
John Orrechio	Director, Division of Investigations, Office of Electric Power Regulation, Federal Energy Regulatory Commission
David Pritzker*	Attorney, Administrative Council of the United States
Rusty Russell	Conservation Law Foundation
Henry Yoshimura*	Director, Electric Power Division, Massachusetts Department of Public Utilities

* Indicates those interviewed on several occasions.

Index

Page references annotated with the letter "n" followed by a numeral refer to the endnotes.

A

Abbanat, Brian, 66
Adams, Charles Francis, regulatory philosophy, 7, 235-36
adjudication (in electric utility regulation), ix, 1, 53-139, 225
  adjudications before the Massachusetts DPU, 55-56, 250-51n8
    1982-1991 (table), 56
  adversarial advocacy in, 59, 60-61
  complexity, 58-59
  consensus building effects on, 125-39
  consensus building mechanisms for, 36-39
  defined, 53-55
  due process requirements in, 53-54
  encouraging stakeholder representation in, 225, 269n3
  increase in use of, 55-57
  initiating consensus building in, 224
  policy making in, 60, 251n12
  prior to 1970, 9-10
  public comment on, 226, 270n6
  PUC commissioner involvement in, 227-28
  PUC staff involvement in, 226-27
  shortcomings, 57-61
  subjectivity of, 59-60
  tradeoffs in, 59-60
  versus rulemaking, 141-42
  in PUC schedules, 54
  See also rate cases; ratemaking
Administrative Procedures Act. *See* APA
Administrative Process, The (Landis), 142
administrative rulemaking. *See* agency rulemaking

ADR (alternative dispute resolution), 27-34
  applications in electric utility regulation consensus building, 34-36
  assisted, 39-40
  benefits of, 249n21
  distributive issues in, 31-33
  fundamental limits to, 33-34
  as integrative bargaining, 28-29
  power imbalances in, 30-31
  PUCs and, 35, 248n15
  trainings, 35, 247n12, 247-48n13, 248n14
  See also consensus building (in electric utility regulation); facilitation; mediation; negotiations
advisory staffs (of PUCs)
  as a consensus-building mechanism, 37-38, 44, 226-27, 248n16, 270n5
  at the DPU, 137, 168-69, 227, 253-54n36, 262n103, 265n31
  versus DSM collaboratives, 124
advocacy staffs (of PUCs)
  as a consensus-building mechanism, 38, 44, 223, 226-27, 269n2, 270n7
  DPU policies, 137, 227, 253-54n36, 262n103, 270n7
"Against Settlement" (Fiss), 33
agency rulemaking
  appeal rates
    federal, 145, 262n8
    state versus federal, 150
  consensus-building procedures for, 146-49
  court refinements of, 144
  evolution at the federal level, 142-46
  judicialization of, 144-45

296 — Index

laws increasing accountability in, 143, 262n4
subjectivity of, 145-46
See also negotiated rulemaking; rulemaking (in electric utility regulation)
alternative dispute resolution. See ADR
alternative power providers. See APPs
Ambrosio, Michael, 189, 267n43
   on the adoption of the New Jersey bidding settlement, 201-2
   on the BPU bidding support switch, 194
   on the negotiation of liquidated damage funds, 199
   on QF inactivity in New Jersey, 190
Amy, Douglas, *The Politics of Environmental Mediation*, 247n7
"An Assessment of Cogeneration and Small Production Policy in New Jersey 1981-1986" (BPU), 191
APA (Administrative Procedures Act)
   classification of ratemaking, 250n2
   rulemaking procedures, 142-43
     DPU preapproval rulemaking process versus, 155-56
     negotiated rulemaking and, 146
   See also MSAPA (Model State Administration Procedures Act)
appeals
   of DPU DSM-related decisions, 127, 261n98
   from DSM collaboratives in Massachusetts, 126-27, 129
   of EPA decisions, 145, 148
   from IRM rules, 180
   of PUC decisions, 44-45, 60, 180, 249n22, 249n24, 251n13, 251n14
   of settlements, 44, 249n23
     Pilgrim settlement appeal probability, 85-86
APPs (alternative power providers), failure protection mechanisms, 197-99
arbitration, nonbinding, 271n14
Art and Science of Negotiation, The (Raiffa), 28-29, 246n4
assisted negotiation. See facilitation; mediation
Attorney General (Massachusetts)
   COM/Electric case intervention, 112
   DSM collaboratives proposal, 98-99
   DSM incentives opposition, 106, 111, 112
   DSM support, 96, 97, 98-99
   NEES case intervention, 111
   Pilgrim case testimony, 71
   WMECo case intervention, 112
automobiles, consensus building in improving standards, xiii
avoided costs, 190, 266n40
   avoided-capacity component, 266n40
   avoided-energy component, 266n40
   calculation variations, 205, 267-68n51
   and DSM investment, 21-22

B

Baldassari, Dennis, 189
   on the utility view in the New Jersey bidding dispute, 194
Barkovitch, Barbara
   on electric utility management failures, 244n9
   on interventionism, 14, 222
Batinovich, Robert, CPUC DSM policy, 15-16
BATNA (best alternative to a negotiated settlement), 28
   diagram, 29, 246n3
BECo (Boston Edison Company)
   DSM available to, 121, 260n91
   DSM collaborative agreement, filing, and DPU order dates (tables), 108, 122
   DSM expenditures and savings, 1987-1991 (table), 237
   DSM expenditures for NUP consultants, 1988-1993 (table), 125
   DSM expenditures in 1987 (table), 96
   Edgar Station power plant case, 84-85, 121
   NEES case intervention, 118
   NRC actions against, 66-67
   Phase III preapproval filing, 122
   Pilgrim history, 66-70
   Pilgrim outage cost claims, 69, 253n33
   Pilgrim-related management changes, 67, 252-53n28
   Pilgrim settlement, 73, 85-86

Index — 297

DSM investment issues, 77, 83-85, 254n45
Pilgrim spending, 67, 68-69, 253n30
  1986-1988 (table), 68
postPilgrim settlement finances, 83, 254n47
See also Pilgrim (Pilgrim Nuclear Power Plant)
BECo collaborative, 113-14, 121-22
  Edgar Station case effects, 121
  NUP-utility relationship, 110, 113-14, 121-22
  illustrated, 109
  Pilgrim case effects, 113, 121
Besser, Janet, 95
best alternative to a negotiated settlement. *See* BATNA
bidding
  bid price cap, 212, 269n60
  bidding block size, 212
  controversial questions on (table), 23
  DSM, 195, 201, 206, 267n44
  reduced responses to, 205
  utility alternatives to, 204-5, 267n49, 267n50
  See also QF bidding
Bird, Ralph, hiring at BECo, 67
Borden, Harold, 189
  on utility QF purchasing in New Jersey, 192
Boston Edison Company. *See* BECo
Bowring, Joe, 189
  settlement process support, 210
  on the withdrawal of the Public Advocate appeal, 203
BPU (New Jersey Board of Public Utilities)
  bidding issue switch, 194, 209
  bidding settlement discussions call, 192
  bidding settlement role, 194
  on QF bidding, 191
  QF policies, 189-92
  settlement adoption, 201-2, 206, 210, 267n48, 268n53, 268n57
  settlement claims rejection, 203
  staff power, 194, 201, 267n46
  staff representatives, 267n43
Breaking the Impasse: Consensual Approaches to Resolving Public Disputes (Susskind and Cruikshank), 246-47n6, 271n14
Breyer, Stephen
  on due process requirements in adjudication, 53
  on judicial review of PUC decisions, 45, 249n24
  on the subjectivity of adjudication, 59-60
Brown, Jerry (Governor of California), DSM policy, 15-16, 245n14
Bryson, John, CPUC DSM policy, 16
Burrington, Steve, 94
by-pass problem, in electric utility regulation, 219

C

Cagnetta, John, 94, 255n57
  on DPU criticism of BECo's DSM efforts, 255n51
  DSM collaborative offer, 98
California
  collaborative DSM process, 18
  demand-side management, 15-16, 18, 245n13
  interventionism in, 18, 219, 269n1
  oversubscription in, 152, 264n21
California Public Utilities Commission. *See* CPUC
Cambridge Electric Company. *See* COM/Electric
carbon dioxide, emission cost values used in Massachusetts utilities (table), 240
carbon monoxide, emission cost values used in Massachusetts utilities (table), 240
case settlements. *See* settlements
caucusing before/during settlement negotiations, 234, 271n18
Central Maine Power, QF bidding implementation, 264n20
Chaisson, Joseph, 94
  on the WMECo NUPs, 112
Chernick, Paul, on Pilgrim potential costs, 71
Chilton, Robert, 267n43
CIPCA (Cogeneration and Independent Power Coalition of America, Inc.), motion against the New Jersey bidding settlement, 203

298 — Index

CL&P (Connecticut Light and Power),
    DSM collaborative revival, 118
CLF (Conservation Law Foundation),
    255n56
  collaboration with NEES, 99, 110-11,
    117-18, 124
  COM/Electric interventions, 112,
    120, 258n75, 260n89
  and the DSM collaboratives, 98-103
  WMECo case intervention, 112
Clinton administration, consensus build-
    ing, xiii
Coakley, Susan, 95
  IRM technical sessions involvement,
    265n32
Cogeneration and Independent Power
    Coalition of America, Inc.
    (CIPCA), motion against the
    New Jersey bidding settlement,
    203
cogenerators (in New Jersey), discontent
    with the bidding settlement, 200
Cohen, Armond, 95, 153
  on the NEES collaborative, 124
"Collaborative Approaches to Conserva-
    tion" (McIntyre and Reznicek),
    129
collaborative process. See consensus
    building (in electric utility regu-
    lation)
collaboratives
  prospective, as consensus-building
    mechanisms, 38-39
  See also DSM collaboratives
COM/Electric
  DSM collaborative agreement, preap-
    proval filing, and DPU order
    dates (tables), 108, 122
  DSM expenditures
    in 1987 (table), 96
    for NUP consultants, 1988-1993
      (table), 125
    and savings, 1987-1991 (table),
      237
  DSM successes, 120, 260n90
  Phase II preapproval case
    intervention, 113
    proposal, 113, 258n77
  Phase III preapproval case
    DPU order, 123
    interventions, 120, 260n89
    proposal, 120, 260n88
    settlement, 120-21
  rate case overturn, 113
  rate increase factors, 113, 258n76
COM/Electric collaborative, 112-13,
    119-21
  frustrations in, 119-20
  NUP-utility relationship, 110, 119-20
  illustrated, 109
  unraveling of, 119-21
comments
  in the DPU preapproval rulemaking
    process, 157-58, 264n26
  from the IRM technical sessions, 176
  on settlements, providing for, 226,
    233, 270n6
commissioners (of PUCs). See PUC
    commissioners
Commonwealth Electric Company. See
    COM/Electric
competition
  in electricity generation, 22-24, 154,
    172
  protecting nascent utility DSM pro-
    grams from, 175
confidentiality in settlement negotia-
    tions, 234, 252n24, 271n18
Connecticut
  DSM collaborative beginning, 97-98
  DSM collaborative revival, 118
Connecticut Light and Power (CL&P),
    DSM collaborative revival, 118
consensus, national, on electric utility
    regulation, ix, 7, 9-13
consensus (in electric utility regulation)
  attainment of, 43-44
  cultivating, 222-23
  in the DSM collaboratives in Massa-
    chusetts, 128-29
  in the IRM technical sessions, 175-
    76, 181, 187
  judicial review of, 44-45, 249n24
  in the Pilgrim settlement, 86-88, 220
  PUC approval of, 44-45, 50, 249n25
consensus building (in electric utility
    regulation), x, 1-3, 27-51, 220-
    36
  ADR applications, 34-36
  assisted, 39-40
  benefits of, 50-51, 220-21
  in California, 18

Index — 299

developing policies for, 234-35
during prefiling periods, 134-35, 137
efficiency in, 46-47
enhancing the legitimacy of the regulatory process, 50, 138, 220
   in the DSM collaboratives in Massachusetts, 128-29, 138
   in the IRM rulemaking process in Massachusetts, 181-84
   in the New Jersey bidding settlement, 209-11
   in the Pilgrim settlement, 86-88, 138, 220
evaluating, 2, 27, 41-51, 249n21
fairness in, 46-47, 48
funding, 229-30
including difficult issues in, 230-31
including stakeholders in, 225-26
including supplemental documentation in, 233
initiating, 224
literature, 41
in Massachusetts, 18-19
mechanisms, 2, 36-39, 220
   table, 37
in New York, 15
paradigm shift required, 222
participant interest satisfaction assessment, 48-49
practicality of, 50-51, 138-39, 220-21
   in the DSM collaboratives in Massachusetts, 130-34, 139
   in the IRM rulemaking process in Massachusetts, 184-87
   in the New Jersey bidding settlement, 211-13
   in the Pilgrim settlement, 88-90, 138-39
principles for designing, 223-36
   table, 223
prospective, xii, 38-39, 225
providing time for, 234
resource savings, x, 41-43, 221, 249n21
   in the DSM collaboratives in Massachusetts, 125-27
   in the IRM rulemaking process in Massachusetts, 177-81
   in the New Jersey bidding settlement, 208
   in the Pilgrim settlement, 85-86

securing PUC involvement in, 226-28
societal benefits, 43, 221
structuring, 232-33
substantive benefits
   analytic approaches, 45-46, 249n26
   evaluative criteria, 46-49, 249n27
   participant insights, 48-49
   PUC approval and, 249n25
   See also ADR (alternative dispute resolution); DSM collaboratives; DSM collaboratives in Massachusetts; integrative bargaining; Pilgrim settlement
consensus building (in public policy dispute resolution), xii-xiii, 3
Conservation Law Foundation. *See* CLF
consultants, exit interviews with, 121-22
consumer advocate groups
   anti-utility protests, 12
   IRM technical session participation concerns, 168
   See also intervenors
cost disallowances (by PUCs), 16-17, 245n15
   in the Pilgrim case, 72, 76
   Supreme Court on, 33-34
Cowell, Stephen, 95, 153
   on the IRM technical session participants, 168
CPUC (California Public Utilities Commission)
   collaborative process endorsement, 18
   DSM policy, 15-16, 18, 244n12, 245n13
cream skimming in DSM programs, 175
Cruikshank, Jeffery
   on ADR, 246-47n6
   on assisted negotiation, 39
   on fairness in consensus building, 48

D

Davis, George, on Pilgrim performance incentives, 82
Dean, George, 66, 74
   Pilgrim case decision concerns, 73
decoupling mechanisms, 25-26, 245n13
demand-side management *See* DSM
Denton, Harold, on the probability of failure of Pilgrim-type nuclear power plants, 252n27

Department of Energy (DOE), negotiated rulemaking in, xiii
Destribats, Al, 94, 153
  on the DPU DSM cost allocation decision, 259n82
  on the DPU environmental externalities decision, 183
Diablo Canyon nuclear power plant, cost recovery-performance ties, 77, 254n42
distributive bargaining, 28
Division of Energy (New Jersey Department of Commerce and Economic Development), opposition to the bidding settlement, 199-201, 267n45
Division of Energy Resources. *See* DOER
DOE (Department of Energy), negotiated rulemaking in, xiii
DOER (Division of Energy Resources) (Massachusetts), 252n23
  DSM collaboratives proposal, 98-99
  DSM support, 96, 97
  IRM proposal, 160
  Pilgrim case decision concerns, 73
  Pilgrim rate case intervention, 69-71, 253n34
  WMECo case intervention, 112
DPU. *See* Massachusetts DPU (Department of Public Utilities)
DSM (demand-side management)
  in California, 15-16, 18, 245n13
  cost allocation/recovery issue, 104-6, 111-12, 256n63, 256-57n65, 259n82
  cost-effectiveness test issues, 21-22, 104-5, 245n19, 256n63, 256-57n65, 258-59n80
  cream skimming in, 175
  direct investment in, 110, 132
  DPU IRM interim order policies, 162, 264-65n28
    table, 163
  fuel substitution issue, 106, 118, 257n66
  in Massachusetts, 96, 130-32, 261n100, 261n101
    utility expenditures/savings (tables), 96, 125, 130, 237
  measuring savings from, 111, 258n72

opposing views of, 259n82
  program design, 132-33
  utility investment in, 21-22, 117, 217-18, 245n20, 259n85
  issues in the Pilgrim settlement, 76, 77, 83-84
  See also DSM collaboratives
DSM bidding, 195, 201, 267n44
DSM rules and, 206
DSM collaboratives, 38-39
  in Connecticut, 97-98
  in Vermont, 230
  versus advisory boards, 124
  versus traditional settlements, 126
DSM collaboratives in Massachusetts, 4-5, 64-65, 93-139
  appeals, 126-27, 129
  background, 95-97
  CLF role, 101
  Connecticut example, 97-98
  distributive issues settlement, 220
  DPU non-participation in, 44, 101-2, 107, 116-17, 128-29, 136-37, 227
  and DSM growth, 131-32, 261n100, 261n101
  and DSM program design, 132-33
  endurance, 93, 137-38
  ESCO interests, 99
  evaluating, 93, 125-38
  excluding issues in, 230
  formation and approval, 97-102
  funding, 100-101, 108
  information sources, 93-95, 255n48
    interviewees (table), 94-95
  innovative features, 132-33
  joint-utility collaborative, 98-108
  legitimacy, 128-29, 138
  litigation, 126-27
  NUP funding, 93, 135-36, 229
  NUP involvement, 98-100, 102-3, 125, 126, 136
  ongoing, 123-24, 137-38
  participants, 93, 99-100, 128, 136
  Phase I, 100, 102-8
  Phase II, 100, 108-17
  Phase II collaboratives, 108-17
    agreement, filing, and DPU order dates (tables), 108, 122
    NUP-utility relationships, 109-10
    preapproval cases, 114-17

structure, 103, 108-9
Phase III, 100, 117-23
policy making difficulties, 133-34
practicality, 130-34, 139
process evaluation, 134-38
resource savings, 125-27, 261n96
technical sessions, 101, 103, 107-8
unique features, 93
utility expenses, 125-26
utility interests, 99, 100
See also joint-utility collaborative in Massachusetts; and individual collaboratives by name
DSM incentives in Massachusetts, 100, 110-11, 132, 261-62n102
DPU decisions on, 116, 259n83
and DSM growth in Massachusetts, 132
opposition to, 106, 111, 112, 132
DSM rules (in New Jersey), 268n55
and DSM bidding, 206
formation process, 206-7, 268n53
roundtables versus technical sessions, 206-7, 268n54
DSM settlement board (for BECo DSM programs), 83-85, 89
due process requirements in adjudication, 53-54
Duquesne Light Co. v. Barash, 33-34

E

Eastern Edison Company
DSM collaborative agreement and preapproval filing dates (table), 108
DSM collaborative demise, 257n70
DSM expenditures for NUP consultants, 1988-1993 (table), 125
Economics of Regulation, The: Principles and Institutions (Kahn), 11-12
Edgar Station power plant
preapproval request, 158, 264n35
proposal, 84-85, 121
Edison Electric Institute, ADR experiments, 35, 40
efficiency in consensus building, 46-47
EFSC (Energy Facilities Siting Council)
state funding for, 173-74, 265-66n36
See also IRM rulemaking process in Massachusetts

electric power plants
Edgar Station proposal, 84-85
technological plateau, 11, 244n7
Zimmer case, 40, 248n19
See also nuclear power plants; Pilgrim (Pilgrim Nuclear Power Plant)
Electric Revenue Adjustment Mechanism (ERAM), 245n13
electric utilities
citizen confrontations with, 12-13
customer cutbacks on electricity usage and, 12
DSM collaboratives proposal in Massachusetts, 98-99
DSM investment, 21-22, 117, 217-18, 245n20, 259n85
electricity options outside the bidding process, 204-5, 267n49, 267n50
energy resource management role, 173, 217-18
industry tensions and uncertainties, xii
interdependence with other resource providers, 220
management failures, 13, 244n9
in Massachusetts, 96
DSM expenditures/savings (tables), 96, 125, 130, 237
resource ratemaking treatment investigation, 152-54
PUC cost disallowances and, 16-17
regulation advocacy, 8
revenue adjustment mechanisms, 84, 245n13, 254n44, 254n46
technological stasis, 13
See also DSM collaboratives in Massachusetts; electric utility regulation; and individual utilities by name
electric utility regulation
beginnings, 7-9, 243n3, 244n5
by-pass problem, 219
consensus attainment in, 43-44
controversies in, 7, 19-26, 34, 217-18
cost adders, 20-21
and electricity generation competition, 22-24
environmental externalities in, 20-21
incentive ratemaking, 25-26, 245n13

interjurisdictional conflicts in, 24-25, 218, 246n23
interventionism in, 7, 9, 13-19, 218-20, 222
minimizing societal costs of electricity, 20-21
national consensus on, ix, 7, 9-13
rate case rise, 11-12
traditional approaches, ix, 1, 50, 218-19
  modifying, 233-35
  shortcomings of, 218-20
and utility DSM investment, 21-22
See also adjudication (in electric utility regulation); consensus building (in electric utility regulation); interventionism (in electric utility regulation); rulemaking (in electric utility regulation)
electricity
  consumer expenditures for, 1
  expansion, 9
  marginal cost pricing, 14-15, 264n22
  societal cost minimization, 20-21
  transmission issues, 24
  See also electricity generation; electricity rates
electricity generation
  bidding questions (table), 23
  bidding rules, 246n22
  by industry, 245-46n21
  cogeneration (in New Jersey), 190
  competition in, 22-24, 154, 172
  controversies in, 23
  environmental concerns, 218
  history (graph), 10
  industrial self-generation case, 126-27, 261n97
  pollution from, 21
electricity issues. *See* electric utility regulation
electricity rates
  calculating, 250n4
  COM/Electric rate increases, 113, 258n76
  history, 9
  graph, 10
electricity-related disputes
  energy resource management and, 217-18
  growth in, 1

  See also ADR (alternative dispute resolution); electric utility regulation
Electrifying America (Nye), 9
Endispute, Inc., Zimmer power plant case, 40, 248n19
Energy Consortium
  energy service charge proposal, 117-18, 123
  NEES case interventions, 111, 117-18
  Pilgrim settlement participation, 74
  WMECo case intervention, 112, 258n74
Energy Facilities Siting Council. *See* EFSC
energy prices and utility rates in the 1970s, 11-12
energy resources
  committed, 185, 266n39
  conservation cost bonuses, 20, 245n17
  displacement controversy, 174, 185, 266n39
  emission cost values used in Massachusetts utilities (table), 240
  MIT Energy Lab optimization approach, 173, 265n35
  New Jersey versus Massachusetts IRM planning and procurement practices, 195-97
  ranking controversy, 175
  solicitation controversies, 174-75, 185
  utility management role, 173, 217-18
  See also IRM rulemaking process in Massachusetts
energy service charges, Energy Consortium proposal, 117-18, 123
"Energy Strategy: The Road Not Taken?" (Lovins), 21, 244n10
environmental externalities (in utility resource decisions), 20-21
  Clean Air Act and, 245n18
  DPU rulings, 257n67, 266n38
  emission cost values used in Massachusetts utilities (table), 240
  evaluation controversy, 174-75, 183-84
  impact-based calculations approach, 173
  joint-utility collaborative debate, 106

Vermont mediation on, 40, 248n20
environmental groups
    anti-utility protests, 12
    IRM technical session participation concerns, 168
    See also intervenors
Environmental Protection Agency. *See* EPA
EPA (Environmental Protection Agency)
    decision appeals, 145, 148
    negotiated rulemaking in, xiii, 147-48, 263n13
ERAM (Electric Revenue Adjustment Mechanism), 245n13, 254n44
ESCOs (energy service companies)
    and the DSM collaboratives, 99
    in the IRM technical sessions, 175
ex parte rules (for regulators), 54, 227
    applicability to rulemaking, 144, 270n8
exit interviews, with consultants, 121-22
externalities. See environmental externalities

F

face saving, in the Pilgrim settlement, 89
facilitation, 39-40, 231-32
    in DPU technical sessions, 107, 169-70, 187, 231, 257n69
facilitators versus mediators, 231, 232
fairness in consensus building, 46-47, 48
Fam, Sherif, 153
Federal Advisory Committee Act, and agency rulemaking, 143
Federal Energy Regulatory Commission. See FERC
Federal Power Commission. See FPC
FERC (Federal Energy Regulatory Commission)
    interjurisdictional conflicts with PUCs, 24-25, 218, 246n23
    settlement judge use, 40
    settlement procedures use, 38, 61-62
FG&E (Fitchburg Gas and Electric)
    DSM collaborative venture, 108
    DSM expenditures for NUP consultants, 1988-1993 (table), 125
Fisher, Roger

    on distributional tensions in negotiations, 32
    on enhancing power imbalances in negotiations, 30-31
    on integrative bargaining, 28-29
Fiss, Owen, on inappropriate cases for ADR, 33
Fitchburg Gas and Electric. *See* FG&E
Flynn, Peter, 94
formal rulemaking, 250n2, 262n2
Fort St. Vrain nuclear power plant, cost recovery-performance ties, 77, 254n42
Foy, Douglas, 95, 103
    on the DSM collaborative process in Massachusetts, 98
    on DSM incentives, 110-11
    on fuel substitution, 106
FPC (Federal Power Commission)
    rate case backlog, 61, 251n15
    settlement procedures, 61
Fratto, Robert, 153
Freedom of Information Act, and agency rulemaking, 143
Freeman, S. David, on the FPC, 61
fuel substitution, as a DSM measure, 106, 118, 257n66

G

Gabel, Steven, 267n43
    on a bidding settlement in New Jersey, 192
generic investigations by administrative agencies, 152
Gentleman, Mary Beth, 153
Getting to YES (Fisher and Ury), 28-30, 34-35
    predecessors (reference), 246n2
Golden, Senator, Pilgrim settlement participation, 74
Golden petition (Pilgrim rate case), 69-70
Goldman, Charles, 189
Government in Sunshine Act, and agency rulemaking, 143
governors, utility regulation support, 8, 243n2
Gustin, L. Carl, 94

H

Hahn, Richard, 153

on the IRM technical sessions, 182
Harter, Philip
　on ADR, 29-30, 246n5
　on consensus building, 222
　on hybrid rulemaking, 144-45
　on negotiated rulemaking, 146
hazardous waste clean-up, consensus building for, xii-xiii
health and safety indicators as nuclear power plant incentives, 77, 80, 89, 254n42
Hicks, Elizabeth, 94
Hirsh, Richard
　on the electric power industry consensus, 11
　on utility regulation conflicts, 13
Home Box Office v. FCC, 144
Horan, Douglas, 74
hybrid rulemaking, 144-45

I

"Improving Negotiation in the Regulatory Process" (Susskind and Morgan), 246-47n6
incentive ratemaking, 25-26, 245n13
Independent Power Producers (IPPs), 22, 195, 264n23, 267n44
inflation and utility rates in the 1970s, 11-12
informal rulemaking. See rulemaking (in electric utility regulation)
Insul, Samuel, utility regulation crusade, 8
integrated resource management (IRM). See IRM (integrated resource management); IRM rulemaking process in Massachusetts
integrated resource planning, versus the DPU IRM model, 160-61
integrative bargaining, 28-29
　diagram, 29, 246n3
　strategies (table), 30
　See also ADR (alternative dispute resolution)
interest satisfaction in dispute resolution
　assessing, 48-49
　in the Pilgrim settlement, 75, 86-87, 88, 254n41
intervenors (before PUCs)
　anti-utility protests, 12
　dissatisfaction with interventionism, 219-20
　distrust of utilities, 13
　funding, 229-30, 247n8, 270n12
　　DPU policy, 101, 256n60
　　industrial, 111, 112, 258n74
intervention (before PUCS), 58
　costs, 247n8
　in the Pilgrim rate case, 69-70, 253n34
interventionism (in electric utility regulation), 7, 13-17, 218-19
　in the DSM collaborative preapproval cases, 116-17, 259n84
　during the era of implied consent, 9, 244n5
　intervenor dissatisfaction with, 219-20
　shortcomings of, 18-19, 219-20, 222, 269n1
interviewees
　on the DSM collaboratives in Massachusetts (table), 94-95
　on IRM rulemaking process in Massachusetts (table), 153
　on the New Jersey bidding settlement, 188
　on the Pilgrim settlement (table), 66
IPPs (Independent Power Producers), 22, 195, 264n23, 267n44
IRM (integrated resource management), including environmental externalities in, 160, 170, 173
IRM rulemaking process
　avoidance of litigation, 180
　MECo settlement, 180, 266n37
IRM rulemaking process in Massachusetts, 19, 151-87, 270n13, 271n20
　background, 152-55
　DSM policies adopted, 162, 264-65n28
　　table, 163
　evaluating, 151, 177-87
　final rules, 177
　　appeals, 180
　　improvement, 181
　　major changes and refinements (table), 178-79

versus the New Jersey bidding settlement, 195-97
formal rulemaking process, 176-77
information sources, 151-52
interviewees (table), 153
interim order on, 159-63, 185
   table, 163
legitimacy, 181-84
objectives, 151, 152, 155, 160
practicality, 184-87
process evaluation, 185-87
process steps (table), 159
proposed regulatory structure, 160-62
   four phases (table), 161
resource savings, 177-81
timeline, 175, 183, 185
See also IRM technical sessions
IRM technical sessions, 151, 159, 162-87, 185-86, 221, 224
atmosphere, 167-68, 186
balancing of interests, 182-83
benefits, 179-81
breadth, 181-82
business concerns in, 184
clarity, 182
comments from, 176
consensus in, 175-76, 181, 187
convergence of opinion in, 171-74, 181-82, 187
   table, 172
costs, 177-79
depth, 171
disagreements in, 174-76
   table, 174
DPU decision for, 162-65
DPU involvement in, 168-69, 186, 226, 227
   staff representatives, 265n32
facilitation of, 169-70, 187, 231
issues included in, 162-63, 265n29
   by session (table), 171
negotiated rulemaking possibilities, 187
participants in, 166-68, 186, 225, 269n4
   table, 167
schedule, 165, 265n30
structures used, 165-66
substantive results, 170-76
technical sessions evaluation form (illustrated), 239

technical sessions evaluation responses, 169, 170, 171, 178-79, 182-83
   table, 238

J

Jersey Central (Jersey Central Power and Light Company)
   bidding experience 1988-1992 (table), 204
   contract for QFs, 190-91
joint-utility collaborative in Massachusetts, 98-108
   CLF role, 102-3
   cost-effectiveness test issue, 104-5, 256n63, 256n64, 256-57n65, 258-59n80
   cost recovery issue, 104-6, 256n63, 256-57n65, 259n82
   DPU approval, 101
   DPU directives to, 102, 107, 256n62
   DPU non-participation in, 101-2, 107
   DPU technical session with, 107-8
   environmental externalities issue, 106
   fuel substitution issue, 106
   objectives, 102, 104
   participants, 99-100
   Phase I, 104-7
      filing agreements, 107
      table, 105
   Phase II, 107, 257n68
   proposal for, 98-99
   structure, 102-3
   technical sessions, 101, 103, 107-8
Joskow, Paul
   on PUC cost disallowances, 245n15
   on state regulators, 14
judicial review of PUC decisions. *See* appeals, of PUC decisions

K

Kahn, Alfred
   consensus-building efforts, 14-15, 19
   on marginal cost pricing, 244n11
   marginal cost pricing policy, 14-15
   on utility rate increases in the 1970s, 11-12
Kahn, Edward, 189
Keegan, Robert, 264n24
Kelly, Kathleen, 94
   on the DPU DSM guidelines, 105

Kilmarx, Mary, 95
Kociencki, Harry, 189
   settlement process support, 210

L

Landis, James
   on the FPC, 61
   on rulemaking, 142
Lawrence Berkeley Laboratory, QF development study, 191
Lax, David, on competition versus cooperation in negotiation, 32, 247n9
least-cost integrated planning, versus the DPU IRM model, 160-61
legitimacy (of the regulatory process)
   consensus building and, 50, 220
   in the DSM collaboratives in Massachusetts, 128-29, 138
   importance of, 124
   in the IRM rulemaking process in Massachusetts, 181-84
   in the New Jersey bidding settlement, 209-11
   in the Pilgrim settlement, 86-88, 138, 220
Lehr, Ron, on PUC commissioner work overload, 57-58
levelization of payments, for QFs in New Jersey, 190
Levy, Paul, 264n24
Levy Commission, 264n22
   utility resource ratemaking treatment investigation, 152-54
liquidated damage funds, 197-99, 212 table, 198
litigation
   avoiding
      by technical sessions, 180
      by the DSM collaboratives in Massachusetts, 126-27
   versus negotiation, 33-34
Lovins, Amory
   on DSM, 22
   on energy strategy, 21, 244n10

M

Manager as Negotiator, The (Lax and Sebenius), 32
marginal cost pricing of electricity, 14-15, 264n22

Mass. D.P.U. 86-36-F, 104-5, 159-63
Massachusetts
   DSM growth in, 130-32, 261n100, 261n101
   fuel charges, 69, 253n31
   preapproval cost-recovery system for utility investment, 156-57
   rate case settlements in, 63, 251n18
   shortcomings of interventionism in, 18-19, 219
   utility DSM expenditures/savings, 96 tables, 96, 125, 130, 237
   utility resource ratemaking treatment investigation, 152-54
   See also DSM collaboratives in Massachusetts; IRM rulemaking process in Massachusetts; Massachusetts DPU (Department of Public Utilities)
Massachusetts Citizens for Safe Energy (MCSE), Pilgrim settlement participation, 74, 87
Massachusetts Department of Public Utilities. See Massachusetts DPU
Massachusetts DPU (Department of Public Utilities)
   advisory staff, 137, 227, 253-54n36, 262n103, 265n31
      IRM technical sessions participation, 168-69
   advocacy staff policies, 137, 253-54n36, 262n103, 270n7
   on BECo's management of Pilgrim, 67, 79
   case load makeup, 54
   on the CLF DSM collaborative process proposal, 98, 101, 255n55
   commissioners
      changes in, 264n24
      IRM technical sessions participation, 169
   consensus building evolution, 235-36
   DSM campaign, 96-97, 131, 255n51
   DSM collaborative Phase II preapproval decisions, 114-17, 259n81
   on cost allocation, 116, 259n82
   on financial incentives, 116, 259n83

interventionist directives, 116-17, 259n84
program design modifications, 115
ratemaking modifications, 115-16
DSM collaborative Phase III preapproval decisions, 122-23
COM/Electric order, 123
NEES directives, 122-23, 260n92, 260-61n93
WMECo order, 123, 261n94
DSM hearings, 97, 98-99, 255n52, 255n54
DSM-related decision appeals, 127, 261n98
electric utility adjudications, 55-56, 96, 250-51n8
1982-1991 (table), 56
environmental externalities ruling, 257n67
incentive ratemaking, 25
intervenor funding policy, 101, 256n60
IRM encouragement, 154-55
IRM rulemaking. See IRM rulemaking process in Massachusetts
and the joint-utility collaborative
approval of, 101, 256n61
comments on the portfolio, 107
directives to, 102, 107, 256n62
DSM guidelines for, 104-5
non-participation in, 101-2
non-participation in the DSM collaboratives, 44, 101-2, 107, 116-17, 128-29, 136-37, 227
Pilgrim cases, 69-72
Pilgrim settlement approval, 77-79, 87
policy-making procedure, 149
preapproval rulemaking process, 155-59
shortcomings of, 158-59
steps in (table), 156
preapproval rules, 72, 156-57, 254n38, 255n52, 256-57n65, 258n79
controversy over, 158, 264n35
division of risks in (table), 157
prudent, used, and useful standard (for utility investments), 154, 155
state funding for, 173-74, 265-66n36

See also IRM rulemaking process in Massachusetts; IRM technical sessions
Massachusetts DSM collaboratives. *See* DSM collaboratives in Massachusetts
Massachusetts Electric Company. *See* MECo
Massachusetts Mediation Center, 169, 177
MASSPIRG (Massachusetts Public Interest Research Group)
DSM collaboratives proposal, 98-99
DSM incentives opposition, 106, 112
Pilgrim rate case intervention, 70-71, 253n34
prefiling settlement concerns, 172
report on Pilgrim, 68, 253n29
WMECo case intervention, 112
May, Thomas, 66, 74
on BECo's desire for a Pilgrim settlement, 73, 85-86
on Pilgrim performance, 82-83
MBSS (model-based statistical sampling) technique, 258n72
McCraw, Thomas, on Alfred Kahn, 14
McGlennon, John, 170
McGuire, Jim, 189
McIntyre, Bernice, 264n24
DPU order encouraging IRM in Massachusetts, 154-55
on the DSM collaboratives in Massachusetts, 129, 261n99
on the IRM technical sessions, 164-65
McMahon, Gerard
on agency rulemaking, 145-46
on negotiated rulemaking, 147, 246-47n6
McNair, Robert, 189, 205-6, 208, 268n52
on cogenerator discontent with the New Jersey bidding settlement, 200
MCSE (Massachusetts Citizens for Safe Energy), Pilgrim settlement participation, 74, 87
MECo (Massachusetts Electric Company)
DSM expenditures and savings, 1987-1991 (table), 237

DSM expenditures for NUP consultants, 1988-1993 (table), 125
DSM expenditures in 1987 (table), 96
DSM program regulation, 258n78
IRM rulemaking process settlement, 180, 266n37
on the joint-utility collaborative, 99
preapproval filing, 111
QF power acquisition approach, 173, 265n34
See also NEES collaborative
mediation (in settlement negotiations), 39-40, 231-32
  deciding upon, 232
  state-sponsored offices, 265n33
mediators
  role in cultivating consensus, 223
  selecting, 232, 271n17
  versus facilitators, 231, 232
  versus settlement judges, 271n15, 271n16
Menkel-Meadow, Carrie, on ADR benefits, 249n21
methane, emission cost values used in Massachusetts utilities (table), 240
Miragliotta, Anthony, 189
Mississippi Power & Light Co. v. Moore, 246n23
MIT Energy Lab energy resource optimization approach, 173, 265n35
MIT-Harvard Public Disputes Program, ADR trainings, 35, 247n12
model-based statistical sampling (MBSS) technique, 258n72
Model State APA. *See* MSAPA (Model State Administration Procedures Act)
Monsanto Company electricity self-generation appeal, 126-27, 261n97
Morgan, Allan
  on factual disagreements in rate cases, 59
  on the judicialization of agency rulemaking, 145
  on negotiated rulemaking, 246-47n6
MSAPA (Model State Administration Procedures Act), 143, 149
  PUC exemptions from, 149, 263n17
  state adoptions of, 149, 263n16

N

Nantucket Electric Company
  DSM collaborative agreement, preapproval filing, and DPU order dates (table), 108
  DSM collaborative demise, 257n70
  DSM expenditures for NUP consultants, 1988-1993 (table), 125
NARUC (National Association of Regulatory Utility Commissioners)
  ADR trainings, 35, 247-48n13
  on PUC reforms, 24
  rate case settlement guidelines, 64, 252n21
  rate case survey, 55, 56-57, 251n9
National Association of Regulatory Utility Commissioners. *See* NARUC
National Civic Federation, 243n1
  utility regulation support, 8
National Conference of Commissioners on Uniform State Laws, Model State APA, 143, 149
national consensus, on electric utility regulation, ix, 7, 9-13
National Electric Light Association (NELA), utility regulation support, 8
National Regulatory Research Institute (NRRI), MSAPA study, 149, 263n16
NEEPC (New England Energy Policy Council), energy conservation study, 97, 255n53
NEES (New England Electric System)
  DSM expenditures, 117
  DSM preapproval filing and DPU order dates (tables), 108, 122
  DSM preapproval filings, 111, 117-18, 124
    DPU directives on, 122-23, 260n92, 260-61n93
    settlement of third, 124, 261n95
  on the joint-utility collaborative, 99, 255-56n58
NEES collaborative, 99, 100, 101, 110-11, 117-18, 256n61
  direct investment approach, 110
  DSM incentive proposal, 110-11, 116, 257-58n71, 259n83
  future prospects, 124
  NUP-utility relationship, 110

illustrated, 109
structure, 103
negotiated rulemaking, 146-49, 263n14
  benefits, 146-47
  as a consensus-building mechanism, 39, 248n18
  encouraging stakeholder representation in, 225
  at the federal level, xiii, 146, 147-48, 263n12
  PUC commissioner involvement in, 227-28, 270n9
  PUC staff involvement in, 226-27
  steps in, 146
  table, 147
  writings on, 146, 246n5, 246-47n6
Negotiated Rulemaking Act, 148, 248n18
"Negotiating Power" (Fisher), 30-31
"Negotiating Regulations: A Cure for Malaise" (Harter), 144, 146, 246n5
negotiations
  assisted, 39-40, 231-32
  delaying, 230-31
  difficult issues in, 230-31
  history (reference), 246n1
  phasing, 225-26
  types, 28
  See also ADR (alternative dispute resolution); consensus building (in electric utility regulation); facilitation; mediation; negotiated rulemaking; settlement negotiations
NELA (National Electric Light Association), utility regulation support, 8
New England Electric System. *See* NEES
New England Energy Policy Council. *See* NEEPC
New Jersey
  dispute over QF bidding, 191-92
  negotiated rulemaking provisions, 211, 268n58, 268n59
  QF development in, 190-92
New Jersey bidding experience 1988-1992, table, 204
New Jersey bidding settlement, 187-215
  adoption of, 201-2, 206, 267n48
  appeals of, 202-3, 208

background, 189-92
bidding experience, 203-7
  table, 204
discontent with, 199-201
due process concerns, 201, 267n47
evaluating, 188, 207-14
expiration, 207, 268n56
formal ruling process, 188
implementation, 203-7
information sources, 188
interviewees, 188
  table, 189
legitimacy, 209-11
major components (table), 196-97
negotiated solutions, 197-99
NUP concerns, 194-95
postsettlement process, 201-3
practicality, 211-13
process evaluation, 213-14
resource savings, 208
revising, 207
rulemaking requirements, 214
settlement group representatives (table), 193
settlement negotiations, 195, 220, 224, 270n13
settlement process, 192-95
stakeholder representation in, 225
utility perspective, 194
utility violations, 211
versus the Massachusetts IRM rules, 195-97
New Jersey Board of Public Utilities. *See* BPU
New York
  consensus building processes, 15
  marginal cost pricing of electricity, 14-15
  public utility commission laws, 8-9
  rate case settlement guidelines, 64
  use of settlement judges, 39-40
New York Public Service Commission. *See* NYPSC
Newman, Andrew, 95
Nickerson, Janice, opposition to the Pilgrim settlement, 79-80
nitrogen oxides, emission cost values used in Massachusetts utilities (table), 240

nitrous oxide, emission cost values used in Massachusetts utilities (table), 240
no-losers cost-effectiveness test, 245n19
Nogee, Alan, 66, 74, 95, 153
  on the MASSPIRG Pilgrim rate case intervention, 70
  on the MECo IRM rulemaking process settlement, 266n37
  on the Pilgrim settlement, 74, 92, 254n39
nonbinding arbitration, 271n14
nonparticipant cost-effectiveness test, 245n19
nonutility parties. See NUPs
"Normative Theory of Public Law Remedies, A" (Sturm), 249-50n29
notice and comment rulemaking process, 143, 250n2, 262n2
  technical sessions versus, 167
notice requirements in settlement negotiations, 234, 271n18
NRC (Nuclear Regulatory Commission)
  and Pilgrim, 66-67, 82, 87-88
  settlement opposition, 79-80
NRRI (National Regulatory Research Institute), MSAPA study, 149, 263n16
nuclear power plants
  cost disallowances, 16-17
  cost recovery-performance ties, 77, 254n42
  health and safety incentives, 77, 80, 89, 254n42
  Palo Verde nuclear case, 35, 247n11
  See also Pilgrim (Pilgrim Nuclear Power Plant)
Nuclear Regulatory Commission. See NRC
NUP consultants, Massachusetts utility DSM expenditures for, 1988-1993 (table), 125
NUPs (nonutility parties)
  funding for, 229-30, 247n8, 270n12
  in the IRM technical sessions (table), 167
  in the Massachusetts DSM collaboratives, 98-100, 102-3, 124, 125, 126
  in the New Jersey bidding case, 192, 193, 201
  in the Pilgrim case, 73-74, 83-84, 88, 91
  See also individual DSM collaboratives by name
Nye, David, *Electrifying America*, 9
NYPSC (New York Public Service Commission)
  on commissioner involvement in rulemaking and adjudicatory proceedings, 270n10
  on rate design settlements, 34, 247n10

O

Oak Ridge National Laboratory collaboratives study, 104, 136
O'Connor, David, 153, 169-70
  facilitation of DPU technical sessions, 107, 257n69
Office of Management and Budget (OMB), federal negotiated rulemaking role, 146, 262-63n11
oil prices and utility rates in the 1970s, 11-12
O'Leary, Marilyn
  on inappropriate cases for ADR, 33
  on tradeoffs in adjudication, 59-60
OMB (Office of Management and Budget), federal negotiated rulemaking role, 146, 262-63n11
OPEC oil embargo and utility rates in the 1970s, 11-12
open meeting laws for PUCs, 54, 250n1, 252n24
Oppenheim, Jerrold, 95, 153
  on the reluctance to appeal rules, 180
organic compounds (volatile), emission cost values used in Massachusetts utilities (table), 240
Overton Park, Inc. v. Volpe, 144

P

Palo Verde nuclear power plant case, 35, 247n11
paper hearing procedures in agency rulemaking, 144
Pareto curve, 28
participants (in consensus building)

Index — 311

including stakeholders in consensus building, xi-xii, 225-26
See also interest satisfaction in dispute resolution
parties to disputes. *See* participants (in consensus building)
Pastuszek, Lydia, 94
phasing negotiations, 225-26
Pilgrim (Pilgrim Nuclear Power Plant)
   BECo outage cost claims, 69, 253n33
   BECo spending on, 67, 68-69, 253n30
   capacity factor required, 71, 76, 80-81, 254n37, 254n43
   cases before the DPU, 69-72
   Massachusetts economic downturn and, 82-83
   MASSPIRG report on, 68, 253n29
   the NRC and, 66-67, 82, 87-88
   postsettlement performance, 80-83, 90
      indicators (table), 81
   potential costs, 71
   power outage, 68, 253n32
   radiation exposure from, 67, 82, 252n25
   reactor shutdowns, 66-67, 252n27
   See also Pilgrim outage and rate cases; Pilgrim settlement
Pilgrim outage and rate cases, 69-72
   BECo perspective, 70
   cost disallowance possibilities, 72
   DPU alternatives, 72
   DPU concerns, 71
   intervenor perspectives, 70-71
Pilgrim settlement, 64, 73-92, 138-39, 231
   background, 66-72
   benefits, 76-77
   core negotiating group, 74, 254n40
   distributive issues in, 32-33, 91, 220
   DPU approval, 77-79
   DSM investment issues, 76, 77, 83-85, 254n45
   DSM settlement board, 83-85, 89
   evaluating, 65, 85-92
   information sources, 65-66
      interviewees (table), 66
   initiation of, 73, 92, 254n39
   innovations, 77
   legitimacy, 86-88, 138, 220
   major components (table), 76
   NUP concerns, 73-74, 83-84, 88, 91
   opposition to, 79-80
   participant satisfaction, 75, 86-87, 88, 254n41
   performance incentives, 76, 77, 82, 89, 254n42
   practicality, 88-90, 138-39
   process evaluation, 90-92
   resource intensity, 58, 70
   resource savings, 85-86
   settlement negotiations, 74-75, 91
   signing, 77-78
   stakeholder representation in, 74, 225
   technical sessions versus contested proceedings in, 224
PJM (Pennsylvania, New Jersey, Maryland Power Pool) billing rate, 266n40
"Points on a Continuum: Dispute Resolution Procedures and the Administrative Process" (Harter), 246n5
policy dialogues, as a consensus-building mechanism, 37
Policy Paradox and Political Reason (Stone), 46-47
Politics of Environmental Mediation, The (Amy), 247n7
Potter, William, 189
   appeal of the New Jersey bidding settlement, 202-3
   on Division of Energy discontent with the New Jersey bidding settlement, 200
Power to Spare: A Plan for Increasing New England's Competitiveness Through Energy Efficiency (NEEPC), 97
practicality of consensus building, 50-51, 220-21
   in the DSM collaboratives in Massachusetts, 130-34, 139
   in the IRM rulemaking process in Massachusetts, 184-87
   in the New Jersey bidding settlement, 211-13
   in the Pilgrim settlement, 88-90, 138-39

preapproval cost-recovery system for utility investment (in Massachusetts), 156-57
prefiling settlements, 61, 126
negotiation process, 134-35, 137, 172-73, 266n37
principled negotiation. *See* ADR (alternative dispute resolution)
Prophets of Regulation (McCraw), 14
prospective collaboratives
as a consensus-building mechanism, 38-39
See also DSM collaboratives
prudence reviews, in cost disallowances, 17, 245n16
PSE&G (Public Service Electric and Gas Company), bidding experience 1988-1992 (table), 204
Public Advocate (New Jersey)
motion against the bidding settlement, 203
opposition to the bidding settlement, 199-201
Public Disputes Program (MIT-Harvard), ADR trainings, 35, 247n12
Public Involvement in Integrated Resource Planning: A Study of Demand-Side Management Collaboratives (Raab), 94
public service commissions. See PUCs (Public Utility Commissions)
Public Service Electric and Gas Company (PSE&G), bidding experience 1988-1992 (table), 204
Public Utilities Regulatory Policy Act. *See* PURPA
public utility commissions. *See* PUCs
Public Utility Company Holding Act (PUCHA), 24
PUC commissioners
consensus-building forums involvement, 227-28
ex parte rules for, 54, 144, 227, 270n8
work overload, 57-58
PUCHA (Public Utility Company Holding Act), 24
proposed reforms, 246n24
PUCs (public utility commissions)
advocacy staffs, 223, 269n2
authority, 243-44n4

balancing role in adjudication, 60-61
beginnings, 7-9
case load increases, 57
consensus-building policies, 234-35
consensus-building role, 222-23, 226-28
cost disallowances by, 16-17, 245n15
Supreme Court on, 33-34
decision appeals, 44, 60, 180, 249n22, 251n13, 251n14
decision lengths, 58, 251n11
DSM policies, 22
dual role, 19, 223
due process requirements for, 53-54
as a funding source for consensus building, 229-30, 270n11
interjurisdictional conflicts, 24-25, 218, 246n23
intervention before, 58
costs, 247n8
interventionism, 13-19, 218-20, 222, 269n1
judicial review of PUC decisions, 44-45, 249n24
laissez-faire approach, 9-10, 13
mediation use, 40
MSAPA exemptions, 149, 263n17
open meeting (sunshine) laws, 54, 250n1
policy making by, 60, 149-50, 251n12, 263n18
rulemaking use, 149-50
settlement approval, 44-45, 50, 115, 233, 249n25
settlement negotiations forbidden by, 230
settlement rejection, 233-34
staff involvement in consensus building, 226-27
staff shortages, 57
synonymous terms for, 243n1
See also adjudication (in electric utility regulation); interventionism (in electric utility regulation); PUC commissioners; rate cases; ratemaking; rulemaking (in electric utility regulation)
PURPA (Public Utilities Regulatory Policy Act), 22, 263-64n19
implementation of, 152

Index — 313

interjurisdictional conflicts over, 24-25

Q

QF bidding, 152, 172, 173, 264n20, 266-67n42
  New Jersey dispute over, 191-92
  versus the DPU IRM model, 161-62
  See also New Jersey bidding settlement
QF rule (in Massachusetts), 152
QFs (Qualifying Facilities) (for electricity generation), 22, 264n23
  BPU policies, 189-92
  development in New Jersey, 190-92
  MECo QF power acquisition approach, 173, 265n34
Qualifying Facilities. *See* QFs

R

Raab, Jonathan
  consensus-building involvement, 3, 66, 95, 151-52, 243n2, 255n50
  on DSM collaboratives, 94
  IRM technical sessions involvement, 265n32
Raiffa, Howard
  on bargaining trades, 28-29, 246n4
  on competition versus cooperation in negotiation, 247n9
  on consensus-building substantive benefit analysis, 46, 249n26
railroad commissions, nineteenth century philosophy, 7
rate cases, 54-55
  decision lengths, 58, 251n11
  duration, 58, 251n10
  electricity-related versus general, 55
  factual disagreements in, 59
  forward-looking, 54-55, 56, 250n5
  fundamental rights in, 33-34
  prior to 1970, 9-10, 244n6
  procedural structure, 54-55, 250n3
  table, 55
  resolving distributive issues in, 32-33, 91, 220
  rise in, 11-12, 55-59, 250n6, 250n7
  See also adjudication (in electric utility regulation); settlements (in rate cases)
ratemaking

classification of, 250n2
controversies in, 218
DPU preapproval rules, 72, 156-57, 254n38, 255n52, 256-57n65, 258n79
  controversy over, 158, 264n35
  division of risks in (table), 157
  incentive, 25-26, 245n13
  traditional cost-of-service, 25
  See also adjudication (in electric utility regulation)
Recommendations for an Enhanced Electric Utility Planning and Procurement Process (Armenti et al.), 207
reg neg
  term described, 262n10
  See also negotiated rulemaking
regulation (of industry)
  impetus, 7-9
  nineteenth century philosophy, 7
  See also electric utility regulation
Regulation and Its Reform (Breyer), 59
regulators
  activist imperatives, 13-14
  failures of, 13
regulatory interventionism. *See* interventionism (in electric utility regulation)
Regulatory Interventionism in the Utility Industry: Fairness, Efficiency and the Pursuit of Energy Conservation (Barkovitch), 14
regulatory negotiations. *See* negotiations
Reilly, William, on the appeal rate of EPA decisions, 145
resource savings from consensus building, x, 41-43, 221, 249n21
  in the DSM collaboratives in Massachusetts, 125-27
  in the IRM rulemaking process in Massachusetts, 177-81
  in the New Jersey bidding settlement, 208
  in the Pilgrim settlement, 85-86
Reznicek, Bernard, 74
  on the DSM collaboratives in Massachusetts, 129, 261n99
  hiring as BECo CEO, 67
  Pilgrim case settlement initiative, 73, 254n39

Rockland Electric, bidding experience 1988-1989 (table), 204
Ross, Leonard, CPUC DSM policy, 15-16
Rouse, Rolly, 153
  on the IRM technical sessions, 182
Rowe, John, 94, 103
  on DSM incentives, 110
  on the NEES collaborative, 124
Ruckelshaus, William, on the appeal rate of EPA decisions, 145
rulemaking (in electric utility regulation), ix, 1, 149-50, 225
  consensus building effects on, 214-15
  consensus building mechanisms for, 36-39
  DPU preapproval rulemaking process, 155-59
    division of risks in (table), 157
    shortcomings of, 158-59
    steps in (table), 156
  formal, 250n2, 262n2
  informal, 143, 250n2, 262n2
  initiating consensus building in, 224
  judicialization of, 142
  in Massachusetts, 19
  notice and comment, 143, 250n2, 262n2
  prior to 1970, 10-11
  public comment on, 226, 270n6
  PUC commissioner involvement in, 227-28, 270n9
  PUC staff involvement in, 226-27
  versus adjudication, 141-42
  in PUC schedules, 54
  See also agency rulemaking; IRM rulemaking process in Massachusetts; negotiated rulemaking
rules
  appealing of, 180
  DSM, 206

S

Salgo, Harvey, 153
  on the IRM technical sessions consensus, 175-76
satisfaction. See interest satisfaction in dispute resolution
savings (DSM), measuring techniques, 111, 258n72
Schneider, Peter, 170

Sebenius, James, on competition versus cooperation in negotiation, 32, 247n9
self-dealing, 191
  BPU disputes over, 266n41
  concern about, in Massachusetts, 174
seminars and conferences as consensus-building mechanisms, 36-37
Sentinel Energy Services Company, DSM collaborative exclusivity protest, 256n59
Sergel, Richard, 94
service boards. See PUCs (Public Utility Commissions)
settlement judges, 39-40
  versus mediators, 271n15, 271n16
settlement negotiations
  confidentiality in, 234, 252n24, 271n18
  as a consensus-building mechanism, 36, 37-38
  encouraging stakeholder representation in, 225
  guidelines for, 38, 248n17
  in the New Jersey bidding settlement, 220, 224, 270n13
  in the Pilgrim settlement, 74-75, 91
  prefiling, 134-35, 137, 266n37
  PUC commissioner involvement in, 227-28
  state policies on, 234-35, 271n19
settlements (in rate cases), 36, 37-38, 61-64
  appeals of, 44, 249n23
  comments on, 226, 233, 270n6
  guidelines for, 63-64, 252n20, 252n21
  increased use of, 62, 251n16
  issues covered in, 63
  in Massachusetts, 63, 251n18
  before the NYPSC, 62-63, 251n17
    1981-1990, table, 62
  NYPSC on, 34, 247n10
  preclusion of, 63, 251-52n19
  prefiling, 61, 126
  process issues, 63-64
  PUC rejections of, 233-34
  See also DSM collaboratives; settlement negotiations
Shapiro, Robert, 153

on the IRM technical sessions, 181, 184
shared savings incentives for DSM, 100, 110-11
Shimshak, Rachel, 66, 74, 95
  on DOER Pilgrim case decision concerns, 73
  on the Pilgrim settlement negotiations, 75
small groups, as used in the IRM technical sessions, 165-66
stakeholders
  including in consensus building, xi-xii, 225-26
  See also participants (in consensus building)
Stalon, Charles, on prudence reviews in cost disallowances, 245n16
statistical sampling, model-based technique, 258n72
Stone, Deborah, on fairness in consensus building, 46-47
Sturm, Susan, on consensus-based negotiations, 249-50n29
sulfur oxides, emission cost values used in Massachusetts utilities (table), 240
sunshine laws for PUCs, 54, 250n1
supplemental consensus-building processes. *See* consensus building (in electric utility regulation)
Supreme Court, on PUC cost disallowances, 33-34
Susskind, Lawrence
  on ADR, 29-30, 246-47n6
  ADR trainings, 35
  on agency rulemaking, 145-46
  on assisted negotiation, 39
  on factual disagreements in rate cases, 59
  on fairness in consensus building, 48
  on negotiated rulemaking, 147
  on tempering power imbalances in negotiations, 31

T

Taylor, Earle, 94
  on WMECo, 118, 119
technical sessions
  as a consensus-building mechanism, 37
  in the DPU preapproval rulemaking process, 158-59, 264n27
  in the DSM collaboratives, 103, 107-8
  Pilgrim case possibilities, 92
  versus the notice-and-comment process, 167
  See also IRM technical sessions
technological stasis
  defined, 244n8
  of electric utilities, 13, 244n8
Technology and Transformation in the American Electric Utility Industry (Hirsh), 11
"Theory and Practice of Negotiated Rulemaking, The" (Susskind and McMahon), 246-47n6
Tierney, Susan F., xi(n), 95, 253n35, 264n24
  on consensus building, xi-xiii
  on the DSM collaboratives and DSM growth in Massachusetts, 131-32
  on the joint-utility collaborative agreement, 101
  Pilgrim case investigation, 71
Tucker, Ben, 94
21E process (hazardous waste clean-up), xii-xiii

U

Ury, William, on integrative bargaining, 28-29
U.S. Department of Energy. *See* DOE
U.S. General Services Administration, Pilgrim settlement participation, 74
utilities. *See* electric utilities

V

Vermont
  DSM collaboratives, 230
  environmental externalities mediation, 40, 248n20
Vermont Public Service Board, caseload and staffing, 1988-1991 (table), 57
Vermont Yankee Nuclear Power Corp. v. Natural Resources Defense Council, Inc., 144
voluntary settlements. *See* settlements (in rate cases)

W

Wald, Patricia, negotiated rulemaking concerns, 148, 263n14
Walker, Michael, 189
 on avoided cost calculation variations, 205, 267-68n51
Wallach, Jonathan, on Pilgrim potential costs, 71
Watts, Wendy, 94
Werlin, Robert, 66, 95, 153, 264n24
 on the DPU DSM incentives decision, 116
 on DPU frustration with utility DSM efforts, 97
 on the IRM technical sessions, 164-65, 176, 181, 184
Western Massachusetts Electric Company. See WMECo
wheeling (in electricity transmission), 23
White, Carol, 94
Wisconsin, public utility commission laws, 8-9
WMECo (Western Massachusetts Electric Company)
 DSM collaborative agreement, preapproval filing, and DPU order dates (tables), 108, 122
 DSM collaborative proposal, 98
 DSM expenditures and savings, 1987-1991 (table), 237
 DSM expenditures for NUP consultants, 1988-1993 (table), 125
 DSM expenditures in 1987 (table), 96
 DSM incentives proposal, 112, 116
 Phase II preapproval case, 112
  DPU decisions on, 115, 116
  interventions, 112, 258n73, 258n74
 Phase III preapproval case, 119
  DPU order, 123, 261n94
WMECo collaborative, 111-12
 cost recovery issue, 111-12, 116, 259n82
 DSM pace controversy, 111
 evaluation and monitoring dispute, 111
 frustrations in, 118
 NUP-utility relationship, 110, 112, 118
  illustrated, 109
 rejuvenation of, 118-19

Woolf, Tim, IRM technical sessions involvement, 265n32

Y

Yoshimura, Henry, IRM technical sessions involvement, 265n32

Z

Zajac, Mort, 94
 on the COM/Electric NUPs, 119, 260n87
zero-sum negotiation, 28
Zimmer power plant case, 40, 248n19

About the Author

Jonathan Raab has been working on energy, environmental, and regulatory issues for over fifteen years. His Ph.D. from MIT is in Energy and Environmental Policy/Resource Economics. He also has an M.S. from Stanford University's Civil Engineering Department in Resource Planning and Management, and an A.B. from Stanford University in Social Sciences. Dr. Raab has written over thirty-five publications, and has taught energy policy and planning courses at both Stanford University and the University of Oregon. He currently runs an independent consulting and dispute resolution practice in Boston, Massachusetts. Raab Associates has advised and assisted public utility commissions, utilities, intervenor groups, the National Association of Regulatory Utility Commissioners, and many other public and private entities. Dr. Raab recently mediated a negotiated rulemaking on incorporating environmental externalities in utility planning for the Vermont Public Service Board that included more than fifteen parties and took over nine months. Prior to beginning Raab Associates in 1991, he was the assistant director of the Electric Power Division at the Massachusetts Department of Public Utilities.